SECRETS AND Wives

SECRETS AND Wives

The Hidden World of Mormon Polygamy

SANJIV BHATTACHARYA

Soft Skull Press

Library of Congress Cataloging-in-Publication Data is available
ISBN 978-1-59376-521-7

Cover design by BriarMade
Interior design by Elyse Strongin, Neuwirth & Associates, Inc.

SOFT SKULL PRESS
New York, NY
www.softskull.com

Printed in the United States of America

You fight your superficiality, your shallowness, so as to try to come at people without unreal expectations, without an overload of bias or hope or arrogance . . . and yet you never fail to get them wrong . . . You get them wrong before you meet them, while you're anticipating meeting them; you get them wrong while you're with them; and then you go home to tell somebody else about the meeting and you get them all wrong again. Since the same generally goes for them with you, the whole thing is really a dazzling illusion empty of all perception, an astonishing farce of misperception.

    —Philip Roth, **American Pastoral**

Contents

believes that polygamy is a righteous path, whatever the actual numbers of polygamists in the group may be. And when I use "wife," I refer not only to women who are legally married, but those who are spiritually married too.

For words like "wacko," "nutjob" and "bananas," I defer to the *Oxford English Dictionary*.

Now to the thanks. This book would never have been possible without the generosity of countless sources, many of whom feature in the book, but not all. Particular gratitude goes to Vicky Prunty and Rowenna Erickson of the now-defunct Tapestry Against Polygamy; Anne Wilde of Principle Voices, who let me stay at her place for a week; Mary and Gary Batchelor; the authors John Llewellyn and Andrea Moore-Emmett, who shared their research and contacts; the people of Centennial Park, who gave my journey such a positive start; Utah attorney general Mark Shurtleff, along with Paul Murphy, Carolyn Nichols and Jessica Eldredge; the Tucker family, especially Christy; and, of course, the scores of fundamentalists, current and former, who trusted me with their stories, not least the wonderful Bob Foster, perhaps the most trusting of them all, who sadly passed away.

I owe a debt of thanks to *Marie Claire*, *The Telegraph* and *The Independent* in the UK for publishing my early articles about polygamy; to Andy Mackenzie at Channel 4 (UK) for allowing me to make a documentary, *The Man with 80 Wives*, about Warren Jeffs; to my editor at Soft Skull, Anne Horowitz; and to my exceptional agent Kate Garrick, without whom I would never have reached the finish line.

But most of all, I thank my family—my parents, Sabita and Ramen, who, as always, were unfailing in their support; my parents-in-law, Carlene and Norm, who looked after me during the writing of the book at the excellent Pepper Jack's Bar & Grille in Grand Coulee; and especially my wife, Tawnya, whose love and encouragement were invaluable throughout the journey. She put up with me disappearing off to Utah for months on end and talked me off a ledge or two along the way. I'm doing just fine with one, thanks.

SECRETS AND Wives

Introduction

When Mitt Romney lost the 2012 election, it was widely reported that the so-called "Mormon moment" had come to an end. Whereas at one time, the M word had been everywhere—on the front page, the nightly news, Broadway—now it wasn't. Obama won and the world moved on. And it felt rather abrupt, the way it happened. After all, this "Morment" had lasted a good few years. It's hard to say exactly when it started—it's not as though a pistol went off—but it was 2007 when I set off for Utah to investigate polygamy, the trip on which this book is based, and even then, you could sense it building in the background, like a swelling orchestra.

At its crescendo, America became a strange and excitable place in which girls flapped hysterically over the *Twilight* franchise, conservatives flapped hysterically over Glenn Beck's conspiracy blackboard, and the musical *The Book of Mormon* swept the Tony awards. There was no arguing with the *Newsweek* headline of June 2012—"It's Mormon in America"—particularly given the Republican primaries earlier that year, featuring both Mitt Romney and Jon Huntsman. Two Mormons bidding for the White House? That's not bad for a religion that makes up only 2 percent of the population.

But one thing became abundantly clear early on: The word *Mormon* didn't focus-group well. The LDS Church knew this already. In 2009, it had engaged the advertising agencies Ogilvy & Mather and Hall & Partners to assess what it saw as a perception problem, and the agencies discovered that not only were most people ignorant of Mormon beliefs, but they were also broadly suspicious of the believers, describing them as sexist, cultish, and secretive. So just as Romney's bid for the presidency got under way, the church unleashed a multimillion-dollar PR campaign devoted to changing its image. The "I am a Mormon" campaign of 2011 featured, among others, a Hawaiian surfing champion (Joy Monahan), a black female mayor (Mia Love), and the lead singer of the Killers (Brandon Flowers). The message was clear—Mormons aren't weird or scary; they're normal and ethnically diverse. Cool, even.

And it worked. A Pew survey following the election found that even though most Americans were no better informed about Mormons or their beliefs, they were more kindly disposed and more accepting in general. It may have been due to the campaign or simply because America had just reelected its first ever black president and a greater tolerance toward once-maligned minorities prevailed. Either way, the church came out of it well. Even though Romney had lost, Mormons had won. The moment had paid off.

Meanwhile, polygamists, or "fundamentalist Mormons," as they call themselves, were going through a similar change. Roughly forty thousand people in America have chosen to preserve the original Mormon doctrine of plural marriage even though the mother church officially gave it up in 1890. For a century, they have survived in hiding, scattered through the American West, and they too suffer from an image problem, to put it mildly. At best, polygamists are viewed as religious kooks, and at worst, they're seen as criminal cults whose men openly abuse and enslave young girls—their sisters and nieces among them. But the situation was changing at the time that this book was written—an effort to revamp the image was under way. Polygamy, it turned out, was having a "moment" of its own, one that fittingly coincided to a large extent with the Mormon one. In fact, in keeping with Mormon history, the polygamy moment started first.

The parallels aren't perfect, but they work up to a point: A controversial figure in the national news prompts unprecedented scrutiny of his culture, while the entertainment world attempts to humanize it. So just as Mormonism came under scrutiny because of the ambitions of Mitt Romney, polygamists came under scrutiny because of the delusions of their leading celebrity Warren Jeffs, the tyrannical prophet of the FLDS, the Fundamentalist Church of Jesus Christ of Latter Day Saints. (Jeffs is currently serving life for child rape.) While the LDS Church launched a PR campaign, the fundamentalists launched legal actions—some to challenge state incursions during the Jeffs investigation, and once even to try to decriminalize polygamy itself. And in terms of popular culture, the Mormon Moment featured *Twilight* and a musical, while the Polygamy Moment commanded our televisions, spanning drama (*Big Love*) and "reality" (*Sister Wives*).

The parallel that matters most in the end, though, is this: The Polygamy Moment was also a success. Over a period of about five years, from 2007 to 2012, the otherness of polygamy was eroded and the dark shadow of Jeffs gave ground to an altogether more wholesome image—that of clean-cut families from the suburbs, a minority striving for acceptance, and a people who ultimately deserve our sympathy more than our loathing.

Three families in particular were instrumental in this shift in the public imagination. The first was fictional—the Henrickson family of HBO's drama *Big Love*, which premiered in 2006. The story of a self-made millionaire with three attractive wives, the show represented the first time that polygamists had been humanized like that in a serial drama, let alone rendered in such aspirational terms—in Season 5, Bill even became a senator.

But it was reality TV that best illustrated polygamy's acceptance by mainstream culture. The Brown family of the show *Sister Wives*, now in its sixth season, clearly lacks the wealth and sex appeal of the Henricksons—the patriarch, Kody, is a folksy, earnest advertising sales guy from Lehi, Utah, and his four wives are similarly unremarkable. But this is their strength; ordinariness is their attribute. By revealing the drab mundanity of lives that were once considered exotic and subversive, *Sister Wives* achieves something revolutionary. It shows a nonconformist culture conforming quite happily to the conventions of reality television, and in so doing, it neutralizes the threat somewhat. Besides, what greater evidence of inclusion into American life is there than your own reality TV show?

That the show even exists is perhaps the most remarkable thing about it. Barely a year or two before its launch in 2010, the notion that any polygamist family would permit television cameras into its home was laughable. Polygamy is a closed culture, steeped in its otherness and willfully withdrawn from society at large. It's been this way for a century—the clay has set. So any reporters who ventured into this world typically found the doors closed and the lips sealed.

But the mold began to break around 2006–2007. And for this, credit must go, ironically enough, to Warren Jeffs. He had brought such disrepute to polygamy over the previous six to eight years that certain fundamentalists felt compelled to break their silence, just to show that they weren't all quite as bad as him. It started during the heat of his trial, when aggrieved plural wives made the occasional foray onto Fox News and CNN. Then, once the media herd got wind, the list grew to Oprah, Anderson Cooper, and Montel. They were mostly from Jeffs's own cult, the FLDS, and they looked pained and wretched in their braids and bonnets, pleading for the government to stop persecuting their children's fathers, who were, after all, only practicing their religion. They cried out for pity, these women, and they generally got it, if only because it's sad to see people defend a system that so clearly subjugates them.

Then another, more telegenic face of polygamy began to appear—wives again, but in modern garb this time, from somewhat less regressive groups. These were the polygamists-next-door, the soccer mom suburbanites in the *Big Love* mold who came to emphasize their normality—we're not oppressed they said, we're just like you. Of these, Kody Brown is the apotheosis, but he came later. The path to the Browns was paved by others, particularly one family based in Herriman, Utah—the Dargers.

Typically, the rare polygamist families who entertain reporters do so reluctantly, often retreating quickly into the shadows afterward. But Joe Darger and his three wives always seemed to relish the limelight. They've appeared time and again, as studio guests, in magazine interviews, and as talking heads. Often billed as "the real *Big Love* family," they present a marketable front—attractive and articulate wives, well-adjusted children, and so on. And they make no bones about their desire to bend public opinion. In fact, if you've seen a real polygamist family on television in America, it's likely to be either the Dargers or the Browns.

This is either a problem or a triumph, depending on your perspective. The image of polygamy that these families project is narrow and specifically intended to present this subculture in a positive light. And yet if you want polygamy to be decriminalized, they're perfect—decent, honorable families who serve as an effective distraction to the uglier headlines that polygamy often generates. This juxtaposition has been a feature of the polygamy moment from the start—headlines about child rape contend with softer lifestyle stories about the Brown wives' favorite recipes, or how the Darger wives handle jealousy. And as Warren Jeffs has drifted out of the news the profile of the Dargers and the Browns has grown.

There was a heady year between 2010 and 2011, when the FLDS story was approaching its conclusion and the Browns were just beginning to enter the public consciousness. *Sister Wives* launched in September 2010, a couple of months before Jeffs was extradited to Texas to face his last trial. And barely a month before he was sentenced to life, bringing the long FLDS saga to a close, the Browns launched a landmark lawsuit that continues to capture the headlines, even as the Jeffs case recedes into history. It happened in Season 2, when the Browns were compelled to leave Utah for Las Vegas because Utah County investigators found them in violation of antipolygamy statutes. So Kody Brown engaged the high-profile attorney Jonathan Turley to try to overturn the polygamy statutes in Utah, a case that will soon be ruled on in Utah's federal court. And the Dargers are right there in the thick of it. They have a book out at this point, and a publicist, and they're busy lobbying on the Browns' behalf. Joe Darger is now a Republican delegate for his home town.

I suspect that something has been lost here, in terms of our understanding of Mormon polygamy in America. While polygamists have gone from secrecy to prime time in short order, both extremes are forms of concealment in their own ways. We understand the Browns only through the warped prism of reality television. And the Dargers have a clear PR agenda, one that they happily admit. Always more inclined to sell polygamy than reveal it, they've given so many interviews by now that their sound bites are as smooth as pebbles.

But polygamy is a much broader and wilder culture than these two made-for-TV families reflect, in a very literal sense at that. Of all the diverse groups and sects in the subculture, the Dargers and the Browns are closely tied to one—the Apostolic United Brethren. Kody Brown is a full member, while Joe Darger is closely aligned. And the many other groups and independents that have not been heard of in this polygamy moment may now never be. It turns out that it's actually easier to hide when you have such public ambassadors out there dominating the conversation.

This book, however, was written at a different time—long before the Browns came on the scene and while the Dargers were just warming up. In 2007, the first season of *Big Love* had just aired and the Warren Jeffs drama was in full tilt. It was a sensitive time, with hindsight, a tentative toe in the pool of publicity for a long-buried subculture so new to the sunlight. Fundamentalists understood why they needed to open up, but they weren't sure how. It was a period of experimentation and risk—the cusp of polygamy's moment.

Looking back, I was lucky. To be sure, I met with a good deal of wariness as I went around knocking on doors—a journalist living with polygamists? Preposterous! But of those families that gave this book a shot, none had TV shows to promote or books to sell. There was no media slickness about the polygamists I met—they were as unfamiliar with me as I was with them, so it was exciting, unpredictable, a little scary at times. But our encounters always felt honest and unvarnished in a way that might be harder these days, when a multiplicity of wives just might get you a TV show.

Dropping In for Coffee

CHAPTER 1

To live outside the law, you must be honest.
—Bob Dylan

*I*N A CITY full of fundamentalist Mormons, the Vermillion Cafe looks about as fitting as a dive bar in Mecca. A Krispy Kreme at Fat Camp. A Radioshack in Amish Country.

It's well known that Mormons don't do tea or coffee—or liquor or tobacco, so sayeth the Lord—and yet here's a coffee shop, smack in the middle of Colorado City, a small desert town on the Utah/Arizona border renowned for its Mormon fervor. They're so Mormon here, they practice polygamy as the Prophet Joseph Smith did, except with some kind of a caffeine clause—so long as you're observing the Lord's higher law about multiple wives, then He'll let the cappuccino slide. The same may go for margaritas and Lucky Strikes, but I doubt it.

It ought to be simple. I've got a couple of hours to kill, and there's a windstorm blowing, and anywhere else in America, I'd go to a coffee shop or a bar. But this place isn't like anywhere else. Colorado City was built, populated and, until recently, governed entirely by polygamists. They don't like passing travelers here. When I first visited back in 2004, the local children flipped me off and yelled abuse while a succession of pickup trucks tailed me and even tried to run me off the road. This was a regular deal back then, a local sport. Things may have improved since—at least today, I managed to drive in unmolested. But there's a line of pickup trucks parked outside the Vermillion. Maybe the welcome committee was just on its lunch break.

There's really no alternative, though. The fried chicken place around the corner is closed, and the pizza place next door only does takeaway. And I can't wait in my car; I've spent far too long in this thing already. It stinks of Cheetos and Snapple. I can't even get NPR on the radio. And just a short walk away is a hot cup of coffee, maybe a brownie, in the first and original restaurant in Colorado City. I know the clientele can see me, the Gentile in his parked car, weighing up his options. The longer I wait, the less choice I have.

So I huddle and squint through the wind, push through the glass doors and make my way to the counter. The eyes are upon me in an instant, and minutes pass before a girl with a big sunny smile emerges from the kitchen. She sees me, and her smile vanishes. She's maybe fifteen, her face a moonscape of acne, her hair swooped up into an ornate wave.

"Do you serve coffee?" I ask.

She points to a machine by the wall: "Help yourself." And she disappears back into the kitchen.

I've seen that look before—part alarm and part curiosity. The look of someone who knows she shouldn't stare but can't help it. I saw it at the grocery store here in town the other day when I asked the ladies in the meat department if I could get "just two chicken breasts, please." The smallest packet on the shelf had twelve. Spot the monogamist.

But the staring goes both ways. Colorado City and its neighbor Hildale have attracted a steady trickle of gawkers over the years, both tourist and media. And lately that trickle has become a flood, given the public trials of their "prophet, seer and revelator" Warren Jeffs, the leader of the Fundamentalist Church of Jesus Christ of Latter Day Saints (FLDS). He became a fugitive from justice in 2004 and was arrested in late 2006, and it's March 2007 now—so this community has seen no end of outsiders staring at polygamists staring at outsiders. And I'm fairly conspicuous, as outsiders go—the East Indian genes, the English accent, the Volkswagen Jetta, the vaguely clueless air. Around here that all spells "media," which is bad enough, but combined with a doctrinal disdain for dark skin, that's two strikes. I may as well be walking around ringing a bell.

The machine splutters a cup of superheated French vanilla, and I turn to find a seat. The room averts its eyes ever so slightly. There's a table by the window, a place to watch the tumbleweed chase the polygamist women to their trucks, the red dust swirling around their long skirts. Two of these women sit at the table beside mine, but when our eyes meet and I smile, they collect their sandwiches and move. Perhaps I shouldn't have smiled— Jeffs taught his followers that Gentiles only smile to lure the righteous into sin. Which would be a wonderful idea, if it worked. I could have done with that smile in high school.

The café looks tatty and neglected. The wallpaper's peeling, the ceiling's crumbling and the walls are bare—no paintings, no calendars, not even a menu. A piece of A4 taped to a door reads REST ROOM in wobbly marker. It's a place past caring about making an impression. And the same could be said of the town as a whole. Half-built homes skirt the perimeter, their frames hollow and roofless, their ribbing exposed. Front yards are heaped with red dirt and firewood, a shambles of rusty trailers and children's bikes. At one time Colorado City was the seat of the Prophet, an example of what a polygamous society could be. But Jeffs spent his last years here draining it of both followers and finances and scattering his elect to recreate Zion in new compounds in Texas, Colorado, Montana and South Dakota. He moved out himself in 2002, commencing a long and colorful descent that has now landed him behind bars and placed the trust on which the city was built in the hands of a state fiduciary. Colorado City's days may be numbered.

Nevertheless, at the Vermillion, life rumbles along. Regulars pour through the door, chuckling about the wind and fixing their mussed hair. They're a tribe apart, no doubt. The men appear to come in two models—either rake thin and bespectacled or beefy giants with sagging bellies. Both share the same pallid complexion, the same preference for denim, the same tidy haircuts and tucked-in shirts with the sleeves rolled down to the wrists. (It's one of the Prophet's laws—there's no right to bare arms here). As for the women, they wear the regulation pioneer getup of long dresses and bonnets, set off by thick socks and sandals. This season's colors are anemic pastels— lavender and lime, cream and cyan—which most women wear plain, since

Jeffs banned patterns. There's no jewelry, no makeup, nothing to offset the general dowdiness. But some latitude has been granted with their hair, so long as it's bunched up in a century-old style. So it's all about the bob and the braids in Colorado City, the waves and curls.

A burst of laughter from the back of the room. A fat girl wearing a cowboy hat is looking directly at me and sniggering. Like—who's that guy, I bet he's media, let's snigger at him. And I can't avoid her. Wherever I look, I can feel her staring. Then some boys join in, although they seem more curious than provocative, as though they've never seen an Indian drink coffee before and anything might happen at any moment.

"I'm Mr. Dutson. I own this restaurant." An old, thin man is leaning over my table. He looks troubled. "Do you mind me asking what is your business here?"

"I'm working on a book actually."

"Have you got any cameras?"

"No, no cameras."

"Because we don't allow any cameras." He points to a sign on the door: NO CAMARAS AND RECORDERS [*sic*].

"I understand."

"We're very private people."

"I respect that."

"So we don't allow cameras."

And with that, he leaves. But now the staring is intense. People have turned around to see what the fuss is all about. And if I look back, they hold my gaze, their stares closing in on me like white blood cells surrounding a foreign body. The Vermillion wants to expunge me like a pustule.

Maybe if I just look out of the window like I planned. Drink my scalding coffee and watch the wind toss the candy wrappers into the air, jagging them around like puppets. Maybe if I focus on the tumbleweed bouncing along, maybe count the tumbleweed, count the bounces . . .

A sheriff's truck pulls into the parking lot and makes a vulturous circle around the café. He's clearly not just popping in for a sandwich. Look at how he's parking, shoving his front grille right up against the window where I'm sitting. It's like he's baring his teeth.

· · ·

The world of Mormon polygamy is like a range of volcanoes, seldom acknowledged but for its eruptions. Every few years or so, one explodes—there's a rape or a murder or a prophet who just plain goes nuts—and for weeks, it dominates the news cycle. Typically the media seizes the opportunity to recall all the other times polygamists have gone nuts over the years, inviting former plural wives to say "they're all nuts, you know," and perhaps some current wives to protest, "no, we're not!" And then the cycle moves on. But all the while, beneath the surface, the magma continues to bubble and seethe. It won't be long before it blows again.

The Vesuvius of this bunch was triggered by Ervil LeBaron, nicknamed the "Mormon Manson." A large, deranged man of considerable charisma, he decided in the early 1970s that his Church of the Lamb of God was the only true church, and that all other polygamist leaders had to submit to him or face "blood atonement." Right away, the bodies started piling up. A vicious internecine feud within his own church led to the murder of his brother Joel and five others. Then two of his wives went and shot Rulon Allred, the leader of one of the biggest polygamist groups in America, the Apostolic United Brethren. Gripped by mental illness, Ervil continued ranting right up until his death in prison in 1981, at which point he'd left a long list of people who had wronged him. Several people on the list were subsequently killed, many by his own children, which led to the hysterical narrative that the list was a hit list, and that his followers would keep going until every last name had been exterminated. As it was, the last murders in the LeBaron saga took place in 1988.

It was three years after Ervil's death when the next polygamy scandal erupted. The Lafferty brothers, Ron and Dan, became convinced that God wanted them to kill their brother's wife, Brenda, and her fifteen-month-old baby. So in July 1984, they did (a story best told in Jon Krakauer's *Under the Banner of Heaven*). Brenda's crime, it seems, was dissuading Ron's wife from consenting to polygamy. Dan claimed at the time that stabbing his baby niece was "no problem," and that God approved, a position he maintains from jail today.[1]

Not four years later, another polygamist, Addam Swapp, grabbed the headlines by bombing an LDS Church meeting house using eighty-seven sticks of dynamite.[2] He left behind a spear with the note, "Jan. 18, 1979," the date on which his father-in-law, John Singer, was shot dead while resisting arrest. Singer had been involved in a protracted battle with authorities over the right to indoctrinate his children to practice polygamy, among other things. And Swapp was ready to stand his ground. When the SWAT teams descended upon his family compound, he engaged them in a thirteen-day siege that culminated in the death of a police officer.

And so it continues, eruption after eruption: John Bryant's sex ranch in Mesquite, Nevada;[3] Arvin Shreeve, the pedophile gardener from Ogden, Utah. None of this is made up. In 1998, John Daniel Kingston beat his sixteen-year-old daughter Mary Ann unconscious in a barn in northern Utah for fleeing from a marriage to her uncle David.[4] And the dust had barely settled on that case when Tom Green, a magazine salesman in his fifties, decided to parade his five young wives and thirty-two children on national television. That was about when I started to tune in.

I remember watching Green on *Jerry Springer*, fascinated by the freak show of this obese, self-righteous man and his fawning harem. It was the way he spoke that struck me—so earnest and reverential about his family and faith even as he subjected them both to the baying Springer audience. It was as if he'd never heard of Jerry Springer before. And perhaps he hadn't. The way Green saw it, he was striking a blow for the Fundamentalist Mormons of America—say it loud, I'm a polygamist and I'm proud. But he got so carried away with all the attention, all the free hotels and limousine rides from JFK, that he cheerfully revealed how, at the age of thirty-seven, he had gotten his thirteen-year-old wife, Linda Kunz, pregnant. Green hasn't been nearly so enthusiastic about doing interviews since his release from prison in 2007.

I was only dimly aware of polygamy at the time. Growing up in the UK, the likes of Addam Swapp and the Lafferty brothers scarcely registered. I just had the vague sense that Utah was "weird" and that polygamy had something to do with it. So the Tom Green circus got me curious. I did a little reading.

I learned that polygamists consider themselves fundamentalist Mormons and that polygamy had been perfectly common in the Mormon Church until 1890 when, under federal pressure, the Church announced a new revelation, known as "the Manifesto," forbidding the practice. Ever since then, diehards like Green—and LeBaron, Swapp, Kingston, Jeffs and others—have declared the Manifesto to be less a revelation from God than a capitulation by the LDS Church. By their lights, polygamy remains a godly principle, to be practiced only by the righteous, regardless of the law of the land. And the fundamentalist communities that these men led, often in stark isolation from society at large, would tend to erupt into scandals on a regular basis for decades to come. These scandals have largely defined the image of Mormon polygamy for the outside world, as a bizarre, fervent and occasionally sinister substratum of America's religious life.

It wasn't until Warren Jeffs became the prophet of the FLDS, however, that the full strangeness and complexity of Mormon polygamy became clear. The FLDS was just one polygamist community of many, about ten thousand strong, that existed not only outside society but outside the law, complete with its own schools, mayor and police force. That this was even possible is tremendously exciting in a country that seems more homogenous by the day. Incredibly, for fifty years, Colorado City was left to its own devices, like an anthropological Petri dish left out in the sun. Inflame a people with doctrine, apply a culture of fear and scorn for the outside world and transfer to a remote desert location. The result? A polygamist who went clear off the reservation.

Jeffs went mad the way Hemingway said people go bankrupt—gradually, then suddenly. No doubt the peculiar incubator of Colorado City played its part, though it can't have been solely to blame since Jeffs was raised in Salt Lake. His wives may be partly responsible too—he did have seventy-eight of them, after all, a prospect that makes me jibber and pull my hair out in clumps. But I suspect what tipped Jeffs over the edge was power. His father, Rulon Jeffs, was the prophet before him, and as Rulon's favorite, Warren rose quickly in the ranks. A quiet, nerdy type given to snitching on his brothers, Warren became the principal of the cult's school in Salt Lake City, where he was known for both the cruelty of his punishments and his dismal jokes at the school revue.[5] And when Rulon was incapacitated by a series of strokes, Warren became his executor, eventually replacing his father when he passed on and inheriting the role of God's chosen messenger on earth. At which point, Jeffs's insanity blossomed. He banned books, television, radio, news papers, the Internet, nonreligious music, cartoons, the color red, sports and any kind of pattern, especially stripes. He even banned laughter, because it caused "the Holy Spirit to leak out."[6]

As with every self-respecting despot, the lunacy of Jeffs's laws was matched by the severity of his punishments. Men who displeased him had their wives and children "reassigned" to worthier subjects. He kicked hundreds of boys out of the community—the "Lost Boys," as they became known—to reduce competition for the younger, often underage, girls (he's alleged to have married one as young as twelve). And then he went on the run, with an armed guard and a giant "chase me" sign on his back, busily building new compounds in Montana and Colorado and erecting a huge temple near the small West Texas town of Eldorado, on a ranch he christened Yearning for Zion. Life was meticulously circumscribed at the YFZ ranch. All sugar and cereals were prohibited. Curtain drapes hung precisely an inch from the floor. And the Prophet held "heavenly sessions" in which five of his wives massaged him at once, while he taught that masturbation was "the most terrible sin next to murder."[7]

It was while Jeffs was on the lam that I set off in pursuit of him for Channel 4 in the UK, filming a documentary called *The Man with 80 Wives*. (Eighty was just the number people were saying at the time, not that anyone knew for sure.) I didn't find him—the FLDS is famed for its secrecy at the best of times, let alone when their prophet is being hunted down by the FBI. So while I managed to speak with several former members, the closest we came to current followers was a lot of footage of women in prairie dresses shielding their faces and shooing their children indoors.

But then Jeffs was caught on August 30, 2006, and in the media frenzy that followed—if not Vesuvian in proportion, then at least on par with Mount St. Helens—a unique opportunity arose. One that explains, in a roundabout way, what I'm doing back here in Colorado City at all.

So far, in media terms, Jeffs is the gift that keeps on giving. First he was a fugitive cult leader with a battalion of wives, building a secret temple in Texas. Then he was caught leaving Las Vegas in a red Escalade carrying three wigs, $54,000 in cash, a laptop and fifteen cell phones.[8] He's since been charged in Utah and Arizona with multiple counts of "rape as an accomplice"—arranging a marriage between a man and an underage girl—and one of his nephews has accused him of molestation. And, even as his followers keep me under surveillance at the Vermillion, Jeffs is on trial in St. George, where he's apparently been throwing himself against the cell walls and denying that he was ever a true prophet.

An opportunity arises from the way that the Jeffs saga is playing within the fundamentalist community. Thanks to the FLDS, polygamy is yet again being associated with abuse and tyranny, and for this reason, many fundamentalists are shamed by Jeffs, in the same way that the Mormon Church is shamed by polygamy. There are at least thirty thousand fundamentalists apart from the ten thousand in the FLDS—a teeming multiplicity of smaller churches and independents. Some command business empires, others are almost destitute; some live in isolated desert communities, others in cities; some are six generations deep, others are recent converts; some wear prairie dresses, others say "tomato." But one thing they all share is that they're tired of seeing polygamy get slammed, and they wish that the media, whom they detest, would understand that there's more to polygamy than Warren Jeffs.

So this is my window, my opening into a hidden world. While the FLDS dominates the news, I'll reach out to the rest of the diaspora and offer to show a fuller picture of Mormon polygamy in America, to present fundamentalism in all its diversity.

It's a small window, I'll admit—a single missing brick in a great wall of loathing for the media that has stood strong for the better part of a century. Typically, fundamentalists have found their encounters with the media to be superficial and tinged with treachery—all those Jerry Springer questions about which wife on which night and how young are the girls. Once the interviews are over, the community typically closes up once again like a wound, even more mistrustful than before, leaving the rest of us with our caricatures confirmed—the polygamists as the Amish, only more sinister, sexualized and hostile.

But lately the winds have been turning. However damaging Warren Jeffs has been, his crimes run counter to a broader tide of tolerance for polygamy among the general public. Mormon presidential hopeful Mitt Romney caught flack for describing polygamy as "disgusting," given that his own ancestors are polygamists. Utah's attorney general Mark Shurtleff has long promised not to prosecute polygamy itself, but only the crimes within polygamy. His office began the Safety Net Committee, which builds bridges between social services and fundamentalist groups. Polygamy is seen less as a moral abomination these days, now that unorthodox family structures are becoming increasingly common, and it keeps coming up during the debates about gay marriage, to which America appears to be inching closer by the day. But most important of all, pop culture has come around. It's no longer cool to throw rocks at polygamists. HBO's hit drama *Big Love* is a huge hit.

So after years of silence, the community has lowered its guard. There have been appearances on the nightly news. While making the documentary on Jeffs, I met several families who welcomed me with open arms. People like Marvin Wyler and his second wife, Charlotte. The kindly old couple left the FLDS but still live in town and still practice polygamy. They invited me in, fed me and let me stay over. I brought them an apple pie from the nearest town, and they explained why they'd left the group but kept the faith. I met a few of their daughters, who sang a song called "Families Are Forever." I had a go on their trampoline. We went through their family albums. After dinner, we watched *Prophet of Evil: The Ervil LeBaron Story*, starring Brian Dennehy, and laughed about how crazy polygamists can be. And I thought, if this is possible in Colorado City, then why not elsewhere?

That's why I'm here. I saw the window ajar and I couldn't resist: here's my chance to enter a hidden world of prophets and their harems, of secrets and wives, before the window closes again. I want to find out why they live this way and how it can work. Are they like me, can we be friends? Could I become a polygamist myself? I'm not much of a patriarch. I only have the one wife and she kind of bosses me about, to be honest. But I like the idea of living outside the law. Not that I understand why polygamy's illegal in the first place.

I want to visit the big groups like Centennial Park and the Kingston group, as well as the smaller ones like the True and Living Church in Manti. I want to meet the independent polygamist families scattered throughout Utah and hang out with them, see their lifestyles up close, find out what they think of other polygamists and what they think of me. And most of all, I want to meet their prophets, their small-town messiahs, to figure out whether they're for real or not. Do they actually hear these voices, or is it a scam? And maybe, by the end of it all, I'll understand why it is that every few years or so, one of these volcanoes goes off.

So I came back to Colorado City, with an apple pie in my backseat for Marvin and Charlotte. But Marvin's out at the moment, and Charlotte's at her post office job until 4:30 PM. That's why I'm here at the Vermillion, blowing on my coffee, pinned to the window by dagger stares. Checking my watch and trying to watch tumbleweed. Trying not to think about the polygamist policeman heading for the door.

The doors swing open, and the glances dart over to the officer's gleaming badge, his squeaky boots, the paunch, the muttonchop sideburns. A few of the diners nod and smile as he slowly swaggers over to my table. HELAMAN BARLOW, it says on his badge.

"Has Mr. Dutson come out to talk to you about taking pictures?"

"Yes, he did. But it's okay, I don't have a camera."

"Well, he's asked me to come and talk to you. He said you've been here for a long time and to find out what you're here for."

"I'm here for the coffee."

"Are you a reporter of some kind?"

"Yes, I'm writing a book."

"A book. Well, Mr. Dutson says you've been here for three or four hours now."

"Hours? I've been here about ten minutes. Not even."

"Hmm . . . that's not what Mr. Dutson said."

"Look, I don't mean to bother anyone, I'm just having a cup of coffee."

"Have you got any ID?"

"Yes, why?"

"Just to make sure you check out, you know."

"Do you suspect me of something?"

"No, no, I just have to make sure."

So I hand him my ID while the rest of the café watches. I'm the guy getting pulled over, I'm the spectacle. Helaman takes my card and walks away. He's on his phone. He looks over at me and smirks.

"Okay." He hands my card back. "So how long do you think you'll be?"

"I'm just having a coffee! I promise I won't bother anyone.

"Mr. Dutson asked me to find out when you would leave."

"But I *talked* to Mr. Dutson, he said it was *fine*." Clinging to the cliff's edge now. Fingers clawing at the earth. "Those people over there have been here longer than me—go and hassle them." Grip slipping, Helaman's boot heel hovering.

"So how much longer do you think?"

"Fine." I get up and gather my things. "If you want me out of here, I'll leave. But there's a name for what you're doing, you know." Oh dear, I'm making a scene. "Police harassment. And especially in this community, you should know better."

The silence is excruciating as I clumsily grab my bag and make for the door. The fat girl sniggers. I glare at her. She glares right back. No one says a word. I'm regretting my little outburst already. I should have saved it. Now I've got to leave and I've got nothing to say—the moment seems to call for some final flourish.

And then I remember, I haven't paid for my coffee yet. So I sidle up to the counter, hold out my wallet and wait once more for the startled girl with the acne. I should just leave a couple of bucks on the counter, but I'm too flustered to think.[9]

The Campaigners

CHAPTER 2

◆ Vicky

Marriage is the chief cause of divorce.
—Groucho Marx

*I*T'S A CHILLY morning in Salt Lake City when I drop in on Vicky Prunty of Tapestry Against Polygamy. I figure I'd better get some background first before approaching real-life polygamists, and Vicky has been perhaps the most prominent voice on the issue in the last decade. A former plural wife, she formed Tapestry in 1998 with Rowenna Erickson, whose experience of polygamy was similarly bitter. Since that time, the two have weighed in on almost every major polygamy trial. They've lobbied the state, harangued the media and provided information to law enforcement and social services. Their goal is plain: the wholesale incarceration of people who live "the Principle."

"So you want to interview polygamists, huh?" says Vicky, when I meet her outside her house. She seems a little manic, as though she's restraining herself from some kind of outburst.

"Yes, I want to hang out with them, see what they're like."

"Ha! Good luck!" she snorts. "Actually, they'll probably love-bomb you. They'll make it look really good. They'll get all their prettiest wives together. It can be pretty overpowering, I imagine. For a male."

Sounds like Laura Ingalls Wilder through a soft-porn lens. Buxom wives in pioneer dresses soothing my brow: "Why, you must be so tired . . ." *Little Cathouse on the Prairie.*

"They're absolutely white supremacist, you know," says Vicky. Pop goes the love-bomb. *Little Bigot on the Prairie.* "They think they're superior to blacks and Jews and gays and—what are you, Indian? Oh, absolutely. But they'll never tell you that. You'll have to dig. Ask them if they've ever had a black member of their church. Ha ha!"

For Vicky, polygamy isn't just about men having more than one wife; it's a whole culture of oppression—child abuse, racism, sexism, religious extremism. All these pernicious isms buzzing around like flies beneath that shiny *Big Love* lid. She can summon her outrage in an instant and take off on a rant against polygamy, the Mormon Church, the state of Utah and the local media without so much as a pause for breath. She uses the dramatic rhetoric of the protest banner. In a letter to Nevada senator Harry Reid, she wrote that "the reality of polygamy . . . is that organized polygamist cults are *merchandising plural wives*" (my italics).

"People just don't understand what polygamy entails," she says, exasperated. All those stories about welfare fraud, forced marriages, underage brides and creepy old men marrying their nieces—they're all true and worse. She rattles off horror story after horror story—some hearsay, others less so—about polygamists battering their children, locking them in closets, holding them under water to stop them from crying. "There are girls desperate to be saved in these communities, and society doesn't care. I mean, it's against the law, so the state should prosecute. It's so hypocritical for the U.S. to bring order to the Middle East, when we have our own Taliban right here."

And there it is, the antipolygamist catchphrase: the American Taliban. I've heard it from other crusaders, other former plural wives who fled. It has a hysterical ring that tends to lower the discourse, but from Vicky's perspective, there's plenty to be hysterical about here. She sees a conspiracy afoot involving the state of Utah, the attorney general and the LDS Church. To her mind, the reason polygamy isn't being prosecuted is because half the Utah legislature is Mormon.

"Watch out for the lion's grin," she says. "It's the dark abyss. Religion, politics, domestic abuse and human rights—it's all here. When you know that both church and politics are all LDS. Oh yes—Hitler, Stalin, Saddam Hussein, they all took control of the media. And that's what's happening here."

"The Church controls the media?"

"The Church is involved. It outright owns the *Deseret News*. And you just have to read *The Salt Lake Tribune*, what they say about polygamy. It's unbelievable."

There's helplessness in her voice; conspiracies are often the refuge of the helpless. For ten years she's tried, but the state of Utah still won't take a hard line. Instead, it's all *Big Love* and liberals letting these monsters off the hook. The argument is slipping away from her. And it won't be long before she lets go once and for all. A diagnosis of breast cancer will prompt her move to Sacramento to focus more on her children than on polygamy. In December 2009, Tapestry will finally disband. But until then, she fights on.

"The government is working with the polygamists now. We give the AG [attorney general] information, but instead of going after these people like normal criminals, nothing happens. No arrests, no subpoenas, nothing. They just don't want to bring attention to it. They want Mitt Romney to be president."

"But they went after Warren Jeffs."

"Yes, but that's a way of distracting attention from the bigger picture. You have to remember, this state was founded by polygamists. It has culturally embraced polygamy. You need to explain that in your book, the whole history of Mormonism—that's what this is about. The LDS Church put money into stopping gay marriage, but they're not doing anything to oppose the fundamentalists who are trying to get polygamy decriminalized. So you have to wonder, do they want this to come back?"

She has a a nice place, Vicky, considering she's paying the rent with a welfare check. She lives here with her six children from two separate marriages, both plural, and she runs Tapestry from her living room, a desktop computer against the wall. Tapestry has never had an office or an income, she says. It's just Vicky, Rowenna, and a couple of generous lawyers.

"I know, being on welfare is kind of like what polygamists do," she shrugs. "I could go get a job and provide for my family, but I've dedicated my life to Tapestry. It's a ministry to me, not quite a religion."

We pull out her family albums, and she shows me her wedding pictures—a much younger, thinner Vicky back then. "I put on a hundred
pounds since I started Tapestry," she says. "That's what activism does for
you. It's the stress. That's Gary, there."

Gary was her first husband, an Englishman she met at Brigham Young
University. She was quite taken with him—he was a musician, a linguist;
he spoke French, German and Italian; and he felt the gospel with a convert's passion. They were vanilla Mormons then, young and fresh-faced,
with no plans for plural marriage. But their faith led them to fundamentalism. And their lives were altered irrevocably.

"This was when we lived in the Rock."

"The Rock?"

"Yes, a big, you know . . . rock. We lived inside it. There's a whole polygamist community at the Rock, it's out in the desert near Moab."

Gary worked as a car salesman in the Salt Lake area, some eight hours'
drive away. So when he was working, he stayed at another, more local
polygamist compound, belonging to the Addam Swapp and John Singer
families—the same Addam Swapp who blew up an LDS stake center with
dynamite.[1] It was through the Swapp family that Gary met Mary, the
young daughter of the Swapps' lawyer, Keith Morrison. Vicky and Gary
had been married for eight years at that time, with three kids. With Vicky's
blessing, Mary became wife number two.

"Here's our wedding. I know I *look* happy. I was actually doing really
well until about three-quarters of the way through when Gary sat down
and started to play the wedding march. I remember just running out of the
door at that point."

Vicky had supported this marriage, even suggested it—it was what the
scriptures demanded, after all. But the reality quickly dawned. The way she
describes it, her charming English husband morphed into a harsh, power-
wielding patriarch who played one wife off against the other. Even when
she and Mary moved into separate homes, there was little improvement.
Vicky was torn up by jealousy.

"It was all divide and conquer," she says. "He would say, 'If you don't
homeschool the kids, I'll have Mary teach them.' He told us if there was a
Christmas tree in your house, he wouldn't come and visit, because fundamentalists don't believe in Christmas. Oh yes. But you see, it all boils down

to the intimacy and the sex. Whenever you structure a relationship where one person can have sex with whomever they want but the others have to be exclusive to that person, you give them a hell of a lot of power."

According to Vicky, there was little room for dissent. "He said, 'Never voice your opinion if it's contrary to mine,'" she says. "He would say, 'I'm the tree, and if you don't like my shade, then you're free to move.'" She also accuses him of having disciplined the children in a way that upset her. "He would tap them on the mouth to stop them from crying or put them in their rooms for hours on end. That was when Mary said to me, 'My baby has a bloody lip, because Gary was making him stop crying.'"

At one point, Vicky claims, Gary tried to exorcise her of evil spirits and even led their children and Mary in praying for her death. "I remember my kids saying that they wouldn't say 'Amen.'"

"What do you mean, 'prayed for your death'?"

"Fundamentalists believe in blood atonement. So the only way a woman can be forgiven is if her blood is shed. Gary used to say, 'You're mine to dispose of,' and, 'Like a dog you'll be coming back to your master.' He said that if I fully repented, then he would decide in the next life whether to forgive me or not. It was emotional abuse."

It should be said that both Gary and Mary strenuously and comprehensively deny Vicky's allegations, and in fact, her entire characterization of their marriage, which they claim is 'distorted and vindictive'*. Where they agree, however, is that Vicky was deeply unhappy and left only three years after Mary joined the family. But she didn't leave polygamy—she left for another polygamist. She became wife number three of Christopher Nemelka. Strongly built, earnest and charismatic, Nemelka remains one of the more eccentric figures on the fundamentalist scene. At the time, he was creating quite a stir in fundamentalist circles for his claims to have translated, through direct revelation, an entirely new book of Mormon scripture. Certainly, Gary was impressed enough to invite him to Vicky's house one day, where she met him for the first time.

"This guy, you should see him," says Vicky. "He pretty much looks like Fabio, the guy in Hollywood with the long hair? So I was like . . . okay! He's quite an intelligent, charismatic and talented man, actually."

---

* For their full response see the third section in this chapter, "The Batchelors"

Nemelka had two wives at the time—Jackie and Marcee (Marcee is Mary's cousin). And they seemed happy to Vicky, which set her thinking. "I was very distraught being the first wife, but was it me being weak, or was my husband not living polygamy correctly? I thought perhaps being a third wife would be different."

"But why Christopher?"

"I actually had a spiritual experience about that. Chris had mentioned this song, he'd written it down. And when we went out to dinner at this soup-or-salad place—all of us, Mary, Gary, myself and the children—I heard the song come on. It was my witness that I should leave Gary and have Chris be the head of our family."

So, a few months later, Vicky visited Chris and his two wives at their home and asked to join their family. "I made it clear that I didn't want an intimate relationship, but that I felt it was necessary that my children and I were part of a family. I believed in the law of adoption, which came from Joseph Smith, where basically you choose which family you want to be a part of. So if a man is more worthy, you can actually join that family."

"You *didn't* want to have sex with Fabio?"

"No, I didn't want a physical relationship. I hadn't been with Gary for a year physically by that time. He called it spiritual fornication because I wasn't, you know, com*pliant*. I wasn't *one* with him in *spirit*. But by that stage, I believed that the only time that it was appropriate for a woman to be intimate with her husband was if she wanted to get pregnant."

It's a little implausible, all this—from the way she talks about Nemelka, it's pretty obvious she was hot for the guy. And sure enough, her plans of chastity fell apart on the wedding night. She claims the other wives convinced her to be a "full wife" and to have "all the benefits." So after a quick prayer, the other wives left the room and Vicky and Chris got down to it. "He's so different to Gary," she says dreamily. "I was so quickly absorbed into him in every way."

Different is an understatement. Nemelka's wives wore matching outfits with plain, drawstring robes and no makeup. And this was in Salt Lake City, not some far-flung desert compound. They were stared at everywhere they went. "I don't know," says Vicky. "I guess people thought we were Amish or something."

For a few short months, it sort of worked. They lived in Vicky's home—for which Gary was paying the rent, in lieu of his child support obligation—and Vicky became pregnant with Nemelka's child. "We were a quintessential polygamous family. The wives were beautiful, he's gorgeous—we made *Big Love* look like a joke." But only three months later, Nemelka sat the family down in the living room and dumped both Vicky and wife number two, Marcee. He announced that he had never believed in polygamy anyway and he was going to stay with his first wife, Jackie.

"I remember running into the bathroom and being sick," she says. "And just jumping into the shower and scrubbing myself raw. It was because I'd had sex with this man—I thought he loved me. And then I realized I was just a sexual object. I'd just been discarded."

Vicky fled to Grass Valley, California, where she remained for a couple of years, hoping for a new life. But it was a tough transition. She had six children with her—seven eventually, including Nemelka's baby—and very little money. They had no car, they shopped at thrift stores, and the plumbing was on the blink, so she took her kids to use the restroom in the park. There were a few ill-judged overtures to patch things up. She says Nemelka tried to woo her back by buying her a new truck, while Nemelka claims that she was begging him to rescue her from destitution. What's clear is that they carried on an intermittent relationship behind Jackie's back until Nemelka ultimately invited her back to Salt Lake, where he'd found her a house. And while Vicky insists that she accepted on the grounds that their relationship was chaste, she clearly had sex on the brain.

"I was working for another nonprofit at the time, JEDI for Women [Justice, Economic Dignity and Independence]," she says. "And I'd come home from meetings, all made up in my little suits, and all he could do was eye me. Maybe there was something appealing about the control I finally had."

Then one day, Nemelka showed up at her door with a massage table. He'd been training as a masseur and was even certified. "I wasn't going to have sex with him," says Vicky. "But when he came over as Mr. Masseur, well, he had me on his massage board and he was massaging my back, you know . . . And then down to my legs. Then his hands went on my lips." Did she say "*lips*"? "And at that point, I gave in."

At this point, I give up. Despite the "happy ending," their relationship continued to deteriorate. Vicky says that she became consumed by guilt, so she withheld sex, which enraged Nemelka until one day, he snapped and threw her to the gravel. But Nemelka's version is the opposite. In the police report from the incident, Nemelka doesn't deny shoving Vicky, but he is quoted as saying that Vicky was "in my face . . . because I won't fuck her."[2]

There have been several legal battles between Nemelka and Vicky over the years, numerous calls to the police, threats and allegations, many concerning the custody of their daughter. But the drama with Nemelka had barely begun when Vicky started Tapestry. It was the spring of 1998, with the fateful massage still fresh in her mind, when she got in contact with Rowenna Erickson, a fugitive from the Kingston group.

"There were about six of us at the beginning," she says. "We started out as Tapestry of Polygamy to help women and children who wanted to leave. But after about a year, we changed to Tapestry *Against* Polygamy." The new Tapestry still wanted to help women and children leaving polygamy—it just also wanted polygamy abolished forever.

It's gone six and the sky has turned to night. Vicky's daughters return from school in a kerfuffle of bags and shoes and chatter. Vicky tweaks the baubles on her Christmas tree and straightens the cards on the shelves. There's two weeks to go before the twenty-fifth.

"I've had a Christmas tree ever since I left Gary," she says. "I just like the holidays. I'm not a Christian or anything." Her faith began to fade in California. Now she claims to be an agnostic. She reaches for a book on her shelf by Carl Sagan, a tribute to rationalism, a feast of debunkery, and for a while, we happily rail against Creationists, the Christian Right, the whole caboodle.

But at the end of it all, she returns to Nemelka. It's as though she's still smitten. "He always believed in fighting for the underdog," she says. "Our daughter would protect the smallest of creatures, and I believe that Chris also had that same desire. I do not see all bad in him." She shows me his book, *The Sealed Portion,* "translated by Christopher." No surname. It's a proper tome, a doorstop. She hands me a leaflet for an organization linked with Nemelka called the Worldwide United Foundation, purportedly to help the poor.

"Chris believes there are people—well, beings—who are way more advanced than we are. They might be extraterrestrials. They're the ones who are giving him all this stuff."

I laugh. "Extraterrestrials?"

But Vicky's not laughing. "There's a homeless guy he talks to who doesn't age. He's been around for hundreds of years. I've never met him, but I try not to judge Chris just because his beliefs are different to mine."

The silence between us is a little awkward. What happened to Carl Sagan?

"So who else are you going to talk to for your book?" she asks.

"Chris Nemelka, for sure. He sounds fascinating."

"Apart from Chris."

"Those polygamists who live in the Rock, they sound good."

"All the people who've been involved with me, basically!"

"And there's this other group, Principle Voices. I've got the number of someone called Anne Wilde." Principle Voices is a propolygamy organization, begun and run by fundamentalists.

"Oh, Anne, yes, she'll give you the rosy version all right. Don't say you've been talking to me. I know Anne. She delivered my baby with Gary."

"Really?"

"Oh yes. We all know each other. My sister wife with Gary founded Principle Voices with Anne. In fact, Mary's still married to Gary."

So two of the chief campaigners on either side of the polygamy issue were married to the same man. Two dueling women with a man at the center. It's so *Adam's Rib*. It's so polygamy.

"Ask Anne, she'll introduce you to Mary."

◈ Anne

> I don't like the sneaking around . . . Actually, I love the sneaking around,
> it is so exciting!
> —Barb, *Big Love*

It was 1999, barely a year after the founding of Tapestry, that Anne Wilde decided to hatch the fundamentalist response. The news back then was all about John Daniel Kingston (known simply as Daniel) who'd beaten his sixteen-year-old daughter Mary Ann unconscious for not submitting to a

marriage with her uncle.[3] Polygamy as a whole was coming in for a drub-
bing, and Tapestry's rhetoric was doing the rounds—oppression, brainwashing, abuse. And this riled Anne, a plural wife herself. So she called her
friend Mary—Gary Batchelor's wife.

"We discussed doing a book to show the sympathetic side of polygamy,"
she says. "Those who were happy and adjusted were too afraid to speak
out publicly."

As the second wife of a prominent fundamentalist author called Ogden
Kraut, she knew something about publishing. So together with Mary and
historian Marianne Watson from the Apostolic United Brethren (or the
"Allred Group"), she set about contacting all the groups and independent
families she could find, persuading hundreds of plural women to tell their
stories anonymously. It's always women who speak out in polygamy's
favor, to counter the impression of their victimhood. The best hundred
stories became the book *Voices in Harmony*. The first thousand copies sold
out in a month.

It was a significant milestone. A culture weaned on secrecy and separation was daring to speak out and demand respect. Once the media cot-
toned on, Anne's phone started to ring. And it has never stopped. The
book led to the creation of Principle Voices, an advocacy organization with
the slogan "Don't talk about us, without us." So whenever the media come
to Utah, like me, in search of real-life polygamists, they visit Anne, the
gatekeeper.

We meet one Saturday morning, at her home by the foot of the mountains. She cuts an imposing figure—tall, with deep-set brown eyes that
wouldn't be out of place with a crack of lightning and a creaky hinge. She
has the air of an occasionally severe schoolmarm. But sprightly. "Do you
ski?" she asks. "Oh you should! I took it up when I was forty. It's never too
late." She doesn't hit the slopes "that often" any more. Anne is seventy-four.

There's a sadness about her home, a mustiness. I was expecting all the
bustle of a plural family, but Anne lives alone. Her chairs look scarcely sat
upon, the cushions are at perfect right angles, it's oppressively tidy. Her
husband of thirty-three years died in 2002, and her children have long
since left the nest. Still, polygamy keeps her busy. When she's not working
at a Mormon bookstore in downtown Salt Lake City, she's at home running Principle Voices, in the same office room where she once worked

for her husband Ogden. The phone calls and emails come from Japan, Australia, Germany, *The New York Times*, Larry King, you name it. This is polygamy's hour, and Anne is at the hub.

"If we don't speak up, we're never going to get it decriminalized," she says. So she tries to demystify polygamy, show its diversity, stop its demonization in the media. She wants people to say "fundamentalist Mormon" rather than "Mormon fundamentalist," and "plural marriage" rather than "polygamy." And she wants to spread the idea that polygamy—sorry, plural marriage—is actually a feminist lifestyle. Plural women can always balance career with family because the other wives provide the daycare. It's a solution for twenty-first-century women who want to have it all! And who wants a man around the whole time anyway? It's nice to have an evening to yourself sometimes. Doesn't absence make the heart grow fonder?

"There's always this focus on jealousy and sex all the time. Why not on love? In polygamy there are more people to love me, and more people for me to love. Let's put it on a higher level!"

"But what about Warren Jeffs?"

"I know," she says, shaking her head. "Because of the FLDS, people think our women are uneducated, barefoot and pregnant. And it's not true! All cultures have problems. There's abuse in monogamy, too."

This is a common riposte from the polygamist lobby—to compare the billions of monogamists of every faith, creed, language, shape and size, with their tightly defined demographic crumb of thirty-eight thousand fundamentalist Mormons (Anne's figures), all beholden to the same scripture, the same history and largely the same beliefs. It's like comparing Asia with Aspen.

Nevertheless, the message is getting across. Anne is delighted with the coverage in *The Salt Lake Tribune*, and on a national level, she senses attitudes shifting. She agrees that *Big Love* is probably helping, though she's not a fan of the show herself (too much sex). But other trends have energized her, like the decline of the traditional family unit. "There are grandparents taking care of grandkids, gays, single mothers, surrogates, lots of other lifestyles. And polygamy's been around the longest—it's probably the oldest type of marriage there is. We believe Adam had more wives than just Eve. This is not just some new innovative whatever like these new surrogacy and IVF things. They probably didn't even know how to do that in Bible days." Who needs IVF when virgins are giving birth?

She shows me graphs and charts. Ever since the book, it seems Principle Voices has become the de facto census keeper for plural marriage. "Here's the FLDS—that's the biggest with 10,000," she says. "Then the AUB, we call them the Allred Group, with 7,000. Then the Kingstons and Centennial Park with 1,500. These smaller groups here are like Jim Harmston's group, and then there are all these independents all over in Utah, Idaho, Montana, Missouri . . ."

Her figures are questionable. She simply asks the group leaders for numbers, and they have reasons to either exaggerate and inflate their significance, or lowball and not draw attention. (Certainly Tapestry reckons Anne's figures are too low).

But it's significant that almost every major group sends representatives to sit on Principle Voices' monthly action committee. To date, the FLDS remains the only group that refuses, and even there the relationship is thawing ever since the raid, when Principle Voices organized fundraising drives to send care packages to FLDS families and write letters to their displaced children. As an organization, it's flourishing. It assists polygamists who've felt the wrath of the law and, on occasion, even appeals convictions. It holds seminars for social services to better understand the fundamentalist community, and vice versa. One ongoing campaign is to alter the welfare claim forms. While Tapestry argues that polygamists burden the welfare system with all those kids and single moms, Anne insists the opposite—that polygamists don't use welfare *enough* because they don't know which box to tick, legal wife or single mother. And remarkably, the wind appears to be at Anne's back. Principle Voices may have originated out of opposition to Tapestry, but it has since outgrown it. In July of 2009, for example, while Principle Voices addressed a huge rally of FLDS members in downtown Salt Lake City, Tapestry was on its last legs, just a few months from disbanding.

To hear Anne tell it, this all began in 2004 with the first meeting of the Principle Action Committee. Simply bringing the groups together for the first time remains her proudest achievement.

"We had it here in my home, and we invited representatives from the major communities. Everyone except the FLDS—you couldn't get in there, at the risk of your life practically! And some of these people had not been in the same room for decades. Some were relatives and friends who used to be in the same group, but they've since split and split again. The next year, we even had the leaders of some groups come. We've got pictures of them talking together!"

She makes it sound like a Middle East peace summit, a convening of fractious groups, each convinced that only they have the true church. Polygamy is far from one happy family. As with Protestants and Catholics, religious groups typically save their greatest hatred for those that most closely resemble themselves.

"We respect everyone's differences," she says. "We're not trying to take over, we're just here to work toward what we have in common. Which is why the chairperson is always an Independent. If it was a group representative, the other groups might feel slighted."

Hypersensitivity and polygamists go hand in hand. Their persecution complex is a product of their history. They've been wounded from all sides—by the state, by the Mormon Church, by cultural prejudice. So long as polygamy remains a felony, Anne will continue to frame it as a civil rights issue, like racism and homophobia: polygamists as an oppressed minority seeking rights and representation. That's why she sees liberals as her best hope for a fair hearing. It's ironic that a conservative religious group should appeal to liberal secularists because other conservative religious groups view them with suspicion. Anyway, aren't Mormons hostile to gays and black people? Just a little bit?

Now's not the time to ask. I want Anne to introduce me to her polygamist friends first. So I ask about her experience of polygamy, and she visibly softens. For Anne, polygamy meant true love.

She came out of the LDS Church, a staunch Mormon who'd been married to another staunch Mormon called Ted for nine unhappy years. When they divorced in the mid-'60s, she had several children and the sense that a new, more religious chapter was opening up for her. She'd read that the LDS Church had changed radically over the years, and she wanted to adhere to the earlier teachings, like polygamy. It was around this time that she fell for a fundamentalist scholar called Ogden Kraut and became his second wife. They were a perfect match.

"We agreed on everything. The only thing was mayonnaise or salad dressing, so I kept a bottle of each in the fridge," she says, cheerfully. Ogden had several other wives after her, each one living in separate homes. But Anne didn't mind. "I felt so sure of my husband's love that I didn't care how many wives he had. And he was such a good man. I wanted him to bring similar happiness to other people."

They couldn't have children together, so they made books instead—sixty-five in all. Anne worked as Ogden's "secretary" and for years, their marriage was secret. Still today, some secrets remain. She won't say when they got married or who performed the ceremony or how many other plural wives would eventually join Ogden's family. She won't confirm whether the first wife consented to the marriage or attended the ceremony or whether she even knew that Anne and Ogden were man and wife for the early years while Anne pretended to the rest of the world that she was simply his PA. She will admit, however, to keeping her relationship with Ogden from her mother, her kids and the LDS Church. "My mother was trying to fix me up all the time, but I'd say, 'Mom, I'm happy with the way things are.' She thought I meant living alone whereas I meant being a plural wife!" Anne laughs. "You kind of have to play games in this thing."

As for the LDS Church, Anne's policy was "don't ask, don't tell." She remained an active member, playing piano at church and writing the newsletter, even as Ogden held fundamentalist meetings at their home. And the kids were none the wiser because Ogden would creep in and out of the house when they were asleep—he'd arrive after they were put to bed and leave before they woke up. "Then later in the day, he'd come back, and we'd work together on books," says Anne. "So as far as the kids knew, I was his secretary and that was that. I wasn't lying; I just wasn't telling them the whole story. I didn't want them to have to defend my lifestyle at school."

For years, Anne remained this secretary with a secret, working with Ogden by day and attending the occasional function by night, always as boss and secretary. "It was exciting!" she says. "It was very romantic and different and adventuresome! And you know, we had a marvelous romance. It was kept alive all the time because it was exciting and different."

There's a word for the woman who meets a married man for clandestine romantic trysts, who shares a knowing glance with him at dinner parties, the thrill of secrets, while the legal wife is at home folding the clothes, none the wiser. Yet Anne only utters the word "mistress" in disgust at the morality of the "outside world," particularly the French. Who are they to judge polygamists, she says? "Our only crime is that our men marry the women and support them and call them wives!" she says. Except for the ones who don't call them "wives," at least not in front of anyone else.

Ultimately, the secret got out. Anne's mother, a devout Mormon, was devastated when she discovered the truth, a disappointment she carried to her grave. The first wife decamped to Arizona with her five children. And when the church got wind, it put Anne on probation and eventually "disfellowshipped" her, removing her from the church rolls on April 6, 2005.

"So, will this be a positive or a negative book?"

"Well, Anne, I want to be fair," I tell her. "I feel that the negative side is well-known by now. What I'm interested in are ordinary polygamists, the people under the radar, the ones who don't make the headlines."

"So how are you going to present the negative side?"

"I'm not sure. I think the whole Warren Jeffs situation will raise many of the negative issues."

She's nodding. Yes, focus all the bad stuff on the FLDS. That's what she wants.

"Did you have any religious background?"

"Not really. But my parents were raised Hindu."

"Oh, is that Allah?"

"No, it's the one where the gods have loads of arms?" She seems content with this explanation. "My parents had an arranged marriage, you know."

"Did they?"

"Yes, my dad came over to England to get a job. And when he had a place to live, he had his parents back in India find him a wife. Then he went back, met my mum for the first time, married her and brought her to London. They're still together." She brightens. Now I'm no longer just some journalist, I'm a weirdo like her. "In my parents' culture they see it as a marriage of families. Big families, too. Both my mom and dad have like, ten brothers and sisters, that sort of thing."

"Like Mormon families! Well, when I introduce you to people, make sure you tell them that."

She said "when." This is a good sign. Suddenly my phone rings. It's sitting on the table between us and I notice the name flash up on the front: "Vicky Prunty." I lunge to grab it and flip it to silent. "Sorry about that,

Anne, I should really turn it off . . ." Did she see the name too? Maybe I should just tell her.

"That's okay. You can answer that if you want."

"No, it's not important." We sit for a minute. It's a little awkward.

"Now you must include the history in your book." *Bing bong*! My phone has one new message. "You know, I really don't mind if you want to make a call."

"Honestly, that's fine. I'll turn it off."

"Because the history is why fundamentalists exist, really. History and doctrine. It's very important. You can't interview these people unless you know the history. You won't understand them. And neither will your readers."

This is Anne the schoolmarm giving me my homework. She knows books, she knows polygamy and she has plenty of advice for me. I need to observe the proper etiquette, she warns. Don't ask the men how many wives they have or who they're married to when you meet them. Don't ask for surnames. Don't ask what jobs they do. Don't ask for any information that might identify them, because if people find out, they risk losing their jobs. Tread carefully, these are sensitive people.

"Here's a funny story for you—Gary Batchelor used to be married to Vicky Prunty from Tapestry Against Polygamy. Now he's married to Mary, the Chairwoman of Principle Voices. So Gary's really stuck between them!"

Why's she talking about Vicky all of a sudden? Should I just tell her that I met Vicky already?

"But I'd prefer it if you didn't mention that in your book."

"Mention what?"

"About Gary being in the middle of Mary and Vicky. Gary and Mary wouldn't want you to. What happened was Vicky became very controlling."

Did she see the phone? Does she know I'm lying? This is a woman who hid her marriage from her own kids for years. She can probably see right through me. It's time I left.

"And then Vicky left to go with another man, Christopher Nemelka. You don't need him in your book either. He's just not even relevant."

"Okay, well . . ."

"Vicky had a child with him. Then she had a child by somebody she wasn't even married to—so you can see the pattern. Ask Gary and Mary, oh they'll tell you about that. Gary's a talker."

"All right."

"But don't put any of that stuff in your book."

◈ The Batchelors

> Every day people are straying away from the church and going back to God.
> —Lennie Bruce[4]

Mary Batchelor of Principle Voices and Vicky Prunty of Tapestry Against Polygamy are used to duking it out in public. They've fought on the letters page of *The Salt Lake Tribune*, as dueling interviews in magazine articles and as talking heads on Fox News. Typically, they try to avoid the fact that they once also fought in private, as sister wives—both of them wary of reducing the argument from a national issue to a personal spat. But in polygamy, politics is personal. And personal shots have been taken.

Usually Vicky is first to the punch. She certainly didn't hold back with me. And Mary's response, even the creation of Principle Voices, has largely stemmed from an urge to defend herself, her family and her faith. It's in that spirit that Gary and Mary agree to meet me at their home.

"We don't want to get into a slanging match here," says Mary, sitting me down at her kitchen table. "See, Vicky will say things about us, and we'll think—'that's not true!' But if we fight back, it just makes her angrier. She's really . . . we just want to move on with our lives." She slaps the table and laughs. "So! What do you want to know?"

Mary's immediately endearing—open and chatty, quick to laugh, with a friendly round face and a thatch of straw-blonde hair. She loves grappling with a conversation, as does Gary, her lean and wolfish husband who sits beside her. And as they tag team the whole saga, they bicker in a charming, married way. Mary doesn't fit the stereotype of the submissive plural wife at all. But then she's not actually living polygamy at present. Ever since Vicky left fourteen years ago, it's just been Mary and Gary. One of the curiosities of Principle Voices is that neither of polygamy's most vocal advocates, Anne Wilde or Mary Batchelor, is actually living polygamy.

Their story starts with Gary, aged eighteen, who was living at home with his parents in England when Mormon missionaries came knocking and changed his life forever. He threw himself into this new faith, flying to Salt Lake and enrolling at BYU where he studied languages. And it was there that he met Vicky. For five years they were married as members of the LDS Church.

Then in the spring of 1986, a chain of events. Gary fell in with a patriot movement, the kind of people who obsess over international banking conspiracies that control the world. They introduced him to Lynn, a member of the Mormon Tabernacle Choir who had inexplicably stopped going to church. So Gary and Vicky went to Lynn's house for dinner to ask what was up, and Lynn told them of a fellow tenor in the choir who had read the *Journal of Discourses*—a collection of sermons from the 1840s and 1850s—and been so shaken up by certain passages that he took them to his bishop. His bishop promptly excommunicated him. This tenor then showed Lynn the passages in question, and Lynn also had questions for his bishop—and he too was excommunicated. So Gary asked "what passages?" And Lynn showed him. And that very night, he and Vicky decided to leave the church. Within a week they would be on the path to polygamy.

"It's like that Monty Python skit where a guy sees another guy dead on the ground clutching a piece of paper," says Gary. "He picks it up and reads it and starts laughing so hard that he falls over dead clutching the piece of paper."

The passages didn't even concern polygamy. They were about the Adam–God doctrine, a long buried Mormon belief that Adam is in fact the ruling god for our planet, not Jesus as the Church now maintains. Apparently Adam, the first human being on the planet, lived for 930 years siring children all the way in order to get the human race going.

"To me, nothing else had ever made so much sense," says Gary. "I know the church did not teach that, because I had never heard it. And I felt deceived. I felt there was an integrity lapse in the church that I couldn't tolerate."

Digging deeper, he discovered that the Church had taught Adam–God until the turn of the century when it started to tuck it away in order not to offend the Christian mainstream. Eventually the Church discounted the theory altogether, as it did with another core teaching about plural marriage. And this too made complete sense to Gary who, even while married to Vicky, retained feelings for another girl he'd once been engaged to at BYU.

"I think internally I had become the kind of person who was simply simultaneously in love with two people," he says. "Plural marriage just rang true to my nature." Vicky wasn't nearly as keen, of course, but she had no choice—Gary had never followed his religious convictions with anything less than total commitment. "It became pivotal," he says. "I was zealously moving in an ideological direction and there was no holding me back. And Vicky could see our marriage being threatened. So she prayed, and the next day she said, 'I have all the answers I need.'" She was in. It was time to find wife number two.

First things first—Gary moved Vicky into a cave. The Rock that Vicky had mentioned is in fact a polygamist community out in the red rock desert near Moab. Lynn introduced Gary to some friends who had blown out chunks of the rock with dynamite and fashioned living quarters inside. It was somewhat rough and ready, but it was theirs, a piece of Zion, and a safe place from which to usher in the last days. The head man at the Rock was a wonderful eccentric called Bob Foster, a man who felt the spirit keenly, and who invited Gary and Vicky to stay. And they accepted, though in practical terms, the move made little sense—Gary worked in Salt Lake, an eight-hour drive away. So during the week, he'd leave Vicky at the Rock and stay at the Singer-Swapp compound further north. He'd been gripped by the whole Addam Swapp story—blowing up the LDS stake center, engaging the authorities in a siege. And the more time he spent up there, the more he saw of Bill Morrison, Addam Swapp's lawyer. And by extension, Bill's daughter Mary, who would visit occasionally. It was the spring of 1988.

"Once, I brought Vicky up from the Rock, and Mary was there," says Gary. "And Vicky said to me, driving home, 'You know, that's someone you could marry.' It was just a silly wisecrack. I wasn't even that interested in Mary. But I saw her a few more times and I realized I had strong feelings for her."

Actually approaching Mary was another matter. She was only nineteen and she didn't come from a polygamist family—it could be a shocking proposition, particularly since she didn't seem in the least bit interested. There were a few ill-judged overtures on Gary's part, notably a letter written in French, followed up by a letter from Vicky insisting that her husband was actually a good man. Mary ran a mile. But a year and a half later, they met again at the Swapp compound. This time, Mary had come around to the idea that polygamy was a true teaching. She was even praying daily for the Lord to guide her to Mr. Right.

"I was just speechless," says Gary. "After all that knuckle-biting, I was thinking, 'How can I get this powerful inspiration and then it doesn't work out? God, do you let people down like this?'" They spent an awkward evening together—Gary, Mary, Vicky and the kids. Gary played a few songs on the piano. But, for a salesman, he wasn't much of a closer—the subject was never raised, Mary left again and Gary was at a loss. Little did he know that Mary was having an epiphany on the drive home.

"I was just struck by this total overwhelming love, and I started crying and . . . I felt like this is my family," she says. "I really didn't even know them but that's how I wanted it—I wanted God to tell me who to marry." A couple of lunch dates later, plans were afoot for the wedding.

Given the extent of the disaster that would unfold—a plural marriage that went so wrong it spawned a protest organization against itself—one might argue that God didn't have a hand in the matchmaking after all. Or if He did, He had His mind on other things, like helping rappers win Grammies or depicting the Virgin Mary in a grilled cheese sandwich. But Gary and Mary don't blame God. They blame themselves. And they blame Vicky. They could all read the writing on the wall.

The stress of the wedding, for starters. All the politics and muttering going on. Mary's parents and grandparents were all there, and none of them approved—they felt Vicky and Gary were too new to the gospel, that they were all in for a bumpy ride. And of course they were right. Neither Vicky, Gary nor Mary had grown up with polygamy. They had no idea what they were in for and there were no guidebooks. There's no *Dr. Phil* for polygamy. All they had was zeal and doctrine and naïvety. And to make things worse, they'd all been fasting for the previous five days. Come showtime, Gary could barely stand.

It didn't take long for things to start falling apart. First Vicky left the reception in tears—at the first few bars of "Here Comes the Bride," it was a case of "There Goes the Wife." Then Mary was shocked speechless when it came to opening the gifts. She'd planned to do it with Gary, back home, a private moment between them. But instead, Gary invited everyone—the family, Vicky, everyone.

"And as we're opening presents, he's giving things to Vicky," says Mary. "Like, 'Oh this'll work for our bedroom,' and 'This'll look good in your bathroom.' And I'm like—*what?* I can hardly say 'no' and take it back. Gary didn't mean any harm by it. But those are the things—when you go into polygamy you don't know how you're going to be blindsided. Vicky felt that if someone gave me something, Gary should decide if she needed it more than me.'"

"It's an interesting philosophical question," says Gary. "A man has two wives, one with rich parents and one with poor parents. Say the rich parents give their old car to the daughter rather than trade it in. So now you have an arbitrary inequity. And the whole spirit of communal living is to make sure that the bounties of the collective are shared fairly between the members. So now the husband has the responsibility to rebalance that inequity by getting the other wife a car that is equivalently nice. That's why plural marriage is so difficult for men. They have to solve problems that you don't have in monogamy."

Meanwhile, polygamy was making Vicky quite mercurial. "You never knew which Vicky you were going to get from one day to the next," says Gary. "One day she's all nice and loving, the next day my clothes are on the front lawn."

I bring up the full list of Vicky's charges—that Gary told her never to voice her opinion against his, that he prayed for her to die and disciplined the children inappropriately. And Gary sighs.

"I'm not going to take the bait," he says. "Her whole portrayal of me and our marriage is distorted and vindictive and calculated to paint herself as the only victim. I could say so much about her . . . but I won't. It was a divorce. Even in the best cases, divorces are full of heartbreak, rejection and allegations. And ours was no different. We were not perfect. We made mistakes. But to try and dismantle all of her contradictions and falsehoods and utter fantasies . . . it's just a vast expenditure of negative energy and it serves no good purpose. My priority is a peaceful home life for our children."[5]

He says that he tried to salvage his marriage at the time by giving democracy a shot—three-way meetings, joint decision making, everyone gets a say. It didn't work—Gary would end up siding with one wife or the other, creating a winner and a loser. But equally Gary couldn't put his foot down either, which became an issue when it came to doling out the money. At first both wives knew what the other was getting, which simply gave them ammunition to argue. Then Gary tried the line, "Tell me your needs and I'll make sure they're met." But then Wife A would want to know what Wife B's needs were first, and if Gary didn't tell her, his clothes wound up on the lawn.

It was a mistake to have both wives live in the same house for the first year and a half—the potential for conflict increased exponentially. Plural wives often mention that they will fight harder over the kitchen than they do over their man. And Gary's final mistake was to invite Christopher Nemelka over at a particularly fractious time in their marriage. Gary was somewhat fascinated with Nemelka back then, particularly his claim to have translated a whole new book of scripture by the powers of revelation. What's more, he came recommended by Anne Wilde, who was similarly enthused. But Nemelka's arrival was the beginning of Vicky's departure. And as bitter and draining as their marriage had been, when Vicky left, both Gary and Mary were heartbroken.

"In our hearts we never really believed she would leave," says Mary. "I was convinced the problems would be worked out." Instead, the acrimony has continued ever since. They fight through Tapestry and Principle Voices; they fight over who gets the kids and when and how they're to be raised.

Ultimately both women would succumb to exhaustion, with Mary standing down as director of Principle Voices in 2008, determined to focus on her family, and Vicky throwing in the towel on Tapestry the following year for much the same reason. And yet even after such a bitter experience of polygamy, Gary and Mary continue to defend plural marriage, even pine for it. Mere experience is no substitute for the magic of doctrine and the promise of salvation. It's as though working for Principle Voices has cemented their belief in the covenant—all those arguments stressing the pros and mitigating the cons.

But the Principle Voices position hasn't calcified in the same way that Tapestry's has. Mary is better able to discuss polygamy's negatives than Vicky can discuss polygamy's positives. While they both share a rhetoric of victimhood and an outrage about the LDS Church and the state, the "anti" lobby seems more impatient. Mary doesn't insist that I agree with her positions, just that I understand them. The more reasonable, less dogmatic campaigners appear to be the ones who believe in 930-year-old men.

But appearances may be deceptive. Dogma still reigns in the lives of the Batchelors. Despite all they've been through, they're quite open to entering the crucible again. It's not something they can be specific about but Mary admits that she has always felt out of balance in monogamy. And jealousy wouldn't be a concern because "jealousy is a vulnerability issue. There was not enough vulnerability between Vicky and me. We were cautious of each other. We should have talked about our feelings and shared all those heartbreaking things together. I may be able to do that with another woman."

Vicky doesn't buy this touchy-feely version of plural bliss. "Women in polygamy always make it sound so good," she says. "'Oh, the wives are like sisters'—all that. But they have to present that image. Mary's the first wife now, so she's been in a fifty-fifty relationship with Gary for all these years. That will end if Gary marries again. She'll be in for a shock. Gary will change. Polygamy changes everything."

I mention to Gary that I can't quite believe he would even consider a second wife, having been so obviously burned. And he gets all excited.

"Exactly! Exactly! That's what you need to understand!" he says. "This is a passionate religion, it's intense. When I learned that the LDS Church was burying some of its teachings, I had this swallow-the-red-pill thing where my mind is blasted open and now I have all this extra knowledge. It's been very rewarding for me to go through this somewhat Siddharthic journey of learning more and more. Now, I feel I'm at the loftiest place that I can be."

Where does this come from, this blazing certainty of Gary's? What kind of potion is Mormon doctrine that he would sacrifice his stability all over again?

"You need to get into some of the doctrine and the history or you'll never understand," he says.

"That's what Anne Wilde told me. And Vicky."

"Seriously, if you want to understand why these people live this way, you need some context."

"Of course."

"It's a fascinating history."

"I know."

"Have you read the Book of Mormon at least?"

Mormon Polygamy—
The First Century

CHAPTER 3

Whenever I see a pretty woman, I have to pray for grace.
—Joseph Smith[1]

As I say, it never ceases to amaze me how gullible some of our Church members are in broadcasting these sensational stories, or dreams, or visions, some alleged to have been given to church leaders.
—Harold B. Lee (LDS President)[2]

A CONFESSION—I HAVEN'T ACTUALLY *read* the Book of Mormon. Not the whole thing. I once managed to skim my way to the book of Ether, but then I needed to lie down. A case of the vapors. It's like literary Ambien with all those wherefores and untos and yeas.

But the story behind the book is fascinating. It begins with a revival, a religious mania that sweeps the land shaking the people into a fever, until they collapse to their knees, crying out for the new millennium, and then rise, resolved to bend society to their new purpose. Known as the Second Great Awakening, it took place in the 1820s and, as Marilynne Robinson notes, "left in its wake the abolitionist movement, the women's suffrage movement . . . Seventh-day Adventists, and the Latter-day Saints."[3] It swept the Northeast like brushfire, scorching with its zeal the entire states of New York and New England. The area around Palmyra, in

New York, was so ablaze with the spirit that it was named "Burned-over District." It was also where Joseph Smith grew up.

During Smith's youth, all the major movements were in town—the Quakers, the Shakers, the Shaking Quakers, the Perfectionists, the Celibates and the free love cult of Oneida, now survived by a successful brand of cutlery. The young Joseph would have witnessed all manner of delirium and ecstasy around him—the spasmodic jerking of bodies and heads, hysterical dancing or crawling around on all fours, barking. Wherever he turned, the air hummed with madness and possibility. His father was saddled in debt and operated a failing farm. His mother, Lucy, a mystical woman, would chatter to the Almighty as she went around the house. In his own way, Joseph was determined to surpass them both. Though he would later depict his teenage self as a simple seeker for the one true faith, Joseph's reputation was that of a rogue known for tall tales and an interest in folk magic. He became a "scryer" or "money digger," a treasure hunter of sorts. Using the props of an occultist, a necromancer's trick bag of crystals and relics, he would divine the location of Indian burial mounds in order to dig up their artifacts. Grave robbing, essentially.

His favored method was to place a special "seer" stone or "peep stone" (basically a rock with a hole in the middle) in an upturned hat and bury his face in it to exclude all light. Then the stones would tell him by way of wondrous visions where the treasure was buried. There were hiccups. Joseph was convicted of fraud in 1826 after being accused by a farmer who'd paid him to locate a stash of silver. And the father of his first wife, Emma Hales, didn't fall for it either. When the two confronted each other one day, a witness to the meeting, Peter Ingersoll, reported, "Joseph wept and acknowledged he could not see in a stone now, nor never could; and that his former pretension in that respect were all false."[4]

And yet over the next few years, he would harness his seer stone and hat to create a new world religion, a faith so powerful it intends to put a man in the White House.

The story goes that in the autumn of 1823, when Joseph was seventeen, an angel called Moroni visited him in his bedroom with news about a calling that he was to undertake. He'd been visited by angels before. There may have been another vision while walking through the woods, three years earlier, but Joseph had trouble keeping his story straight on that one.

In his first published writing about that period of his life—a good fourteen years later—he failed to mention the event altogether. Then he produced a version of the story in which he claimed he was sixteen at the time of the vision. Some years later, he claimed he saw not just "the Lord," but also two personages and a pillar of fire and many angels. Come the published version in 1840, however, he'd lost the pillar of fire and the angels and said he was fourteen, not sixteen. And the two personages were God and Jesus Christ. That's the version the Mormon Church goes by today.

In any case, it was the vision in his bedroom that truly set things into motion. The angel Moroni, hovering at the foot of his bed, told him about some gold plates on which was engraved the full history of the former inhabitants of America. The plates had been buried in the Cumorah hill 1,400 years earlier, and Joseph was to dig them out and translate them. Evidently the text was a sort of hieroglyphics, a language Joseph described as "reformed Egyptian." But God had also included with the plates a couple of seer stones, known as the Urim and Thummim, which He had primed specifically for translating them. Scripturally speaking, the batteries were included.

Then things got complicated. First Moroni said, "Now is not the time," but Joseph went and dug up the plates anyway, at which point he was thrown to the ground by a mysterious force and the plates vanished into thin air. Moroni promised he'd return them when the time was right, and that Joseph should keep coming back to the same spot every September 22 to check. So he did, and a few years passed with no joy. But then he married Emma Hale in 1827 and that very September, he found the gold plates in a stone box.

When Joseph first brought the plates home, he refused to show anybody because, he said, "No man can see it with the naked eye and live."[5] This sounded reasonable enough to his wife, Emma, who became his first secretary in his new calling. And though Emma never lost faith in Joseph, neither could she explain how he translated the plates while they were left on the table, wrapped in a cloth. His method was to stare into his peep stone in a hat and dictate the new scripture to Emma. (He couldn't transcribe it himself, as he was illiterate.)

Seeking funding for the publication of this new book, Joseph soon enlisted the farmer Martin Harris as both his secretary and underwriter for the first printing of his Book of Mormon. And just like Emma, Harris was forbidden a peek at the plates, lest God strike him down. So during the translation, a blanket would divide the room, with Joseph and his stones on one side and Harris on the other taking dictation. So it would have gone, had Harris's wife not interfered—she wasn't fooled by Smith's peep stone routine and demanded to read what they'd written. And Martin, who was clearly getting an earful at home, would cajole Joseph daily to let him show her their work. Finally he relented and Martin took the first 116 pages back to his skeptical wife. And, in an ingenious move, she stole the manuscript and challenged Joseph: "If this be a divine communication, the same being who revealed it to you can easily replace it."[6] But still, Joseph wriggled free. He claimed to have received a second revelation forbidding him to retranslate the first 116 pages, as Lucy Harris had asked, just in case the devil found the stolen portion, altered it and published it in a different form. God, he said, had a backup plan for just this eventuality—another set of smaller plates, the plates of Nephi, which covered the same history, albeit a condensed version with a slightly different slant, so Joseph was covered in case of any inconsistencies in translation.

Not surprisingly, Martin Harris wasn't Smith's secretary for much longer. He was replaced by Oliver Cowdery, who had a much less troublesome wife and was also considerably more literate than Harris. But again, Joseph's method seemed to render the actual plates incidental. He'd leave them wrapped on a table and bury his head in a hat, and somehow the scripture would appear to him out of the blackness. In this way, the "translation" was completed, and by 1831, he'd published the Book of Mormon. After which, an angel appeared and whisked the plates back up to heaven.

The only evidence that the plates ever existed is the testimony of the eleven so-called witnesses, whose names are listed on the first page of the Book of Mormon. Joseph reportedly took Cowdery, Harris and a man named David Whitmer into the woods where they saw an angel enveloped by a brilliant light who produced the plates and said a few words. But their accounts of the event differ and their stories changed over time. Harris started off saying that he "saw them with the eye of faith" and that "they were covered with a cloth." But years later, he said he "saw the angel turn the golden leaves over and over."[7] David Whitmer first said he saw the plates lying on the ground in a field. Then later, this became a lavish account of a table that appeared heaped with all kinds of plates and records.

In Fawn Brodie's 1945 biography of Smith, *No Man Knows My History*, she suggests that this "makes it all the more likely that the men were not conspirators but victims of Joseph's unconscious but positive talent at hypnosis." The claim is supported by an account of how Joseph persuaded a further eight witnesses to sign a declaration saying they'd not only seen the plates of gold but had handled them. Brodie writes:

> He assembled them in a room, and produced a box, which he said contained the precious treasure. The lid was opened; the witnesses peeped into it, but making no discovery, for the box was empty, they said, 'Brother Joseph, we do not see the plates.' The prophet answered them, 'O ye of little faith! . . . Down on your knees, brethren, every one of you, and pray God for the forgiveness of your sins . . .'

For a divine text, the Book of Mormon has come in for no little criticism. It's drearily written—the phrase "and it came to pass" is said to appear at least two thousand times. There is no great poetry, no Sermon on the Mount—its chief concern is with battles and feuds. Mark Twain famously described it as "chloroform in print." Harold Bloom, who considers Joseph Smith a "religious genius," has this verdict: "[I]t has bravura, but beyond question, it is wholly tendentious and frequently tedious."[8] And Fawn Brodie has this to say about Smith's literary chops: "He was chiefly a tale-teller and preacher. His characters were pale, humorless stereotypes; the prophets were always holy, and in 3,000 years of history, not a single harlot was made to speak."

In terms of straight forgery, an estimated twenty-five thousand words of the Book of Mormon are lifted from the Old Testament and two thousand words from the New Testament. The lifts come straight from the King James version of 1611, the one with which Joseph was most familiar, and they reproduce the grammatical and stylistic errors of translation that Bible scholars have since corrected—which would suggest that it's not an ancient record at all but an attempt by a nineteenth-century American to mimic one.[9] And whatever its merits—its audacity, for example, in purporting to present three millennia of human history—they are outweighed by the simple fact that it is almost certainly untrue. Not just the small print—the whole thing.

The abridged version is that around 600 BC, an Israelite named Lehi sailed from Israel to Central America and established a Hebraic culture in the Americas until about 400 AD. Lehi's sons, Nephi and Laman, were bitter rivals whose armies fought constantly. The moral, upstanding Nephites were "white and delightsome" as the early editions of the Book of Mormon had it. (When the church caught flack for overt racism, it replaced the phrase in 1981 with "pure and delightsome.") The nasty, mischievous Lamanites, on the other hand, were cursed with dark skin. The Book of Mormon is at heart the story of a race war.

The battles continued on and off for hundreds of years. There was a lull around 33 AD, when Jesus, fresh from his resurrection, appeared in the sky above them, to tell them to give peace a chance. So they did, for about two hundred years, but then war broke out again. And this time the Lamanites went on a rampage and slaughtered every last Nephite, including the valiant General Mormon, who died on Cumorah hill. His story might have died with him, had his son Moroni—the angel who visited Joseph in the bedroom—not preserved his father's legacy on gold plates and hidden them for future generations to discover. Only in the Mormon version of American history are white people the victims rather than the perpetrators of genocide.

The problem with all this is the central claim that Native Americans are in fact Lamanites, descendants of Israel. There's simply no evidence to support it—not a shred. No trace of Hebrew in the ancient languages of Native America, no Hebraic influence in the artifacts and archeology and no evidence of the scores of great cities of the Nephite civilization. Whole cities we're talking about. Not a sign.

Smith had devoured the Bible as a boy, so it was natural enough for him to identify with the Hebrews. And, as Fawn Brodie points out, there was another book making the case for the Hebraic origin of Native Americans that was published a few years earlier.[10] But the genetic markers of Native Americans have been studied and all signs point to an ancestry in the people of Northeast Asia, who crossed the Bering Strait.[11] There's no reason to postulate a link to the Middle East, and yet Mormons insist that the evidence isn't all in yet. It's the argument Creationists use against evolution, and the oil industry has employed about global warming—we're not sure, there are alternative theories, it's too early to say.

The church insists that the Book of Mormon is a work of literal history, not metaphor or myth. And yet their only attempt to find proof is a small, token department called FARMS—the Foundation for Ancient Research and Mormon Studies, based at BYU—which sends archeologists to Central America in the hope of finding something, anything, that will relate to the Middle East. It hasn't happened yet. But a dearth of evidence has never held back a religion. One of the church's most popular defenses of the book—one worthy of Stephen Colbert—is that the book is its own proof. That is: the book that says it was written by God must have been written by God because it says so in the book and God doesn't lie. (Now hand over 10 percent of your income.)

It's said that the Book of Mormon is simply too genius for an uneducated gadabout like Smith to make up himself. But in fact, the ideas are quite fitting for an unschooled rube of the early nineteenth century. The antipathy toward blacks, for instance, is in tune with the practice of slavery. Joseph maintained that blacks were the descendants of Ham, one of Noah's three sons who had committed one of the Bible's more obscure crimes, when he saw his father sleeping drunk and naked on his bed. Noah awoke and promptly cursed Ham, declaring that his son would be a slave. The Biblical story is notoriously difficult to interpret, but according to Joseph, Ham's descendants were cursed with dark skin, which by Joseph's reckoning has a connotation of cowardice. As per the Book of Mormon, we all began life as spirit children in heaven prior to taking bodies on Earth, and there was a war in heaven between the followers of Lucifer and the followers of Jehovah. But a third of the spirits didn't pick sides, opting to sit on the sidelines waiting to see who won. For this fence sitting they were cursed with black skin when they took physical bodies. It was a similar curse that Noah inflicted on Ham.

Ideas like this proved immensely popular. Of all the cults to emerge from the Second Great Awakening, only Mormonism became an international religion. And this is Smith's genius—he pitched his product perfectly. Mormonism spoke directly to the yearnings of his believers, their self-image and their optimism—it's quintessentially American. As Richard and Joan Ostling write in their book *Mormon America*, Mormonism is "a religious version of the American dream."

The flattery alone. From day one, Mormons refer to themselves as saints—sainthood isn't earned through good works; it's part of the sign-up package. When Smith taught that Americans were God's chosen people, he was tapping into a tradition of American exceptionalism. This is a nation bursting with pride in its independence from colonialism, its famous freedoms—the New World was too good *not* to be holy. How else do you explain Manifest Destiny? And so the teleological arguments for the Book of Mormon flow easily: this is the Promised Land, therefore the Israelites must have come here; we're God's chosen people, therefore Jesus must have visited us.

Furthermore, the prize is bigger. Mormons can expect the world, quite literally. They're encouraged to receive direct revelation from the Lord, and if they do right in this life, the men at least can expect a promotion in the next, to the level of a deity. This is why they tithe, why they say "heck" instead of "hell"; it's why fundamentalists practice plural marriage at the risk of prosecution. Not to commune with God in heaven, but actually to become gods themselves, with dominion over entire planets.

The implications of this prospective godhood are earthshaking for a purportedly Christian faith. No longer is God an ethereal, ubiquitous, invisible presence but a former man of flesh and blood, who ascended in the Mormon fashion. Early Mormons believed that God was Adam, and that Adam was in fact the father of Jesus. But this so-called Adam–God doctrine has since been disavowed by the Mormon Church, which insists that the title in fact goes to Jesus, who reigned over Earth in his premortal form, before his corporeal birth in a manger. Nevertheless, the principle remains true, as a famous Mormon maxim has it: "As man now is, God once was; as God is now, man shall be."[12] And it won't be much of a wait either. "Latter Day" implies that the end is nigh, and godhood is around the corner.

In the interim, however, there would be suffering. Certainly Smith's followers suffered terribly. Wherever they laid foundations, the Mormons were loathed and routed—from New York to Ohio to Missouri to Illinois. Men were tarred and feathered, stripped and horsewhipped, their homes and businesses set ablaze, their women and children abused. Even God seemed displeased, sending them a crippling plague of cholera in 1839. As a result, persecution became a theme of the Mormon story. It imprinted itself upon the Mormon character. And however painful the persecution was to endure, it also galvanized the people and renewed their commitment to the mission. Part of the problem was that they were trying to settle what was then the western frontier, a wild and violent country of drifters and men of questionable pasts, given to hunting rather than farming. These frontier types felt threatened by the self-proclaimed saints, with their communistic way of living, their ant-like work ethic and their utter allegiance to Prophet Joseph. And the rumors of polygamy didn't help. Though the Mormons denied it for years, it was well known that Joseph was practicing plural marriage. Of all the revolutionary doctrines he'd created, this would be his ultimate undoing.

Scholars reckon he came upon the idea around 1830, when he was working on a "translation" of the Bible and found evidence of polygamy in the Old Testament. (It's not hard to find; Abraham, Jacob, David and Solomon were all open polygamists.) He didn't announce his revelation on the subject until much later, but there's no doubt he'd been practicing plural marriage before then. The relevant scripture in the Book of Mormon is the fourth verse in section 132 from the Doctrine and Covenants:

> For behold, I reveal unto you a new and an everlasting covenant; and if ye abide not that covenant, then are ye damned; for no one can reject this covenant and be permitted to enter into my glory.

Joseph was by most accounts a Clintonian prophet—charismatic, a convenient liar and quite incapable of keeping it in his pants. By the time he died, he'd accumulated thirty-three wives according to most, though there may have been more. And of these, according to historian Todd Compton,[13] eighteen were single, four widowed and eleven married and cohabiting with their spouses when he married them. Of the married women, most were married to church members who were probably happy to offer their wives to the dashing young prophet. And contrary to claims that polygamy was just a means of caring for older, unattached women during tough times, most of Joseph's wives were teenagers or in their twenties. There's little doubt he was having sex with them. Several wrote as much in their journals.[14]

As a spiritual justification to sleep with other women, section 132 worked wonderfully. It amounts to a chat-up line about the premortal existence. Mary Lightner wrote in her journal: "Joseph Said I was his, before I came here . . . I was created for him before the foundation of the Earth was laid."[15] In other words, "We're kindred spirits who were matched up in heaven, but by some mix-up in this life, we got married to different people. So let's put things straight back at your place." And to inoculate himself against charges of adultery, he claimed that all marriages were invalid unless they were performed by proper Mormon priesthood authority.

Joseph knew just how explosive his new doctrine was, so he kept schtum about his extracurricular conjugation for years, telling only a handful of people. But many of those who found out were outraged. When Oliver Cowdery discovered his affair with Fanny Alger, a sixteen-year-old live-in maid, he left the church, having written to his brother of "a dirty, nasty, filthy affair."[16] According to one elder, Mosiah Hancock, Alger had been a part of a trade—in return for Fanny, Joseph gave her uncle Levi a girl named Clarissa Reed.

But no one was angrier about the Alger affair than Joseph's first wife, Emma. As soon as she found out, she threw Alger out of the house. (It's believed Joseph then tried it on with her replacement). And clearly, his subsequent announcement in verse fifty-four, section 132 was designed specifically to keep Emma in check. It's an open threat:

> And I command mine handmaid Emma Smith, to abide and cleave unto my servant Joseph, and to none else. But if she will not abide this commandment she shall be destroyed, saith the Lord; for I am the Lord thy God, and will destroy her if she abide not in my law.

It was polygamy that killed Smith, in a roundabout way. The Mormons had settled in Nauvoo, Illinois, and were gathering strength—they'd built an impressive temple, raised a small army, and the prophet was acquiring a taste for power. In 1844, the year of his death, he not only announced his candidacy for president of the United States but also established a secret Council of Fifty, whose meetings remain a mystery to this day—no records were kept and the LDS Church is typically revealing nothing.[17] But we can presume it discussed how best to expand and apply its mounting economic and military power. Smith had plans for a theocracy, and he was making his neighbors nervous.[18]

Meanwhile, Smith's polygamy was creating enemies. One William Law, whose wife Smith had repeatedly propositioned, joined with a group of other dissenters to establish a newspaper, the *Nauvoo Expositor*, expressly for the purpose of discrediting Smith. It only ever published one issue, the June 7 edition, attacking Smith for his political ambition and in particular his practice of polygamy. Joseph denied the charges, lying easily and with passion, motivating his followers to destroy the printing presses in retaliation. But this ignited their enemies. Polygamy was one thing, but an assault on the free press was an attack on the Constitution—it was the perfect excuse. The mob that set after Smith eventually closed in on him in a jail in Carthage and stormed the building. In the fighting, the prophet was shot and killed.

Smith's martyrdom was a fitting close to an extraordinary life. Not only did his murder cement his legend, but it also secured the future of his religion. In his death, he intensified the Mormon persecution complex and ushered in the leadership of Brigham Young, an altogether more resolute and pragmatic man. It was Young who led his people out west to find a homeland, Young who built the Temple, the roads and the cities in Utah. And it was Young who began the rebranding of the land of Utes as a Holy Land, assigning place names plucked from the Bible and the Book of Mormon. He noticed just enough similarities to flatter his flock that they were indeed the new Israelites and that he was in fact America's Moses. After all, there was a lake like the one in Galilee and mountains like those in Sinai. He had a beard, Moses had a beard. And ... that's about it.

Once again, however, the polygamy issue became contentious. Abraham Lincoln was the first to turn up the heat in 1862 with the signing of the Morrill Anti-Bigamy Act, but it didn't work because most probate judges in Utah were Mormon bishops. Then president Ulysses Grant tried to pursue Brigham Young for lascivious cohabitation, but nothing came of it. Then the church, feeling emboldened, decided in 1874 to force the issue and challenge the constitutionality of the antibigamy law. It submitted a test case—that of Brigham Young's secretary, George Reynolds, who was indicted of bigamy when his second wife admitted to being a plural wife.

The case made it all the way to the U.S. Supreme Court, just as the church had planned. But in the final verdict, they lost. In *Reynolds v. the United States*, justice Alexander Waite ruled that "Laws are made for the government of actions, and while they cannot interfere with mere religious belief and opinions, they may with practices."[19]

The reasoning is daft—that religion is a matter of beliefs rather than action, that it ought to exist only in your head. So Mormons ignored the decision and continued to practice polygamy, what with God's law being higher than man's and all that. But the pressure was telling, and the church began to divide: diehards like John Taylor, who would become the third prophet of the Mormon Church, insisted that polygamy was an immutable law, while Brigham Young, ever the pragmatist, was backing away from the issue. Young wasn't alone. Many Mormons had entered polygamy in the 1850s because they thought the Millennium was upon them, but when nothing changed, they asked Young to dissolve their unsatisfactory marriages. So in 1871, Young flip-flopped and said that polygamy was no longer essential to reaching the highest degree of heaven: "A man may embrace the law of celestial marriage in his heart," he said, "and not take the second wife."[20]

The pressure kept mounting. The Edmunds Act of 1882 didn't only render polygamists ineligible for public office and jury duty, it also meant that Mormons could be prosecuted for unlawful cohabitation, which was far easier to prove. And so the "cohab hunts" began—federal marshals swooping down on communities throughout Utah and southern Idaho looking for violators. A Mormon Underground was created in which men hid near or within their own homes in secret compartments and cellars called "polygamy pits." Almost one thousand Mormon men, and a few women, were jailed during this time. For some it was a badge of honor. Some even turned themselves in.

It was in this climate that the crucial 1886 revelation took place. John Taylor, the president of the church, asked God whether or not he should end polygamy. He'd long been a defender of the practice and had gone into hiding, himself, from January 1885, when federal officials ordered his arrest. God gave him an answer in September 1886, while he was hiding out at the house of a John W. Woolley. God told him that "my everlasting covenants cannot be abrogated nor done away with but they stand forever."

Only three months later, the seventy-eight-year-old Taylor married the twenty-six-year-old Josephine Roueche.[21]

Most modern polygamists claim their legitimacy from the 1886 revelation. But did it even happen? The only witness was John Woolley's son, Lorin, who claims he was one of John Taylor's bodyguards at the time. And while the fundamentalists believe him, the LDS Church doesn't. A later church president, Heber J. Grant, even called Woolley "a pathological liar."[22]

Lorin Woolley's story was that John Taylor retired one night to pray on the polygamy question, while Woolley himself stood guard outside his door, the only entrance to the room. He saw a light under the door and heard voices—Taylor was chatting with first one person, then another. And so it went until dawn, after which Taylor emerged from his room and said, "I had a very pleasant conversation last night with the Prophet Joseph."[23] The message was plain: polygamy was to be sustained. (The third voice was Jesus's, apparently).

That Lorin Woolley waited until 1912, some twenty-five years later, to mention this momentous event is his first credibility problem. But he has others. According to Woolley, the very next day Taylor held an eight-hour meeting attended by thirteen people, five of whom were given copies of his revelation and then ordained with priesthood authority—Lorin and four others. But the other four men left little record of these ordinations and did not speak of the meeting to anyone else prior to Woolley's story. And the other people listed as being present reportedly said nothing of the matter in their journals. There's no record of Lorin Woolley serving as a bodyguard to John Taylor—he was a little slight for the job anyway. And he was quite the storyteller. He claimed, for instance, that he was once a spy for the church and then a spy for the U.S. Secret Service.[24] He claimed to have met Mahatma Gandhi along with several U.S. presidents[25] and to have been visited by the likes of Joseph Smith, John Taylor and Jesus Christ.

Nevertheless, fundamentalists believe him. They have to—without Lorin Woolley, there wouldn't be much left of polygamy. But they also distrust the LDS Church on this matter, since it has denied the authenticity of the 1886 revelation in typically shady fashion. The revelation is said to be handwritten on a piece of paper that was found among John Taylor's effects after his death. But the church won't release the paper for authentication, nor the journals of several other alleged attendees of the eight-hour meeting. It all gives credence to the fundamentalist claim that something stinks in Denmark and the church has apostatized.

After Taylor's death in 1887 came the final blow. The federal government gave the Edmunds Act sharper teeth, making plural marriages felonies and forcing wives to testify against husbands. The renewed act even threatened to dissolve the legal entity of the church corporation and confiscate church property over $50,000. So the next church president, Wilford Woodruff, caved in. On September 24, 1890, he issued the Manifesto—an official Church document stating that members were not to practice polygamy anymore, but to obey the law of the land. It signaled the start of the church's transformation, a journey from the fringe to the mainstream.

The going was rough. The Manifesto was widely jeered. Gentiles saw no admission that polygamy was wrong—only advice to submit to the law. And Mormons saw only political expediency, not a bonafide revelation from God. "It's a press release, not a revelation," says Anne Wilde, noting that it begins "To Whom It May Concern" and not "Thus Saith The Lord."

What's clear is its insincerity. Even Woodruff appeared to be playing both sides. He hedged desperately, insisting that God had written the Manifesto, so any impression of political expediency must have been His idea—perhaps God was simply trying to protect the church? And his fellow church leaders looked for loopholes. There was no outright condemnation of plural marriage, so maybe they could take extra wives in Canada or Mexico without breaking American laws? Maybe God would permit the occasional lie if it was to help other members of the church? The wheels of hypocrisy were turning. While outwardly opposed to the practice, the church was winking at it all over the place. Between 1890 and 1904, the number of church-approved plural marriages was at least 250. And the numbers went up after Utah was given statehood in 1896—statehood that had been granted specifically because church leaders promised to clamp down on polygamy. In 1910, *The Salt Lake Tribune* listed more than two hundred Mormon men, including six apostles, who had taken post-Manifesto wives.[26] The Mormon reputation was beginning to morph—from that of a sexually deviant cult to a deceitful church whose leaders couldn't be trusted. And neither version held out much prospect for acceptance into mainstream society.

So when Heber J. Grant became president, he called an end to the duplicity. At the General Conference in 1931, he announced that the church would not only excommunicate polygamists, it would assist the state in prosecuting them—this from a man guilty of post-Manifesto cohabitation himself in 1899. Nevertheless, even Grant maintained his deniability. "We never believed polygamy was wrong and never will," he said in a 1937 interview. But "one of the cardinal laws of the church is to obey the law."[27] The polygamists were driven underground once more, this time hounded by both the state and their own church. But they were a determined lot and accustomed to persecution. They swore their children to secrecy, kept their families close and gathered in secret. And in this way, polygamy has prospered ever since.

When the Saints Come Marching Out

When a religion has become an orthodoxy, its day of inwardness is over: the spring is dry; the faithful live at second hand exclusively and stone the prophets in their turn. The new church, in spite of whatever human goodness it may foster, can be henceforth counted on as a staunch ally in every attempt to stifle the spontaneous religious spirit, and to stop all later bubblings of the fountain from which in purer days it drew its own supply of inspiration.

—William James, *The Varieties of Religious Experience*

There is a piece of famous advice, grand advice even if it is in German, to forget what you can't bear.

—Saul Bellow, *Herzog*

$\mathcal{I}$T's APRIL 1, the Sunday of the LDS Church's biennial National Conference weekend, and anywhere between a billion and a trillion Mormons are pouring out of the conference center. The men and boys look chipper and corporate, their dark suits so stiff the hangers might still be in the jackets. The women resemble an army of Martha Stewarts or small-town news anchors, supreme in their assurance that their salvation is secure, their linens spotless and their soufflés certain to rise in this life and the next. No one rushes or dawdles or crisscrosses the rows, and this goes for the children too. The orderliness is immaculate. Their pacing and posture is so even, so metronomic that I'm thinking of microchips and slow-release medication, of Nurse Ratched, George Orwell and *Invasion of the Body Snatchers* starring Donald Sutherland. Outside of Japan or the insect world, I've never seen anything less unruly. It's so very ruly it's terrifying.

I thought it'd be a good idea to explore Salt Lake City, the spiritual home of polygamy and the seat of the Mother Church. And this is more or less what I'd been expecting. The modern church is known to be acutely corporate and straitlaced; mostly conservative, Republican and obsessed with family values; and determined to preserve America's moral center against a rising tide of turpitude. And yet this same church was once considered morality's greatest enemy, a threat to the social fabric. For the first sixty or seventy years, Mormonism was seen as a heretical cult infamous for its sexual degeneracy (polygamy), theocratic tilt (allegiance to a prophet) and pseudocommunism (living "United Order").

So the Mormon story is one of dramatic reversal, a church that changed its stripes. A former affront to heartland Puritanism is now a bastion of the same. The one-time communitarians are now capitalists and political allies of the Christian evangelicals who frankly can't stand them. There are those who admire the church's metamorphosis, its ability to adapt— missionaries proudly point to the sign on the corporate headquarters building that reads THE CHURCH OF JESUS CHRIST OF LATTER-DAY SAINTS and say, "See how the words 'Jesus Christ' are bigger than all the others? The Church changed that specifically to appear more Christian."

But others find the church's mutability dishonest. Fundamentalists accuse the church of having betrayed its core principles, with polygamy as just the start. There's also the Adam–God doctrine that so exercised Gary Batchelor. Not to mention the whole about-face in the church's attitude toward black people. Until 1978, black people were expressly forbidden from holding the priesthood. But then the church reversed this position, under Prophet Spencer W. Kimball. And this was no minor tweak— for Mormons, the priesthood is the key to partaking in the sacrament, receiving temple endowments, the sealings of marriage and admission to heaven. All Mormon men hold the priesthood. Today, Mormons speak about June 1, 1978, as a day on which prayers were answered and a burden was lifted. Church members were sobbing with joy.

But surely President Kimball's Kleenex breakthrough was long overdue? After all, 1978 was twenty-three years after Rosa Parks and fifteen years after "I have a dream." Jimi Hendrix was dead and Muhammad Ali's best years were behind him. Mormons remain prickly about the subject today, insisting that their institutional racism is a thing of the past and can't we all just move on. In March 2013, the church even amended the section describing the 1978 declaration by saying that the ban it lifted (on black people entering the church) was iffy from the outset: "Church records offer no clear insights into the origins of this practice," it now says. But many fundamentalists reckon that the Kimball declaration was as forced as the 1890 Manifesto on polygamy. So a cloud still hovers. It's probably fair to say that there wouldn't be so much prejudice if it wasn't for those Mormons.

Nevertheless, the church's strategy of capitulation and assimilation appears to be paying off. For all its scorn of evolution, Mormonism has followed an archetypical Darwinian path out of a teeming free market of religions—competition, adaptability, success and expansion. Now the church in the United States is more Bible-y and corporate than many of its Christian peers.

Certainly it's richer. Per capita, Mormonism is comfortably the wealthiest religion on the planet, though the church has always been typically secretive about actual numbers. By some estimates, revenues of church-held businesses amount to upwards of $7 billion per year, and that figure is dwarfed by the church's immense property holdings worldwide. Frank Zappa once said that the only difference between a church and a cult is its real estate portfolio. According to Anson Shupe and John Heinerman, authors of *The Mormon Corporate Empire*, the most detailed investigation yet, church assets amount to $11 billion. But that was back in 1985. The church has grown considerably since. It boasted thirteen million members at the latest accounting, each one of them tithing 10 percent of their incomes—gross, not net.

What's extraordinary about Mormon growth is that it appears to defy orthodoxy. Here is a faith which was conceived not in the primitivism of bygone millennia, but in the early nineteenth century, during Reason's greatest advances, and it has flourished ever since in their midst. No doubt the missionary program yields its harvest of souls—few churches are quite so dedicated to proselytization. And Mormons do like to procreate, a channel of expansion that polygamy turbocharged in its early years. But here again, Mormon families are a rebuke to the convention that social advance begets lower fertility rates, not higher.

There was a piece of hype that followed the church in recent years, one that it rather enjoyed—that of the Fastest-Growing Religion.[1] It was never proven but there's little doubt that its global reach is extending. Now that the racial barriers have been lifted, the growth markets are increasingly overseas. The ratio of non-American to American Mormons has more than tripled since 1980. And this all sits perfectly with the church's stated plan to convert the entire world and usher in the destructions, followed by the Second Coming of Christ, after which they can all become gods in the next life, with whole planets to control for eternity. Given the context, their bid to put a "saint" in the White House is relatively modest.

Spend a few days in Salt Lake City, however, and the prospect of Mormon power is a shuddering thought. And not just because of the dismal liquor laws. In the Downtown District surrounding the temple, the streets are vast, vacant and alienating; the intersections are barren expanses; pedestrians look lost and cowed. It's Brigham Young's fault for stipulating that the streets should be wide enough to turn a horse and carriage. He surely envisioned his Mormon Mecca as a hive of bustling saints, busy consecrating their profits to his beloved church. Instead he created a scene from *28 Days Later*, peopled only by missionary drones stalking the streets searching for new souls. Even cars look adrift on the giant streets of Salt Lake City, stranded at red lights for eternities, watching tiny pedestrians traverse immense crossings.

Mind you, there's a cool side to Salt Lake City, if you can find it. The coffee shops have emerged as salons of the alternative SLC, the Gentile City, caffeinated and groovy, where friendly students at the University of Utah will come to the rescue of a dismayed out-of-towner. There's some Gentile solidarity going on. Go to the Sugar House neighborhood, they say. It's cool there. Check out Ninth and Ninth, there's a gay gift shop.

But even these pockets are under assault. They've torn down historic buildings in Sugar House to make way for a dull residential project. And in downtown Salt Lake, the church has flapped its mighty checkbook and demolished whole blocks in the gust. By 2012 the church promises another mall near Temple Square, some residential living and—essential to any swinging metropolis—a BYU campus.

I learned all this on a bus tour of the city. I like bus tours. I like the seniors and their plastic bags, the chatty guides, the gift shop. Our guy taught us that the Salt Lake Valley is "the biggest hole on earth—seventy miles wide and fifty miles deep." And that Brigham Young stopped the wagon trails and said, "This is the place," at a place now called Heritage Park, where they do pony rides and you can buy actual Salt Lake salt.

But I also learned that Mormons can't be trusted with their own history. A case in point: the bronze engraving at Heritage Park commemorating the Donner Party, a wagon train bound for California that became snowbound somewhere in the Sierra Nevadas and resorted to cannibalism to survive.[2] The engraving makes no mention of the cannibalism, which is like commemorating O.J. Simpson without mentioning the murders. And this is typical—the Mormon Church is obsessed with its history only to the extent that it can be sanitized and revised for present purposes.

On the one hand, the church is clearly committed to the preservation of its past—it employs scores of historians in large, well-funded departments. The church history archives contain fifty thousand collections— thirty-nine thousand more than the Library of Congress. Members are encouraged to explore their family trees and pioneer heritage; the immense genealogical library is their pride and joy. And yet the past it presents is a propaganda reel. Should a Mormon historian dare to dissent, then the church simply excommunicates. The last purge was in 1993 when a series of scholars known as the September Six were thrown out, including the openly gay scholar D. Michael Quinn, who had notably drawn attention to post-Manifesto polygamy within the church.

The most egregious display of church revisionism is in Temple Square. Take the Joseph Smith movie, for example, which plays every ninety minutes at the Legacy Theater and reduces the prophet's complex story to an infantile exercise in myth and popcorn. Gone are Smith's years of money digging, his fascination with peep stones and his taste for other men's wives—instead we see him heal the sick and buy a slave his freedom. Gone too is Joseph's haughty, aquiline beak—the actor cast looks more like Ewan McGregor. And for all the camera's ogling of the handsome and earnest Mormons, it similarly fetishizes their tormentors, the toothless mobs of drunken Gentiles, their faces riddled with sores. Leni Riefenstahl, eat your heart out.

The revisionism continues throughout Temple Square. In the North Visitors Center, a life-size diorama depicts Joseph Smith reading the golden plates directly from a ring binder, while Oliver Cowdery sits across the table from him—no blanket, no peep stone, no hat. And there's not a single mention of polygamy anywhere. The silence is deafening. Not a word about Joseph Smith's thirty-odd wives or the polygamy of subsequent church presidents. Of all the topics that the church would sooner avoid, polygamy and magic are up at the top, but there are others. The racism is one. Also the "garments," or "magic underwear," or "Joseph Jammies" that are said to operate like force fields, saving the wearer from getting mangled in car wrecks and such.

Then there are the baptisms for the dead, which sounds like a George A. Romero movie but may actually be creepier. It's a ritual that combines two of the church's core characteristics—a hunger for world domination and a fondness for tampering with the legacies of the departed, a tradition dating back to Joseph Smith's plundering of burial mounds. What happens is that every week, Mormons gather at temples with names of the deceased and undergo proxy baptisms on their behalf. And the baptisms are recorded in an immense database, deep within a mountain in Utah, which members are busy filling with all the names they can find. The practice caused a stink in the mid-'90s when the American Jewish Committee objected to the baptism of Holocaust victims and the creation of a record that robbed them of the very Jewishness for which they had died. So the church took the Jews off their lists—two chosen people at loggerheads. But the work continues on other fronts. Gandhi, Pope John Paul II, Elvis and Hitler have all been posthumously baptized, as has President Obama's late mother, Stanley Ann Dunham.

The tour stopped at Brigham Young's home, the Beehive House, a hokey attraction on the tourist beat. Missionaries with stars-and-stripes badges approached me like shop-floor sales staff. One Sister Wickley busked her way through showing me the bizarre exhibits in the glass cases.

"This is a bracelet that Brigham Young wore. Guess what it's made of."

"I don't know."

"Hair. His own hair. And see this, this is made of hair too. They made a lot of things out of hair."

"Why?"

"I dunno. I guess, you know, pioneers—they made use of everything."

"And what's this?" Near the hair bracelets was a book with a weird half-Russian looking script.

"Oh that's the Deseret alphabet—they tried to start a new language."

"I guess it didn't work out."

"I guess."

I liked Sister Wickley, her whole shruggy, I-just-work-here attitude. But she didn't lead the tour; Sister Godfrey did. And Sister Godfrey had fallen into a bowl of smug when she was a baby. With her nose in the air, she led us through the house, past the latter-day clothes folded on latter-day beds.

"Hands up who can guess why the boys' rooms were smaller than the girls' rooms?" she said. A mother elbowed her boy, and his arm shot up. "Because the boys were out working!" he said. And Godfrey and the boy's mother exchanged a look that, if smugness could create electricity, would have powered a small city.

Incidentally, hands up who spotted Godfrey's attempt to diffuse Mormonism's patriarchal reputation? The boys may have had smaller rooms than the girls, but there's no mention of Brigham Young's rampant polygamy. Nor his declaration that men could simply claim the wives of lower-ranking men if the women conceded.[3] Needless to say, Young was the highest-ranking priest at the time.

"I just love walking through this house," Godfrey breezed. "It's as exciting as walking through Noah's Ark!"

Come the end of the tour, the sisters handed out pencils and forms and asked for the numbers of friends who "need to hear the gospel." All kinds of "friends" came to mind, but then the girls started singing. "Because I have been given so much, each day I must give . . ." I tried to escape, but there was singing outside, too. You can't escape hymns in Temple Square. Singing missionaries stalk the grounds. The strains of their voices waft through the white hospice architecture, accompanied by the soft pad of Hush Puppies and a general geriatric murmur. Your only hope is to keep moving. Stop for a second at a diorama or map and they appear suddenly by your side, smiling in pairs, like *The Shining*.

The missionary thing, I don't get. As if lecturing perfect strangers about the meaning of life weren't patronizing enough, they put teenagers on the job, dispatching them to all corners of the Earth to gather souls for the Lord as if they're rounding up shopping carts in a parking lot, the only other job they're qualified for. It wouldn't be so bad if they were more like Sister Wickley, more at peace with their teenage cluelessness. But it's Godfreys that the church is known for. Smugness emanates from the temple like a fog. It's as native a feature to Salt Lake as vanity is to Los Angeles or niceness is to the Midwest. The old joke goes that St. Peter's giving a guided tour of heaven and as they walk past a big room with closed doors, he whispers, "Sssh, it's the Mormons. They think they're the only ones up here." Some fundamentalists describe it as "Club LDS syndrome." And the church is especially clubbish in Utah with the temple as some kind of VIP area—not even Mormons can get in without being on the list (having a valid temple recommend).

I'm assuming that as with most velvet-rope parties, the temple is actually crap on the inside. The closest I got was when a missionary outside showed me a ring binder of snapshots of the temple interiors, like a real estate catalogue. Evidently this holy of holies, this gateway to infinity, consists of a series of pristine, Regency-style rooms through which saints wander about in white outfits and white slippers, their voices reduced to a whisper. (The white uniform is a house rule; there's a store in town called White Elegance full of temple attire and accessories.)

But the rest is a mystery. Not for Gentile ears, anyway. What happens in the temple stays in the temple. Upon receiving their all-important temple endowments, Mormons swear never to reveal what goes on there, making the sign of disemboweling themselves and then slitting their throats. Or so says a *Frontline* documentary on PBS. So it didn't go down too well when a hidden-camera video went viral in October 2012, revealing all kinds of solemn oaths and secret handshakes.

But these aren't the Mormon secrets that intrigue me. I'm interested in the cracks in the façade, the stress fractures. The pressures of Mormonism can be particularly hard on the young, who must go through a relentless routine of meetings, family home evenings, societies, clubs, boys' groups, girls' groups, scout groups. And at every turn they are measured against the standards expected by their parents, friends, community and bishop. All that judging takes its toll. Again the jokes speak volumes. "Why should you only ever take two Mormons when you go fishing? Because if you take one, he'll drink all your beer and smoke all your weed." And another: "What did the Mormon girl do when they broke out the alcohol at a party? She put her clothes on and went home."

As Sister Godfrey sang, I recalled the studies that have found that good Mormon and Christian girls who have sworn to premarital chastity are secretly having anal sex instead.[4] There's a joke here about loopholes, but I'm not going to make it; there's a dark edge to all this, after all. Utah is the number one state in the republic on at least two counts—the density of Mormons and youth suicide among young males.[5] Is it reasonable to presume a connection between the two? As believers so often tell atheists: just because you can't prove it, doesn't mean it doesn't exist.

Before leaving, I decided to confront the Mormon Church on some of these issues. Not the anal sex and suicide, but the polygamy and revisionist history. So I left the singing missionaries and the endless photographs of Gordon Hinckley among happy black children and I made an appointment with the LDS Church publicity office. Months later, a chipper, corporate-looking man named Mike met me in the lobby of the giant church building and led me to a man named Ron Barney, a church historian and apologist of thirty years standing. Ron's a deliberate man with a round friendly face, but on the day we met, there seemed a certain steeliness about him—he knew what was coming.

"So, Ron, the gold plates. In the diorama, Joseph Smith's just reading them, there's no peep stone or blanket. It didn't happen like that, did it?"

"Well, no one knows. Joseph never talked about how he received these things."

"But not a single mention of a peep stone?"

"I agree he used peep stones. He came from an environment where the practice of magic was pretty common."

"So why not mention it somewhere in Temple Square?"

"We're embarrassed. We're ashamed that Joseph Smith was involved in that stuff. You ask any of those ladies out there in Temple Square, and they don't have a clue! But in the historical community we say, 'Yeah, the evidence is abundant.'"

"What about baptism for the dead? It doesn't seem right to turn the dead into Mormons by these proxy ceremonies."

"We don't! That's a misunderstanding, you know. We just give the dead the choice to accept Jesus in the hereafter—our feeling is that everyone deserves that choice, living or dead."

It's a fair point—if you believe in eternal life, why not give the dead the same opportunities as the living? The logic is appealing, never mind that such acts of spiritual altruism seem to veer into the realm of trespass.

I brought up polygamy and section 132 in the Doctrine and Covenants, and Ron sat back in his chair and smiled. "Okay, well, we surmise that Joseph enquired about polygamy among the Old Testament patriarchs," he said. "And we surmise that God gave him a response in about 1831. But it was all under a veil of secrecy. Joseph didn't write anything down about that. All he wrote was the revelation itself."

"So he did practice polygamy."

"Sure! We know there was polygamy in the early Mormon Church. We have the Fanny Alger story and all the other women, but again, it was so secret, all we have are fragments. Crumbs. What people have done is take these fragments"—and he gets up to put five random dots on his white-board, drawing lines between them—"and they say, 'Maybe it's a dog.' But in reality, if the full record was to be there . . ." More dots, more lines. "They'd realize, we're talking about an elk!"

"So it's definitely a mammal."

"Well, we're not sure. In the absence of Joseph Smith, you cannot draw a proper picture of early polygamy. It's all guesswork."

"How many wives did Joseph have then?"

"I don't know. Is it twenty-seven or thirty-three? See, I don't care. What difference does it make?"

"These are wives you're talking about."

"Sure, but we've been attacking this for two generations and we still don't know."

"But they existed, they were real. Why isn't there any mention of them in Temple Square?"

"Because we're ashamed. It's not the norm of America today, and we'd just as soon forget about it. When I say 'we,' I mean, the institutional religion. We don't talk about the Mountain Meadows Massacre* much either, for obvious reasons."

"So isn't the past being edited for present purposes?"

"You haven't been reading what Mormon historians have been saying. We never shy away from it. Never."

"In Temple Square you do."

"Well, that's the public aspect—people aren't interested in history, they're more interested in electronic gadgets and movies and all that stuff."

"So you underplay polygamy because it's too complicated a subject for most people. It's best left to historians."

"Correct."

Ron sounds like Jack Nicholson in *A Few Good Men*—the public can't handle the truth about polygamy. Of course, it's not the public that's the problem. And I can see why fundamentalists are antagonistic toward the LDS Church. They've been pariahed by this organization whose approach to history is guided by embarrassment and shame. There's something profoundly distasteful about a church that desperately distances itself from the daily lives of its ancestors even while celebrating their other achievements. It's intellectual dishonesty and Ron has no answer for it.

The longer I spent in Temple Square, a dreary propaganda park of Mormon drones and singing missionaries, the more I sympathized with the polygamists. I was reminded of something Gary Batchelor told me— that when the fundamentalists broke away, the church lost many of its most independent, colorful members, the ones who had the courage to strike out on their own and live outside the law if their principles demanded it.

It's time to find Mormonism's adventurers.

---

*In which a Mormon militia, on September 11, 1857, massacred a wagon train heading west of approximately 120 unarmed men, women and children, simply in order to deter federal troops from entering the Utah territory. The Mormons disguised themselves as Native Americans for the attack in order to blame the atrocity on the local Paiute Indian tribe, a deception that was encouraged by Brigham Young.

Centennial Park

CHAPTER 5

❧ Movie Night

We don't create a fantasy world to escape reality, we create it to be able to stay.

—Lynda Barry

I'M IN COLORADO City, the beating heart of Mormon polygamy, on the border between Utah and Arizona, and I'm watching a movie with sixteen young fundamentalist girls, all of whom are singing along to the soundtrack. And I can't quite believe what I'm witnessing. Because this isn't some Christian "values" movie or an old-school Biblical epic or even a G-rated Disney effort that managed to scrape past the polygamist censors. We're watching *Lagaan*, an Oscar-nominated Bollywood movie made in 2004. The song's in Hindi so the girls don't understand a word they're singing, but they're keeping up pretty well all the same—some have seen this four-hour movie ten times already. Some are even on their feet performing the dances, each one dressed up in sashes and wraps and makeshift saris in bright blue, green, pink and red; every forehead has a bindi. And this is all taking place in the reception of the Mohave Community College, only a few hundred yards down the road from the Vermillion Cafe.

Who knew that there was a Bollywood following right here in the heart of Mormon polygamy? Actually, Bollywood doesn't cover it—this is more of a cultural evening. The girls' mothers have brought in trays of home-made Indian snacks and sweets and saffron rice. I provided the chicken curry and the ethnic presence. And before the screening, we ate in the library, listening to Ravi Shankar on iTunes, surrounded by wall hangings of Rama and Sita on horseback and the baby-blue Krishna playing the flute. I'm apparently the first Indian these girls have met, so they peppered me with questions. Yes, I've been to India. Yes, it's awesome. No, I don't understand a word they're saying either.

"Oh what I would give to speak Hindi," says Lori Wyler, the librarian, a roly-poly plural wife in her sixties, with bright, sparkling eyes and a gleeful smile. "It's such a musical language." She presses her palms together and bows—"*Namaste!*"—and gives out a delighted laugh.

This evening is all Lori's doing. She became obsessed with India following the breakdown of her plural marriage some fifteen years ago. It started with rooting around on the Internet, where she found *Autobiography of a Yogi* by Paramahansa Yogananda on Amazon. And now she has quite a collection of Indophilia. These wall hangings, the Ravi Shankar—it's all Lori. She's a fan of the *Matrix* movies because there's a song in one of the soundtracks with lyrics from Hindu scripture. She tells me that one day she'll make a pilgrimage to the Lake Shrine Temple in Malibu where the Yogananda built a sanctuary.

It was Lori who introduced Colorado City to *Lagaan*. She bought seventeen copies and handed them out to her friends—you must sit through it all, she told them, it'll make you cry. Quite why *Lagaan* struck such a chord is hard to say. It's a sweet enough film, G-rated, and, according to Roger Ebert, "enormously entertaining." When the fate of a poor Indian village rests upon a cricket match against its loathsome British masters, it takes a dashing young peasant boy to rally a team; unite Hindu, Muslim and Christian; and fill them with the belief and purpose they need to defy the odds and overcome. An underdog sports movie, in other words, full of the kind of values that go over so well here—patriotism, family and faith.

But for Lori, the lead character played by Aamir Khan is Christlike. "That's what Jesus did. He united all these people and asked us to look beyond the surface and he stood up to authority and . . ." Lori can talk all night about Aamir Khan. So could most of the girls here, I suspect—they whimper every time he gets a close-up.

There's something wonderful about Mormon fundamentalist girls singing in Hindi. It's a commercial for diversity and the magic of movies, the end of prejudice and peace on Earth. And yet their own fundamentalist culture is riven with division and sectarianism, the disease of religious societies, a form of entropy. These girls, for instance, are not of the FLDS, the predominant church in this area; they don't follow Warren Jeffs or eat at the Vermillion Cafe—Bollywood movies are unthinkable for *that* crowd. These girls come from the Centennial Park community, which broke away from Colorado City in 1986 and built a new town just a couple of miles down the road. Following the split, the remaining group called itself First Ward, eventually rebranding as the FLDS, while Centennial Park was known as Second Ward, though it bristles at the implied inferiority of "Second." Both groups practice placement marriage, whereby spouses are chosen for each other by priesthood elders who claim privileged access to God. Though they differ somewhat in their customs, their core beliefs are broadly identical.

The split was painful and messy—families were carved in two and assets sold off. And the FLDS has only salted the wound since—their members are forbidden any contact with apostates, with no exceptions even for immediate family. So even though the two communities shop at the same stores, should an FLDS sister see her Centennial Park brother, she must not approach or even talk to him, just in case she is found out and her salvation is denied. Instead their eyes meet and silent decisions fly between them. If they both need bananas, say, and just happen to find themselves near the fruit at the same time, maybe they can get away with some surreptitious muttering in the produce section. This scenario is real—the brother from Centennial Park told me himself. If you could parse the glances at Foodtown, you would know the history of Colorado City.

But Centennial Park isn't the only group to be alienated by the FLDS. Lori's husband, Marvin, for instance, stuck with the FLDS during the Centennial Park split and obediently avoided contact with Second Warders. But he has since been excommunicated himself for objecting to the tyrannical regime of Warren Jeffs, so now his family lives exiled in its own neighborhood. This is the same kind and chuckling Marvin who lives with his second wife, Charlotte; we watched the Ervil LeBaron movie together. In a way he was lucky. Many excommunicated men also lose their families—their wives and children are reassigned to other men and they go willingly, terrified of losing their salvation. But Marvin's family stuck by him, and together they sought the comfort of a smaller breakaway group. After a lifetime of devotion to priesthood hierarchy and a presiding prophet, there was no question of going it alone. They chose a group loyal to an abrasive, rotund man named Winston Blackmore, a former leading figure in the FLDS who was banished to Canada by Warren Jeffs. Marvin couldn't leave for Canada himself—he would have to sell his home, his land, and these things aren't so easily achieved in Colorado City, where a church trust owns most of the property. So Marvin would secretly tune in to the services in Canada by phone, playing the sermon over his loudspeaker. It was only Marvin and a few others, though. Needless to say, Blackmore's group doesn't associate with Centennial Park, or vice versa. Such Brotherhood among the brethren.

As for Lori, she left Marvin and struck out on her own. She says she felt smothered by his overbearing zeal. Besides, the bitterness of all this splintering upset her. So now she doesn't hold to any group or sect. She has embraced her apostasy. There were years of estrangement, but now that Marvin also feels the sting of alienation, they're beginning to spend more time together. They recently drove eighteen hours to Canada to try to make contact with one of their daughters, Lucinda, but she's a "Warrenite"—a follower of Warren Jeffs—and she refused even to come to the door to see Marvin, which hurt him terribly. They left a box of things for her at the gate and drove the eighteen hours back home again.

When *Lagaan* is over and the British are defeated, the girls politely thank Lori for creating this little moment, and they return to the fundamentalist schisms of Short Creek. A few girls actually live in Colorado City where the tension is the worst—Colorado City is where the FLDS is based. Most, however, return to Centennial Park, where I've been staying for the last few days. Centennial Park was where I cooked up the chicken curry this afternoon. It's the kind of place where moms spend the afternoon dressing their daughters up in pseudosaris and cooking Indian snacks from recipes off the Internet, ever mindful that these very daughters are intended as future plural wives. Centennial Park, I'm discovering, is a whole different story.

❖ Settling In

Our business here is to be Utopian, to make vivid and credible, if we can,
first this facet and then that, of an imaginary whole and happy world.
    —H. G. Wells, *A Modern Utopia*

They run a slick ship at Centennial Park. On my first day, a man called
Mark meets me in the car park and plunges me into the day ahead. It's all
been figured out: first there's church, a full three-hour grind. Then Mark's
cousin David, a man with three wives and thirteen children, takes me in
for Sunday lunch—an immaculate spread of gleaming silver and ornate
napkins and polished glasses for red wine and white. The wine part is a
surprise. I'd thought of my journey into Mormon polygamy as a form
of wacky detox, but apparently it's only the vanilla Mormons who don't
touch the stuff—the fundamentalists of Short Creek are all about a tipple.
I guess with families that large, you need a snifter to tune it all out.

A few bottles later, I'm whisked back to the church building for an
evening class about polygamist hero John Taylor. And I find myself in an
orderly pew, in a hushed hall, listening to a dreary man read in a dreary
monotone from a dreary book. All this, just as my food coma is kicking
in—a belly full of pasta and wine, knocking me out like Rufalin. Only
I can't give in to it. Not here. Not in church. ("Who's that Mexican guy
snoring and drooling down his front?" "Oh, just the journalist, it's his first
day. I think he's drunk.")

A tap on my shoulder. "Hi, are you that book writer?"

"Yes, that's me."

"I'm Nephi*," says the guy sitting behind me. "You can stay in my house
if you like."

And just like that, I'm in. The closed world of Mormon polygamy has
given me a key to its front door. "I just leave it in the flower pot on the
right," he says. "You can stay as long as you like."

Nephi's not a polygamist as such. He's a fundamentalist who isn't actually living the Principle, not right now, anyway. He lives alone in a house a

---

*Nephi's name has been changed.

block away from the church building. After the lecture we sit in his kitchen where he explains the situation over a bottle of Syrah.

"See, I'm not exactly the poster child for all this. I split up with my third wife last year, and she lives with the kids down in Hurricane." Hurricane is the nearest town to Short Creek, twenty-two miles away.

"You mean your third sister wife?"

"No, I've had three wives, but only one at a time. Yup—three marriages and three divorces. Ha ha! That's why they probably don't want me speaking to you."

"Who doesn't?"

"The Priesthood."

He means the Priesthood Council, or "the Brethren"—a group of seven men who control all things in Centennial Park, on account of how God speaks more clearly to them than to anyone else on the planet. Marriages are at the very top of their agenda. They decide who marries whom around here. All three of Nephi's marriages were the Brethren's idea, though Nephi is quick to add that he was responsible for the divorces, not them. The first two were a case of too young, too foolish. The third was a more solid match—they had five children together—but it fell apart last year because she didn't want to live polygamy. So she took the kids and moved out of town.

"So now what?" I ask him. "Are you looking for a wife who does want to live polygamy?"

"No, no, it doesn't work like that. You don't go looking. God decides. God tells the Priesthood through revelation. I don't know what I'm going to do just yet. My problem is chasing girls—I confessed it all to the Elders. I was really worried about it. I wanted to know that I'm going to have another wife, you know? There's a lot riding on it when you talk to the Priesthood. But they weren't shocked at all—they just said, 'That's a common problem, don't worry.'"

"They've probably heard it all by now."

"Right. So basically, I'm good. The Priesthood wants to give me more wives, I've just got to behave myself for a while."

It sounds uglier than he intends, this business of the Brethren "giving" men wives as a reward for good behavior. But it's the language that offends more than the principle. Because in Centennial Park the Priesthood speaks for God, and God bestows blessings upon the virtuous, blessings like wives and children. It's right and proper that the well-behaved should be favored with marriage.

Of course "give" usually suggests "take" somewhere down the line. The members of the Priesthood are only men, and Centennial Park has a trust to which members tithe. And Nephi has never struggled for money. He buys and sells land for development and he's good at it. If he should stray, then perhaps a donation would encourage the Priesthood to forgive him? An extra wing on the school library?

To suggest such a thing would only offend. Nephi's a believer. On his walls, as for every home in Centennial Park, he has a picture of the Priesthood Council—a panel of their individually captioned portraits. Next to them are pictures of his own family, including a huge group shot of some 160 people, all the progeny of his polygamist father. As far as Nephi's concerned, God talks to the Brethren. When it came to the marriage of one of his daughters, for example, "all seven Elders prayed on it and they all came up with the same guy."

He also believes in polygamy, and not just because the scriptures say so. For Nephi, polygamy "makes sense." It's "logical." These are the arguments I keep hearing from fundamentalists, these appeals to reason and logic.

"I think it has carnal validation," he says. "Men want to spread their seed, so they want to have more than one partner. But women, by the time they sleep with you, it's just to seal the deal. You know what it's like—once you've slept with a woman you can't shake her off! Women want to be 'enveloped.' And you can't be enveloped by more than one man. So girls that sleep with two guys, they either love one or they love neither—they can't love both at the same time, they're not hardwired that way. But a man can envelop two women at once."

This idea that women can't love more than one man at a time sounds a bit iffy, a bit convenient. I can hear my wife protesting: "Why not?

"You should have brought her," says Nephi. "We could have converted her for you."

"Yeah, well, good luck. When I asked her if she'd be able to handle a couple more wives, she was like: 'Let's get one to do the dishes, one to do the cleaning . . .' She sees them more as staff."

"Did you ask her if you could have sex with the staff? Oh come on, you're useless! Give her a ring, let me talk to her, I'll negotiate this whole deal for you."

He's a good laugh, Nephi. He shows me to the spare room and I move in. For the next few weeks, I'll be waking up in Centennial Park.

The first thing I learn about Centennial Park is that they're big on waving here. They wave from the streets, from their cars, at intersections. And it's not just kids or people I've met—*everyone* waves. And smiles. It may as well be doctrine at this point: Thou shalt practice polygamy and thou shalt wave at the little Indian guy who's here to judge us.

And I love it. Brothers and sisters of Centennial Park, if I can just bear my testimony on the waving thing—it works! In fact, I get a giddy feeling just driving around town. It's the waving, and the opulence, the sheer newness of the place, all the freshly minted mansion homes, one after another, each one with scores of bedrooms and giant yards. Centennial Park is the Beverly Hills of Mormon polygamy and it's booming—new homes are being built all over the place. There's still no Main Street yet—no strip mall, no shops, no café, no "town square" for all those moms to park their strollers and have a natter. So it feels a little formless, a town without a center—the only place where the community gathers now is a meeting hall in town that triples as the church, the high school and the stage for community functions. It's all function and austerity here. But I rather like it. There's a purity of purpose to Centennial Park, an air of discipline. If people lounge about in hammocks, there's no sign of it, not even when the sun's beating down so hard the asphalt shimmers. In Centennial Park, the Mormons are always in motion.

Most days, I wake up and throw open the windows just to listen. It's the soundtrack to an idyll out there; the peal and chatter of harmonious domesticity, the squealing children, the urging moms, the sweeping of red sand from driveways, the chug of distant diggers, the occasional squawk of a chicken. It's glorious stuff, rustic and comforting. And it fits the southern Utah accent—a round and clipped inflection reminiscent of the West Country in England, a farmery burr that reminds me of cider and meadows and the Glastonbury Music Festival. They don't just go down to the creek here; they go clurr down to the creck.

If I'm lucky, the phone will ring and I'll be invited to lunch or dinner with one of the families who have dared to invite me in. And I'll get a chance to practice those rules that Anne taught me—no surnames, no "how many wives?", no diving into the dinner before someone has said grace. But I'm discovering they don't really mind all that out here. I get the tour, I meet the kids, they tell me all about those pictures on the walls—the ones of the Brethren and the one with the lineage of prophets from Joseph Smith on down. And as we sit down to burritos and tossed salad, at tables laid by armies of obedient children, a young girl with dimples and pigtails will say a few words to heavenly Father—thank you for the burritos, thank you for all my moms and thank you for our guest Mr. Sanjiv.

And I think: *Is this for real?*

The window boxes blooming, the spotless carpets, the sunshine catching the Thomas Kinkade on the wall. In one house, every child lines up to shake my hand and bid me welcome. In another, the little helpers clear up after dinner and stack the dishwasher and wipe and sweep, the older children marshalling the younger ones, while mom number three tells me how fortunate they are to be insulated from the degradations of the outside world.

"Hugh Hefner lives with three women and he got his own TV show! If you ask me, that man has the morals of an alley cat, but who cares as long as he's not marrying them and making a commitment? The president has an affair in the White House. Is it any wonder the government is so disapproving of us?"

She pops in a VHS of Charlton Heston's *The Ten Commandments*, and the younger children all sit rapt on the sofa munching cookies. "Come, I want to show you something." In the living room her teenagers have invited some friends over to work on their homework together. "You wanted to know what our young people do in their spare time, so this is the sort of thing. Everybody, this is Sanjiv. He's writing a book about us." And they wave: "Hello, Sanjiv."

My skepticism ebbs and flows. I'm walking through a catalogue of Mormon living here, page by page—a world where crockery is never broken, socks are never lost and voices are never raised in anger. This mom—we'll call her Ruth—seems to think of me as an inspector with a checklist: Are the children grateful? Is the food nutritious? Is their entertainment Bible-based? Her challenge, though she never states it, is plain:

"Look around and tell me what's wrong with our way of life. Name one thing." And I don't blame her for being defensive or putting on a performance for dinner—I'd break out the silverware too if a journalist came over with his notebook. This is new territory for us both.

It was a recent decision by the Brethren to allow reporters into their community, and these are just the first, cautious steps. Only a few families have volunteered. Often only one wife of three in a family will speak to me; others stay silent, reproving figures in the background, busy with children and laundry, their ears burning. It's not done, to expose yourself here. What's to be gained? Don't you know our history? Outsiders have never been kind.

As one lady explained to me with dripping disdain: "The Amish are 'quaint.' We don't get 'quaint.'"

Ruth mentioned Hugh Hefner. Everyone mentions Hugh Hefner. We think of polygamist women scrubbing pots and pans, but they also watch *The Girls Next Door* on E! Hefner has become part of the rhetoric that polygamists deploy when confronted with outsiders. He's an emblem of society's double standard and Gomorrah at their gates. He's a riposte: who are *you* to judge *us* when *you* glamorize *him*?

But Hefner is also a comfort. In a culture that has defined itself out of opposition, it helps to have your talking points iconized and wearing silk pajamas. Centennial Park is a bubble. Part of its appeal is that everyone and everything is familiar here, especially the conversations, so people can settle into their talking points like armchairs. Everyone knows where everyone stands, at least on Hefner. But this is another prickly subject—the uniformity of opinion. In fact there's a talking point about this very thing. Well aware that their veneration of the Brethren looks a little lockstep, they protest that their culture is free and diverse, and everyone chooses their own destiny, their politics and particularly their wives.

"No one is forced to marry anyone they don't want to marry," Ruth says. "*No one.* Now, I don't know if that's what's happening over there." She points toward Colorado City. "That's what we hear in the media, but we don't always know whether to trust it."

If the choice in wives is as free and diverse as their choice in politics, then it's a narrow field indeed. Over dinner with the polygamists of Centennial Park, one overriding worldview becomes apparent, quite aside from the scriptures. They watch Fox and vote Republican here. They don't believe in global warming because they "don't believe in Al Gore," and don't get them started on the Clintons or the current administration. They are the kind of patriots who detest the government—their loathing of federal power is a century old. The world is going to the dogs, what with rocketing divorce rates, boys in gangs, girls getting abortions and everyone on drugs. Can you blame them for protecting their pristine polygamist bubble? How else can they stay uncontaminated? Isn't it their right to protect their children?

For years, their resentment of state persecutors was said to manifest in wholesale welfare fraud, a practice known as "bleeding the beast"—but the people of Centennial Park reject the idea with vigor. They've never heard of "bleeding the beast," they say. They don't go to the state for handouts; they believe in self-sustenance. But their antipathy to the government is so strong that when the conversation turns to the Iraq war, their sympathies often lie with the Iraqis.

"Those people didn't want democracy, but America imposed it on them," Mark told me. "It's the same with us—they want to impose themselves on us, and if we won't change to be like them, they just want to wipe us off the face of the earth!"

The war may be the only issue we agree on. As a blue state liberal who's pro-choice, pro–gun control and pro–gay marriage, I'm an alien in Centennial Park. But that's okay, I've always been an outsider of sorts. Growing up in London as a second-generation Indian, I'm used to the curiosity of others and the questions they ask to unwrap whatever mystery I present. Moving to Los Angeles only compounded my difference, and the questions evolved in turn. So when the Centennial Park Action Committee (CPAC) invites me to a grilling one evening at a café, I'm quite looking forward to it. My only concern is that it might be at the Vermillion, but it appears Second Warders don't eat there. They eat at the Merry Wives Cafe just off the highway, a thriving new enterprise with excellent burgers. Even the cafés tell the story of Short Creek.

I'm positioned at the center of a group of some twenty-five people and they ask me questions in turn, peeling back the layers one by one. They hear "England" and smile—so many of their ancestors came from there. Did I know that the Timpsons, one of the founding families of Centennial Park, owns a chain of shoe stores in the UK? They hear "Hindu" and ask about Allah, as Anne Wilde did. Have they not seen *Lagaan*? Their daughters have.

But Hindu will do—what dismays them is that I don't believe.

"I'm not a person of faith," I tell them.

"I know, but you're not an atheist."

"Yes I am."

"What—you don't believe in *anything*?"

After some bafflement and shrugging, though, they seem to give me a pass. Perhaps "India" and "Hindu" are sufficiently foreign to be of some reassurance. I don't fit the mold of past persecutors. And wasn't there something on Discovery about how "they've got polygamy in India"?

So it's done. In a few quick strokes, their curiosity is satisfied. Now they want to know what I think about them. Will I be negative? Will I sensationalize? There's a self-obsession about Centennial Park, a product of its isolation, its history of persecution, its conviction in its righteousness. They have that embattled sense that serves religious groups so well. They named their junior high school Masada after that fort in Israel in which the Jews committed mass suicide rather than surrender to the Romans. A little grim for a junior high school.

Their agenda is this: they want the decriminalization of polygamy, public sympathy for polygamists and a firm demarcation between Centennial Park and the FLDS.

"We're not them, you know," says Susie Timpson, gently. One of the key members of CPAC, Susie is a waddling mass of motherhood and soothing noises. "We're not the FLDS. Our people have a choice. We don't force here, no. Our children watch television, they read books, they go to college. We can get you figures on how many go to college, but it's higher than out in the world. It's so sad what's happening over there with the young girls being forced. And I know that's the sensational story, but we don't do that."

The principal of the high school invites me to speak to the students, so one morning, I stand before them, the teenagers of Centennial Park. For an hour I rattle through my fitful story—how I switched subjects at college, dabbled with music and fell into magazines; how I traipsed through India, apartment-hopped through London and wound up in Los Angeles. It's the story of a rootless wanderer blurting from chapter to chapter, trying to discover who he is, and it strikes no chord with these kids. They know their roots, they've been marinated in their history. Their identity is the principle subject of their education.

So come question time at the end, they ask me nothing about my life, the story I've just told them. They want to know only how I see them. What will my book say? Will I be fair or will I sensationalize? The same questions I heard from their parents.

A word on church. I only went the one time, on my first day here, but once was enough. It reminded me of Dunbar in *Catch-22*, a soldier who so fears death that he creates and wallows in tedium, figuring that each minute he spends bored lasts longer than those in which he is engaged. He would have appreciated the Sunday meeting in Centennial Park. The minutes last for hours. This is worship without the fever or the show. There's no band here, no clapping hands, no pounding on the pulpit, no hugs, no jabbering in tongues—no attempt whatsoever to jazz up the Almighty. It's boiled vegetables, no salt. Fundamentalism minus the fun. It's one of the reasons they call polygamy "the Work."

The service begins with the Brethren sitting in a row on stage, seven grave men in dark suits, facing down their flock. They wait for silence, for the last whisper to a fidgeting infant, and then a man in the center stands and clears his throat. He doesn't smile or offer a reading or a homily. He merely mutters some community announcements—something about a house raising and a class on food preservation. (Polygamists are big on food preservation what with the apocalypse just round the corner.) Then he calls on someone to "bear their testimony." After which he calls upon someone else, and then another. And so on it goes until your brain slips into a semicoma and your will to live has drained into a puddle on the floor.

These words—testimony, testament, testify—are said to stem from a time when men would take oaths by placing their hands over their testicles to demonstrate their sincerity.[1] The equivalent of "I swear by my balls that I'm telling the truth." But church isn't anywhere near as entertaining as that. For fundamentalist Mormons, bearing testimony means winging it on stage. No one knows who will be called, so no one is prepared and the service becomes a procession of busking mumblers expressing their gratitude for um, heavenly Father and um, also for um, the Priesthood. As an introduction to the spiritual realm, the gates of exaltation and ecstasy, it's even duller than the Church of England assemblies I remember from school. Back then, at least there was mischief to be had—surreptitious ear-flicking and missiles, the call-and-response of flatulence and giggles. These are the things I associate with "Our Father Who Art in Heaven."

First up is a near-blind old man called Brother Marvin who tells stories about the miracles he's experienced—like the time in Los Angeles when he forgot to bring his directions but he found the Holiday Inn anyway. Hosanna. Then a dour man called Brother Ray threatens to cancel the community dances if the boys and girls don't stop getting into "entangling alliances." He is followed by a Brother Joseph who admonishes the younger members not to judge the Work by the weakness of the "administrators," because they're only human—which sounds a bit like he's having his cake. I thought these men represented God? Brother Joseph also brings up the idea of "the shelf." If something doesn't make sense, he says, don't reject it, just put it on "the shelf"—it might make sense later. This goes for anything that doesn't fit with, or flatly contradicts, the Book of Mormon or the Bible—anything that might challenge their faith. So presumably that's where one puts all the evidence for the theory of evolution or the DNA findings about Native Americans. A big shelf, in other words. Sturdy.

The service only livens up when John Timpson takes the stage. A stout, toady man with a belly like a marching band drum, he stands with his head back, wiping the tears that trickle down his cheeks with long, drawn out strokes of his hankie. His tongue lolls on his lower lip. His bulging eyes scan the crowd.

"Reject God, and Lucifer will tie a chain around your neck and drag you away!" he booms. The tears roll. "And I tell you this because I was given a responsibility to tell you by my father. And I mean GOD ALMIGHTY!"

This is more like it. Timpson is the president of the Council, the most senior member of the Brethren. And he uses his pulpit to remind them of the mission. No defensiveness, no hedging or triangulation—Timpson states it plain. The world is falling apart out there, false churches abound, particularly the Catholic Church, and Satan is on the march. But here in the bubble, they are safe. Centennial Park is the only true church on the planet. God is with them, here in this room.

"Because Brother Joseph restored the Priesthoods, Melchizedek and Aaronic," he says. "They're here on earth somewhere. And if they're not here in this room, then go find it!"

This is the raison d'être for Centennial Park—they believe the priesthood is the key to Zion, the last remaining hope for mankind, the only passage to the Celestial Kingdom. And it's here, this priesthood, it's in the room. I'd originally thought that the priesthood referred to actual priests. But the way Mormons talk about it, it could be a calling, an ether, a certain kind of knowledge. And as John Timpson booms and bellows, I do feel a curious sensation, as though a truth has dawned and I have been led to a particular and compelling realization: that I don't actually understand what he's going on about.

What is this "Priesthood"?

◆ First You Get the Priesthood

DUDLEY: Do you think you've learned from your mistakes?
PETER: Oh yes, I'm certain I could repeat them exactly.
  —Peter Cook and Dudley Moore[2]

It's all about the priesthood with polygamists—who's got it, where is it, who gave it to whom and where did they lose it? (Check at the front desk, maybe someone handed it in.) If the maxim for Watergate was "follow the money," for fundamentalism it's "follow the priesthood." Or to paraphrase Tony Montana from *Scarface*: "In this religion, you gotta get the priesthood first. Then when you get the priesthood, you get the women. Then when you get the women, you get the planet."

The priesthood is many things. Colloquially it refers to the Priesthood Council or the apostles—the very top brass in any polygamist group, and for that matter, the LDS Church. But strictly speaking, the priesthood is the authority that God gave these men to represent Him. Mormons believe that God sent the apostles Peter, James and John in person to give the priesthood to Joseph Smith and Oliver Cowdery by the laying on of hands. Then Joseph passed it on to a bunch of other people, like Brigham Young, and he passed it onto the next generation, and so on. And whoever has it now is officially God's delegate on Earth. It's one of the fun parts of Mormonism, this comic book idea that holiness can be conferred through touch, like tag or hepatitis.

There are several kinds of priesthood going around: the lowest form is the Aaronic, which relates to baptism; then comes the Melchizedek, which relates to the laying on of hands; and then the highest form, a subset of the Melchizedek priesthood, known as the High Priest apostleship, which is the kind that God gave Joseph Smith, the kind that confers the right to seal people in eternal marriage. It's this last kind that fundamentalists squabble about. They talk about the "keys to the priesthood"—particularly the "sealing keys"—and they want to know: who has the keys now, who has the power?

The rule is that once the keys are passed from person to person by the laying on of hands, only God can take them from you. So from Joseph Smith on down, it's a game of succession. The LDS Church believes they were handed from Joseph Smith to Brigham Young to John Taylor and down the line of church prophets to the present prophet in charge. But fundamentalists depart from this lineage at precisely the point where the church renounced polygamy. They believe that the priesthood went to John W. Woolley, then his son Lorin, who then "called" six other men to his council, whose pictures hang on every wall in Centennial Park: John Yates Barlow, Joseph Leslie Broadbent, Joseph Musser, Charles Zitting, LeGrand Woolley and Louis Kelsch. With the exception of the Order (also known as the Kingston group), every Mormon fundamentalist group or independent claims its authority from these men.

The birth of this new organization in Salt Lake City caused great excitement. It was the 1930s and times were tough in America, especially for polygamists who were feeling the wrath not only of the law but also of the

LDS Church. So one of the first things Lorin Woolley did was send a party down to Short Creek to establish a community there, as a refuge for those who'd been excommunicated for living plural marriage. And things came together quickly. Their religion was under assault, and they were resolved to protect it, no matter what. It was a time of great zeal and mission and unity. But it was brief.

In 1944, the entire Priesthood Council was thrown in jail for bigamy and were offered immediate release only if they renounced polygamy. Some refused on principle—it was unthinkable to capitulate on a divine teaching—but others accepted, reasoning that it was God's way of granting their liberty, so that they could return to their multiple wives. And just like that, the seeds of division were sown, seeds that would bear fruit time and again. The story of the priesthood is one of infighting and rivalry, backstabbing and guile—all the human failings these aspiring gods had set out to rise above. After 1944, fundamentalists quickly separated into opposing camps, complaining constantly about the other side—that they hadn't "called" their Priesthood Brethren properly, for instance, or that while hands had been laid on properly enough, other requirements had not been met, such as divine visions or the presence of holy messengers and such. These Pythonesque quibbles over regulations and ordinances are, to this day, among the keenest disputes in fundamentalism.

By 1951, the group split for the first time. One member, Rulon Allred, announced that he had received the priesthood from the ailing prophet Joseph Musser and promptly broke off to establish a church of his own, the Apostolic United Brethren, now one of the largest groups with some 7,500 members. It was a controversial claim. There are those who argue, for instance, that Joseph Musser was too debilitated at the time by a series of strokes to lay hands on anyone, and that Allred actually placed Musser's hands on his head himself to get the priesthood out of him. There are those in Centennial Park today who who claim that Allred didn't get the priesthood at all, but just an ordinary blessing, and anyway, you're not meant to grab the priesthood like a bag of swag and bugger off like that, you're supposed to stick around and build up Zion.

As it happened, there was a brief respite from sectarianism following the Allred split. When the governor of Arizona launched an infamous raid on Short Creek in 1953, it was a grievous blow on the face of it. Many of the fathers were behind bars, and their children were taken into custody. But it had a galvanizing effect. Nothing unites people better than an external oppressor. So the Priesthood set about rallying the faithful, sending men down from Salt Lake to round up their flock once more, replenish them with fire. The rest of the '50s and '60s were a golden age, a time of rebuilding and purpose, under the stewardship of the Prophet Leroy Johnson, or Uncle Leroy, as he was known. Water systems were installed, along with telephone lines and plumbing. Roads and a high school were built. The kingdom was rising once more.

But then Uncle Leroy grew old and infirm, much as Joseph Musser had before him. And the same pattern repeated itself. Like cowboy builders who prey on retirees, power-hungry polygamists have consistently exploited priesthood holders who have been rendered vulnerable by age or poor health—it's virtually a tradition. As Uncle Leroy's condition deteriorated, two clans emerged to dispute his succession. One supported the claim of Marion Hammon, an imposing figure from Salt Lake City, who'd come to get Short Creek on its feet after the raid. The other backed the Barlow family, who laid no claim to priesthood succession but were powerful nevertheless since they had the ear of the ailing Uncle Leroy and were in close with the keeper of the storehouse, Fred Jessop, who oversaw all the town's supplies. As senility overcame Uncle Leroy, he fell into the Barlows' grasp. They became his full-time caretakers and denied others access to him. It was a power grab, pure and simple.

The Barlows began to beat the drum for a new regime of one-man rule. At the time, the prophet's position at the head of the Priesthood Council was considered administrative—he was a leader for the sake of order, not because he had enhanced priesthood powers. But the Barlows argued otherwise—that the prophet did have a higher form of priesthood, and only he possessed the divine calling to appoint new members to the Priesthood Council. There were scriptural precedents for this, as there were for the opposing arguments—even a newly minted religion like Mormonism was rife with quarrels of interpretation. But politically, the case was clear: The Barlows* had Uncle Leroy under their control, so it suited them for the power to be concentrated in his hands.

---

*Members of the Barlow family in the FLDS refused all requests for interview

By 1980, Short Creek was starkly divided. Barlow parents stopped sending their children to school because Marion Hammon was the administrator. Friends avoided each other in public, rumors were rife. It all came to a head one day at a meeting that Short Creekers recall as clearly as the Kennedy assassination. The only Council member present was Alma Timpson, and he openly criticized the Barlows for exploiting Uncle Leroy, at which point the Barlows and the Jessops called him a liar and walked out. They had defied God's representative on Earth. It was a dark time.

Upon Uncle Leroy's death, the Barlows got their wish—Marion Hammon was forced out, while their choice, Rulon Jeffs, was anointed instead. Hammon set off down the road to build Centennial Park, taking approximately a tenth of the people with him—the name came about because it was 1986, a century after John Taylor's revelation on polygamy. Meanwhile, Rulon Jeffs's reign fell into the familiar pattern. He suffered a number of strokes, and this time it was his son Warren who exploited him, using methods straight out of the fundamentalist playbook—he became his caretaker, his gatekeeper, his executor and ultimately his usurper.

Clearly the priesthood system has weaknesses. The rules about seniority and succession are ripe for exploitation. But so long as polygamists remain caught up with points of order and small print, there's no changing it. The one lesson that may have been gleaned from all this, however, is the peril of one-man rule. It remains the biggest bone of contention between the FLDS and Centennial Park.

Centennial Park operates through a council of seven who consult God together until they're unanimous on the subject at hand—a system of checks and balances, in other words. The FLDS however, defer to a solitary leader, and unfortunately for them, the last man was Warren Jeffs.[3] But their argument for an all-powerful prophet has a valid Mormon pedigree. Joseph Smith himself stated he was the only one who could get revelation.[4] He also stated that that "revelations and commandments come only through the one appointed,"[5] and that the day would come when the Lord would send the "One Mighty and Strong" to put the world to rights:

And it shall come to pass that I, the Lord God, will send one mighty and strong, holding the scepter of power in his hand, clothed with light for a covering, whose mouth shall utter words, eternal words; while his bowels

shall be a fountain of truth, to set in order the house of God and to arrange
by lot the inheritances of the saints . . . [6]

Leaving aside the stuff about his bowels being a fountain for a minute, this passage has been responsible for no end of Mormon madness over the years. Fundamentalist history is full of men who have laid claim to the "mighty and strong" title.

In Centennial Park, however, they point to other passages that suggest that councils, in which all members possess the same authority, are a better system. By this thinking, all priesthood holders are able to receive revelation—their powers are equivalent in that sense. What distinguishes them are the revelations themselves, which are tied to one's position in the community. One Council member explained it thus: "Revelations to you are legitimate for you and your jurisdiction. If you have a family, then you can receive revelations that direct that family. But you can't receive a revelation for the church, that's not your jurisdiction—that's the president's prerogative." The president can, however, receive revelations about your family, if you're a member of the church. It's a hierarchical business, revelation, and this is why Priesthood Councils aren't nearly as even-handed and democratic as they purport to be. Seniority is important, the number of years served on the council, a man's wealth and standing in the community—the Priesthood Council is as political a body as the board of any corporation.

The importance of hierarchy in fundamentalist groups is the principle reason why the groups keep splitting and separating, the fission of sects that is the affliction of all religions. There's a clear incentive to create two hierarchies instead of one, because two groups means twice the number of apostles who, as the most powerful members, get the pick of the ladies. Fundamentalists don't say this to reporters, for obvious reasons, but it slips out now and again—the higher up in the Priesthood hierarchy a man is, the more wives he can have, and the more wives a man has, the more exalted he is on Earth.

It sounds crude, but just as when Nephi talked to me of the Priesthood "giving" him more wives, it's more the language that offends than the principle. Because in Centennial Park, the principle is sound—of course the Priesthood seniority should be blessed with more wives because the Lord knows that they are righteous enough to treat them all well. And of course a man with ten wives can be said to have mastered the Work more than a man who has only two.

"Everyone wants to be a leader," Marvin Wyler told me in an offhand moment. "Leaders always seem to get more wives. And the more wives you have on Earth, the more exalted you are—they all try to say that's not the case. But it is. The nature of the devil is greed."

◈ Going Plural

In every dream home a heartache
And every step I take
Takes me further from heaven
Is there a heaven?
　　—Bryan Ferry[7]

Jared* remembers the split of Colorado City more clearly than most. It was a pivotal time. He was an adolescent just beginning to define himself, and the pillars of authority were crumbling. He was with his father at that famous meeting where the Barlows called Alma Timpson a liar and walked out. He watched them leave, and he was scared—they were rejecting a member of the Council, a representative of God, and he knew just where his dad, Lorin, stood on the matter. When the exodus began, his father glared at him and said, "You move from that chair, and I'll knock you back in it."

But just as the Priesthood's grip over Colorado City was slipping, so too was Lorin's hold over Jared. He was an alcoholic, a distant and miserable father who stashed bottles of vodka all over the yard. He made a pittance working at a sawmill, and Jared's mothers were overwhelmed trying to keep the thirty-strong family going on such little money. So increasingly, Jared was left to his own devices. And increasingly, he started to rebel.

It was the 1980s, and the community was electrified by the renegade

---

*Jared's name has been changed

prophet Ervil LeBaron, who had threatened to kill the leaders of all the significant fundamentalist churches, particularly Uncle Leroy Johnson. LeBaron's wife and stepdaughter had already shot the polygamist Rulon Allred dead, and after LeBaron himself died of a heart attack in 1981, he left a hit list for his followers. So Colorado City was on high alert. A team of town fathers would take shifts driving around town, monitoring all the entrances, while the next shift stayed back at the school building, watching movies. Jared and his pals used to sneak up on them and steal the keys out of their cars and lock all the doors; they'd light bonfires in the yards; they'd find an open window and pelt them with tomatoes and put a rod through the door handles so that when the men came running out to catch them— bang! They couldn't get out. Schoolboy mischief.

Then one day Jared went too far. As part of the split, the Centennial Park people were to hand over the school building to the First Ward, the very school that had been built and run by Marion Hammon, the leader of the Centennial Park community. So out of reverence for Hammon's work, and not a little pride, the entire community got together and cleaned and scrubbed and swept the place until the building, once the lifeblood of the community, could be passed to its new owners in immaculate condition. Given the animosity of the split, it was a tremendous gesture. And the First Ward's response spoke volumes—it promised to demolish the building at the earliest, and bulldozers were duly massed nearby. So Jared saw an opportunity. He and his pal Chris decided to grab a bunch of rocks and smash a few windows before the dozers moved in. Just for the hell of it. They must have done thirty windows in all.

But they were seen, and when word got back to the Elders, the entire community of Centennial Park turned against him.

"My dad beat the shit out of me," he says. "He said he was ashamed that I was his son. I'd go to a meeting and everyone would look at me like I was the devil. As far as they were concerned, I was just a no-good son of a bitch."

For three months he was forced to return to the school to clean up the mess he made—sweeping up the broken glass, chiseling out the mortar in the frames and working to pay for replacement panes. He'd desecrated the work of the community and he had to put it right, even though as soon as he was finished, the building would be demolished. It was harsh work—his hands were all cut up from the shards—and he was alone. His friend Chris had gotten off lightly; only Jared was the town pariah. So sitting up there alone, looking at his bloody hands, he faced a choice. He could either leave the community and strike out on his own—forget the Priesthood, it was breaking up anyway. Or he could stay put and prove them all wrong—the Elders, the whole community and especially his father.

He tells me this now, a slightly balding, softly spoken man, sitting on the back porch of his mansion home. Jared's wealthy now, with two wives, six children and, as far I can tell, a wonderful life. But he still carries an ember of that determination within him. He's still proving them wrong.

Emma* thought about leaving too, though for quite different reasons. The daughter of Marion Hammon, she was a devout girl growing up, quiet and unassuming. She also had a poor relationship with her father, a common story in fundamentalism. He was ferociously strict, booming and powerful. He yelled in church, people were terrified of him. And he was so busy, what with being a leader and the patriarch of an immense family of seventy-five children and nineteen wives, that in the rare event that he actually spoke to Emma, he seldom remembered her name.

Still Emma's memory of him is generous. When Emma's half sibling Sara Hammon left the group, she accused her father of abusing her from the age of five. But Emma thinks the charges are "outlandish." And she's no trite apologist for plural marriage. She doesn't regard her childhood through a Hallmark filter. Growing up in a huge plural family was hectic, bewildering and impersonal. And when her father died, with Emma still in her teens, she considered other options. "The thumb was lifted," she says.

Her first thoughts were of leaving: "I wanted something else. I wanted to go to horse-riding school in Phoenix and do dressage." She had a horse already. All she needed were the requisite school credits to get into a riding academy, so she started cleaning motels to pay for night school at the Mohave Community College. But it all petered out; her dreams died in Colorado City. She couldn't leave her mother, as so many of her siblings had. She couldn't risk disappointing this pious and long-suffering woman

---

*Emma's name has been changed

whose faith had both forced her into such a difficult marriage—with a man more than twice her age—and enabled her to endure it. "It would have crushed her if I would have walked," she says. "She would have felt like a failure."

So Emma stayed. But what her mother didn't know was that she started seeing a boy around this time, too. And not just any boy, but Jared Zitting, who trashed the school. There was no sex at that stage, just kissing and fumbling, but they knew it was wrong—dating is *verboten* in Centennial Park. Only God decides who hooks up with whom. The belief is that, somewhere out there, there's a kindred spirit to whom Emma is eternally paired and the only way to find this person is through fervent prayer. When God hears her prayers, He tells the Priesthood whom she's meant for (He might cc: Emma too, but no promises). Then the Priesthood tells Emma and she either submits to God's will or she defies Him. All dating does is complicate matters, steams up the lens. Say Emma develops, for sake of argument, "the horn" for Jared, how's she going to know if said "horn" is of the flesh, or if it's a message from God?

"If you start courting a girl and she gives her feelings and emotions over to you, then it's harder for her to make the right choice," Jared says. "So I felt that I had dishonored her when we kissed."

So the lovebirds broke it off and Emma went to the Priesthood Council to ask whom she belonged to. At the time, the Council consisted of only one man, Alma Timpson, ninety-three—the rest of them had passed away and no new members had been called. Timpson responded with a question: "Anyone you have special feelings for?"

"I'm not here to get what I want," she said. "I'm here to figure out what God wants."

"Yes, but if you have a connection, maybe it's because you're kindred spirits from a past life," said Timpson. "Go on, tell me who this person is."

For the first two visits, Emma held out, but eventually she buckled and blurted out Jared's name. So Alma went off to pray about it and, sure enough, God gave him a thumbs-up. The wedding was set for two weeks' time.

"I know what it looks like," says Jared. "Like Brother Timpson said, 'Sure, go ahead,' and God wasn't involved at all. But I don't think God speaks to these men with a clear voice all the time. I think Brother Timpson prayed on my name and just didn't have any bad feeling about it. Sometimes the Priesthood doesn't even know that God's speaking through them. There's times I'll have a question and I'll pray on it. Then at a meeting, one of the apostles will answer that question for me without even knowing it."

As much of a miscreant Jared may have been growing up, his faith had never faded. And that was one of the rocks Jared and Emma clung to when their marriage hit choppy waters. The first four years were manageable, but years five to eight were tough. "I got a job and I was earning more money than he was," says Emma. "It got a little bit weird right there. Then I had to quit my job and . . . at seven years, divorce looked like a good option. We talked about it. It was real."

It didn't happen. They stuck it out, worked hard and scrimped and saved. Jared's framing business flourished while Emma became a model mom with an immaculate home of folded clothes, fluffed cushions and children who studied the gospel. And they all sacrificed for a common goal: to build their dream home. So there were no holidays or expensive purses or trips to Vegas or movies and restaurants. This house, they promised, would be paid for in cash. The Zittings were determined to get ahead.

Now the home is built and Emma and I are out in the yard taking it in. She doesn't scream polygamy, Emma—she looks like Chrissie Hynde in a long skirt, with a funky shag hairdo. We pass a gorgeous rock garden into the huge games room for the kids and go up through three floors of bedrooms, some junior, some lavish. It's a mansion. And it was obviously built with at least three wives in mind, perhaps fifteen kids or so. Jared has always wanted to live the Principle, as Emma has always known.

But when it actually happened, neither one had any idea what they were in for. They went plural four years ago, a full fifteen years after they'd got married.

"We'd only just paid off our debts, the mortgage, the cars," says Emma, wistfully. "We were just about to do all those things we'd been denying ourselves all those years. And then . . ."

"You didn't want Jared to have more than one wife?"

She scoffs. "What do you think? Would you want your wife to have a second husband?"

"I'm not a polygamist, Emma. I don't subscribe to this religion where . . ."

"Yes, yes, and you would think that you would get so submerged in this life that it's like breathing. And when you talk to some women, that's what they say. That's the 'right' answer. But I told Jared, if I'm going to do this interview, I'm not going to give you the 'right' answers."

Emma didn't want to do this interview. This was all Carol*'s idea, the second wife. She's a young blonde of twenty-four with big green eyes, gleaming bunny rabbit teeth and a quick, breathless way of talking, like a child. It was Carol who persuaded Jared who persuaded Emma to let me try to persuade her in person. And it wasn't easy—Emma grew up in a culture that doesn't trust outsiders, particularly journalists. She has uncles, aunts, grandparents who were arrested, even thrown in jail for polygamy. But Carol was keen, a relative newcomer to the scene. Not a convert exactly, but she was raised outside the polygamist dominions of Colorado City and Centennial Park.

"It's hard moving into someone's house that they've lived in for fifteen years," she says. "You break a plate and it's like 'aargh!'" She's driving me down from the baseball fields to her home, talking at a terrific pace. "It's hard seeing yourself as family. And you know when you marry a guy, he doesn't care which way you put the dishes in the dishwasher, but when you move in with women, it's different. I mean, me and Emma, we're different. *Different.* She's a very homey person and I was hyper and doing stuff. But you know, I'm just talking, you probably don't want to know all this. Have you got any questions? What's your book about anyway? I mean the *angle*?"

Carol lived in Colorado City until she was four. Then the split went down and her family left town, just the four of them—her parents, her brother and her. They moved to the tiny town of Kanab about thirty-five miles away. But they had only left to escape the animosity of the split; they never lost ties with the Priesthood. So Carol was baptized in the church at nine, even though she lived "out in the world" till she was twenty, going to public school, dating boys and participating in all the other activities of a nonfundamentalist life. And her home was never plural. Her parents weren't even that religious for that matter, at least not until they decided to move back when she was done with high school.

---

*Carol's name has been changed

"Growing up, I used to love visiting Colorado City. I had like four or five cousins who were my age, and we had sleepovers, it was great. So when my parents moved back, I was like, 'yeah!'" Carol went back with them and eventually moved out to live in one of her uncles' homes in Centennial Park. She started working as a gym teacher at the Colorado City Academy and stayed for three years.

Then all her single friends from Kanab started getting married. And Carol wasn't sure what to do—should she stay in Centennial Park? The politics, the culture here, it was a lot to take on. But she also knew that she wanted children, desperately. And that from the age of sixteen, she'd known that she couldn't have them on account of ovary problems.

"That's why I wanted to be a plural wife," she says. "I didn't really care what number, as long as it wasn't first. That was my main goal. I just wanted to have kids."

So she approached John Timpson, the president of the church—the big guy who spoke in church the other day with the tears rolling down his cheeks. At first she asked him about some other guy she'd had her eye on. But Brother Timpson dissuaded her.

"He knew what I wanted," says Carol. "Someone I didn't have to drag to church, who was a good dad, and wasn't an alcoholic. But this guy was two out of three. So I asked him if there were other options?" When Timpson suggested Jared, she laughed out loud. "It had always been a family joke. I always used to say he was the cutest old man I've ever seen."

The first step was to meet Jared and see if she felt comfortable. So she made an appointment with him for lunch one day. And for nearly three hours they sat there, chatting, laughing, getting along just dandy. Jared had no idea that she was scouting for a husband; he thought she wanted a job. He even asked if she was interested in applying, at which point Carol goofed. "I just asked him, 'How do you feel about getting married?' And he's like, 'What?' Splutters his drink, whatever. And I'm like, 'Oops . . . well I've talked to the Priesthood, and they feel good about it. Now it's for you to pray about.'"

It all went down at a secret picnic in Larson Park where Jared was meeting his oldest sister. She's in the FLDS, so she's not strictly allowed to see Jared, but she'd had a baby, and her mom had mentioned to Jared that if he so happened to be at Larson Park at this certain time, then the whole family would be there and he could see the baby. So he arrived with Emma and the kids. And there was a picnic, and it was lovely. Then one of the Council members pulled Jared aside and told him in private that everyone felt good about Carol joining his family—everyone meaning Carol, her parents and, crucially, the Council.

"I knew what was going down," says Emma. "The way they looked over at me when they were talking. Call it intuition. So we got in the car afterward, with the kids in the back, and I said, 'Who is she?' He's like 'What?' I said, 'Just tell me. Who. Is. She?' He said, 'Carol Hammon.' And it was like a kick in the gut. I couldn't breathe. Because I babysat Carol, I knew her. Her dad is my half brother. But that was it. Did Jared ask, 'Do you want to do it?' No. Did I have a say? No. You're told, not asked. And two weeks later it was a done deal."

The weeks leading up to the ceremony were excruciating. "I was terrified, scared to death. I could hardly eat. Every insecurity you can possibly imagine came up, every jealousy. I couldn't even own it enough to say that this is my choice even though it hurts like white-hot pain. I felt betrayal, I felt grief, I felt helpless—you can go down the whole list and put an X by it. But if I had stood in his way, I would have lost him. Jared never would have left me, but I would have lost his respect and his love. And he would have done it anyway. He was clear about that."

When she got her breath back, Emma argued with him. Jared recalls quite a grilling. "She said, 'So if I leave you, I'll get your house and all your money, and you'd give it all up for Carol.' And I said, 'Have it all. I can't let my conscience be dictated by someone other than myself. I'm going to do what God directs me to do, and you can choose whatever you choose, you're a free person.'"

Emma suggested that Jared keep Carol out of sight in a separate house on the other side of town, as far away as possible. But Jared wouldn't have it. "I don't want to be a part-time dad to my kids. To me, it's really not living the law the way it's meant to be lived. It's like pretending I'm on a business trip."

For wives to live in separate houses would be "a lot easier," says Emma. "The home is much harder to share than the men." But polygamy is meant to be hard. And in Centennial Park, there are no shortcuts.

Separate homes might be fine for the wussies up in Salt Lake City who are afraid of the LDS neighbors finding out, but those excuses don't fly in a fully fundamentalist community. The object of plural marriage is to help people overcome their flesh—all the emotions, jealousies and insecurities—and still live harmoniously together. No wallowing. No whining. After all, this is the family you're hoping to abide with in the next life, in Mormon heaven. Better get used to it down here. Gods don't get into arguments over who left the batch in the dryer.

· · ·

One of the hazards of going plural is that people start fainting around you. Weeks after they married, Jared introduced one of his most faithful clients, a Mormon man, to "my other wife, Carol." He keeled over right there in the office. A similar thing happened when Jared first brought Carol to the house to tell the kids. His ten-year-old, Marcus, fell straight off his chair.

The kids were happy, though. Carol was young, she was fun—as a teacher at the Colorado City Academy she had taught most of them sports at some point. And the kids helped Carol through the awkward first few months, a time of peculiar loneliness. It's not as if she and Jared were inseparable, like honeymooners. She hardly knew him. "Usually people get married and jump in bed or whatever, but not us," she says. "I didn't love him, he wasn't coming near me. It was weird—I was in someone else's house married to a man I didn't really know."

It took a long time for Carol to feel at home. The kids weren't hers and they always ran to their mother first. She'd often walk into the living room and find the family there, all perfectly happy, as they were before she arrived, and she'd hover awkwardly at the edge. At other times, her single friends would call up, "Hey Carol, what are you doing, let's go out!" And she'd have to tell them, "I'm babysitting six kids right now."

But it was harder for Emma, for obvious reasons. So she suggested a few ground rules to make life bearable. No intimacy outside the bedroom, for starters—none of that *Big Love* stuff where Bill Paxton goes through the house kissing all his women and pinching their asses. "That way, I could treat it more like a business proposal," she says. It was agreed that Carol would work for Jared, as his accountant, so that Emma could remain at home, queen of her domain. And life would follow a certain routine—Emma would pack lunches for Jared and Carol as they set off in the morning, and she'd make dinner too on weeknights, while getting weekends off. It's still hard for her to see Jared leave the house every day with this young blonde, leaving her, in her late thirties, back home with a pile of laundry. "No one wants to be the old maid," says Emma. "We all want to be the young gust." But Carol's jealous too—she doesn't have as deep a relationship with Jared as Emma has. She doesn't have the same maternal bond with the kids.

"It upsets me when people say, 'Oh, you let him have other wives, so you must have no feelings about it,'" says Emma. "I'm human, you know. I just can't afford to feel the jealousy and the insecurity. What if my kids saw me being vulnerable and they thought, 'Mom's unhappy, so that isn't for me, this life'? I've become more and more like my dad. I don't allow myself to be vulnerable. I'm a lot colder. I have to be. You have to have insulation in this life."

It's now been four years since Carol arrived. And though the strife began on day one, they've mellowed enough to submit to these interviews. I sat down with Jared, Carol and Emma individually, each one deliberately out of earshot of the other. If this were a documentary, we'd cut between one quote and the next. It's a cross section of a plural marriage.

> **Emma:** When Carol came around, I had to give Jared up. I don't want to go into the gory details. It wouldn't even be justified to go into how hard it was when you see what Christ went through. And then there was the house we worked so hard for. And the kids. Oh, I was choking to death.
>
> **Carol:** She was very accepting. She basically told me this is what I want my kids to become and I would love it if you could help me.
>
> **Emma:** The kids were the hardest part for me. I told Jared but he was not very kind about it in the beginning. I think men have to learn—if they don't, it makes living this life so hard it wouldn't be worth it.
>
> **Jared:** I had to forcefully say: "Those kids are not only your children, they're my children and Carol's children." And she said, "Screw you." And I said, "No, that is the case. It has to be."
>
> **Carol:** Jared's always the bad guy. I remember once we were going to go on a business trip up to Sacramento, but he bailed out at the last

minute. He said, "Why don't you go—I need to be with my family now." Can you imagine? "My family."

Emma: My mothers never fought, they held it together. So I never verbally abused anyone—that's important to me. You can't just vent and rail against somebody and expect it to be all right tomorrow. Once you pound a nail in a board, you can pull the nail out but the hole's still there.

Carol: I don't know what I was mad about but I didn't think that the rest of the family was outside the door. When you're accused of something instead of asked, that makes me go ballistic. If Jared comes back and the first thing he says is, "What were you thinking, why did you do this"— then I'll say, "Screw you." And I'll say it for an hour. I remember saying, "I'm done with you, just done." And when I went upstairs, Ladonna [Jared's oldest daughter] was crying. She thought I was going to leave. So the new rule is if you're mad about something, take it into the barn.

Emma: English people call fights "barneys," do they? Have they been to our house?

Carol: But I think it's good for Ladonna to see that if I don't like something, then I can stand up and say so. Women in this religion have this reputation that they always stand down.

Jared: Carol is a hot-blooded girl. She's thrown her cookies at me and screamed and yelled and hit me and I have to unconditionally love her the moment after she did that. I can't say "screw you." Look what God's asking her to do. I think Emma gets a kick out of watching Carol and I go through relationship struggles that she and I went through years ago. I think it gives her confidence that there's ground that has been gained that's of value.

Emma: Okay, here's a scenario. He tells Carol, "Let's take the kids to the movies at 3 PM." Then he calls me and says, "I don't want the kids going out unless they've done their jobs and their homework." So Carol walks through the door and says, "We're off to the movies!" And I say, "But they haven't done their jobs yet." And she gets upset. And she takes the kids. You see? That's a very small-scale scenario. Very small.

Carol: Like I said, Jared's the bad guy. I never feel any hatred toward Emma.

Emma: If I thought Jared was in control, I wouldn't be participating. This is where faith comes in—I think God's in control. Absolutely. It's not a lifestyle I chose. I'm doing this for religious reasons, for the next life. And there's no choice but to be all right with it.

Jared: When Carol calls and says, "Hey, can I take the kids down to the creek and play in the sand?" Before, I used to say, "Sure, if you think it's a good idea." But now I say, "Let me think about that." Because maybe she's bullshitting me for a minute and she's out to get even with Emma on something. Maybe it's the other way around.

Emma: Carol's not a planner. She doesn't sacrifice today for later. She's one of those immediate-gratification people. I didn't go on cruises and have big rocks on my fingers, we didn't even go to the movies—we lived on my paycheck of $2,000 a month and we invested in his company. Then Carol shows up: "I got credit card debt, I got to pay for my dress . . ." But she can't possibly appreciate what she didn't live through. So I've had to just let it go.

Carol: Sometimes I need to take Emma out and say, "Let's go and do something crazy, let's just have a bottle of wine and go out on the porch and let the kids do the dishes."

Jared: Carol had a reputation for being a flirt and that bothered Emma. She wasn't sure if I was going to go off the deep end and become a different person—start racing around with this young little thing and forget who I am.

Carol: There was an issue with me dressing the way I did, so I had to wear a dress every other day, to try and be more ladylike. It's been a bit of a struggle.

Jared: Carol and Emma are like night and day different. Do I wish they could be more alike? Yeah, it'd be great. But they're not.

Carol: Emma is perfect, she does everything perfect. I don't know how she puts up with me—sometimes I have laundry all over the place.

Emma: Carol is perfect for me. I couldn't have custom-made somebody that could work me as hard as she does.

Another hazard of going plural: women start avoiding you in case the polygamy thing rubs off on their husbands. Polygamy as a virus. And this goes for fundamentalist women too. Take Emma's sister, Florence, who lives down the road. Of all the women in Centennial Park, she's probably the hottest—tan, thin, glamorous in her Ray-Bans. But after six kids with her husband, whom she adores, she lives in constant fear that he'll come home one day with a younger woman, a Carol, to upset her applecart for good.

"She won't do things with us anymore, because she's scared. White-knuckle scared," says Emma. "She almost can't tolerate Jared now. But she's still here in the community. It could easily happen and she knows it. She's already had some work done."

Florence isn't the only one who has stopped coming over to the house these days. The chief salesman in Jared's company isn't likely to pay a visit either, not after the last time. He's an outsider, but a close friend, so Jared wanted their families to get to know each other, to develop that comfort level. So he invited him over for a barbecue. It was a disaster. His wife went charging upstairs to look at the bedrooms, asking Jared personal questions about why Carol didn't have any kids and whose bedroom was whose. At one point she suggested that if Carol would marry someone who's already got a wife, she might well go for her own husband. At the time, Carol was out in the yard shooting hoops with him and the kids.

"It was horrible," says Jared. "And this guy was so embarrassed. He tried to shut her up, but he couldn't control her."

The reactions of "outside people" are hard to judge. There are the fainters, the blurters, the disapproving Mormons and the openly disgusted. It's often best to just keep your plural secrets to yourself, but that path has its pitfalls too. Take the guy at the coffee shop for example, who sees Jared and Carol come in every day for cappuccinos—what's he to think when one day Jared shows up with Emma? "I think Jared's having an affair," he whispers to Carol, the next time he sees her. "She's got dark hair, about so tall . . ." And Carol has to feign shock. "Oh my God! Are you sure? Actually, you know what? That sounds like his sister. But thanks for letting me know . . ."

And then the following week, they see this same guy at the movies in St. George. Whenever Jared takes the family to the movies, he never holds both of his wives' hands at the same time, there's no sense in drawing attention—usually one wife will get the popcorn with the kids while the other finds some seats with Jared. But what if Jared's holding Emma's hand and not Carol's? "I know people stare at us, they're all trying to guess, is he, isn't he?" says Jared. "But we only have this problem in Utah. In Las Vegas no one cares! Maybe I should move there!"

I'm back on the porch with Jared on a routine summer's day. Emma's horse is neighing, the cows are lowing and the kids and the wives are out raking manure into the lawn. "Great," says Jared. "I can just see the headline: polygamist women spreading manure outside while the husband watches on the porch."

"Well, it's true."

"I'm blaming you. If I didn't have to do this interview, I'd be out there with them."

It's nice to see the kids at work. They're doing their chores as good kids are supposed to do, but they're complaining too, which is a relief. Some of the kids in Centennial Park are so perfect they scare me. Jared's kids whine and answer back. The oldest sister, Ladonna, sixteen, wants to go upstairs and listen to her Ludacris CD. The oldest boy, Marcus, fifteen, wants to show off his first car, a 1963 Mustang. But Carol's out there with them, mucking in while Emma sees about cleaning the house. And Jared's giving orders. "Come on now, put your back into it!"

"This lifestyle forces a man into a leadership position," he tells me. "When I married Carol, she would ask, 'Is this Emma's way of doing things, or is this how you want it?' And to be honest, I never really thought about it—for the last fifteen years, when it came to the house or the kids, I just left it to Emma. So Carol would say, 'You're in charge, not Emma, so how do you want it?' And for the first time I had to define how to care for the children, how to keep the house, what kind of food I prefer the kids to eat . . . And Emma would say, 'You're changing everything because Carol showed up.' There's no winning."

A case in point—the backsplash. The wives have been squabbling over the décor of the new house. Emma wanted Victorian, Carol wanted Mediterranean, and there's no mixing the two, they're completely different. So, faced with an impasse, Jared started picking out stuff himself. But Carol complained, "It's our house too, we deserve a say." So he said, "Okay, you and Emma agree on the interior for the basement and I'll do whatever you want." And after a month of battling through it, Emma and Carol finally settled on this particular design with a backsplash.

"But when it was finally done, Carol pulls me aside and says, 'I think that backsplash looks like shit, but Emma loved it so I made her a deal—she could have that, but I was going to have my way on the upstairs kitchen.' And I said, 'Wait a minute, that wasn't the deal. We're not doing trades here.' And this big argument broke out. Emma was pissed because she didn't agree to the trade and Carol was calling it a Southwestern-style backsplash when it was actually Spanish-style. Carol was pissed because Emma steamrollered her when it came to talking to the contractors. So now, basically, I'm at the point where I'm going to uninvolve them again."

"Nightmare."

"So you know, when people say, 'It must be such an ego boost having two women,' yeah, I can see why they think that. But I'm either pissing off one or appeasing the other."

"So when will you be ready for number three?"

"Whenever the Lord thinks I'm ready."

"Shouldn't you get the hang of two first?"

"Actually, I hear that three's easier. See with two, one wife's right and the other's wrong—so whichever way you go, you're screwed. With three, you can balance it out."

He seems optimistic about the prospect of a third wife. And he's not the only one. Emma likes the idea of Carol adjusting to a wife-invasion just as she had to. "Carol doesn't care to talk about it," she smirks. "She's facing what I faced—fears, doubts and insecurities that Jared's going to get a lovely little wife who's going to bow at his feet and do everything he wants. I tell her, 'Jared's going to get that blonde, blue-eyed sixteen-year-old, and it'll all go out the window.' And it's a joke, but it's reality as well. And she knows it."

But Carol insists she's also up for a third. "I came into this to be a plural wife. I didn't really care what number wife I was going to be as long as it wasn't first. So why not? He's already sleeping with someone else. What's one more?" And she's fine with having no say in the matter. "It doesn't matter to me who it is—if Emma and I can get along, then anyone can do it. And we wouldn't be living this way if we could pick and choose."

"Anyway," says Jared. "We could do with another pair of hands to rake that shit into the lawn!"

◈ The Skeptical Fundamentalist

> Take good care of what the priests say
> 'After death it's so much fun'
> Little sheep don't let your feet stray
> Happiness is easy
>   —Talk Talk[8]

To attack religion has a fish-in-a-barrel quality. It's all too easy to point out the hypocrisies, the blood-soaked histories and the dearth of evidence for these imaginary friends. So when an atheist challenges religious faith, it's considered unsporting, insensitive, even arrogant, while believers who claim a favored relationship with the creator of the universe are somehow seen as humble.

Well, I don't buy it. Beliefs are too important to be left uncontested for reasons of etiquette. It would be rude *not* to challenge a man's faith in a place like Centennial Park where religion is the bedrock of society. It would be as if I didn't take them seriously. And I do. Besides, Mormons aren't too concerned with protecting my feelings. I'm just a Gentile, after all, whose dark skin is a curse from God.

So when one of the Priesthood Council tells me that he's keen to answer any questions, I leap at the chance. Brother Marcus Cawley* is known as something of an intellectual in Centennial Park. He's the wise old man, the one with two doctorates. He's also the main reason why Centennial Park has allowed me in. Of all the proponents of the community's new openness, Brother Marcus is out in front.

But barely five minutes into our meeting, he throws me a curveball. "I consider myself a skeptic," he says. "As you mature, you realize there is no way to prove that God exists and no way to prove that he does not exist. And I believe heavily in reason and logic."

A skeptical fundamentalist? Isn't that an oxymoron?

I remember Marcus from church—he opened the service on the day I arrived, the seventy-one-year-old mumbler with the piercing eyes and the strangled voice, his swept-back white hair showing its stained roots like tobacco fingers. As one of the most senior apostles in Centennial Park,

---

*Marcus Cawley's name has been changed

he has on countless occasions liaised with God on whom the young girls and boys of Centennial Park should spend their eternities with. And he's telling me not only that he's a skeptic, but also that he's a fan of the Greek philosophers, a reader of science journals and a subscriber to the position, so offensive to so many believers, that the world is billions, not thousands, of years old. "I don't think it's reasonable to reject science," he says. "If it requires recognizing that the Bible was amiss, then so be it. Like the Flood. I think it's nonsensical to believe that water covered the whole earth, I don't think that's even possible . . ."

I'm stumped. Admittedly, I approached this interview with some pretty strong doubts about fundamentalism. I suspected it of being a protest, a Luddite squall against modern life, against the Babylon that presses upon its gates, threatening to contaminate its innocents with lust, liquor and doubt. But at the same time, a hypocritical protest, because fundamentalists turn to Babylon's doctors when they are ill, craving all the benefits of the world they rage against. I was tempted to characterize them as nostalgists who totemize some books while burning others, and as literalists for whom truth is calcified in texts—for whom texts are divine and free of metaphor. I imagined them digging in their heels as the world transforms with technology, war and social revolutions, clutching at the past like a child holding onto mother on the first day of school. And I sensed that they cast this cowardice as courage, their incuriosity as wisdom, their rigidity as strength.

So am I to revise all this now that I'm faced with a doubting fundamentalist?

Not entirely. As we wade in, Marcus's faith seems secure enough. He finds the Mormon conceptions of God and man "logical." And it is in some ways easier to grasp. Their God, for example, isn't an ethereal mist, but an exalted man and father—a family man of "body, parts and passion." God has feelings, He's comprehensible. And He's not alone up there—there's a whole council of gods with him, 144,000 in all. And together they regulate the affairs of the celestial realm where the Gods live—the two lower realms are the telestial (the lower order) and the terrestrial (where we are now).

For Marcus, the celestial realm is where the mystery of life begins. God has a world to run up there, so first of all, he starts populating it with spirit children whom He fashions out of something that Joseph Smith called

"Intelligence," a strange refined matter that is at the core of all life. It has no beginning and no end and lives forever. Marcus reckons physics may someday discover what Intelligence consists of.

Once God has created enough spirit children, He's ready to build a world where they can take on physical bodies. So He goes to the Council to get permission to build this world—even gods need building permits. The Council then assigns him a fellow god to act as a liaison between Him and the Council, effectively sending back progress reports once building is underway. In other words, planet Earth is a construction project and gods are like foremen with hard hats making sure the workers stop catcalling the girls and get back to work. It's all so practical and pioneery, so suited to fundamentalists who are, incidentally, huge in the construction business.

"This way, there's order in all things," says Marcus. "The one that's appointed to work with heavenly Father reports back to the Council with an accounting of what's happening." So that bit in Genesis where God looks at His handiwork and "saw that it was good," that's not God being cocky, it's the Council approving God's work so far. "They're telling God 'Okay, you've got the green light to move on to the next phase.'"

The point of all this is so that the spirit children, now encased in physical bodies, can get to work on improving themselves until they become gods themselves and celestialize the entire planet. As far as Marcus is concerned, Joseph Smith was one of the guys that made it—he was exalted to god status and today he's up in the celestial realm hanging out with Jesus.

"I believe that Joseph Smith was one of the greatest psychics that America ever produced," he says. "He was up there with Edgar Cayce and Arthur Ford." Marcus's skeptic credentials are fading. Cayce was a quack psychic in the early twentieth century who predicted that California would slide into the ocean and that the United States would discover the "death ray" that destroyed Atlantis. Arthur Ford, meanwhile, was a fellow charlatan who was exposed for a high-profile stunt in which he purported to contact the dead Harry Houdini. (Houdini's widow, it was revealed, had slipped him the inside information he needed).

Marcus protests that psychics aren't always 100 percent accurate— sometimes they bring back false information because whatever they receive has to be filtered through their brains and nervous systems. It doesn't necessarily mean they were frauds. But nevertheless, it muddies the waters—if their information cannot be trusted, why believe them?

"There were things Joseph said that weren't true," says Marcus.

"But you accept that he had these visions, the angels and all that."

"Yes. Because Joseph Smith wasn't a liar."

"So the truth of his revelations boils down to the strength of his character?"

"Yes. I'm not saying he was spotless—he was just trying to organize a church and deal with people and inevitably you get entangled. But he couldn't have been a charlatan, because he would never have suffered so many persecutions—he would have made his message a little more palatable."

This argument—that polygamy must be a divine command because no man would choose such an unpopular doctrine otherwise—sounds a lot like the argument that God created homosexuality. After all, who would choose to have sex in public toilets, risking arrest and the destruction of an otherwise promising pop legacy?

"But Joseph Smith said that the Bible is the inerrant word of God."

"As far as it is correctly translated."

"And the Bible maintains that the world was created six thousand years ago."

"But there's so much evidence against that, it's hard for me to hold that view. When I see evidence that I don't think I can controvert, then I have to rearrange my thinking."

"So it isn't the inerrant word of God then. And Joseph Smith was wrong."

"There are inconsistencies and you're always trying to reconcile them. But you can do that and still have faith. The most important part of religion is human beings trying to make society work. The ethical practices."

Clearly there's wiggle room in Marcus's theology, considering his acceptance of science and the fallibility of scripture. But it appears he's being whittled down. Science and reason are forcing him into contortions. Since the prophet's teachings are demonstrably inaccurate, there must be other reasons to say that he speaks for God. Look at his character, say, or the righteousness of his followers or the endurance of his church—the reasons hop from place to place, the standards slip and slip. It feels churlish to point out that the ethical practices Marcus is talking about are anything but, at least by most modern standards. Is it ethical to deny women the priesthood?

"I know, everything has to be equal these days. People ridicule the idea in Genesis, where the Lord told Adam and Eve, 'The woman's heart will turn to her husband and he will rule over her.' But we see it all the time. When we put people together, the woman's heart does turn to her husband, she relies on him. Those roles are there in our genes, they go back to cavemen. The feminist movement wants to deny that, and they're not succeeding. Women who are trying to be like men aren't happy—they get to be thirty-five years old, they haven't had a child, and it's too late. They've cut off their nose to spite their face."

"But feminism isn't the issue. Why is there a spiritual gap? Is God male?"

"God is both male and female. There's a mother in heaven and a father in heaven. The reason we don't pray to mother in Heaven is because the man holds the priesthood, and the woman only holds the priesthood through her husband. So women can't administer like men, they can't lay on hands and invoke the power of the priesthood. They can only ask God to heal a person."

"Seems chauvinistic."

"I'm not saying it isn't. That's just the order that God established in Genesis."

Now he sounds more like a fundamentalist—don't blame me, blame God, they're his rules. When I move on to the gay question, Marcus chuckles. He's rather enjoying this to and fro. I tell him that I'm all for gay marriage, that I've always thought weddings are pretty gay anyway and so what if homosexuality is a sin? Plenty of sinners get married.

"But marriage is an institution for family life, that's the purpose of it," he says. "And homosexuality does not establish family because you can't have children in that union. So it's a mistake to call two homosexual people a marriage. I think they should have all the legal privileges attached to marriage, just don't call it marriage."

"It's the coinage you object to?"

"Yes! I don't have any problems with homosexuals. But I resent how they seem to say, 'You have to look at it the way we look at it.' Well, I don't. For example, I don't believe that they're born homosexual and can't change. There's an organization that helps people to change their orientation."

How this myth has persisted, I do not understand. But then Marcus is in his seventies; there was bigotry in the water when he was a kid. And given the kind of bluster that ranking religious leaders have been emitting about gays, Marcus is actually on the enlightened side. The Vatican, for example, announced that men with "deep-rooted homosexual tendencies" can't become Roman Catholic priests but that "transitory" tendencies up to three years old are fine.[9] Admittedly, "deep-rooted" does sound pretty dirty, but what's a transitory tendency? Being gay on a bus?

Marcus and I bat the gay thing back and forth for a while—I say it's genetic, he insists it's a lifestyle like yoga or vegetarianism, and so we are at an impasse. The irony is that polygamists have typically resisted the "lifestyle" label when it comes to their own lives—they feel it diminishes their calling. And it is a little more encompassing than yoga, I'll give them that— you don't find sixteen-year-old girls escaping sinister yoga compounds in the dead of night and appearing on Larry King. But equally, polygamy can be either taken up or given up like a course at Bikram's studio. When polygamists play the civil rights card, they identify their own plight with that of African Americans or gays, people who can't choose to be otherwise. And given their own positions on blacks and gays, it's a strategy that wears increasingly thin.

It was Marcus who brought up *The Bell Curve*, the notorious book of 1994 by a Harvard psychologist and a scholar from the American Enterprise Institute that suggested that black people had lower IQs on average than white people. "You couldn't prove cultural bias in the tests," says Marcus. "And I studied behavioral sciences, so I know the methods that they used and their methodology was impeccable. But that book got slammed. It goes against political correctness. And it's the same with homosexuality. If you establish that they aren't born that way, then you'll get a similar backlash. Political correctness has created a climate where it's not acceptable to study these things."[10]

This is a familiar complaint—about the PC thought police restricting speech, progress and all things good. And yet no one has benefited more from political correctness than fundamentalist religious groups. They want to be protected from prejudice on account of their religion so that they can propagate prejudice in the name of their religion. To what extent can a tolerant society tolerate the intolerant? This is the question polygamists pose to America, the same question that radical Islam poses to the Western World.

When *The Bell Curve* came out, Marcus wasn't surprised—he knew in his bones that black people weren't as smart as whites. "I lived through the '30s and '40s, when IQs were a big deal. And you could see it, the black children weren't achieving the same as white children at school. So sure, I thought there was that difference. I just didn't have the evidence until this book."

The Bell Curve was cited as an example of scientific racism—science's tendency to give credence to ugly racial theories and provide supporting arguments for genocide. Certainly twentieth-century science has given fresh momentum to anti-Semitism. And to the delight of the religious right, Darwin's champion T. H. Huxley was an inveterate racist while the abolitionist movement sprang from churches.[11] But science was more often a support to existing prejudices than a root cause. As with Marcus's reaction to *The Bell Curve*, the racism was already ingrained and seeking evidence for its cause. And the cause came straight from scripture.

The argument goes that when Cain killed Abel, God punished him by marking him with dark skin. But Marcus isn't convinced: "The Bible doesn't say anything about dark skin, I don't find it in the Hebrew." Then there's the issue of Cain's descendants. Somehow the strain of Cain survived the Flood, even though the only survivors were Noah's children—so it's assumed that the black gene was carried through the line of Ham (one of Noah's brood). But Marcus isn't sold on that either: "They say Ham's wife had the blood of Cain, but according to the Bible the descendants of Ham were the ancient Egyptians, and they were Semitic, not black. I think it's just something that's come about because people need to explain their prejudices against black people on religious grounds."

"So where do you stand on the LDS Church giving the priesthood to black people in 1978?"

"They shouldn't have done it."

"But you just said the scripture is unclear, it's all a way of rationalizing existing prejudices . . ."

"I know. That's why I'm more sympathetic toward the blacks than my colleagues. But I'm not in a position to say I would give them the priesthood. That's not my call."

So ultimately, his fundamentalism reasserts itself, the abdicated responsibility: "It's not my call, it says so in the book." And for all his protestations of skepticism, Marcus is convinced of his afterlife, of what awaits him "beyond the veil." If you've lived a good life in the Priesthood work, you qualify to have someone meet you at the gates, to ease the transition from the physical to the spiritual world, like the cars that greet first-class passengers at the airport. And the spiritual world is a wonderful place of imagination and creativity, a dream world come to life.

"In the physical world, we can imagine things, but we don't have anything until we build it physically," says Marcus. "In the spirit world, physical restrictions no longer apply. What you create with your mind is reality, so it depends on your disposition and character. If you feel you fell short of what you could have been in this life, then you create a hell, and you need to repent and get over it, to get in a better frame of mind. There's a movie that depicts this better than any I've ever seen. *What Dreams May Come*, with Robin Williams."

I'm not sure I can bring myself to associate Robin Williams with heaven. And as for my afterlife being a product of my imagination, I'd go a step further—the whole concept is imaginary.

"What about hell, Marcus? What about the lake of unquenchable fire?"

"That's the Christian hell. We don't believe in that. That came about because the Israelites felt oppressed from all sides and they developed a persecution complex. Along with this complex is the sense that some day they would be vindicated, a feeling of revenge: 'The time will come when every knee shall bow and every tongue confess that Jesus is the Christ.' But Joseph did not ascribe to that concept, he said hell is a state of mind. When you realize the opportunity you had in this life, and you didn't take it—that's hell."

"But I've been given the opportunity to receive God's word and I'm not taking it. So what happens to me?"

"When you die, your spirit stays right here in a dimension that we can't perceive—that's the spirit world. Some spirits want to get back into this life, some don't even know they're dead. If in life you gave yourself to the pleasures of the body, that's what you're going to want when you're dead— you'll want to have a body. So you'll linger around physical bodies trying to participate in that world. That's what ghosts are."

"Let's say I didn't succumb to the flesh. I just didn't buy into the Book of Mormon either."

"Well, you can't get into the celestial kingdom without being baptized."

"So for me to become a god, I'd have to return to this world to be baptized."

"Or you can have it done by proxy—that's what baptism for the dead is."

"So if someone baptizes me by proxy, while I'm up in the spirit world, then my spirit will be whisked up from the spirit world to the celestial sphere."

"No, not to the celestial sphere. You can't go into the celestial sphere until you have a body and you're resurrected. Until then, you just stay in the spirit world."

"So why bother doing the ordinances at all? Why not just hang out in the spirit world with Robin Williams?"

"Because the Earth as a planet has to progress as well, it has to be celestialized or it's going to be destroyed. The Earth is our world, so if the Earth is celestialized, then that will be our celestial glory and we will dwell thereon. But a lot of things have to happen before that."

Marcus just used "thereon" in a sentence. That's a lifetime of reading scripture for you. But for one of God's representatives on Earth, Marcus doesn't seem to have the arrogance or dogma I was expecting. I don't share his prejudices and convictions, but we get along; I admire his decency, his curiosity, his willingness to talk. And I trust him—just not enough to pick my wife, necessarily. So I tell him as much. It's a warm exchange.

"Well, you know, Sanjiv, I'm placing a lot of trust in you here too," he says at the door, shaking my hand. "I'd appreciate it if you could change my name, because polygamy is still illegal and . . . you just never know."

And as I drive back down Highway 22, watching Centennial Park recede in my rearview mirror, Marcus's words stay with me. Here's a fundamentalist who wants to engage with society at large, to forge his faith in the kiln of arguments with outsiders. And yet he's afraid of prosecution. And it seems wrong.

Texas 2008

CHAPTER 6

> We submit to the majority because we have to. But we are not compelled
> to call our attitude of subjection a posture of respect.
>
> —Ambrose Bierce, *A Cynic Looks at Life*

*T*HEY TRIED RAIDING the polygamists before. It didn't work out
so well.

It was the summer of 1953 and governor John Howard Pyle of Arizona
took it upon himself to whip up the moral panic over polygamy and then
stomp on it with massed cavalry and rippling flags. His reelection was due
the following year and he was a rising star in the Republican Party, tipped
to be a presidential candidate. And this looked like a political slam dunk—a
Christian monogamist on a mission to "protect and defend the helpless"
against the Short Creek polygamists, a deviant cult engaged in white slavery
and child brides, "the foulest conspiracy you could possibly imagine." He
even had senior members of the Mormon Church cheering him on.

But the governor was in for a surprise. When his men arrived on July 26,
guns cocked for the showdown, they were met not with violence, but by
four hundred fundamentalists singing "God Bless America" beneath a
raised U.S. flag. His men arrested 36 men that day, and took 86 women
and 236 children into custody, dispatching them to small towns all across
the state. But the charges didn't stick. After six months the women were

freed and the men were offered a deal to plead guilty to conspiracy, a misdemeanor, which they accepted. They were given a year's probation. And the public, who were supposed to rejoice at the liberation of so many poor, victimized young girls, instead recoiled at the reports of families torn apart, of mothers separated from their children. So Governor Pyle lost his bid for reelection. His presidential hopes were in tatters. And for fifty years, no subsequent governor dared tackle the so-called polygamist problem again.

The polygamists, on the other hand, returned to Short Creek convinced that God had won and that they could now build up their community without interference. They were the halcyon days, right after the raid. Persecution had both fortified them and magnified their trust issues with the outside world, so now they had a scar to cherish, a story for their grandchildren, a newly minted nimbus of martyrdom hovering over them all. The raid had also given fresh meaning to their ancestral fear and loathing of Gentiles—it made the Crickers that much more huddled and suspicious and ultimately more prone to the manipulation of the wrong kind of prophet.

Warren Jeffs was born two years after the raids, the fruit of Pyle's folly in many ways. As prophet he exacerbated the isolation and the extremism of Short Creek—there would be no contact with outsiders or apostates, no pollution by their media, no trust whatsoever. Every time a woman escaped the cult and spoke of the horrors within, the cult closed up behind her, surrendering nothing, not even words. And so the hysteria mounted, year upon year. The very rhetoric that motivated Governor Pyle—white slavery, brainwashing, the merchandizing of women and children—now rushed to fill the FLDS's own obstinate silence. And the din only grew when Jeffs started siphoning off his selected few to a new ranch in Eldorado, Texas, called Yearning for Zion. The world watched them build a gleaming white temple in the middle of cowboy country, and the questions began to clamor: Why the temple, why Eldorado, were they expecting the apocalypse, were there plans for a mass suicide? And still the FLDS regime of silence held firm, even when Jeffs was captured and convicted of sex crimes.

But eventually the pressure took its toll. Someone who claimed to be a girl calling from inside the ranch sent up an alarm, and the gates came crashing down. The state of Texas charged in to the rescue: they removed 439 children from the ranch and scattered them through shelters from

Amarillo to Austin. The raid on YFZ Ranch in Texas became the biggest child-custody case in U.S. history. And like the first one, it didn't work out so well.

The phone calls began in March 2008. A girl called Sarah Jessop Barlow was calling the NewBridge Family Shelter in San Angelo, claiming to be from YFZ Ranch. She said she was blonde, blue-eyed, sixteen and pregnant, the seventh wife of a much older man called Dale who forced her to have sex with him and beat her viciously while another woman held her eight-month-old baby. If she was caught trying to leave, she said, her husband would lock her in a room and not allow her to eat. It was exactly what the Texas authorities had been waiting to hear.

Sarah's story chimed with those of so many polygamous cult escapees over the years, dating from the early days of the Mormon Church right up to the modern era of Tapestry Against Polygamy and campaigners like Flora Jessop. Flora fled the FLDS twenty-two years ago, claiming forced marriage and sexual abuse, and she has been a dogged opponent ever since, devoted to helping women leave a life that she believes enslaves them. When the FLDS bought the Eldorado ranch, she was the first to warn the townspeople about their new neighbors. And she lent credibility to Sarah's cries for help, because Sarah was calling her too at the Child Protection Project, at which Flora is executive director.

So on April 3, 2008, Texas sent its armored personnel carriers and SWAT teams and K9 units to the gates of YFZ Ranch. They came armed for a prison break at Pelican Bay, but instead they found mothers and children. The scene that unfolded was both dramatic and ridiculous, an effect heightened by the excessive costumery on both sides—the twenty-first century soldiers, bulked up like gaming avatars in Kevlar and visors, rounding up the nineteenth-century women and children. A total of 133 women and 439[1] children were removed, first to the Fort Concho complex an hour away, and then to a nearby sports coliseum where they remained until Child Protection Services workers found them shelters. Meanwhile SWAT teams scoured the ranch for documents, family photos, any lists or registers of marriages and children. When they battered down the doors to the temple itself, fifty-seven FLDS men ringed the gates, kneeling in prayer and sobbing.

Texas attorney general Greg Abbott tried to neutralize the drama of the situation. "This is something that Child Protective Services deals with all the time," he said, unconvincingly. "When they find that a child is in a home of four children where one has been sexually assaulted, they will remove them all to make sure they're removed from a zone of danger. This happened to be a home with four hundred kids, as opposed to four kids."

But his premise began to crumble almost immediately. They couldn't find Sarah.

She kept calling after the raid, but she never revealed herself fully. She was scared, she said, because her sister wives had told her that her baby would be taken away. They also told her that CPS workers were trying to poison her with food in shiny wrappers. She said she'd been assigned to a new husband now, Merril Jessop, the leader of YFZ Ranch, and that she'd been moved, but she wasn't sure where to. And it all sounded very compelling, but it led nowhere. So as the days passed, doubts began to niggle.

Flora Jessop wondered how she could have been abused by Dale Barlow when Dale lived in Short Creek—he had never even entered YFZ Ranch. (Sarah told her that she gave Dale's name because she was just trying to protect her sister in Colorado City). Then the police of Colorado Springs said that they, too, knew of a "Sarah" who made calls about abuse. Her real name was Rozita Swinton, an African American woman of thirty-three who allegedly suffered from multiple personality disorder. She had quite a history—in previous cases she'd posed as thirteen-year-old Dana, who was being abused by a youth pastor; as April, whose uncle was taking her to an abortion clinic; as Jennifer, who was locked in her basement. When Texas Rangers searched her home, they found piles of material about the FLDS—Swinton was obsessed, hence her detailed knowledge of names and doctrines. She also knew that the FLDS denied the priesthood to black people and devised racist statements in her calls.

The news that the raid had been predicated on a hoax didn't deter the Texas authorities one bit. Attorney General Abbott insisted that they'd gathered plenty of evidence in their search that pointed to underage pregnancy and bigamy. "The case really doesn't hinge upon that particular sixteen-year-old," he told Larry King. "Once investigators, in good faith, go into the compound . . . the case is on its own after that."

Already it's the invasion of Iraq—the faulty evidence, the hysteria about evildoers, the Texan cowboy and a crusader's sense of setting people free. No doubt the young women of YFZ were supposed to greet the state troopers like liberators. And when it was clear that Sarah was a hoax—that the weapons of mass destruction didn't exist—the justification broadened and grew more vague. It's not about Sarah; it's about all of the children, all kinds of crimes. And still the authorities maintain, "We were right to go in, given the information we had at the time."

But as in Iraq, the problems multiplied. What evidence the state once claimed was fizzling away. The Department of Family Protective Services had maintained there was a "pervasive pattern of underage marriages," that thirty-one girls between the ages of fourteen and seventeen were pregnant, mothers or both. Within weeks, there were only seventeen women left in the disputed age group. One of the previous suspects turned out to be twenty-seven years old.

There were numerous allegations of cruelty and mistreatment against Child Protective Services. On the day that mothers and children were separated, witnesses from the Hill Country Community Mental Health Center spoke of "crying, begging children [who] were ripped from their devastated mothers . . . the floor was literally slick with tears in places. A baby was left in a stroller without food and water for twenty-four hours and ended up in the hospital." Even the judge forbade breastfeeding mothers to stay with their children (she later reversed her decision for all children up to one year old).

That Texas was in the grip of anticult hysteria came out time and again—in its treatment of the entire compound as a single household, for example, instead of nineteen separate residences; or in the alarmist announcement by the head of the Department of Family Protective Services that according to his interviews young boys may have been sexually abused and forty-one children had evidence of broken bones (no charges resulted). The best example, however, was when investigators found a bed in the temple with disturbed sheets and a strand of a woman's hair. The speculation was immediate that it was an altar of sorts for polygamists to ritually deflower their virgins.

The FLDS's response to all this was surprising—they spoke out. Having maintained a strict silence throughout the arrest and conviction of their prophet, they chose this time to launch a full, multimedia PR campaign for the return of their children. Several websites went up to document the raid, explain FLDS beliefs and to argue its case with the state.[2] For a cult supposedly prohibited from using any media, it was a sophisticated response. Women appeared on *Larry King, Anderson Cooper, Dateline* and *Oprah*, all pleading for their children or railing against the evils of the state. They invited reporters onto YFZ Ranch, figuring that the place had already been desecrated. One man told *Dateline* that after the breaching of the temple, it may as well be burned down.

Their public appearances were a mixed success. Certainly they inspired sympathy; sadness was etched on the mothers' faces. When Larry King gathered seven women together, they made a dismal sight, like extras from some miserable movie—all seven in watery blue and aquamarine dresses, their hair in waves. Only three spoke, and then in the kind of rehearsed robotic style that screamed "cult member."

> **Larry:** So to your knowledge you've never seen a younger girl marry an older person.
> **Sally:** Not that I'm aware of.
> **Larry:** Marilyn, have you?
> **Marilyn:** Not that I have ever seen.
> **Larry:** Esther, what about you?
> **Esther:** Not that I have ever seen.

Nevertheless, public opinion was shifting. The herding of families onto buses, the swabbing of cheeks for DNA samples, the armed SWAT teams at the temple gates—it all smacked of state power run amok, particularly since no criminal charges had yet been filed and the grounds for the raid had proven false. Texans complained about the assault on individual freedoms. Utah Mormons recognized in the plight of the mothers their own ancestral persecution. And the FLDS soon found other allies of no small influence—media commentators who accused governor Rick Perry of Texas of using "Gestapo tactics,"[3] lawyers for the Liberty Legal Institute, the ACLU and not least the Texas Rio Grande Legal Aid who represented many of the women.

It was the last of these who secured the return of the FLDS children to their parents. On May 22 they won an appeal in the Third District Court in Austin when the court ordered the judge of the lower court to reverse her decision and send the children home. Immediately the state made its case to the state supreme court, but the ruling was upheld 6–3. Texas had lost—the children were going back to YFZ Ranch. The court criticized the CPS for not having sufficient evidence to take such extreme measures. The state had argued that the parents were flight risks, but was there anything more than anecdotal evidence to support that? And couldn't other options have been explored, like only removing the most at-risk children like the pubescent girls and leaving the rest, or removing the alleged offenders for that matter?

The decision was a humiliation for Texas—a giant tab at over \$12 million and an embarrassment for the authorities.[4] It was particularly devastating for those campaigners who had applauded Texas for taking a stand. When the children were sent home, antipolygamy campaigner Flora Jessop was close to tears—"who's ever going to touch them again?"

The propolygamy camp, however, rejoiced. It became fashionable in the aftermath to beat up on Texas, the armed Goliath going after the little guy. But the attorney general deserves some sympathy here. It would be enormously cynical to presume that his motives were anything other than the rescue of a girl who, as far as he knew, was being abused daily. There wasn't time for a softly-softly approach, given Sarah's phone calls—action had to be taken. Imagine the outcry had he dragged his feet and the abuse was real.

And for all the accounts of the authorities' heavy-handedness—waving guns in a breastfeeding mother's face and so on—there is also evidence of the state's sensitivity. The CPS made every attempt to provide foster care that was in keeping with the children's upbringing—fresh food, not processed food, no television, homeschooling and so on. They provided a "tip sheet" for care workers that explained FLDS culture as they understood it—to avoid red toys since red was a prohibited color, to expect a certain helplessness on the part of the mothers, not to admonish prejudicial statements from the kids. This document was widely criticized by fundamentalists as evidence of prejudice; the FLDS's lawyer Rod Parker slammed the authorities for just listening to the FLDS's enemies and not doing any investigation themselves. But this is a typical move of the FLDS, to withhold all information about itself and then to accuse others of not having the right information.

Besides, the raid exposed just how difficult it is to glean information from the FLDS. One of the state's motions spoke of "an orchestrated conspiracy of silence" among the mothers and children, and it was plain to see in court. During one hearing, a Louisa Bradshaw told the court that she didn't know who lived in her house with her, how she came to be there or where she lived in the past. Clearly the FLDS still resists communicating with outsiders, and by several accounts, it remains firmly in thrall to Warren Jeffs. His picture still hangs on the walls of children's bedrooms on the ranch, and he continues to be worshipped, sex criminal or not. Even after the state released pictures showing Jeffs and an alleged twelve-year-old girl kissing, full-throated, Bradshaw said that Warren Jeffs was "a perfect being to me." And her husband, Dan Jessop, told reporters, "You see far worse, immoral, disgusting, gross things than a girl kissing a man in the streets of your own community. And you and I don't know if the state of Texas fabricated that."

Is this not problematic? Is the state wrong to be concerned about a culture in which parents exalt a known pedophile? And is there any doubt that children have suffered within the FLDS? So many former members have spoken out, and they tell one ringing story—that marriages are forced and dictated by the prophet, that girls are often underage and boys are often expelled to make more girls available for the older men. These stories are not rare. Jeffs himself wrote in 2003: "I say, in the name of the Lord, there is no underage marriage in a Priesthood marriage, in celestial marriage. God has the right to rule. The Lord had me take these two underage girls on purpose, to show that I and we, this people, are with him, with God, not fearing man."

No doubt there's truth to the charge that hysteria infected the Texas decision. Perhaps next time, law enforcement will act with more restraint, taking abuse allegations individual by individual, rather than at a full sweep. But the state's impulse to act rather than dither must be applauded. And the outcome has been positive in many ways. The stiff punishment of those who take underage wives, for instance, and the assurance from the FLDS that underage marriages will henceforth be a thing of the past. It's notable that the FLDS has opened up for the first time, to positive effect.

So they repeated the trick—they let Oprah in and National Geographic, albeit for performances rather than interviews, well aware that the media, so hungry for access, can be easily manipulated. But if this encourages them to emerge more fully, then that's no bad thing. They know that Gentile lawyers won their children back for them, and they did so in defense of quite secular principles: the protection of parental rights by curbing the state's ability to remove children from a home without sufficient evidence. If the FLDS can carry this momentum and further open up their society to the outside world, they may never again see state troopers bearing down on their gates.

Naturally, fundamentalists see otherwise. Mary Batchelor of Principle Voices described the raid as a giant backward step. Even Mark Shurtleff was quick to point out that fundamentalists were now less likely to report crimes in their communities, their trust in outsiders having been damaged. But it's understandable why Utah's attorney general might look to characterize Texas's achievement in a negative light. It throws into sharp relief his own state's inability to effectively prosecute crimes within polygamy. Even Warren Jeffs managed to wriggle free: In July 2010, the Utah Supreme Court overturned his conviction for the crime of rape as an accomplice, in a hugely unpopular decision that was essentially based on a technicality.

Meanwhile, the raid continued to bear fruit. The attorney general's insistence that evidence had been gathered for criminal trials panned out better than anyone had hoped. According to a report by Texas Child Protective Services, twelve of the girls removed from the ranch are victims of sexual abuse, since they were spiritually married between the ages of twelve and fifteen. So far, twelve men have been charged with crimes ranging from bigamy to aggravated sexual assault to conducting an unlawful marriage with a minor. And thanks to DNA evidence, the guilty verdicts have arrived quickly, each one with a heavy sentence. Back in 2005, Texas sharpened its laws against underage marriage and bigamy, so that today, bigamy has been elevated from a Class A misdemeanor to a first-degree felony if the victim is under sixteen. As a result, the son of the leader of YFZ Ranch, Merril Leroy Jessop, was sentenced to a staggering seventy-five years for his marriage to a fifteen-year-old girl.

But the case that surely settles any lingering arguments about whether the Texas raid was justified is that of Warren Jeffs. The raid secured the evidence that led to his incarceration, for life, for the sexual assault of two young girls, aged twelve and fourteen. The raid yielded the diaries, the audio tapes and other documents that the prosecution used to bury him so effectively, not to mention the DNA proof that Jeffs conceived a child with the older girl. It confirmed much of what the propolygamy lobby had once dismissed as prejudice and hysteria. In fact, if it wasn't for the raid, there's a good chance that Warren Jeffs would be free today.

The trial of August 2011 was extraordinary. Jeffs was reliably deranged throughout, electing to represent himself for long stretches, which meant a series of rambling tirades, or "revelations" in which he cursed not just the jury, but also the prosecution and Judge Barbara Walther, the very judge who had adjudicated the original raid. And yet as he complained pointlessly about religious persecution and proclaimed "I protest!" over and over, trying to derail proceedings, the prosecution took him apart using his own words. They quoted from his many dictations over the years—full accounts of his "heavenly sessions" with the fifteen-year-old girl, with whom he had conceived a child. They quoted from his diaries, which detailed specifications for the temple bed and removed all doubt as to its sordid purpose. "It will be covered with a sheet," the diaries said, "but it will have a plastic cover to protect the mattress from what will happen on it."

And jurors were brought to tears as they listened to hours of audio tapes of the prophet not only training girls in how to be a "comfort wife"—how the girls were to "assist each other" sexually during the process—but also a full and gruesome recording of his rape of a twelve-year-old girl. It begins with him telling the little girl, who is crying, to "take your clothes off" and "just don't think about the pain." He commands the other girls in the room to back away—it's believed they tied the twelve-year-old to the ceremonial bed for him. And then he rapes her.

As the court listened to him grunt and pant on the recording, Jeffs sat in the courtroom looking straight ahead, expressionless. It was as if, even in his madness, he knew that his fate was sealed.

To Be a God

In the Judeo-Christian scheme . . . terms like "messiah" and "son of God" are regarded as unique ranks beyond the aspiration of any mere mortal. In other religious traditions, however, godhood can be more accessible. In Chinese religions, in Hinduism, or in the religions of Classical Greece or Rome, an individual might attain divine status in life or be elevated to it after death . . .

—Philip Jenkins, *Mystics and Messiahs*

*I*T SEEMS ARROGANT, this Mormon aspiration to become gods in the next life. As though heaven's not good enough, so they had to go and upgrade their afterlife and out-eternity the Christians. Their craving for godhood seems greedy and overambitious, unseemly for such a professedly humble people. If they flashed it about like rappers, that would be one thing, but they give the opposite impression—that of simple, hardworking folks who lead modest, pious lives in keeping with their pioneer roots. They wear Levis and eat at Olive Garden. They're thrifty and unpretentious, salt of the earth. But in the next world, they want more than Jay-Z would dare to dream. Mormons want their own planet. One each, thank you very much.

I wanted to be a god myself at one stage. Not a Mormon god with my own planet, or a Christian god with a beard and staff, but a worker of miracles, something more along Jesus/Marvel superhero lines. It began in my teens. I'd sit on my bedroom floor, eyes closed, trying to close out my grubby, sullied life in South Wimbledon and turn my brain toward what I imagined were its hidden, supernatural reserves. I'd read about these reserves at my local library, in books like *Develop a Photographic Memory*, *Enhance Your Brainpower*, *How to be a Psychic* and *The Mysteries of ESP*. According to their sleeves, all I had to do was follow their instructions and I could be whoever I wanted to be—a suburban superhero with a whole armory of magic powers such as mindreading, hypnosis and levitation. I'd be able to heal the sick and walk on hot coals, remember everything I ever read and, by some little-known process of remote mind-matrix trans-mosis, become pure pheromone to Janine, the blonde girl who lived down the street and sometimes took the same bus to school. She'd never noticed the little Indian kid following her home every afternoon from a safe fifty yards. Well, she'd notice me now, she'd feel the aura, it said so in the book. I'd exude.

Everything seemed possible back then. As the physical changes of ado-lescence took hold, I resolved to install a few changes of my own, fashion this clay into something sensational. And I had a whole stack of manuals to help me do it—such is the magic when books and naïvety collide. As far as I was concerned, if it was shelved in the nonfiction section, it was true. And it staggered me that this earth-shattering knowledge was gathering dust on a library shelf. Why did people read anything else? Didn't they realize that humans only use 10 percent of their brains? Hadn't they heard of the kid in Russia who could move salt shakers with his mind alone?

Religion had nothing to do with it back then. In our home, God played a cameo role—an art house cameo who did nothing to move the plot along. The only person who ever mentioned God was my mother, and she'd only mention Him when a misfortune befell the family—something truly calamitous like a broken vase or me leaving my football kit on the bus. Her palm would come up—slap!—to her forehead and she'd wail: "Eesh, this is my fate, this is how God punishes me, every time, *every* time . . ."

She seemed to live in constant fear that her children would amount to nothing and all her labor and sacrifice would be for naught. And for my mother, life itself was a sacrifice, especially her marriage to my father, which was arranged by their parents and, as far as I could tell, a disaster.

But I was twelve, I didn't understand the complex burdens they bore, the hopes and fears they'd brought from India to England, from innocence to marriage, the sheer scope and nuance of their disappointments. From what I could tell, all they had in common was their resentment of each other. They seemed to blame each other for their unhappiness, which they perpetuated, and to this day, I recall home as a bitter place in which my mother's muttering was punctuated by my father's fits of temper. So I would hide in my room and work on my superpowers. If I could tune out my parents and my own pop-up brain spam about Janine down the road, then I could escape all this. I'd levitate and fly out of the window.

On Sundays after her bath, my mother would light an incense stick and pull out two photographs of Hindu saints—small black-and-white portraits of an old man and woman sitting cross-legged, with a nimbus glow around their heads. She told me nothing about them beyond their names—Sri Ramakrishna and Sarada Devi. "Oh this is, you know, Indian guru from Calcutta," she'd say, dismissively. "I just say little prayer and that's all." As if she was embarrassed by these old-country superstitions. There was no question of foisting them onto her children. If Ramakrishna's holiness wasn't obvious to me, it was irrelevant.

We were lapsed Hindus, you could say. More lapsed than Hindu. Besides those little photos of saints, all that endured of religion were a few pieces of wall art, some vestigial habits of diet and tradition. We didn't eat beef in our house, which seemed fair enough. Certain kinds of people didn't eat certain kinds of animals—this much was familiar. But other customs I found mysterious, like the oppositional magic of feet and forehead. I was never to touch books with my feet, for instance, since it showed disrespect for learning, and if I did, I was to touch the book to my forehead to erase the mistake. And when elderly relatives arrived from India, we would touch their feet and then touch our foreheads, as though transferring something. I remember the shock of seeing my mother the first time that she swooped down at the feet of her cousin and then looked up at me, expecting me to follow suit. I stood there, confused. She tugged at my shoulder, embarrassed—"Go on, do pranam on Uncle . . ." Pranam? What was pranam? He's been on a nine-hour flight and there's a hole in his sock. Why can't I just shake his hand?

The only time we left the house on account of our faith was for Durga

Puja, the celebration of the mother goddess that lasted a week, around October. Every year, the same routine. In a chilly community hall in Battersea that Alcoholics Anonymous used on Mondays, an idol would be installed—a noisy sixteen-armed goddess riding a tiger and killing demons at her feet. Around her were the familiar Hindu trappings—the fruit and flowers, the priest chanting in Sanskrit, the flames, the incense, the chatter of women in the next room doling out plates of kechuri, a thick stew of rice and lentils. Every so often a man would blow on a conch shell and my mother would thrust pieces of coconut and apple into my hands and push me toward the idol—"Go!" Go and do what? Give a statue fruit? I didn't understand. The garish idols, the adults walking around barefoot, the chanting—none of it made sense in a Battersea town hall, on a rainy Saturday afternoon. And no explanation was given—how Durga came to be riding a tiger or why she had all those arms. God simply wasn't discussed in our family, not even at puja.

As far as I could tell, the adults came chiefly to compare their children. Moms would stalk the hall flashing insincere smiles and passing casual boasts about who got accepted to which school on what scholarship. They were to be feared, these women—they grabbed you by the cheeks and pitted you against their own. Some bragged about how Bengali their children were, how their girls sang Tagore songs and cooked fish curry. Others bragged about how English their children were, how their boys played rugby and went on skiing holidays. But my parents, for their part, cared little for the nuances of this cultural no-man's-land I was living in. All that mattered to them were school certificates and grades, a clear emblem of our standing in this vicious little society. They just assumed that I would fall in line with Bengali tradition and become a doctor or an accountant and have an arranged marriage to a girl from Calcutta. And of course I recoiled. Perhaps arranged marriages made sense in India, where mother goddesses went around stabbing demons with spears. But not to a teenager in South London.

My cultural dislocation only intensified as I got older. I grew apart not only from my parents, but also from the other Bengali kids who seemed so studious, so bland. We were inheritors of our parents' ambitions—mild-mannered squares destined for sensible jobs. I stopped going to puja; it was my protest. I thought of myself as an island, a man without a tribe. It was a romantic idea, but then I was a teenager. Romantic ideas were all the rage.

So again, I wound up in my room, yearning for escape while my parents bickered downstairs. Except this time I'd outgrown my psychic phase. I wanted to be a kung fu superhero instead. I wanted to be like those little Shaolin boys who smashed bricks with their heads and walked away smiling and doing somersaults. I wanted to pummel bullies and win the girl and never walk in fear again—me, a ninety-eight-pound weakling!

But something else happened. I learned that kung fu wasn't the only sphere of superhuman activity. Alongside the stories of eighty-year-old Shaolin masters who had mastered the "death touch" were reports of scraggly old sadhus who could walk barefoot through fire, hold their breath for hours and survive for years on only grapes and water. And all these stories seemed to lead back to India. The firewalkers were Hindu. The guy they sealed in a glass box and threw into a swimming pool—he was Hindu. Even the Shaolin masters trace their lineage to India. Kung fu was brought to China by Buddhist monks, and the Buddha had been a Hindu prince.

And that's how I got religion. It was a roundabout quest for superpowers. Hinduism just seemed to push my buttons, at least on paper. It didn't claim to be the only true religion. There was no central church, no pope, no governing corporation. It was older than the others and wackier—a vast canopy for religious adventure where almost anything goes. You could worship rocks, trees, monkeys, snakes; sex could be filthy and smoking weed was practically recommended. I was looking for a club I could belong to, and those Hindu saints looked more like me than St. Francis of Assisi. And many were Bengalis, like the saint Ramakrishna from my mother's photos. His famous disciple, Swami Vivekenanda, once lived only a few miles from where my mother grew up in Calcutta.

So little by little, I morphed from what I imagined was a rootless enigma to what I imagined was a Bengali Hindu. I fooled myself that I did have a people after all, and some of them had magic powers. All the stuff about the material world being an illusion, and life and death being a cycle, that was all well and good. But I was in it for the superpowers, just as Mormons aim to be gods and Christians yearn for heaven. Every morning I would crunch my legs into an excruciating half lotus and follow my breath in and out, chanting mantras. I even tried them in Sanskrit as a kind of incantation. Trying to be a still pond, as stoic in the face of good fortune as bad. But progress was slow. I couldn't tune out the chatter. I'd scold myself for losing focus and then scold myself for scolding myself. But still, I believed. I saw the Creator's hand in all things, even rifling through the thoughts in my head. It was a comfort to know that my private morality was being noticed, that there was order and fairness to the universe. Faith made me less fearful; it reassured me that a mighty force was guiding all things. And I felt less distant from others; I liked to imagine a small, eternal candle burning within us all, a reminder that we are all one spirit. It's a puny Hallmark image, I know, and I recognize it now as a salve for the loneliness I felt as a somewhat shy teenager—prayer was, in some ways, a simulacrum of company. But I took comfort in my little candle and took it with me to India in my early twenties where, for the best part of a year, I roamed the country hoping for transcendence, that moment that I'd read about—in the nonfiction section—in which I'd be able to see in all directions at once, and for an instant, be one with the entire, grand swirl of creation.

As it happened, most of my cosmic experiences tended to happen with the aid of crumbly charas, a glittering night sky and the wobble and twang of sitar music. The temples were too cacophonous, too redolent of the filth and stink outside their gates. And I never did find myself a guru. In fact, as the months passed, I became increasingly disillusioned with the so-called holy men of India. The newspapers were filled each day with stories of Brahmins abusing lower castes, beating the boys and raping the girls. The real miracle, it seemed to me, was how so many people could endure such injustice and still prostrate themselves before men in robes for the privilege of touching their feet. I became that rare spiritual tourist in India who leaves less religious than he was when he arrived.

My faith fell away once and for all when I returned to India for the Mahakumbh Mela in 2001, officially the largest gathering in recorded history. It was a religious festival, a mass bathing of tens of millions in the river Ganges in the belief that the waters would give the soul *moksha*, or salvation, an escape from the cycle of rebirth. I didn't buy into the moksha aspect so much, but I hoped that the sheer scale of the event would awe me back into belief. I'd always loved Hinduism's weakness for mythic scale, its thousand-horse chariots and oceans of milk.

But the Mela shoved me further into skepticism. The event was spectacular, no doubt—the sea of pilgrims, the feast of colors, the naked sadhus wielding tridents. As a testament to man's hunger for the divine it was magnificent. But I found little nourishment. The sadhus wanted alms or hashish; they would tell your fortune for a few hundred rupees. The naked ones charged for pictures and the circus acts charged more, like the monk with the padlock through his testicles or the guy who could tow a tractor with his penis. The most popular of all was a man who had held his arm aloft for twenty-four years, until the flesh had atrophied and the skin had webbed over his scrunched fist. He had a crowd around him at all times. He looked as though he was asking to be excused.

I found myself waist-deep in the filthy Ganges on an auspicious day for bathing. The mist rose off the river, and the sadhus were silhouettes against an orange disc sun. I splashed what may have been dysentery on my face and said a prayer: Please God, protect me from dysentery, in fact, protect everyone from dysentery, especially the little children. Actually, if you could eliminate dysentery altogether . . .

But then this Swiss guru called Shin arrived next to me on a white horse, brandishing a trident. "Let us greet my sun," he announced, and made a beckoning motion with his hand. "And here is my wind, coming to greet me."

I knew this guy. He lived in the tent next to mine and considered himself an incarnation of Siva even though his passport read "Gideon." "Gideon had to die so that I could take a physical form," he told me, in a ponderous Germanic brogue. "He had extreme pains. When the kundalini comes, which is the creating energy of worlds and suns, the vibration is like six thousand volts. Because I am fire. I came like a sun in the high. I am Mahaprabhu and this is my creation."

Every morning, Shin would wake me up with his bongo drums and his silly cosmic dance. He also appeared to have a permanent and giant erection flapping away under his robes. A strap-on, presumably—it was about a foot long and almost always ready for action. And there it was, while I was trying to pray for the end of dysentery—Shin's lingam waggling about like a divining rod.

The next day, I contracted an acute intestinal infection. My appendix swelled to the size of a grapefruit and I was stretchered out in an emergency jeep. Later that week, God delivered an earthquake to the state of Gujarat, killing at least twenty-five thousand. Shin and his gang, however, made it back to Switzerland just fine.

I was done. God was going on the back burner.

Over the last decade, I have leaned toward atheism—not so much a belief as a lack of belief. God is not a given. I'm told it's unfair to demand proof for God—after all, psychoanalytic doctrines aren't exactly provable either, and no one gripes about them. But religions are seldom content to exist merely as ideas, open to debate. They seek political dominion and special treatment in the tax code. They want to influence our laws and lifestyles, and as such, they demand vetting every bit as much as the other theories we live by, those by which our cars drive and our planes fly. I'm with Thomas Paine when he writes, "My mind is my own church."[1] And so far, my spirituality, such as it exists, is childishly simple. Be kind, help the less fortunate and so on. I suspect that overcoming our physical nature, our "flesh," may be a high ground to which we should aspire, but I couldn't say for sure. And as for the afterlife, I haven't a clue. But it's okay to gaze into the void and wonder. I know enough to know I'll never know enough.

But I remain wistful about my days as a believer. Even if God was a placebo, He still served His purpose. There's something exhilarating about a world of miracles and magic. I liked believing. I like that Journey song, "Don't Stop Believing." I believe in Journey. I believe in small-town girls, living in a lonely world. I just don't believe in heaven or reincarnation or that when I close my eyes and concentrate really hard, I somehow gain an audience within the Lord of All Creation. And if that means I've lost faith, then so be it. At least my hope is intact. I've never really understood the substantive difference between faith and hope, anyway. Like that *Onion* headline, "Bush to Increase Funding for Hope-Based Initiatives."

In *The Power of Myth*, Joseph Campbell describes religion as a defense against religious experience. The doctrine, the concepts, the sheer drive toward the spiritual short-circuits our potential for transcendence. It's like *Moby Dick*: dogged pursuit of the whale may kill you, and you may never find it. What transcendence I have experienced has tended to come from relationships, music and books, often from humor. Laughing until the beer shoots out of my nose is, for me, a profoundly spiritual moment. And in the interim, I'm content to hope for the supernatural rather than swear by it. I still want visions and intuitions that I can't explain, I want to hear the winds whisper and feel the stars align. Atheists can dream too.

Legalize It

Sunlight is said to be the best of disinfectants; electric light the most efficient policeman.
—Louis D. Brandeis

Bigamy is when you have one wife too many—monogamy is the same.
—Unknown

*T*HIS IS THE madness of the law against polygamy in Utah: If a married man sleeps with another woman, it's adultery, and no one bats an eyelid. But if he does the same thing as a fundamentalist Mormon and calls the second woman his wife, then he's committing a felony and risks prison. At its limits, it's a law against vocabulary, a ludicrous statute. So I say, bin it. Set the people free! Fundamentalists are right to call foul.

In most states, bigamy is a crime of fraud: A guy marries a rich widow, fleeces her and tries to move onto the next one without divorcing the first. But in Utah, that wasn't good enough. Fundamentalist Mormons don't register their plural marriages, so the second marriage is notoriously difficult to prove, as federal agents discovered when they went after them in the late 1800s. So they changed the law, broadened the definition to include sexual cohabitation. Now, all a man needs to do to break the bigamy law is have sex with multiple women *whom he considers his wives*. He needn't attempt to marry them legally. His crime is not the sex, but how he regards the sex—as part of a marriage or as part of an adulterous affair. If it's the former, he's a criminal; the latter, he's not.

In Utah's defense, the bigamy law is seldom enforced. Though polygamists are wedded to the idea that they're persecuted by the state, the last conviction for polygamy alone was in 1974. Attorney general Mark Shurtleff has stuck to his policy of only prosecuting polygamy in conjunction with other crimes—a way of putting the boot in.

Nevertheless, the law remains on the books and fundamentalists want to know why. It may be one of the last daft inequities in American law, after the suffrage movement and the advances in civil rights and gay liberation. What is the objection to polygamy? That it's un-Christian? Sexist? A threat to the nuclear family and the holy institution of monogamy? Certainly it seems harder to defend these positions now that the American family is changing so swiftly. While traditional marriage crumbles and divorce becomes a drive-through proposition, matrimony's self-appointed defenders are busy trying to prevent marriage's only remaining enthusiasts—the gays—from joining in. Meanwhile, everyone's adopting—gays, celebrities, infertile or otherwise. And the surrogacy and in-vitro businesses are booming. So while polygamists hide and skulk in Utah, sperm is being sold in glossy catalogues and pretty Harvard pre-meds are lining up to donate their eggs before the fall semester.

The Warren Jeffs saga illustrates that polygamy's status as a felony makes true criminals harder to prosecute. Illegality is a bogeyman that polygamist leaders use to control and terrorize their followers—it's an excuse for secrecy, a cover for real crimes. And it makes everyone a victim, demanding of sympathy: if a man is charged with child abuse, it's not about child abuse, it's about the state picking on polygamists or the media demonizing them, or it's because he was abused himself as a child and no one reported it because they were afraid of the state arresting them for polygamy. These are the arguments that circulate within the fundamentalist echo chamber. Blame cannot be apportioned. Perpetrators are portrayed as victims and guilt is deflected from place to place.

But polygamy has always been illegal. The last time it was debated in the courts was 1878, in the case of George Reynolds, Brigham Young's secretary. It was a test case of straightforward polygamy for religious purposes; the LDS Church had hoped to plead his freedom of religion up to the Supreme Court, win, set a precedent and put the issue to rest. But it lost. Chief Justice Waite commented that polygamy was indigenous to the Asiatic and African nations and entirely unbecoming to descendants of Europeans.[1] And it was decreed that Reynolds's freedom of religion extended only to his beliefs, not his actions, so states were free to criminalize polygamy if they found it reprehensible.

And reprehensible was putting it mildly. Polygamy had been famously labeled one of the "twin relics of barbarism" at the Republican Party convention in Philadelphia, 1856. Slavery was the other—as though having a few wives was tantamount to treating people like animals. But for the churchgoing majority, it clearly was. And *Reynolds* can be seen as a direct appeal by Christians to preserve the so-called holy institution of marriage, their fear being that polygamy posed a threat to civilization itself, that it was an affront to the natural order. But the opposite is true. Many societies throughout history have permitted polygamy. In fact, polygamy may have been more common than not in the pre-Christian world, from the ancient Jews to the Hindus to the Confucianists, the Celts and numerous Native American tribes.[2] And in the present day, it is still practiced throughout much of Asia, Africa and the Islamic world.[3]

Admittedly, many contemporary societies that permit polygamy are far from ideal. Often, there is a large gulf between the rich and the poor, so the women tend to be monopolized by the wealthy, leaving the paupers without partners. And this surplus of unmarried men is a recipe for social havoc. According to evidence from India and China, where female infanticide and sex-selective abortion are commonplace, these poor, unmarried men tend to fight and steal and rape; they form mobs and burn things; they feed the demand for prostitution. One might assume that if young Muslim men were being nagged to put up shelves in the kitchen, rather than being disenfranchised—by societies that condone polygamy, incidentally—then they'd probably be less likely to blow themselves up. These are strong arguments, and apart from the one about exploding Muslims, they've been made most recently, and most eloquently, by Joseph Henrich, an eminent scholar from the University of British Columbia.[4] In 2011, the Supreme Court of British Columbia in Canada debated polygamy's decriminalization in a landmark case, and Henrich's research, completed specifically for the court affidavit, played a key role in making, and winning the argument against.[5]

He makes a compelling case. Drawing on reams of research, he describes societies that permit polygamy as roiling with dysfunction. Besides all the rape and crime and prostitution, polygamous cultures tend to diminish the rights of women, drive down the age at which girls get married and magnify social inequality, even to the point of tyranny.[6] And I'm sure he's right. When he speculates that the rise of monogamy has been a force for equality and democracy in the world, it sounds plausible enough. But he appears to approach the polygamy issue from the perspective of social policy, and if that's the concern, then I suspect there are equally good arguments for the prohibition of all intoxicants, firearms, transfats and cars that travel over sixty-five miles-per-hour. As for social inequality, what could be more American? If lawmakers are concerned with narrowing the chasm between the haves and have-nots, they could start by amending the tax code to be more like, well, Canada's.

But America is not Canada. As Fred Gedicks, a professor of law at BYU, notes: "There are lots of things that we would be better off without. Forms of extreme pornography, for example, or hate speech. But the guiding principle of American constitutionalism is that the government doesn't get to decide what those are. The idea that the government will say that 'it's a bad society that allows polygamy' presupposes that the government knows what a good or bad society is." This is a country of rights that must be preserved even if the resulting social ills are glaringly obvious. One such right is gun ownership, which has accounted for untold tragedy over the years. Another is the right to privacy and sexual freedom. It may well be true that monogamy has contributed to the enlightenment and advancement of Western culture, but it's still not universally popular. In America, the divorce rate is 50 percent and that doesn't even count all the couples who *want* to get divorced but haven't got around to it. So despite centuries of opposition, polygamy endures, that old primitive bastion. In fact, it's as defiant as ever. Over the last few years, the fundamentalist community has been waging a dogged battle in the law courts to take down the bigamy statute,[7] once and for all.

Take the case of Rodney Holm, for example. A police officer and member of the FLDS, Holms had taken Ruth Stubbs as his third wife in 1998. He was thirty-two, Stubbs was sixteen, and Holm was duly convicted in August 2003 of two counts of unlawful sex with a minor and one count of bigamy. But Holm appealed the bigamy count on the grounds that they were only spiritually sealed, not officially married. He was denied by the Utah Supreme Court, but chief justice Christine Durham wrote a spirited dissent, arguing that Utah's bigamy statute was unconstitutional. And this spurred the fundamentalists to unite; they figured they had a chance in the U.S. Supreme Court. Principle Voices rallied the troops to pay tens of thousands of dollars for Holm's petition, a lengthy document that argued that the *Reynolds* ruling is outdated.[8] It also challenged the right of states to regulate relationships that occur outside marriage and said Utah unfairly targets polygamists in its bigamy prosecutions.

It was a muscular effort to change the law, and the opposition recognized it. The Family Research Council filed an *amicus* brief—an interested party brief—in vigorous opposition to Holm's appeal. And the state of Utah reminded the court that Holm's bigamy was with a sixteen-year-old, so any arguments about consenting adults were moot. And it worked—ultimately the U.S. Supreme Court refused to hear the appeal.

With hindsight, fundamentalists concede that Holm wasn't the most wholesome of martyrs—he was, after all, guilty of sex with a minor. So they pinned their hopes on a second case, *Bronson v. Swensen*, that didn't involve any minors at all. Three people walked into a Salt Lake marriage license office one day—Gene Lee Cook, his wife and his then fiancée J. Bronson who asked the clerk for a second marriage license, to enter into plural marriage. Sherrie Swensen was the clerk on duty that day, and she had no choice but to deny them. So the Bronson party went to the federal court and filed a civil law suit against the state of Utah for denying them the right to marry.

Hopes were high. Not only was this case unsullied by sex crimes or other misbehavior, but there were a host of compelling legal precedents to cite. For instance, there was the 1992 case of the Lukumi Babalu Aye Church in the small town of Hialeah, Florida, in which an Afro-Caribbean congregation practiced ritual decapitation of chickens in religious ceremonies, and the town's people passed an ordinance against it.[9] The Supreme Court struck down the ordinance—if you can kill chickens for culinary reasons, then why not for religious reasons? Similarly if you can sleep with multiple women for recreational purposes, why not for religious purposes too?

The most powerful legal precedent to cite, however, was *Lawrence v. Texas* that reached the U.S. Supreme Court in 2003. *Lawrence* established that sodomy between consenting adults was the right of every American, and fundamentalists have been in a lather ever since. The case was straightforward enough. John Geddes Lawrence, a fifty-five-year-old medical technologist was caught having anal sex with a hot dog vendor in the privacy of his home in Houston—a game of hide the wiener. He was convicted under Texas's sodomy laws, and his appeals reached the highest court. And the ruling came down 6–3, that homosexual conduct could no longer be criminalized, and furthermore, that society could not enact laws that target a distinct class of individuals simply because the majority finds their conduct to be morally repugnant.

It was a bombshell decision. The court had rejected morality as a legitimate justification for a state's criminal laws. Justice Anthony Kennedy wrote in his opinion: "The issue is whether the majority may use the power of the state to enforce those views on the whole society. Our obligation is to define the liberty of all, not to mandate our own moral code."[10] And immediately conservatives started flapping about judicial activism and the gay agenda. There was talk of *Lawrence* as a cluster bomb, wreaking havoc all over the place, tearing holes in the fabric of society.[11] It was the slippery slope argument all over again, a favorite of hysterical conservatives for whom two men holding hands is the start of an inexorable moral slide into bestiality and sexual chaos. Today it's sodomy in Texas, tomorrow it's a depraved new world in which men are rutting with geese and sock puppets in the Home Depot parking lot. There's no end in sight.

Justice Antonin Scalia led the charge in his dissent, stating that "state laws against bigamy, same-sex marriage, adult incest, prostitution, masturbation, adultery, fornication, bestiality and obscenity are ... called into question by today's decision."[12] (There are state laws against *masturbation*?) He was joined by Rick Santorum, the former senator for Pennsylvania, who took the opportunity to raise the specter of "man on dog" action.[13]

But no one was more articulate on the subject than James Dobson of Focus on the Family, who declared on *Hannity and Colmes* that "you could have polygamy. You could have incest. You could have marriage between a father and a daughter. You could have two widows, or two sisters or two brothers." I have to admit, the "two widows" thing sounds pretty hot. Lonely women in black dresses, their mascara smudged from tears ... "Once you cross that Rubicon," he continued, "then there's no place to stop. Because if a judge can say two men and two women can marry, there is no reason on Earth why some judge some place is not going to say, this is not fair. [Why not] three women and three men, or five and two or five and five?"[14]

Gays are the gateway drug for this lot: let the sodomites run free and all bets are off, we'll all be stalking the streets, humping anything that moves and grunting like warthogs. Interestingly, polygamists also see homosexuals as a portent of doom, an unspeakable depravity that has no place in God's country. In that respect, they're not unlike the Mormon Church, which put its considerable weight behind the Prop 8 campaign in California to limit the definition of marriage to the straight kind. But fundamentalists wouldn't dream of protesting *Lawrence*, not a chance—they know that *Lawrence* opens the door to polygamy's decriminalization; they understand how useful the sodomite agenda might be.

And this is their dishonesty of expedience. They're employing arguments they don't believe because they stand to gain an advantage. It's reminiscent of the way the Intelligent Design lobby encourages schools to "teach the controversy" and give minority views a hearing, rather than teach in terms of right and wrong.[15] These aren't conservative arguments but liberal ones, from the school of multiculturalism in particular, something that conservatives have traditionally opposed. Polygamists are similarly adopting the liberal tolerance toward minorities while spitting "liberal" from the other side of their mouth.

But they do stand to benefit from advances in gay rights. After all, if little Emma can have two mommies, why not two mommies and a daddy? Aren't two mommies and a daddy "better" than no daddy at all? And what about bisexuals—shouldn't they be legitimately permitted to marry a partner of each gender? If the courts denied this, wouldn't that be denying the person's sexual orientation, which underpins at least part of the gay marriage argument? Besides, what is the substantive difference between a bisexual plural marriage and Mormon polygamy?

To date, the courts have been wary of Lawrence's power. They're loath to unleash it on every appeal that comes their way. Not only Rodney Holm, but also *Bronson v. Swensen* failed to ride Lawrence to victory, since the plaintiffs were said to lack standing—that is, they weren't sufficiently harmed by the laws the plaintiffs sought to overturn.

But in the latest and stiffest challenge to the polygamy laws, the standing argument has already been swept aside. When the Brown family, of *Sister Wives*, came under investigation in September 2010 for violating Utah's polygamy statute, the family members were forced to leave the state and move to Las Vegas. So there's no question that they'd been harmed by the time they filed suit against Utah's governor, attorney general, and deputy attorney general. The state's attorneys tried to get the case dismissed, but the judge refused, and in January 2013, the first arguments were heard.

So far, it looks very much as though Judge Clark Waddoups may well decriminalize polygamy. Early in the proceedings, he asked about the difference between a polygamous relationship and one in which an unmarried man simply chose to have intimate relationships with three women. He even wondered aloud whether the state was cracking down on a religious practice. There was a lot of talk about abuse and underage marriage from the other side, but there are already laws against those things.

At the time of this writing, a judgment is still pending. But it's not unfeasible that the case may ascend yet further to the U.S. Supreme Court. After all, Justice Sonia Sotomayor made a point of bringing up polygamy in the recent arguments regarding Proposition 8, California's ban on gay marriages. She asked Ted Olson, the attorney looking to overturn Proposition 8, whether permitting gay marriage would lead to polygamy. He said no and shooed the question away somewhat, trying to avoid the association—gay marriage concerned the denial of freedom to a specific class of people, he argued, whereas polygamy was about "conduct." And anyway, he said, polygamy is terribly complicated: "Multiple marriages raises questions about exploitation, abuse, patriarchy, issues with respect to taxes, inheritance, child custody, it is an entirely different thing."

But is it? When the Browns' lawyer, Jonathan Turley, told NPR that polygamy was "where the gay and lesbian community was almost exactly 10 years ago, before the ruling in Lawrence v. Texas," he made conservatives shudder. There's little question that the old arguments are falling away and that the move to legitimize polygamy is in the ascendant. In Turley's words, "there is a grander, more magnificent trend that you can see in the law, and that is this right to be left alone."

It might sound as if I'm siding with the polygamist lobby on this one, but that's not true. What polygamists want is decriminalization, not legalization. They don't want the contract, the license, the state interference. Fundamentalist Mormons just want the state off their backs so that they can succumb more completely to the autocracy of their religion.

They want the freedom to practice a religion that restricts their freedom. And that's fine, I don't disagree with them on the government thing; the state does seem like an intruder on what should be a private compact. In that respect, we're all polygamists—man, wife and government engaged in the legal contract of marriage. It's like Doug Stanhope says: "Who says to their girlfriend—baby, I'm so in love with you, this thing we've got together is so awesome we've just got to get the government involved! We need judges and lawyers in this shit . . ."

But the government's in my marriage whether I like it or not. And if I don't get a choice, I don't see why polygamists should, particularly given the volcano factor. Admittedly, the pragmatic problems are forbidding—issues like adoption, custody and divorce are complex enough with just two spouses, let alone seventy-eight, which is the number Warren Jeffs had. But still, if ever a little regulation could do some good . . .

The Order

CHAPTER 9

❖ Mixed Socks and Secrets

> You remember how he would trust strangers, and if they fooled him
> he would say, 'It's better to be fooled than to be suspicious'—that the
> confidence trick is the work of man, but the want-of-confidence-trick is
> the work of the devil.
>
> —E. M. Forster, *Howards End*

I T's A FREEZING winter's night in Salt Lake City and I'm having dinner with Anne Wilde at Chili's. She's in a buoyant mood. She even buys me a margarita. "Now you really should try to talk to the Kingstons," she says, reaching for her cell phone. "Let me see if I've got Rachel's number."

I've heard of the Kingstons, otherwise known as the Order. They've been in the news since the late '90s for a host of lurid stories involving incest, forced marriages and domestic violence. According to Anne, they number at least 1,500 members, which makes them one of the bigger groups. But what sets them apart is their unique organization and economic system. The Order is a kind of microsociety dominated by the Kingston family and dedicated to consecration, a Mormon tradition whereby members donate all their worldly possessions to the church. It comprises two bodies, separate but nearly contiguous: the Davis County Cooperative Society, which owns a business empire believed to be worth $200 million,[1] and the Latter Day Church of Christ, whose prophet, Paul Kingston, holds the purse strings of the co-op. While the links between the two are complicated and closely guarded, what's known is that Order members typically work at Order-owned businesses, or "stewardships," and for miserly wages at that. Furthermore, they're encouraged to consecrate their entire incomes and possessions to the Order, which then permits them to withdraw only that which they need for their austere, frugal lives. And payment comes in the form of credit slips for use at Order "stewardships": the money flows straight back into the group's coffers. In the pantheon of polygamous cults in Utah, the Kingstons are perhaps the most intriguing.

"They've had it very hard over the last few years," warns Anne. "So they might be a bit more private than the others." And with that, she dials a woman named Rachel Young, by all accounts the sister of the prophet Paul Kingston,[2] and sets up a meeting for me, the next morning at 10 AM.

So at 9:55 AM, I'm pulling up outside a little red brick building on State Street in downtown Salt Lake City, an anonymous brick box with the shutters pulled down and only the address on the door. No names, no "Open" sign, no hint of life within but for a sliver of tube light peeking through the window's edge. The girl on reception seems young and fragile, with buckteeth and an erupting complexion. Her face quivers with alarm when I walk in.

"Hello, I'm here to meet Rachel."

She looks at her desk and grabs a pen. "Um . . . she's not here."

"I have an appointment at ten?"

"But she's not here."

"That's okay, I'll just wait."

While I sit, she picks up the phone, hides her face behind her hands and whispers into the mouthpiece. For a few minutes, nothing stirs. Then a curly-haired woman comes down the stairs. "Hi, I'm Rachel," she says.

She's smiling, her hand is outstretched. She looks fortyish, mumsy. She leads me up to an apparently abandoned office, where the shelves and desk have been swept empty but for a few strewn paper clips. And here I meet Carleen, heavily pregnant, whose face appears to have frozen into a mask—a stretched, anxious smile, with glassy, inset eyes, again signaling something like alarm.

"This is my office," says Rachel. "We're doing some moving around. I'm actually into accounting and finance." The "actually" seems odd.

"I've taken the last few years off to be with my family," says Carleen. "But I've been active in the community-services division of the co-op. Last year we had a car seat safety class, parenting classes, homemaking classes . . . things such as that."

Why is she telling me this? So much information, unprompted. We sit at the bare table and smile at each other with fading sincerity. Somehow even the slimmest window of silence lets a gust of awkwardness fill the room. Taking baby steps, I thank them for meeting me and tell them my reasons for coming. It's the standard pitch—their group is significant, I want to learn about their lifestyle and beliefs, to be introduced to families, to meet their leader and try to see the world through their eyes if I can.

Then Rachel offers a spiel of her own. She tells me how the Davis County Cooperative was founded during the Depression by five families who formed a cooperative to survive, and it now comprises several businesses and a membership of maybe one thousand.[3]

"One of the founding rules of the Cooperative is freedom of choice," says Rachel, "so we welcome all religions. We just have a requirement that we work together as the heavenly Father intended. Basically, the Golden Rule: you treat others the way you want to be treated. Even an atheist could be a part."

"An atheist?" I ask. "So I could join?"

"Absolutely you could apply."

"What are the benefits?"

"You'll always have a job. If I lose my job, I can go to members of the co-op, and they will most likely look out for me. We have zero unemployment. Anyone who wants a job gets a job."

"Or if your house burned down," Carleen adds, "our members would give you food, clothes, they'd find you somewhere to live."

"I don't have to be a polygamist to join?"

"We do have some polygamists, yes," says Rachel. "But we have members who are LDS Mormons as well. It's very diverse. We don't believe you have to be the same religion to work together."

Now I'm confused. "I thought religious principles were at the heart of this, polygamy being one of them."

"One of the founding principles was freedom of choice."

"Yes, freedom of choice," echoes Carleen. "Free agency."

"That means I can't impose my beliefs on you. We believe in working together," says Rachel. And she smiles and looks at Carleen, who smiles back.

"But my book is about polygamy . . ."

"Not all the founders practiced plural marriage, actually. A lot of people in the co-op don't," Rachel says.

"But I'd thought you were a church of some sort. And polygamy was one of the beliefs."

"No, that's a common misconception." Smile. "There is a church that some members of the co-op go to. But it's not a requirement. It's called the Latter Day Church of Christ."

Finally! After half an hour of slipping tackles, the church spokesperson is admitting that she is in fact a spokesperson for a church.

"So what is it that distinguishes your church from others in terms of its doctrine?"

Rachel adjusts herself in her seat. "The founding belief is—and Carleen might have her own, she has the right to believe what she wants—but my founding belief is that I want to do what my heavenly Father wants me to do."

"Which is what exactly?"

"We believe in the original principles of the LDS Church."

"You're fundamentalist Mormons?"

"I don't call myself a fundamentalist Mormon. I believe my beliefs are fundamentalist Christian. We read the Bible, the Doctrine and Covenants . . ."

"But mainstream Mormons read those scriptures too, as do other fundamentalist groups."

"Yes, it's amazing how many similarities there are."

And I study Rachel's face for sarcasm here. Nothing. Perhaps she feels she's actually being helpful.

"I want to know what makes your group different."

"I'd say the distinction isn't so much in the church, but in the cooperative."

"And some groups are more extreme," says Carleen. "Like the way the FLDS dress. We don't do that. And I know they practice assigned marriages, and we don't do that in our group at all."

"Is that it? Those are the only differences between you and the FLDS?"

Rachel shrugs and sighs. "Yes, we believe in the Golden Rule."

She looks at Carleen.

"And free agency," says Carleen.

They might not quite be lying, but they dodge and weave, returning always to buzzwords like "free agency" and "Golden Rule." They're spinning the co-op into a Benetton commercial, a Utopia of free will and diversity that would throw its doors open to a darkie atheist like myself. And yet already I feel less like a journalist than a cross-examining attorney, eggshelling around the elephant in the room. When can we actually talk about polygamy?

Rachel appears to have seniority here. While she "answers" the questions, Carleen mostly nods, staring at me in her mildly crazed way, as though she's perpetually reminding herself to smile. When I ask what the pluses of polygamy are, they warm up a little, tag-teaming the arguments like a double act, the same arguments I heard from Anne Wilde. "More moms means free day care," says Rachel. "Yes, so women can pursue careers," says Carleen. "And having several wives makes men better husbands," says Rachel. "Oh yes, much more sensitive and patient," says Carleen, nodding.

"So how do you live the Principle, Rachel?" I ask. It goes quiet for a moment.

"Well, my way might not be Carleen's way," says Rachel. Always this proviso of freedom of choice. "But in my situation, we each had our own homes. So my husband had his own closet at my house and the same at other houses."

"He feels like he's camping every night!" says Carleen, gleefully.

"And sometimes he'll leave his suit in the other house and I'll have to call my sister wife!"

"Yes, but then the socks get mixed up!"

And they laugh and laugh. They laugh so heartily that I laugh along with them, more out of relief at the break in tension. And yet I suspect there's something deliberate about this, a message being sent. This is polygamy: mixed socks and happy, laughing wives.

"That's exactly the kind of detail I want in my book!" I say, eager to capitalize on the mood. "I want to make it personal and everyday. I want the jokes and funny incidents. How can you help me?"

And they look at each other. "Well . . ." Carleen starts to speak, and then Rachel. "No, after you." And they both fall silent. The jolliness of the socks is wilting.

"If people could see the damage that is happening to our kids because it's against the law," says Rachel. "You know, it's amazing. If I was coming out of the closet as a homosexual, I would be patted on the back: 'Good for you!' But if I say I'm a sister wife and I like it, then they'll put my husband in jail."

First Carleen nods in agreement, then she shakes her head in sadness.

"Doesn't Hugh Hefner have a bunch of women that live with him?" says Carleen. "Of course society thinks that's just fine, but when it comes to taking care of them and calling them your family, then that's criminal."

But he does take care of them, I want to say, they live in a mansion. Now's not the time, though.

Rachel looks to Carleen. "You ought to get him a copy of the similarities between what the Utah government is doing to what the Nazis did to Jews." And Carleen makes a note of it. "She's been making a list, it's very interesting. So did you have any more questions?"

I look at my notebook scribblings. It says "Golden Rule blah blah," "mixed socks!!!", "Hefner?" and "Nazis??"

"Yes, I think there's a few more things . . ."

◈ The Hypnotist

Once you wake up and smell the coffee, it's hard to go back to sleep.
—Fran Drescher

I had an inkling they weren't going to tell me anything. A few days earlier, I'd met Rowenna Erickson, who cofounded Tapestry Against Polygamy with Vicky Prunty. Born into the Kingston group, she left in 1992 and has been the group's fiercest critic ever since.

"Oh, they'll paint you a pretty picture," she said, hoisting herself up the few steps to her front door, in the suburb of Taylorsville, Salt Lake City. She's an elderly woman now, with a dodgy hip, but beneath her thatch of brown hair, her eyes are quick and lively. "They'll tell you that I'm bitter and scorned, but I'm not. I'm just telling the truth. And I'm telling you, the Kingstons are not a pretty picture."

Rowenna first spoke out against the Kingstons in the early '90s. But it wasn't until 1998 that her attacks attracted Prunty's attention and led to the creation of Tapestry. That was the year that sixteen-year-old Mary Ann Kingston ran away from home to escape her marriage to her thirty-two-year old uncle David Ortell. She returned to her mother, Susie, who called her father, John Daniel—commonly known as Daniel—who arrived at the house late at night, dragged Mary Ann into his truck and drove her to a ranch in Washakie, near the Idaho border. There, he led her into a barn, removed his belt and beat her savagely, covering her with bruises. Hours after Daniel had left, Mary Ann ran five miles to the nearest pay phone where she reached the sheriff of Box Elder County.

Unlike many abuse victims within polygamy, Mary Ann did not retract or temper her account to protect family members. Her testimony put both her father and her uncle behind bars, though their sentences were slim. Daniel had faced the possibility of fifteen years in prison for second-degree felony child abuse, but he served only twenty-eight weeks, of which twenty-six weeks were on work release.[4] His brother David received ten years for incest and unlawful sexual conduct but was released after four.

But Mary Ann's greatest triumph was in lifting the lid on a cult unlike any other in America, one that even other fundamentalists regard as sinister. In addition to a sprawling business empire and a unique approach to consecration, the Order has a reputation for incest. And breeding takes place at a terrific rate. The current prophet, Paul Kingston, is said to have more than 250 children, several of whose mothers are his half sisters.[5] His brother Daniel is believed to have in the region of 120.[6] According to Rowenna, the Kingstons claim Jesus as their genetic ancestor, which explains all the inbreeding: they want to keep the bloodline pure. But no Order member would ever reveal such a sacred teaching. They don't even admit that they are members at all. The leaders never show themselves or grant interviews; information about their families is limited to hearsay from former members. The first rule of the Order is you must never talk about the Order.

What makes the Order remarkable is the control it exercises over its flock—economic, spiritual, psychological, marital. Members aren't confined to an isolated compound out in the desert—they live in the suburbs of Salt Lake County. *Big Love* country. The wives all live in separate homes, giving the appearance of single mothers, dressed in no distinctive garb, their surnames changed to mask their identity. This is the Order's power, its ability to infiltrate as a shadow population, disguised and dispersed and yet possessed of an unshakeable loyalty to their prophet. And anecdotally, they flout not only the laws circumscribing marriage, but those concerning incest, child labor, statutory rape and welfare fraud. More than any other group, the Order forces the question: to what extent can an open society tolerate a secret society in its midst?

To the people of Utah in 1998, the news that a vast polygamous family was breeding its own cheap labor through incest came, understandably, as a bit of a shock. But Mary Ann wasn't done. She launched a civil suit in August 2003, seeking more than $110 million in damages, a potentially crippling sum. In its original incarnation, the suit named close to one hundred Kingston businesses and 242 Order members, all of whom were allegedly complicit in her unlawful and abusive marriage. It stated that she was pulled from public school after the ninth grade and put to work in the accounting office of Standard Restaurant Supply, an Order stewardship. And that "David would visit Mary Ann on unexpected nights to obtain sex . . . Mary Ann's relatives and the other family members knew of the . . . sexual abuse but did nothing to report it or stop it."[7]

The initial accusations were followed by a lot of paperwork shuffling back and forth between the adversaries, and some tough talk on the Order's part—it claimed to have evidence that Mary Ann was a liar and a drug user and Daniel didn't beat her at all. The Order also made numerous challenges to the suit's legality and filed a number of counter-suits for defamation. But ultimately, the tangle of litigation proved too expensive to continue, and in April 2009 both sides called it quits and walked away.[8]

"It wasn't the result we wanted," says Rowenna. "But we tried. And things happen for a reason, you know? From what I've heard, the Kingstons don't even need to be brought down from the outside. With all that incest going on, they're doing it to themselves."

Rowenna's a rare breed. Most people who leave the Order remain silent, unwilling to risk the wrath of their former families or church. But Rowenna continues to speak out. She considers it her mission to be a thorn in the Kingstons' side. "They stole so much of my life," she says. "I won't let them forget it."

She was born into the cult in 1939, when the group was in its infancy, and she was fifty-three when she left. And curiously enough, it was all her mother's fault. A Mormon from Idaho, she'd heard about a group that practiced polygamy and how they'd seen the savior and all sorts, so she urged her husband, Rowenna's father, to sign up. He was a Lutheran by birth, and skeptical, so he only joined grudgingly, without ever practicing polygamy or consecrating his property as the church advised. It's unusual that he resisted polygamy while his wife yearned for it, but Rowenna explains her mother's zeal as a symptom of a more deep-seated fragility. She'd been raped when she was younger and had suffered the stigma of a young Mormon girl who'd fallen pregnant out of wedlock.

"She wanted to live this wonderful religion to feel better about herself," says Rowenna. "To overcompensate for feeling wrong because of the abuse."

Rowenna's was a typical Order childhood, one of rote prayers, the keeping of secrets and the blind veneration of their prophet, Charles Elden Kingston. She learned to avoid outsiders because outsiders might ask questions, and if they did, she learned to lie. And when she turned twenty-three, Elden decreed that she become the second wife of his first born, Leon. That's how it worked: God told the leader who to match up with whom, just as in Centennial Park. Leon was arguably quite the catch—he stood a decent chance of succeeding his father, at least by the principles of birthright and monarchy. But he also happened to be married to Rowenna's sister; they had five kids. So their two-bedroom house in Murray (a suburb of Salt Lake County) was especially crowded by the time Rowenna moved in.

"When it was my sister's turn to sleep with Leon, the kids would sleep in the other room with me," Rowenna says. "And my sister would sleep with the kids when it was my turn. I don't like to revisit that time very much."

Her sister was devastated at having to share her husband. She became suicidal, confused—is this what God really wanted? And Leon was miserable. Not only had he been passed over for the leadership when Elden died, but the new prophet, John Ortell, had ordered him, a law graduate, to work in one of the co-op's shoe stores. Meanwhile, Rowenna was slowly cracking under the pressure. The secrecy was stifling. She had to hide in another room whenever they had company—no one could know that she lived there as the second wife. And they lived in dire poverty, with their pitiful wages and the pressure to consecrate. She eventually moved out to a tiny two-bedroom of her own, where she took her eight children and somehow managed on only $500 a month.

Then one Thursday afternoon, she was watching Phil Donahue on TV. "They were doing something on hypnosis and I saw someone get a root canal without any anesthetic. And I said, 'Well, I'd love to be able to do that.' And I got books from the library about hypnosis—hypnosis for self-improvement, that sort of thing. You know? Well, I started putting my daughter into a trance. Because I've always been a psychic, you know. When we were younger, we'd play cards, and I'd know what was in my brothers' hands. Oh yes. And I had strange visitations, experiences with other beings. One night, I woke up at midnight, and there was this man standing on my bed. Oh my heck, I screamed bloody murder and dove under the covers! When I finally came out, there was nobody there. But see, I'm not crazy. I know I'm not."

She took a course in hypnotherapy and started learning about brain

states, emotional conditioning, behavior modification and how suggestions become beliefs. And she began to realize how brainwashed she'd
been all these years. The Order, she became convinced, was engaged in
mind control.

"That hypnotherapy course gave me the courage to stand up to the
Kingstons," she says. "It told me I wasn't crazy, I was right to feel what
I was feeling. And I sat down and wrote them a letter. I felt like I was a
victim, and their religion had victimized me. And they excommunicated
me! They've never excommunicated a plural wife before or since, so that's
quite an honor!"

Today, her sister and Leon remain part of the Order, and they live right
next door. You can see Leon's house through Rowenna's kitchen window.
"Oh, they can't stand it!" she laughs. "They see the media come up the
drive to do interviews with me and they know I'm telling all the Order's
dirty little secrets. But there's nothing they can do! Ha ha! I just call Leon
the landlord now. He still owns this house I live in. My kids call him the
sperm donor!"

She clambers up from her chair and hobbles to a bookshelf—"Hold
on, I want to show you something." And she returns with a stack of documents, letters, court filings, what looks like a board game. "Oh that's Polyg-
opoly. Just a bit of fun me and my kids came up with." Community Chest
cards like "You're having another baby—collect $200" and "You've been
approved for welfare—collect $1,000."

"Here, look at this one: 'You got direction on your half sibling'! Direction means the Lord told you who to marry. But what it really means is not
direction, it's erection! Ha! Ha!"

"But Rowenna, it's not about sex, it's about the Principle, the Higher
Law," I say.

"Oh *sure*. In my opinion, Joseph Smith had a sexual addiction. Polygamy
is one big eternal fuck. These men think they're going to be having sex
eternally. And all the women are going to be eternally pregnant."

"The Centennial Park lot didn't strike me as sex addicts."

"I don't know about them, but the Kingstons are very much into the sex
part. Some of the men in the higher echelons even have little cots in their
offices where they can have afternoon delight. They make appointments
with their wives according to who's ovulating when. Oh yes! Some people

say, 'Well, that's their business, I don't care.' But I do care. I know the harm and abuse that comes from this lifestyle. Now I'm going to show you a picture, I don't want you to be shocked. But it's . . . you know. Porno."

She hands me an eight-by-ten-inch print and turns away. "We call this guy Porno Joe. It's Joe Kingston—he's the prophet Paul's brother. I'm not even going to look while you look at it, it's so embarrassing. I don't know if he used a tripod, or if he had one of his other wives taking a picture. But some of his kids discovered the pictures and they sent them to me. I felt like it was a cry for help."

It's a picture of a large man with a mustache—Freddie Mercury's chubby brother—doing the business with a similarly chunky woman. They're in the spoon and splay position, bellies slumped onto the sheets, meat firmly in its mitten, and Joe's looking straight at the camera, as though he's studying his reflection in the lens.

Rowenna has other less salty delights in her stash. Tapes of interviews with old Kingston women, copies of religious meetings and Order documents, the rules of the co-op, the writings of old Kingstons, great wodges of press clippings. And as we pore through them one afternoon, she regales me with horror stories from the Order. Dead babies, beaten children, rape and torture. Almost everyone who so much as thinks about leaving the Order contacts Rowenna eventually. She hears it all.

But after every anecdote she returns to the healing power of hypnosis, what it all means and how she's moved past it—"how hypnotherapy saved my life," in other words. And not just her life. There was one woman, apparently, who left polygamy, but couldn't find peace until Rowenna introduced her to her dead grandmother. She has also put her grandchildren into trance and sent them back to ancient Egypt where they saw aliens who could make the big building blocks weightless. It sounds a bit cuckoo to me, as though she's replaced one cult with another, but I don't want to disappoint her. "You know, I'd love to try hypnosis sometime," I say.

And before I know it, I'm lying on a couch upstairs and Rowenna's saying, "You're feeling relaxed." What's the harm? I've been hypnotized on stage before, it's all a scam. The guy said, "You're feeling hot," so I took off my pants and everyone laughed. But I knew what I was doing.

Within a few minutes, she's got me in a "good place," a place where I feel happy—I'm back in L.A., up Fryman Canyon on a beautiful sunny day looking out over the San Fernando Valley.

"Is there a bird flying nearby?" Rowenna asks.

"Yes, a sparrow."

"I like to think of a dove, maybe, or an eagle. I realized that my spirit guide was an eagle once and I was flying on its back, through the air."

Okay, so a sparrow's not bird enough. How about a goose? No, a chicken. It's like I want to roast my spirit guide. Oh, I know. "Hummingbird."

"Okay, they're beautiful as well. Now imagine the hummingbird comes over to rest on your hand."

Lucky I didn't go with goose.

"Is there a light in the distance?"

Well, the sun's out. "Yes."

"Is the light coming closer?"

"Er . . ."

"Imagine the light coming closer and closer, and nearer and nearer . . . How does that feel? Just feel that light all over you . . . Now is there a personage or a figure in that light? Maybe a spiritual guide, someone who may have passed on . . ."

I've tried this stuff before—focus on the light, breathe, wait for the unicorn and the man with the beard. That's what I was going for in India, and it gave me appendicitis. But this is what fundamentalists swear by, the visions and voices. Maybe in the Order they hear the voice of Paul Kingston booming down at them. Maybe that's what Carleen was tuning into that day when she had that glazed look, like a newscaster with an earpiece: *Don't tell him anything, Carleen. He's a demon from hell sent to invade God's kingdom.* As if a demon would pick a hummingbird for his guide animal.

Mind you, maybe Carleen does actually see me as a demon. They don't want me around, that's for sure. The Order is nothing like Centennial Park. No Mondavi Cabernets and Bollywood movies here. No "come and stay, the key's in the flower pot." What are the chances a Kingston will let me stay over? When I mentioned it to Anne Wilde, she laughed. She said no one's ever seen the inside of a Kingston home, not even her. But why? What are they hiding? Is it really the dark world of abuse that Rowenna talks about? Or is it all superholy—do they see their homes as sacred ground, which a Gentile would only defile? I know there's nothing sacred about Porno Joe's place . . .

"Three and you're coming out of your sleep . . ."

Great, now I've got that image in my head again.

"Four and your eyelids are fluttering . . ."

Hummingbirds, think hummingbirds.

"Five and you're awake and alert!"

Rowenna's looking over me, beaming. "You really went somewhere! What did you see?"

⬥ Origins

> Daniel said to the King [Nebuchadnezzar], "In your dream, you saw a great statue of a man who was very powerful . . . Then you saw a stone that was cut out of the mountain without hands, and it hit the statue on the feet. It broke the feet into pieces and the whole rest of the statue broke into pieces. Then it grew to a mountain, and then filled the whole earth."
>
> Then Daniel said to the King, "This is the meaning of the dream. The statue is a symbol of the kingdoms of the earth . . . The stone cut without hands is heavenly Father Kingdom that will be set up in the latter days. This Kingdom of God will fill the entire earth and will never be destroyed."
>
> This is our time and that Kingdom is the Order, the only place on earth where you can live all of heavenly Father's laws.
>
> —*Teacher's Manual Course B-2*, Age 6–7

The Kingston heritage is as long as that of Short Creek. It stretches back to the first wave of fundamentalists who rejected the 1890 Manifesto and struck out on their own. But the groups soon diverged. Short Creek sought physical isolation, whereas the Kingstons laid roots among the Gentiles and Mormons of Bountiful, just north of Salt Lake County. They sought separation of a different sort, a form of "economic communalism," as historian D. Michael Quinn has pointed out.[9] And this foundational decision has given the group a quite different character.

The story of the Order is that of its prophets, a dynasty of harsh men from the Kingston bloodline, possessed of ruthless ambition and idiosyn-cratic ideas. Charles William Kingston was the first to create a stir in the early 1920s. A pamphleteer, he published one of the first books about the famous Taylor revelation, titled *Laman Manasseh Victorious*.[10] He was also given to visions of his own, once announcing that Jesus had visited him in a dream, accompanied by God. "I noticed neither of these men wore any jewelry, watches, tie pins, cuff buttons etc. Their clothing was plain street dress, spotlessly clean. The suits were dark suits."[11] (Naturally he came up against skepticism. Surely Jesus would wear white? Charles argued that he often went around in cunning disguises).

His wife and kids were believers, as was his son-in-law Clyde. And his son, Charles Elden, was even claiming to receive wisdom through his own dreams. But Elden differed from his father. He wasn't content to write jour-nals and articles; he wanted power. It was Elden who founded the Order in 1935 at the age of twenty-five, during the agony of the Depression, and set about consolidating his position at the top.

First, he declared a law of consecration, whereby members were to give all their land and possessions to him, Charles Elden. The Lord had told him as much in a vision, up a mountain in Bountiful. Elden and his two wives began what he called a "United Order," a reference to the early Mormon ideals of communal living. He also devised a strict ranking of God's favored people, with himself ranked at number one, Clyde at number two and his father Charles William at number five. Then, in 1940, he called a momen-tous meeting that transformed the Order forever. It was the meeting at which he unveiled the Law of Satisfaction, or "One above Another."

"Every individual," Elden explained, "is responsible to the one above him in exactly the same way as if that individual was the Savior himself." And in case that wasn't clear: "You are bound to me just the same as if I was the Highest God in the Heavens."[12] In other words, every Order member should treat the person above them in the hierarchy—whether it be the head of the house, or the boss at work—as though he were a God. Elden was demanding unswerving obedience from a workforce that was ulti-mately answerable to him alone. He can't be faulted for a lack of audacity.

Order members have assured me that "One Above Another" isn't as autocratic as it sounds. Evidently the one above is supposed to be Christ-like and submit if the one below insists, in order to maintain harmony.[13]

But former members tell a different story. "If you even think a bad thought about the one above, then you're at risk of eternal damnation," said one. "And if they tell you to do a thing that's wrong or illegal, you just do it. They're the ones that will pay for it. But you'll be rewarded in heaven."[14]

It's fitting that the architect of this law had a fetish for severe discipline and beat his children from infancy. Elden saw virtue in hardship and austerity—he demanded that babies be bathed in cold water, that there be no wallpaper on the walls, if there were walls at all. In the early days, the group was known for living in tents and going about barefoot, wearing blue coveralls for clothes, tied together with string.[15] It was the philosophy of the hairshirt, one that chimes with Mormon history, all those stories of how the saints suffered on their harrowing journey to the West. But it goes to an extreme with the Order. There's a sense of Monty Python's Four Yorkshiremen. "I'm not saying we were poor, but twenty-seven of us lived in a hospital Dumpster eating muesli made out of gravel and piss." "Gravel? We would *dream* of gravel!"

According to Rowenna, however, Elden's frugality may have led to the death of his third wife, Grace. She'd fallen ill after giving birth, and the conditions at Elden's home were grim: It was January, the place was freezing and Elden believed more in prayer than doctors. Three days after the baby was born, Grace died. "Of course her parents were outraged, but they were conditioned to keep quiet," says Rowenna. "So they never reported her death, they just buried her at this place in Bountiful called the Holy Spot. Even Grace's daughter didn't know. She was raised by Grace's mother, who told her that she was her mother. And Elden was so guilty about it, he dug her up, cut her little finger off and carried it around in his pocket for a long time. I know, when I first heard this story, I wouldn't have believed it either. But one of Grace's nieces told me herself."[16]

This macabre picture of a tortured Elden scarcely sits with the grand vision he portrayed of himself. A year before his death, he wrote a prayer that Order members recite to this day: "With my divine birthright, I have unlimited health, knowledge, intelligence, sympathy, tolerance, realization, ambition, courage, patience, vitality, forgiveness, perseverance, energy, obedience, joy, satisfaction, cleanliness, beauty, confidence, determination and independence, which cause my personality to penetrate and influence all of God's creations."

And yet, the very next year, 1948, he was diagnosed with cancer. Cancer of the penis, according to Rowenna—"I had my friend in the attorney general's office get a copy of the death certificate." His family labored for three days to keep his corpse from rotting in the month of July, fervent in the belief that he might resurrect at any moment.

Elden's successor was his brother, John Ortell, an appointment that was imposed rather than decided by any process of representation. According to Order literature, the policy is plain: God decides. "The Lord picks the leader of the Order," reads one of the teacher's primers for the Order school. "There is no way that such an important position can be decided by man with his limited understanding. The only thing we can choose is whether we will personally accept him."[17]

Elden may have built the foundation, but Ortell built the empire. During his thirty-five-year reign, he oversaw immense growth in the Order's business and property portfolio, its population and ultimately its power. And he achieved this by being, if anything, an even more severe custodian of Elden's values: frugality, physical discipline and secrecy. He was Stalin to Elden's Lenin. He casts a longer shadow.

A famously tightfisted man, Ortell drove an old Chevy and lived in a ramshackle single-story house on 500 East in Salt Lake City. He once boasted that he wore the same black shirt every day for over a year. His was the economy of miserliness—child labor, pitiful wages and the sacrifice of Order mothers, struggling to raise their teeming broods on a shoestring. It was under Ortell that the Kingstons developed a reputation for Dumpster diving—whole families heading out at night with flashlights and boxes to fish expired food out of the bins at the back of grocery stores.[18] He even stood up in church one day and laid down a law about how many squares of tissue should be used when you go to the bathroom. (Three, in case you're wondering—you use it, fold it, use it again, fold it again and use it again. So sayeth the Lord.)[19]

He welcomed welfare payments, in keeping with the classic polygamist reputation. In 1983, the state of Utah sued Ortell for welfare subsidies received by his alleged wives. Investigators charged that four of his wives were fraudulently collecting child support for twenty-six children. Ortell admitted no wrongdoing but paid the state $250,000, and the case was dropped. At the time, investigators estimated his wealth at $70 million.[20]

Deceit, secrecy and obfuscation became something of a hallmark of the Order. Members deliberately changed their surnames to obscure their Kingston roots. Rowenna, for example, was married to Leon Kingston, but adopted a surname, Erickson, which she found in a telephone directory. Carleen goes by the name Cannon and Rachel by Young even though both are daughters and wives of Kingstons. A *Salt Lake Tribune* investigation in 1998 revealed that Order members used false social security numbers—the numbers of dead Kingstons. And the lines between corporation and church are so blurred that the church and the business have often shared the same mailing address. For years religious services were held at Standard Restaurant Supply, an Order stewardship. The church used to share a PO box with the clan's attorney, Carl Kingston.[21]

And Ortell was a savvy business player, a tax code loopholer of the first order. When he died in 1987, he left nothing to his children, but none of them objected. He'd arranged for his vast land holdings to be deeded to corporations in which his immediate heirs were officers. And his remaining fortune was willed to the Latter Day Church of Christ, which his heirs now control. Since donations to churches are tax-exempt, he avoided millions in probate taxes. As Reed Richards, chief of the Criminal Division of the Utah AG's office told *The Salt Lake Tribune*: "If you can get your kids on corporations that control your assets and in the hierarchy of your church, you can beat the system."[22]

Another of Ortell's signature achievements was an acceleration of incest within the Order. He used to work on the co-op's dairy farm in Davis County, where he developed theories about genetics and inbreeding in cattle, and it's widely reported that he applied these theories to his own children in order to purify the Kingston line—the supposed Jesus genealogy that Rowenna was talking about. And yet I've been told by one of the Order's lawyers that this is a terrible libel. "There was incest in the group long before Ortell," she said, with a straight face.[23] And there was—just not quite as much.

Ortell's father, Charles William, had never married incestuously, for example, but Ortell's first wife was his niece, Coreen. He married three of his nieces in all, with a half sister thrown in. Sadly for Coreen, she suffered several miscarriages, perhaps as a result of the close incest, (though more sinister allegations have been made).[24] But her inability to conceive only diminished her in a society so dedicated to procreation. Particularly since Ortell's second wife, Ladonna Petersen, was proving so fecund, bearing him nine children.

Ladonna occupies a huge role in the story of the Order. Quite literally—she was morbidly obese. But she also wielded enormous influence over Ortell. Something about the two seemed to click: Ladonna the ditzy, helpless female with a shrewd talent for manipulation, and Ortell, the all-powerful patriarch who would do anything to make her happy. It's said that in polygamy, a man may have several women but only one wife—the role of chief wife, or as *Big Love* terms it, "boss lady," is seldom acknowledged but common enough. And Ladonna was Ortell's—not just his legal wife, but also the one who monopolized his time and attention and money. Ortell would typically spend five days of the week at her home, splitting the other two days among his twelve other wives.[25] And only Ladonna's children have risen to positions of power within the group. Her seven sons include the current prophet Paul, his child-beating brother Daniel, Mary Ann's uncle/husband David, Porno Joe, Hyrum, Jesse and Jason Ortell, whose fifteen-year-old half sister and wife Andrea died while pregnant with their first child.[26] *The Waltons* it ain't.

For the most part, Ortell hardly knew his children. He never publicly acknowledged them, and in private, according to the reports of ex-members, his role was mostly limited to that of a brutal disciplinarian. He considered himself quite the expert when it came to beating kids. One technique was to slap babies repeatedly in the face until they stopped crying, often leaving them too swollen and bruised to be taken out in public.[27] It was important to begin this process from birth, so as not to let bad habits creep in, and mothers who instituted such child abuse would be rewarded with two-year-olds who minded. "But not too close to the ear," he cautioned his daughter Luann. "It might cause hearing loss."

He didn't believe in doctors but in herbal remedies and home births, choosing to deliver many of his children himself. But most of all Ortell believed in fasting, an old Order tradition. Elden used to say that each day of dry fasting was worth three days with water. Charles William would tell of a zoo where the lions were not fed on Sunday and it almost doubled their life span. And Ortell, for the last twenty years of his life, embarked on punishing fasts throughout the month of January, sometimes going for forty-two days on end. He had a tumor, and he believed if he starved it, he could kill it. The Order history books describe the regime: "Brother Ortell would begin with from three to ten days dry fasting. Then he would begin to drink 4 ounces of water three times a day. At the end of the third week, he would change that to 4 ounces of grape juice three times a day for the other three weeks."[28]

As a result of Ortell's rule, countless babies have been beaten black and blue and half sisters have been married off to half brothers. Doctors have been shunned in favor of fasting and prayer. And the horror stories that abound from this medievalism are often gut churning. Some Order members would die at the end of their fasts. Others, like Jill, a four-year-old girl whose legs were badly burned by candle wax, suffered terribly for want of simple medication. Ortell refused to take her to the hospital, insisting that her burns be treated with mineral water instead, and when her legs became infected he pulled the rotting skin off himself, with tweezers, no painkillers in sight. The poor girl was in agony, and her scars remain.[29]

It was August 1987 when Ortell fasted for the last time. He'd fallen sick—some say he caught something from his pigeons (yes, the prophet kept pigeons). And this time his fast simply brought him to the brink, incoherent and weak, unable to move from his sickbed at Ladonna's Salt Lake City home.

As word spread among the faithful that Ortell might die, influential elders read passages from the Bible in church to prove that Brother Ortell would prevail. But Ronald Tucker wasn't convinced. At the time a thirty-year-old coal miner and lifelong member of the Order, he was traumatized by the news and wanted to help somehow, so he went to Ladonna's house to offer a hand. After all, Ortell was also his father.

He found a disturbing scene—a shriveled old man lying naked on a bed, bony and wasting away. "If you tried to put a sheet on him, he'd rip it off," says Ronald. "He wouldn't stand for underwear either. He just lay there on his back, in silence." Around him were several of Ortell's other sons, mostly from Ladonna's family—Paul, Daniel, Porno Joe, Hyrum—and some other elders like Merlin Kingston, Ortell's brother. They took it in shifts to care for him, desperately trying to keep him alive. "We dropped grape juice into his mouth with a straw, we broke slivers of dates up into pieces no bigger than a match head to feed him, but his body just couldn't take it. We watched him die for two weeks."

At one point, Merlin decided that the way to revive him was to rustle up breast milk from lactating Order mothers and give him an enema with the stuff—perhaps that way, he would gain the strength to eat. But Ladonna stopped it. She said, let Brother Ortell go in peace.

"The day he died, August 25, 1987, we were doing CPR on him," says Ron. "I was the one giving him mouth-to-mouth—nobody else dared, he was pretty rough looking. Hyrum was doing the chest compressions. Joe, Paul and Daniel were throwing hot water on him, to try and shock his system into waking up. This went on for twenty minutes after we knew he was gone. You could see the blood vessels coming up on his skin. Rigor mortis was setting in. I said, 'That's it, we're done.' Everyone was crying, Paul, all the brothers. I was the one who had to shut Ortell's mouth and eyes at the end."

For the next few hours, the family consoled each other around his bedside, remembering that families are forever and that if they were good, they would see Ortell on the other side. "His other wives started showing up at the house," says Ron. "But what got me was they wouldn't go into the actual room. Ladonna would sit by him and touch his arm, but the other wives didn't feel enough of a bond."

Ron's own reactions were mixed. He'd scarcely known his father; virtually none of Ortell's kids had. The last time Ron and Ortell had spoken in any meaningful way was almost twelve years before. He feared him and revered him and yearned for his acceptance. "So I was really sad. I always felt if I could just be a little better, prove my loyalty to the Order more, then he would accept me as a son. If I just had more time. And that was the thing: we all thought we'd have more time. Because we'd been told time and again that Ortell could choose when he died. That he could live forever if he wanted to. I believed that when he went, someone as important as him, he wouldn't just die, but Joseph Smith would come and escort him to the other side. I wasn't the only one. It was pretty devastating."

◆ Meet the Tuckers

> I, RONALD TUCKER, being full converted to and in harmony with the laws and principles administered by the COOPERATIVE SOCIETY OF DAVIS COUNTY, feeling that the application of these laws and principles will bring about better conditions among all peoples.
>
> I voluntarily transfer all claim and title to all my possessions to said society as a GIFT.
>
> I also agree to turn the result of my labor, together with the results of my wife and family's labor to the society, as long as we are members.
>
> In case I or we ever withdraw from the society, I or we claim no equity whatsoever in the society.
>
> —*Agreement between Cooperative Society of Davis County and Members Belonging to the Same*

I first meet Ron and his wife Christy at their home in southern Salt Lake City, a charming little place at the circular end of a leafy cul-de-sac. A bunch of their children have joined us in the living room. Christy brings some chips and dip, Ron offers me a beer. "We drink in this house now," he says. "We gamble. We're making up for lost time!"

He looks like a Kingston, Ron. That is, he looks like his father—big round eyes on a pasty white face, dark hair and glasses. So many of Ortell's children came out looking the same, male or female, that at an Order dance or wedding, "You'd see them all lined up, and it was like one of those computer morphs from one end to the other," says Ron. But very few of the "morphs" had any kind of relationship with their father. Ron didn't even know who his father was until he turned eight, a fairly typical story in the Order. He knew that Ortell was the leader and he came by the house maybe twice a year to spank the kids and sleep with his mom. That was the leader's job, he thought—he did the same in every house. And if anyone asked who his dad was, his mom had taught him to say, "Harold Tucker, he's a truck driver." But Harold Tucker didn't exist, as Ron well knew. The other kids had stories about airline pilots and army soldiers—always people who could plausibly be out of town.

Why his mother suddenly decided to tell him the truth, he has no idea.

And in practical terms, it changed little. Ron was told to stick to his Harold Tucker story more doggedly than ever. He couldn't tell a soul, not even people within the group. And Ortell didn't magically turn into a dad— there was no father-son bonding, no games of catch, he didn't even come over more often. In fact, to call him "Dad" would result in a beating for sure. And Ortell gave savage beatings. "He'd have you go out in the yard and get a board for him," Ron says. "If you cried, he'd hit you harder."

Ron remembers his reaction to the news. "I thought, 'Wow, I'm half Kingston!'" he says. "I thought that was pretty cool because the Kingstons are the leading family in the Order." Even as an eight-year-old, he knew the Order's obsession with stock and ancestry, that some families were more equal than others. But he soon realized that simply having Kingston blood wasn't good enough. There was another, removed, "inner circle" within the Order, an elite that current members are loath to admit even exists. But Ron knew it was real because his best friend Paul was part of it. They did everything together.

Paul Kingston is now the prophet. And Ron is an apostate, an exile. Taken together, their parallel stories illustrate an ugly reality of the Order, a caste system built upon an aristocracy of blood. Strictly speaking, Paul is half Kingston too, like Ron, but no one ever saw him that way, least of all Ron. Because Paul was Ladonna's son. And that meant he was raised with money, favored in marriage and groomed for high office within the Order. The same went for his brothers and sisters. Paul was never in doubt as to whom his father was because Ortell spent most of his time at their house. They may even have played catch. But Ortell didn't care for Ron's mother Marion nearly as much. So Marion had to work a minimum wage job all her life; her family remained poor, her children were destined for grunt work. "I'd go over to Paul's house at Christmas time and I'd never seen so many presents, they were all over the floor," says Ron. "I remember thinking, 'Wouldn't it be neat to have a rich father like they did?'"

Mostly it was Ron and Paul and Paul's brother Hyrum. They got up to all kinds of mischief in the early days, sneaking out at nights to roam Salt Lake City's Liberty Park and setting off fireworks and explosives. They had access to all kinds of stuff through a guy in the Order called Vern—bottle rockets and M-80s and silver tubes, whatever they wanted. When Hyrum got a job at the Eastside Market, they raided the beer and cigarettes and sold them to the kids at high school. Harmless stuff, really. "We were really close, me and Paul," says Ron. "Close as any brothers."

But the caste system kicked in early. It was Order policy, for example, to put the children to work in stewardships from a very young age, regardless of child labor laws. So every summer, from the age of twelve, Ron was shipped out to work at Order businesses in Utah, Idaho, Colorado—wherever. Once he reached ninth grade, he left school altogether to work full-time. But not Paul: Ladonna insisted that her children were not to be "shipped" anywhere, they would stay home with her. And their school work came first: the Order would send her children to college. Ladonna shielded her boys from labor, spoiled them. Paul would simply say that he needed to rest for school, and she'd see to it that he was excused from whatever job he was expected to do. One time, Ron recalls Paul whispering to him, "You want some ice cream? Watch this." And he groaned and gripped his stomach until Ladonna came running. "What is it Paul, what do you want to make it feel better?" Paul said "ice cream" and Ladonna went to the store to buy him some. "I was shocked," said Ron. "Because sugar isn't allowed in the Order. It's seen as badly as the Mormon Church sees cigarettes or coffee. But Paul could get whatever he wanted."

The favoritism was so stark, it upset Ron's mother. But she had no voice in the matter. "Ortell told her that kids are like money," says Ron. "The ones that are in school are like putting money in the bank. They grow and learn—it's like getting interest—and when they're finished they can do more for the Order. But sometimes you need cash, so some of the kids have to be used right now. And I was one of those kids."

Ron and Christy married as teenagers, at eighteen and nineteen respectively. It wasn't forced—they liked each other. And in this respect at least, the Order gave them what they wanted. But life was hard from the outset. The Order moved them from fixing sewing machines in Colorado and Wyoming to mining coal in Utah's Bear Canyon, where they stayed for twenty years. The money was pitiful and conditions were appalling. Accidents were commonplace; Ron's eldest son Jeremy nearly died when a rock cracked his skull (the accidents continued until the mine's eventual bankruptcy in 2008).[30] And though the mine was notorious for exploiting undocumented workers, providing horrendous working conditions and so on,[31] the illegal immigrants were often earning more than their bosses.

As an Order member it was Ron's purpose to build up the kingdom, to consecrate as much of his income as possible, so by the time he retired in 2001, after twenty years, his salary was all of $6.25 per hour.

While Ron was hard at work, Paul was getting an education. He'd finished high school as student body president and star athlete on the swimming team and cross-country teams. To complete the picture, he was even dating a cheerleader, Karen Smith, a fresh-faced Mormon girl who expected they would marry. And for a while Paul may have flirted with the idea himself—according to the *Salt Lake Observer* in 1999,[32] he came close to converting to the LDS Church in the spring of 1978, the second half of his senior year. A date was set for his baptism, but he didn't show up—he left his friends hanging at the Tabernacle baptistry. And the following September he married Patricia Brown, the granddaughter of one of Charles William Kingston's sisters. Eleven months later came number two—his half sister Deborah. He had entered the fold.

Ron was digging coal when Paul was at the University of Utah graduating in business and law. And when Ortell died, Paul sailed past three older brothers to become president at twenty-seven. He was made number nine in the Order's ranking system—apparently the original number nine had left, so the slot was left vacant. Ron was later granted number eighty.[33]

Paul's ascent was no surprise to Ron. The prophet's grooming had begun long ago. As they turned seventeen, Ron was probably closer to Paul than his own brothers, but then things began to change. Paul began to shadow Ortell on his rounds, from stewardship to stewardship, observing how the Order operated. He'd appear at stewardship meetings, sit in the corner and take notes. "The brothers were forming a tight circle, excluding everyone else," says Ron. "It was kinda disturbing. It got so you couldn't really talk to him anymore. I just thought it was me, that if I lived my life better, they would have trusted me as a loyal Order member. I always told myself that it was my shortcomings. So I'd just do my best, be the best coal miner I could be and build up the kingdom that way—they'll see. But now I look back, it was just a power thing. They were keeping it in the family."

Paul's grooming is reminiscent of Warren Jeffs, another son of a presiding prophet, another father's favorite. They are the inheritors, the gentry of polygamy: young princes with the requisite bloodline and smarts to propel them to power. It's a sign of modern polygamy's maturity that the groups are no longer led by traditional prophets, men of magical visions and charisma and a talent for scripture. Today the prophet is a corporate steward, a CEO, a politician. Their groups have grown, they make money; the cult is a business now, to be run by suits like Warren and Paul. And perhaps this is the source of their insecurity; they know they lack the legend of their fathers. So they try to outdo them in other ways: they take more wives, produce more children and lay down laws and punishments that are even more severe.

The friendship between Ron and Paul was as good as dead by the time Paul became president. The gulf was complete. And Ron was hurt. They'd grown up together, best friends, and here they were barely speaking, and he didn't know why. A coldness had come over Paul. "I'd talk to him about my kids, what kind of future they could have in the co-op. You know, Jeremy's a bright boy," says Ron. "But Paul just said, 'He'll mine coal, that's where we need him.' He didn't see anything else in them. My kids didn't mean anything to him. It's real upsetting to be that close to someone and then realize that he's just going to use your kids for slave labor."

But none of this could be said. Now that Paul was the prophet, Ron could no longer be frank or familiar with him. He felt subdued in his presence. "He's the prophet, you know, so God's gonna pour knowledge down into him whenever he needs it on any subject. So I reverenced him."

At that time, Ron's faith was of granite. He knew in his corpuscles that the Order was the only reason that the Earth even existed. "When you see a shooting star, that's a world that failed and the Gods destroyed it," he chuckles. "That's what I believed. And the only reason this Earth hasn't been destroyed is because we have this small remnant of the true blood of Israel left. So as long as the Order survives, God will preserve the Earth."

Ron chuckles a lot as he tells me his story. Not because he finds it funny, but because now he can hear how weird it must sound to an outsider, how obvious the lies had been and how tragic, and embarrassing, that he'd fallen for them for his first forty-two years. It's a complex chuckle, part relief, part sadness and not a little awe at the power that the Order once had over him. "We used to recite these memory gems. Things like 'Please protect Brother Paul and all our stewardships.' And 'Help me to grow where I'm planted'—that's another one. In other words, you're stuck here."

In some respects, his faith sustained him. The belief that he was one of God's chosen gave Ron a sense of superiority over outsiders, a layer of insulation against the prejudice he encountered, particularly from LDS Mormons. "You consider yourself so far above them, it's like listening to infants talk about something they don't understand," Ron explains. "You think, 'That's how it looks to you, but you're never in your life going to understand the things we know and live every day.'" (Another of Ortell's children, Luann Kingston, explained it thus: "People outside the Order didn't matter, they were going to hell anyway. It goes: the Order, then outsiders . . . and then everyone that's not white.")

But equally his faith was crippling him. For instance, he'd taken a second wife five years after marrying Christy. It was a terrible marriage, a poor match that ultimately ended in separation, but Ron believed they were meant for each other. She was his half sister, and he believed that their children would be so pure that they would stand out "like lions among sheep. That's what we were taught the kids would be after a couple of generations. There were people saying how Hitler had the right idea but he was trying to do it without God's help. Well, we had God's help."

So every weekend, he'd go and stay with her in Bountiful, a few hours north of Huntington. But the marriage disintegrated before his eyes. She had an affair and eventually left the group to be with this new man. And the split hit Ron hard. He fell into a deep depression. As miserable as the marriage had been, the break up was debilitating, but not for the traditional reasons. Ron wasn't simply grieving his plural marriage. He had lost his eternal salvation. "If you're Paul or one of his brothers and you've got ten wives and one of them leaves, that's not really a big thing. But if you only have two, and you have a breakup, it's very rare that you ever get another plural wife. So I was really worried that I wouldn't have a family in heaven. It was like the death of a really close family member. It was every bit as hard."

Then there was the other overriding fact of his faith-filled life—that it sucked. It sucked bad. Ron was being exploited by his bosses, by his church and family members. He was living in dire poverty—a family of ten in a horribly dilapidated home, no TV, on little more than $1,000 per month.

"We were so poor, I feel ashamed that I put my kids through it," says Christy. "But we had so little space, we were living on top of each other. There were so many leaks in the roof, I just put a plant under each one. We had skunks clawing up through the floor. I remember sweeping the porch outside one day, and looking at our place. It was the kind of picture you see from Africa. Real poverty."

They ate meat only if Ronald and his brother-in-law Sean went hunting for deer. They grew their own potatoes out back and kept chickens for eggs, but other than that, it was mostly raw oats. The Order swears by raw oats. And Ron swore by the Order. He adhered to all of the group's bizarre dietary beliefs. He believed store-bought cereals caused cancer, ketchup made you infertile, sugar was the devil's crystal. And Ron raised his family on the Order's favorite cure-all, an herb called comfrey. A weed, really. As a good Order family, they grew their own. "We used to have 'green drink,'" says Ron. "Comfrey, garlic and parsley. It's disgusting, but it's supposed to protect you from radiation. They said it would save us from a nuclear holocaust." When an article appeared from UCLA suggesting that comfrey actually *causes* cancer,[34] he believed, as he was told, that it was merely the devil conspiring against the Order. After all, the Lord had spoken. In the Teacher's Manual for the Order school, it reads: "When Brother Charles was living at the mine, he saw an AD in a magazine for comfrey plants. The Spirit of the Lord told him that was something the Order needed. So he sent away for five comfrey plants. Comfrey has been one of the greatest benefits to the health of the people of the Order of anything we have ever had."[35]

Ron and Christy have a daughter named Emily, who drank "green drink" and avoided sugar and ate raw oats. But at the age of seven, she started throwing up and complaining of severe headaches. None of the Order's remedies were working. Christy knew that taking her to a doctor would be frowned upon, but what other choice was there? So she took her in and the doctors were outraged that she hadn't brought her sooner. Emily had a tumor in her brain stem, and they recommended immediate surgery, the insertion of a shunt, a device that would release pressure by diverting the fluid from her brain to the abdominal cavity. But Christy couldn't even raise the suggestion without inviting a storm of opposition. Surgery would be the end of Emily, she heard. Her mother was horrified that she was even considering it. People told her, "You shouldn't have let her eat all that cereal!" Her aunt learned in a dream that Emily would be cured if she stopped eating potato chips.

"Everyone was saying 'Have you checked with Paul that it's okay? You'd better check with Paul first, maybe it's not a tumor.' And I said, 'I saw the MRI scan myself! If your child hurt his leg and you could see the bone sticking through the skin would you ask Paul if it was broken?' Of course I didn't ask Paul for permission. We did the surgery. But I talked to him afterward, because I felt I was supposed to. He said, 'Just tell her not to watch so much TV or stand so near the microwave.' I didn't dare tell him that we didn't even have a TV in our house," says Christy. "That lowered Paul in my eyes."

It was a glimmer of Paul's fallibility—not enough on its own to shake her faith, but together with other signs, other warnings, a terrifying picture was forming, one she could scarcely look at straight on. And Christy wasn't the only one with doubts. A silent skepticism was welling within Ron, too, and their oldest son Jeremy. And none of them dared tell the others; it was just too risky. The Order was strewn with stories of family members who'd been disowned, excommunicated, forbidden contact with their families. Within the Order, church came before family. And yet their home was roiling with doubt.

Christy's tipping point was Paul's refusal to marry off her daughters. Marriage is everything in the Order, and it's always the prophet's jurisdiction. Typically, the boy has a dream about the girl he wants to marry. He then takes the dream to Paul, who permits him to approach her parents. The parents allow him to approach the girl, all being well, and then the girl has a dream about the boy, which she takes to Paul. And only then does Paul decide, in his limitless wisdom, whether the two should be wed.

It sounds sweet in theory, all that dreaming. But inevitably, the pretty young girls were often married off to Paul's brothers—Ladonna's seven boys. By the time the Tuckers left the Order in 2001, the brothers had over eighty wives between them.[36] Certainly the odds favored Christy's daughters finding their way into these inner circle families, a prospect that filled both Christy and Ron with dread. These were older men, three times the age of their daughters, and they had a reputation for cruelty. Christy tells me the story of how one of Paul's brothers locked his wife in a room for three days, a vivacious and free-spirited girl of nineteen or so. "She had no food, a bucket to go to the bathroom in, and a Bible. And she could only come out when she was the kind of person that God wanted her to be. After that she was like a wild horse that had been broken."

There were other possibilities, boys who would come by the house asking after their girls. It is so accepted within the Order that the brothers get the pick of the girls, that Order boys who aren't of royal lineage often try to score points with—or induce dreams in—girls who aren't yet on the brothers' radar, girls under fourteen. Christy has a niece, Michelle, who was eleven when she had an eighteen-year-old asking after her. "He'd come and jump on the trampoline with her. He'd tell her that he'd got direction on her," says Christy. "And remember when Tim started coming over for April? He was eighteen, I think. They used to go out hiking, they had grass fights. He carved their names into a rock. Oh, we kept a good eye on them, as you can imagine. How old were you then, April?"

She blushes. A pretty girl, sitting quietly by her mother. "I was, like, nine," she says.

"Yes, that's right. Nine," says Christy.

Nine.

But the boys stopped coming over just as soon as her girls were of marriageable age. And Christy wanted to know why. Her oldest daughter, Julie, had turned sixteen, and all her friends were getting married. Why not her? (In the Order, sixteen isn't considered especially young for marriage. As another Kingston daughter, Luann, told me, "At sixteen, you're an old maid.")

"Well, we found out that Paul was telling boys who were interested that they should get direction on someone else," says Christy. "Because, in our family, we had black blood."

Again, the Order's obsession with blood. This time, the issue was contamination, a charge that has dogged the Tucker family for years, that in Christy's recent genealogy lurked a black man. According to the Tuckers, this was almost certainly one of the reasons that their lives were so arduous and their incomes so meager.[37] The rumor stemmed from her mother's history. She had been married to Ortell years earlier, but she left him and left the Order and "on the outside" married Christy's father and had five kids, only returning to the Order once they'd divorced. Ortell never forgave her for leaving. And the rumors began that Christy's father had black blood in him, that he himself was the son of a black man, and Christy therefore, and all her children, were stained.

"From what I understand, Ladonna had a dream that anyone who ever left Ortell would marry someone with African American blood in them," says Christy. "So they felt like my sisters and I were partly black, and anyone in the Order who married them, their bloodline would be cursed."

It didn't matter that there isn't anything remotely black about Christy. Ladonna had had a dream, and that was all that the Order needed. Just a sniff of a rumor of a brush with blackness, and all bets were off: Christy's family would never become gods in the celestial kingdom. And if you can't become a god, you can't be with your family in heaven. Devastating stuff for a believer.

Even this, though, Christy could endure. She could forego her after-life, and she could bear being a pariah in this life. She could even accept that her prophet was the kind of man who would disseminate malicious lies among his followers out of a generational grudge passed down by his father. Perhaps this whole thing was a test.

But she drew the line at the condemnation of her children. "I realized that our kids would never be married. People actually told us, 'Your children are better off staying in the Order and never marrying than leaving and marrying outside. Because at least here, they'd be working to build up the kingdom.' And I just couldn't say that to my kids. My kids are not just cheap labor."

Meanwhile, Ron was beginning his own doubtful journey. He wasn't tainted by Christy's "blackness," since he could theoretically marry again and have more kids, free of the curse of Ham. But he'd seen pictures of Christy's grandfather; he knew he was white. And come the funeral, there he was in the casket—a white man. So Ron wanted to know: "How can a prophet believe something that's not true?"

The questions started and he couldn't shake them. It was a form of private torture, a duel with the voices in his head. But he had to settle it—he had to know for sure if the Order was true. What else was left? A life for his family as minimum wage workhorses, part-Negro pariahs with unmarriageable sons and daughters. Was it worth it? Was this a true calling? Ronald decided to look up diaries and journals of early members and get to the bottom of the Order's claims to be the one and only true kingdom of God on Earth.

He came upon the writing of Clyde Gustafson, number two on the

Order's list and Christy's grandfather on her mother's side. He'd written a series of pamphlets in 1976 called "The Sacred Things of the Order," and among them was the story about the time Elden had fasted in a cave in Bountiful for three days and Jesus came down to give him the keys to the priesthood. "But Elden never said that," says Ron. "That story was written by Clyde and he said Brother Elden never told him about any vision. It was just Clyde's imagination." The exact quotation is: "Brother Elden was not very talkative when it concerned other beings that had visited him in the past, so a lot of this is my own impression of what happened."[38]

And this begged the question: If the vision was true, why did Elden not talk about it?

Why leave the telling to Clyde's imagination? And if it was false, why did he permit the lie to gain footing? Were Order members being misled about their own history? Was the history being revised by current leaders?

Ron also pored through the diaries of Clyde's wife, Orlean. She'd written a lot about the early days of the Order, how the men had fasted and prayed desperately for the keys, which never came. It didn't tally with what the Order was teaching. And Ron learned that both Charles William and Elden had vigorously disapproved of underage marriages. "Charles even wrote it down. He said, 'If we ever did this, we would cease to be the Kingdom of God.'"

But it wasn't just the Order that was withering in Ron's eyes; the Book of Mormon was too. "It seemed like once I opened my mind, it got bombarded. I was constantly hearing stuff." One night, for example, he was watching a TV documentary about a tribe. They looked Asian to Ron. But then the narrator said that they were South American, and a light bulb went off. "I'd heard that the DNA shows that American Indians are Asians, not Israelites like the Book of Mormon says. But when I saw those people, it hit me—they *look* like Asians."

Another TV show, this time about Julius Caesar: The camera's panning over the battlefield where there are still artifacts and trenches in evidence, and again, Ron has a realization. "The battle on the Hill Cumorah was supposedly three hundred years after that, with twenty times more people, and they haven't found a *single* artifact. Not one. And I read something about how they haven't found a single Nephite coin in the whole Americas, but every other civilization left coins. Jeremy went online and bought some 2,300-year-old coins from the Middle East. I was getting to the point where I couldn't believe that I believed what I used to believe."

At first, his skepticism was private. It had to be. Ron the patriarch was responsible for his family's salvation. He was "the one above." It was his job to keep everyone in line, hold family meetings and make sure the children recited their memory gems. He didn't know that both Christy and Jeremy were going through a similar experience. Jeremy too had been researching the Order and had come up short. He was particularly dismayed with the Order's callous reaction to his mining accident. He'd nearly died, and his boss's first concern was to find a replacement. Disillusionment was rife at the Tucker home.

"I didn't want to shake their testimony by telling them my doubts," says Ron.

"And I was afraid he would leave me if I told him mine," says Christy.

"And I thought they would disown me if I said anything," says Jeremy.

So the façade continued, each one wrestling with their questions in private. Ron began to withdraw from the church. He stopped going to meetings and functions. He thought his doubts were a test from the devil, a test of such magnitude that it would take a visit from an angel to set him right. Christy went the other way: "I thought, 'No, I'm going to get my testimony back, I'm going to go to everything.' And I was getting madder and madder at Ron, because he wouldn't go to anything."

Then one Sunday morning, it came to a head. Christy was getting the kids ready for church while Ron was sitting on the couch in his robe. So she confronted him—why wouldn't he come to church anymore? And Ron looked at her, fear in his eyes. "He said, 'If I tell you, then you'll think I'm worse than you already think I am,'" says Christy. "And that just about knocked the wind out of me. So I sat down and he told me everything. And so did I. It was an amazing morning. We didn't make it to church that day."

That week, they went to visit Merlin Kingston, the last surviving member of the Order's first family. Merlin was the brother of Ortell and Elden. It was Ron and Christy's last attempt to salvage their faith—they still wanted the Order to be true, they wanted Merlin to show them that their life had purpose and meaning. And when they arrived, Merlin seemed ready. He had all the holy books laid out with bookmarks—the Book of Mormon, the Doctrine and Covenants, the writings of Charles WIlliam Kingston and Orlean and Clyde Gustafson. But instead, the scales fell from their eyes that day, once and for all.

"He said there never was a laying on of hands in the Order, but Brother Elden was born with that birthright—he had the authority before he was even born—so those keys automatically came to him. In other words, the Order didn't have the Priesthood. They just fasted and prayed all day to get it, but after a few years they decided 'Well, we must already have it.' And when he said that, I just sat back and chuckled. He thought he convinced me. And Christy thought he convinced me too. But I was at a point where I didn't know whether to laugh or cry. It was like getting hit with a ton of bricks. It crushed me. The whole thing is just someone's dream."

He was devastated. He couldn't sleep. His world had fallen apart. "I felt a freedom, like we didn't have to do this anymore. But at the same time it was real scary—what are we going to do now, you know? I've been a coal miner all my adult life, I've got ten kids. It was so hard to deal with. So many things. I felt like I could cry at any time, day and night. I don't know how to explain it—everything I believed my whole life wasn't true. My whole world, the world that I lived in and believed and experienced. It wasn't true. It was gone. It was like my former self had died. It's like waking up one morning and having someone tell you you're not who you think you are. If you ever lost someone real close to you, it takes time for it to sink in that you're not going to see them anymore. That's the closest way I can describe it. I just couldn't take it all at once. It took me years to work through it." Two years, roughly, for the worst to pass. But they were only the injuries of impact. Rehabilitation would be a longer, more arduous road. Ron was forty-two at the time. Even now, as he's talking to me, you sense the realization still seeping—that his talents, his youth, had all been stolen.

There's nothing simple about leaving the Order. Even after extensive discussions with Christy and Jeremy, the prospect alone was terrifying—a new house, new job, a new life, and all when Ron's in his forties and he has ten kids. His whole life, he'd been taught that beyond the security of the Order lay a jungle where people lie and cheat and steal. No place for the pure of heart. The Tuckers lived in a tiny isolated community full of Order people, way out in Huntington Canyon. As far as they knew, the outside world was the Bronx in the '70s. After dark. All the time.

And there were all kinds of practical obstacles. Like getting their money out, for example. Most of it was tied up in their house and savings. The house part was complicated because they didn't own the land, only the building. And their savings were under the control of Alana, the Order cashier. Incredibly, Ron had no records; he didn't even know how much he had. In the Order, according to Ron, savings go into a hidden "secret account" of which only the Order has a record. The only way members can figure out what they have is by asking Alana, the cashier, and hoping that she will tell the truth. Some Order members try to keep their own records, tracking their spending and savings from every paycheck during their entire working career. But inevitably, most lose track.

Ron isn't the only Order member to tell me about the "secret account," but he's nervous talking about it—"I might get in trouble with like the IRS, I don't know." It certainly sounds like a peculiar system—with undeclared savings and no paperwork—but the Order's financial system has peculiarity written into its code. It's built upon a racket whereby members are required to consecrate all that they own—their entire inventory—so that when they die, it all goes to the Order. "So if I wanted my mother's couch and bedroom set, I'd have to buy it from the Order," says Ron. "But if there's a debt there, then the children inherit it. It's hideous to me, how old I was before I opened my eyes."

The Order refused to give Ron any of his money unless he signed a form inoculating the Order from litigation. "It basically released them from any claim or blame or wrongdoing that I might want to hold them responsible for now or later," says Ron. "And they said I had to sign it before they would give me my money or my kids' savings or anything." So Ron refused and called Paul. Paul wasn't in. For two weeks, his calls were dropped, his messages not returned.

"So I found a picture of me, Paul and Hyrum with three girls at a school dance," he says. "It was a homecoming dance at Viewmount High, which was a public school. And it goes against Order standards to go to a school dance. It wasn't allowed, to go out in couples. And they were teaching that Paul had lived this perfect life, that's why he was the prophet today. So I copied that picture up and wrote on the back, 'If Brother Paul had ever not lived up to Order standards, could he be the leader of the Order today? Number 1: Going to a school dance.' And I left numbers 2 to 10 blank, so he knew I had more examples. We did a lot of stuff as teenagers. And I gave it to my girls to give to all the other kids at school, knowing that they would show their parents."

The very next day, Paul called to arrange for Ron's check. He got $50,000 for his house and $14,000 for his savings. It was a radical move on Ron's part, to take money out of the Order—that money was considered a down payment on his salvation. Christy's mother begged her to leave some on her balance, if only a dollar.

Jeremy was the first to leave. He couldn't bear to wait around. His uncle Jake, another skeptic close to Jeremy's age, had left and bought a house in West Jordan, a large place where he could host other families who wished to transition out of the Order. So Jeremy moved in with him. And Christy and Ron brought the rest of the family six months later. It was 2001, and they were out in the world. Free.

Things fell fortunately for them straightaway. Ron got a job doing yard work with his brother-in-law Sean, who had left shortly earlier, and in the first day, he was making better money than he ever had at the Order. "I was scared to leave because the one thing about the Order was, you'd always have a job and a home and food on the table, even if it was only raw oats and beans," Ron says. "They told us that employers would lay people off in a heartbeat and people were out of work, and their homes were repossessed. But what they didn't tell you was if you're prepared to work for Order wages, you can always get a job. You can go to McDonald's."

The Tuckers were on their way. They found a decent house to live in, the first one they'd ever chosen for themselves, and they set about adjusting to life on the outside. It wasn't easy. The psychological burden was immediately telling. All those questions that had previously been settled by Paul—where to work, what job to do, where to live—now Ron had to answer for himself. And it was bewildering. The safety net of the Order was gone; he could no longer rely on the Law of One Above Another and tell himself that he was just obeying orders.

"I used to think that hard times were just a test from God," says Ron. "I equated misery and sacrifice with salvation. But when you leave, you realize success and failure are your own fault. I couldn't blame Paul anymore."

The family was also haunted by the Order's more ominous warnings, that they would suffer some kind of divine retribution for leaving. The teaching on apostates is clear: they provoke God's wrath. Sometimes God punishes apostates and sometimes He punishes others for the sins of apostates, but either way, leaving the Order makes God mad, and there was a string of bodies to prove it, former members who had suffered accidents, drug overdoses, depression, even suicide. Christy and Ron knew of several such casualties personally, half brothers and sisters of theirs. Their tragic stories are circulated among the faithful as "I told you so's" to keep the troops faithful.

The transition from the Order into mainstream society is filled with manifold traumas: the burden of responsibility, the dizzying choices, the fear of punishment, the spiritual uncertainty and social alienation. These pressures all mount at once, along with the dawning of one's own naïvety and exploitation, and the grief and shame that naturally follow. And they are triggered by the most ordinary details. Something as basic as money, for example, takes on a whole new aspect outside the group.

Order members are raised with a bizarre relationship to cash. Cash is bad. It's what Gentiles use, and its value is confined to the terrestrial world. In the Order, money is measured in units, which are just like dollars— the rate is one unit per dollar—except units are holy, they can be taken to heaven. Dollars are converted to units only when the money is consecrated. In other words, money is somehow spiritually cleansed by being given to the Order. And units are converted to dollars when they are drawn out and converted to cash, something that the Order strongly discourages. Members are urged to keep as much of their money in units, within the Order's control, as possible.[39]

So when Ron worked down the mine, he was paid in units, which automatically would go on to his Order bank account—not the "secret account," but just his regular one. And when he shopped at Order stores, the cashier would take the units off his balance. Never in his career did Ron receive a paycheck or have a checking account, a credit card, an ATM card or check-book. The only times he handled cash were when he asked Alana, the Order's cashier, if he could convert some of his units.[40] And she wouldn't simply make the transaction—Ron would have to make a case first. Why did he need to make this special purchase that couldn't be made in an Order store? How important was it? Often she'd say, "We don't have

$30 for your daughter's birthday party, can you make do with $10?" And Ron would have no choice but to accept.

So after he left, Ron found himself receiving a paycheck for the first time and wondering what to do with it. "The first time I went to an outside bank, my stomach was in knots. Because as I was driving up to the window, I remember thinking, 'What am I going to tell her that I need the money for?' I wanted $100, but I was thinking, 'I wonder if she'll give me $50? Maybe I should just ask for $20 . . . but I really need $50 . . .' I was shaky, I was sweating when I got up there. I said, 'I need like $50 out of my checking because I've got to get some groceries and my daughter needs some school stuff and . . .' And she's looking at me. 'Okaaay. It's your money.' And right away I thought, 'Damn—I should have asked for $100!'"

This kind of story used to embarrass Ron. But his experience is a common one—every ex-Order member I speak to tells of their trepidation around banks, a sick, nervous feeling approaching the teller and a surge of relief, exhilaration and guilt afterward, holding the cash in their hands. Some speak of circling banks three or four times in their cars before plucking up the courage to walk in. Others have just folded in the confusion and told the teller, "I've just left the Kingston group, please help me, I don't know what to do." Which creates quite a scene.

But the Tuckers are past all that now. They even have a sideline in ATM machines—it's their job to keep them filled. The first time Jeremy stocked it, he had to withdraw $3,000 from the bank. "I was so dizzy when I walked in," he says, "my sight almost went. I nearly fell over."

Life is good now for the Tuckers. Ron has a fruit business, selling the stuff door to door, and Jeremy is starting a flooring company with two friends. Christy's thinking about becoming a flight attendant. And their daughters are getting married. The girl who was left on the shelf, Julie, married a Mormon doctor and moved to Texas. It wasn't the happiest occasion, though, because they married in the Salt Lake Temple, so Christy and Ron weren't allowed in, which left a sour taste. But the family's together and happy and, other than Julie, free from religion. There's no church, no doctrine any more.

"The freedom is exhilarating," says Christy. "It's easier to breathe now that I don't have to lie anymore. I see honesty as a privilege. And I hate it when I'm forced to lie, even if someone asks me if they look good in this dress and they don't!"

But the Order will never be out of their lives entirely. It's in their heads. When Ron went to a Subway for lunch the other day, he thought of the Order. He'd been going there for a sandwich every day, and then one day, the guy behind the counter acknowledged him—he said, "Hi." But Ron flinched. "My first reaction was, 'I'm not going back there again. I don't want anybody noticing me.' That was how I grew up. I spent my whole life trying to stay hidden." He made a point of going back the next day.

Several of the Tuckers' relatives remain in the group. Some even remain in contact, filling them in on the gossip, their own family news. It's rare for them to see Order members anymore—the only times are at funerals, excruciatingly awkward affairs. But every so often, one of the Order kids will come by their house, in secret, to talk to them and see what life outside the Order is like.

That's what the Tuckers hope for these days. They want to be there for anyone else who, like them, wants to leave, but doesn't know where to turn. And they want to warn the world about the Order. That's why they're talking to me. They see the newspapers and the way polygamy is becoming more acceptable, and they worry that the truth is being distorted. The Order is something to fear, they say. It's not *Big Love*.

"They want to control the world," says Christy. "And I know that sounds ridiculous, but that's what they're trying to do. And they're doing it by breeding. I don't want to stay in Utah because there's a good chance my grandkids might marry a Kingston boy. By that stage, they might be running the state government. In twenty years you're not going to know who's a Kingston and who isn't."

It's the numbers that worry them. When I ask my friends in L.A. to guess how many children the seven brothers have between them, I hear 200 or 300. Not even close. According to Rowenna and the Tapestry lawyers, the number is over 650.

Ron grabs a calculator. "Okay, that's just Ladonna's seven sons," he says tapping away. "So if just half of their kids keep breeding at the same rate, that's . . . 90 children each. Hold on—that's nearly 30,000. In one generation. And if half of 30,000 has 90 kids each . . . that's nearly 1.5 million. And a generation in the Order is just twenty years. They're breeding themselves into political power. At meetings, they pass a piece of paper around with the candidate's name you're supposed to vote for. The Order always votes as a block. Soon they'll have enough to sway the statewide elections. Elden prophesied that they would control the world after the destructions."

It's the usual prophecy of doom: When the apocalypse comes and God purges the world of wickedness, the Order will rise and rule the Earth for a thousand years. And the day is fast approaching. True to fundamentalist form, the destructions are a common topic at meetings.

"Everyone was just waiting for it because life was such drudgery—'Oh when the destruction comes!'" says Jeremy. "They taught us that we'd be able to just walk up to the mansions on the hill and just take whichever one you want because all the Gentiles will be killed."

"There's going to be a race war—that's another teaching," says Ron. "They call it the white horse prophecy—it was supposedly given by Joseph Smith. Basically there's a white horse, a black horse and a red horse. The black horse attacks the white horse—which is the race war—and just when it looks like the white race will be annihilated, the red horse steps up and saves them. That's the American Indians atoning for what they did to the Nephites."

"Yeah, that's why we need weapons and ammunition to protect our homes."

There's no shortage of guns and ammo in the Order. Ron remembers the time when one of the seven brothers bought "stacks of AR-15s and HK223s and 308s. I bought a couple from him. He had all kinds of semi-auto pistols and stuff." Ron's friends would Sheetrock guns into their walls at home. And at the Dixon building on Third South and Third West—in the days when it belonged to the Order—"they stashed about thirty assault rifles for when the government collapses. Everyone had ammunition—we got it for wholesale prices. I've still got cases of it downstairs. Thousands of rounds. I was so ready!"

Of course the fear is that the Order's guns might one day be used for harm—the traditional cult scare that the prophet might command his followers to violence. And with polygamy's track record of religious-inspired violence, it's hard to dismiss these fears out of hand. Not least because the Tuckers don't.

"Oh, the younger ones are waiting for that," says Jeremy. "I even talked to guys who said, 'If only Paul would give the word, we could go do it . . .' They're one revelation away."

They said the same about Warren Jeffs—former followers who spoke with the credibility of cult insiders about Jonestowns and terrorist attacks. But they didn't happen. And it sounds improbably hysterical, this idea that Paul Kingston has an army at his feet, ready to kill at his command—it can't be true. But why would the Tuckers take this stuff so seriously? They're reasonable people, they have no motive to exaggerate or lie. They're not selling their story or hustling for a book deal or appearing on television regurgitating soundbites about the American Taliban. They're not raising money for a foundation. There's no outstanding civil suit, no bid for a settlement—they have nothing tangible to gain from the Order's demise.

I tell them about Carleen's version of the Order—a world of free agency and mixed socks where there's no mention of a race war or guns or poverty. And they laugh, all of them—Christy, Ron, Jeremy, the kids.

"Carleen's just being a good Order member," says Ron. "She's never going to tell you the truth. She's protecting the Order, that's her only reason for talking to you."

It's past 1:00 AM now. We've been talking for eight hours straight. The kids are yawning and slinking off to bed. But Ron can't stop. Each memory drags out another like tissues from a box, and he can't rest until he's told me everything. He runs downstairs and returns with a box full of Order stuff. Pay slips, letters, family photos. He shows me the Order's credit system, how a green card meant you had to okay the amount at the office, and yellow meant you had a limit. "Look, this is me and Hyrum there in the photo. That's Paul in this one." The emotions are complicated—he wants to explain but he's not sure I'd ever understand what these people once meant to him and what they mean now.

"See this," says Ron. "This is the only present Ortell gave me." He shows me a pocket tape measure that runs for all of ten feet. It says MASTER MECHANIC on it. "It was the one time in his life that he actually thought about me. He gave me this in 1986, the Christmas before he died. He bought my mom a big box of them to give to all the kids."

My first thought is, if he bought a box of them, then Ortell wasn't really thinking about Ron, not personally anyway. But I can't bring myself to say so. Not now. He's holding his tape measure tenderly, turning it over in his hands.

"I remember when my mom handed it to me, I just got so choked up I couldn't talk. And she thought I was offended, like I expected a better present. But I told her, you know, how happy I was to get it. And I still . . . I'd be really bothered if something happened to it. It's a family tie, I guess. I don't know how to explain it. He's still my dad."

"But Ron, he didn't care about you," I tell him.

"I know, I know. He never once called me to see how I was doing. I always knew that if I never called him again, it would probably never dawn on him that I wasn't around. Now I can look back and see how he really was, and what he was doing. I remember as a kid reading about slave owners in the South, how they'd have children with some of their slaves, and then bring those kids in to be slaves in their houses. And that was hard for me to imagine—how could a father do that? But that was exactly what Ortell did. He had his favored family. And he had other families that he knew would be their servants."

It's 1:30 AM. Christy's exhausted. I'm worn out myself. The kids are asleep. And Ron's standing there, looking at his tape measure and looking at me. He's okay. He's holding it together.

◈ Pure Fruit

> They made their father drink wine that night also, and the younger daughter went in, and lay with him . . . So the two daughters of Lot were with child by their father.
>
> **—Genesis 19:31–36**

> No man can cause more grief than that one clinging blindly to the vices of his ancestors.
>
> —William Faulkner

Ask other fundamentalists about the Kingstons and they respond, "Oh, just lovely people, very good businessmen and the children are *so* well

behaved, but—well, I shouldn't say, but they do, you know, practice . . .
incest." A shake of the head. A sigh. Such a shame that such fine people
should go and ruin it like that. As though the child labor, the slave wages,
the exploitation, that's all just fine. But consanguinity? Now, they're letting the side down.

Other groups are typically hesitant to throw stones, given the "glass
house" factor. But for the Kingstons, incest has an added dimension; it's
more than just an occupational hazard, an inevitable by-product of a
limited gene pool—it's doctrine, a facet of the group's blood obsession,
the idea that its lineage goes back to Jesus, even to Abraham. Blood as a
spiritual birthright. And the doctrinal precedent is right there in the Book
of Mormon. The Book of Abraham tells how Sarah, Abraham's wife, was
Abraham's half sister. From this marriage sprung forth the chosen seed of
Israel.

Today, there's so much incest going on in the Order that the family
trees contort like grape vines wrapping around each other. From the cult's
inception, incest has been one of its greatest stigmas and weaknesses, particularly in terms of the risk of prosecution. But the Order shows no sign
of phasing it out—quite the opposite. Incest is on the rise. Ortell had a
bigger appetite for consanguinity than his father, Elden, and likewise
Ortell's children, the seven brothers, are all maintaining the tradition with
gusto. According to information provided by Rowenna and the Tuckers
to the attorney general's office, Paul has married at least three of his half
sisters; his brother Daniel has married four; David has notched up several
nieces and half sisters, as has Jesse. And Porno Joe married his aunt.

And yet there has been little prosecution over the years. Since attorney
general Mark Shurtleff took office in 2000, there have only been two incest
convictions, and each time as an adjunct charge to a crime of statutory
rape. Mary Ann's uncle/husband David was successfully convicted in
1999, and a year later Mary Ann's cousin Luann Kingston fled the cult
too, charging Jeremy, her nephew/cousin/husband. He served just under a
year.[41] Of the two, only Luann has spoken publicly about her experience, a
happy story because she managed to leave with both of her children—or
as her aunt Coreen accused, "You took pure-breeds out of the Order." She
herself is a pure-breed, an Ortell clone like Ron Tucker; she has the same
pale complexion, the dark hair and glasses. Now remarried to a Mormon,

they live in a small home in Roy, with five children, two from her marriage to Jeremy.

"So I wanted to talk to you about incest, Luann," I begin. And she puts her finger to her lips. We must wait for her children to fall asleep. She doesn't want them to hear this. It's not just the incest. In the Order, incest is part of a broader and more disturbing picture of underage sexuality, abuse and secrecy.

Luann was both Ortell's daughter and niece. Before marrying her mother Mary (number three), Ortell had married Mary's sister, Coreen (number one). But there was never any warmth, paternal or avuncular, in her life. From the off, her family fell out of favor because Ladonna, the all-powerful second wife, felt threatened by Mary; she didn't like Ortell going over to Mary's house, so she'd pull all kinds of tricks to stop him. "She would come with him sometimes and sleep on the couch," says Luann. "Then suddenly, she'd be having a miscarriage or something, moaning and crying so they wouldn't forget she was there. On my mom's wedding day, Ortell didn't come over till 10 PM. And even then he didn't stay. He went back home to Ladonna."

Like Ronald, Luann spent her early years unaware that she had a father at all, let alone that it was Ortell, God's representative on Earth. When she found out, she was crestfallen. "I knew we would never have a relationship, because he was the leader and he had so many responsibilities. When he died a year later I really didn't care."

There was always abuse in the home. According to allegations made in court documents, Luann's older brother Arthur victimized not only Luann but her cousin Mary Ann and Mary Ann's sister Krista. He has never been convicted of these crimes, though he was once sued by Krista (it came to nothing). As Luann got older, she resisted, one day actually slapping him in the face. And Arthur started pounding her. "My aunt walked in on him hitting me, but she went after *me* for not staying away from *him*. Later that night, we had a family meeting and my mom read out of the scriptures and that was it—no one was actually talked to. This isn't a rare case. Since I've come out, I've heard other people say, 'I was molested in the Order,' and they just push it under the rug. I had no idea I could prosecute, I just felt helpless."

By Luann's telling, Arthur remained disturbed throughout his youth—he was kicked out of several high schools, moved from steward-ship to stewardship, from the mine to the ranch in Washakie. Now he has left the Order and married a girl named Shari with whom he has chil-dren, and Luann is convinced that those children are in danger. But there are other perspectives on Arthur. Some insist that he is a victim of abuse who was easily manipulated, and that he has changed. And then there is the Order's position, that not only was Arthur a perpetrator, but so were Luann and Mary Ann, the two girls who left, damaging the Order's reputa-tion as they went. The true victim, by this account, was Krista, who so hap-pens to remain in the cult. Krista has sued Arthur* for abuse and Luann and Mary Ann for helping him.

"They said that I was watching out for him and Mary Ann was helping him," says Luann, visibly exasperated. "They tried to come up with this lawsuit before—last time they said we knew about it but didn't do any-thing, and the judge threw it out. So now they're raising the stakes, making us accomplices. It's a thorn in my side, it's not something I want out in public, but at the same time, it wasn't my fault. It was something that hap-pened to *me*."

Questionable sexuality was a recurring feature of Luann's upbringing. At twelve she was encouraged to work in Order businesses, but to do so, she had to look older than she was, so her mother put her in short skirts and makeup. "You're not allowed to hold hands before you're engaged, and yet they say, 'Dress like a slut and come and work for us,'" she laughs. In fact, dressing sexy was a lesson that Luann was taught in school, by Daniel of all people, the man who beat Mary Ann in 1998. "Daniel flat out said that it's okay to wear something low-cut for your husband. And he would tell the twelve-year-old girls this."

Some days Luann would miss school to stay home and look after her sister Orlean's one-year-old baby because—according to Luann—he'd been beaten so badly "his face was black and blue from ear to ear." The boy's father, Jesse, was Orlean's half brother, one of Ladonna's seven sons. Luann alleges that he would take her into the bathroom, with her little boy, and show her how to discipline him properly. "That was why I had to stay home, because she wasn't allowed to take him out of the

---

*Arthur has refused to respond to repeated requests to interview

house—if the neighbors saw, they'd call DCFS [Department of Child and Family Services]. And this was a regular thing until the boy learned to mind."

Since both of Luann's sisters are married to Ladonna's sons—to their half brothers, in other words—a similar fate awaited her. And sure enough, when she turned fifteen, her mother engineered a meeting with Paul in his office. Shortly afterward she was put to work in Paul's office, where she was told, within weeks, that Jeremy was asking for her. Jeremy's mother was Luann's mom's sister, making him a first cousin; but Jeremy's father was Luann's half brother, making him a nephew. Luann would be his fourth wife.

She reluctantly submitted to the marriage. It was a miserable life. She lived with her mother, and every four days or so, Jeremy would show up, expecting a tidy house and dinner on the table. At first she rebelled, but that just led to screaming arguments. And then Jeremy accused her of cheating, with the Order's hierarchy rallying to his support. One day at church, a tearful Ladonna told Luann, "You know Jeremy deserves better." The Prophet Paul told Luann to stop the betrayal. Her pleas of innocence counted for little. No one trusted her because she'd been close friends with Mary Ann.

So Luann escaped. She discreetly stashed whatever money she had, packed her belongings and, with the help of Ron and Christy Tucker's daughter Julie, moved out. It was a nerve-wracking time. Her sister was in the house that day, so Luann took her kids and went to meet Julie a mile away to decide on when to move. And she saw that Julie had brought thirty people from the local Mormon church to come and help her—a whole fleet of trucks, at her disposal. Reality struck. She was leaving the Order. It was happening. She went straight back to the house with her kids to finish packing, but she found her sister there waiting, hysterical. Somehow she had figured out what was happening.

"She ran up to the car and was banging on the window, screaming 'You give me those kids, you do not deserve those kids.' So I just sped out of there and left the kids with Christy's sister Cathy. That was when we did the move. It was amazing. It took them an hour and we were done."

The Order has always tried to keep its pure-breeds away from public scrutiny, particularly the ones who don't come out as perfect as God intended. Whether the Order's share of birth complications and disabilities is any greater than in society at large is impossible to say, but the anecdotal evidence is disturbing. Luann has no shortage of examples.

"I have a half brother Russell who married his cousin on his mom's side, Debbie, and they have three kids with microcephaly. That's the one where they have the smaller heads? His second wife has one too and there were also dwarves in Merlin Kingston's family." Merlin is John Ortell's brother, one of the oldest patriarchs in the group. He made it a point to marry several nieces and to have their children intermarry; this produced three dwarfs and two deaths due to multiple deformities.[42] According to Luann, stillbirths are common. "Daniel's son Job married his cousin on his mother's side, and they had a baby that didn't have eyes or arms or legs—it was basically a tomato, is how they explained it. That's what people said it looked like."[43]

Luann alleges that they buried the "tomato" in the backyard without a word to the authorities—no report made of a birth or a death. And, according to Ortell's warped theology, these casualties of interbreeding were excusable, the product of sin, if anything. "His explanation was that any perfect child will be worth any number of stillborns or mutations." By Luann's reckoning, several tiny, mangled skeletons have been fed to the worms in Kingston backyards.

"My neighbor Spring was one of Paul's wives," says Luann. "She was also his half sister. She was due around the same time as my second child, and everybody's cars were at her place in the middle of the day—her mom's, Paul's, her sister-in-law Hannah's . . . And just when I was coming home, Hannah was leaving, so I said, 'Oh, did Spring have her baby?' First she acted like she didn't hear me, so I said it louder. And she's like, 'Yeah, she had a boy,' but she looked like she'd been crying. And the next thing I know, Spring's outside, with her oldest kid, and she hasn't got her baby. She was trying to avoid me, so I didn't say anything to her. It was just a weird situation. Then I heard from the girls at the office that the baby was stillborn. But Spring acted like it never happened. They don't announce the birth or the death when that happens. They just bury the baby."

When I asked Carleen about incest, she didn't exactly deny it. "Sure, we absolutely think anything involving underage children is wrong and we don't approve," she said.

"But, I don't mean children necessarily. I'm talking about a brother and a sister getting married."

"Absolutely, if an older brother was to abuse a younger sister, then that's abuse."

"What if they're both of age?"

"If they're consenting adults, then, well, I personally wouldn't do it, but we don't think the law should have anything to say about it."

"Isn't there a danger of genetic mutations in the children?"

"That's really so exaggerated in the media. They did a research project on it and the chance of having a healthy baby for a couple that's not practicing incest is 97 percent and the chance for a couple that is practicing incest is 94 percent. So it's only a 3 percent difference."

"So if a brother wants to marry his sister, you believe they should be allowed to do so, as long as they're consenting adults?"

"I don't think they should be prosecuted."

And this is the crux of the Order's argument, that consenting adults should be free to marry regardless of their familial relationship. It's a tactical shift away from the traditional polygamist line about freedom of religion and constitutional rights. This time the argument is one of sexual freedom, plucked straight from the liberal playbook, a line of reasoning better suited to the ACLU. Still, it's a better argument than some of the others that have been raised around this issue. Like the one about how incest has been around for ages, or "it's in the Bible," both of which apply equally well to slavery[44] and infanticide.[45] Or the one that almost found traction at the fundamentalist youth rally organized by Principle Voices in 2006. Some of the Order children wanted to wear slogans reading "So you think I should never have been born?" Their elders talked them out of it in the end, but only out of fear of raising the incest issue at all. After all, incest is a much harder sell than polygamy. On the continuum of sexual sins from premarital sex right up to bestiality, incest is way up there, two stops past polygamy.

Anyway, isn't the answer to that question, "Yes, of course you shouldn't have been born"? If you agree with the laws against incest, or rape for that matter, then you don't want to see children born that way. And incest is always a queasy subject. The narcissism alone is hideous—it's as close as you can get to breeding with yourself. But I've always believed that the chief argument against it is the one about birth defects—incest increases

the risk of malformed babies, just as drunken driving increases the risk
of an accident. It's the victims who make the case, which is why Carleen's
burst of scientific research is intriguing. Is she right? Does incest really
only increase the risk by 3 measly percent?

As it turns out, no. But she's right about one thing. As Dr. Robin Bennett, the senior genetic counselor from the University of Washington
explains, "The taboo of consanguinity far outweighs the actual health
risks." In other words, it's not as bad as we think. Dr. Bennett was part of
the team that produced the research document that Carleen was probably
quoting, a paper that estimated the increased risk of health problems for
the offspring of first cousins.[46] For congenital effects, the increased risk
was only 2.8 percent, but for the much broader category of "adverse medical outcome," the figure went up to 31 percent. And yet, surely the latter
category is the most meaningful? We fear medical problems, sickness and
disability—what does it matter if they set in at birth or when you're fifteen
or even older? To fixate upon conditions that are only obvious at birth, like
cleft palates, while ignoring metabolic problems and mental disabilities,
which may transpire over years, is akin to building a case against drunk
driving solely on fatalities rather than on all the other casualties.

Furthermore, the research concentrates on first-cousin unions, the only
type for which there exists any half-reliable data. In the Order, however,
many of the marriages are at least one step closer than that. While geneticists describe first cousins as third-degree relatives (because they have
one-eighth of their genes in common), they describe uncles and nieces,
for example, or half siblings, as second-degree relatives (they have one
quarter of their genes in common). First-degree relatives are parents and
children, or siblings. The rate of health defects does not double in proportion with the number of shared genes—health problems aren't quite so
algebraic—and there's no clinical research even to guess what the rate of
defects might be for unions between second-degree family members. But
it's safe to assume that the risks increase. "We assume the risks are somewhere between those of first cousins and those of first-degree relatives,"
says Dr. Bennett. "But the risks have also likely been overestimated."

Still, the Order keeps compounding these risks. While the research
focuses on one generation of first-cousin incest, the Order has practiced
much closer incest for successive generations, going back seventy years

or more in some cases. There are many children in the Order who have only one grandfather, for example—that is, their parents are half siblings. Should the offspring of this half sibling union mate with the offspring of a second half sibling union, which again shares the same father, then the risk increases.

Certainly the health problems, when they arise, can be horrendous. For example, in 2005 the *Phoenix New Times* reported that up to twenty children in Short Creek had a rare and incurable genetic disorder known as fumarase deficiency, a condition that had hitherto only exhibited a few cases worldwide.[47] It's a punishing affliction—symptoms include severe mental retardation and physical deformities, acute epileptic seizures, an inability to walk or sit upright, severe speech impediments. According to researchers, thousands within the FLDS—all of them descendants of the Barlow and Jessop families, which comprise almost half the population—may carry the recessive gene that causes the condition. (A recessive gene is the kind where if you have one, then you don't manifest the disorder, but if you have two, you do.) Once members of the two families began to breed, this recessive gene was passed along very quickly and broadly, as is the way in a limited polygamous mating pool. And the chances of their children carrying two genes and therefore manifesting the disorder increased dramatically. This is how risk magnifies through a program of inbreeding.

But Dr. Bennett maintains that if the mating pool were free of these recessive genes, then incest might not increase the risk of health problems at all. And the data that exists on the subject is so sparing and problematic—and there are so many other complicating factors—that it's difficult to isolate the incest risk from all the others. "The studies haven't separated out if there was fetal alcohol syndrome involved," she says, "and sometimes in incest cases women try to abort their pregnancies because they've been raped. We really don't know what the risks are."

In fact, she maintains, the whole health-risks argument is shallow. "I find it kinda crazy really. I mean, a lot of women take risks when they have children. Women with diabetes risk their children having all sorts of problems, but we don't forbid them from having children. Women who are older have a greater chance of problems, but we don't say you can't have babies after you're thirty-five. I think the scientific argument to say that you can regulate someone's reproductive life is immoral. It's not an official position, but I feel pretty strongly that it's not anyone's business whether you should have a child or not. And that's not to minimize that there are genuine risks associated with consanguinity."

One by one the arguments against incest seem to be faltering. The popular myths exaggerate the risks, the scientific data isn't sufficient to support them and anyway, the risks argument is immoral. What's more, there are, in the annals of consanguinity, several extraordinary cases that appeal to our sense of injustice. They're usually along the lines of a brother and sister who are separated at birth, meet up later as adults entirely unaware of their former connection, and fall in love. Should they be prosecuted for their marriage? What if they've been together for years already? That was the case with Allen and Patricia Muth from Wisconsin, who had several children together— they lost their appeal in 2005 and were both sentenced to prison terms of eight and five years respectively.[48] And of course, it seems wrong, particularly in the light of the Supreme Court's *Lawrence* decision, which appeared to establish that the law would not impose a moral standard on matters of private, sexual practice between consenting adults.

But the incest law will not topple so easily. In fact, in Utah, which already goes further than many states by forbidding first-cousin marriages— unlike, say, California—the law is in the process of being strengthened. In May 2008, three brothers from the notorious LeBaron family found DNA evidence to show that their polygamist father, Ross Wesley LeBaron Jr., had fathered children with his own daughters, in accordance with the so-called pure seed doctrine.[49] The accused claimed that they used artificial insemination, thereby slipping through a loophole in Utah law, but a bill has since been passed to close that very loophole and lengthen the statute of limitations from four to eight years after the act is committed. Esteemed geneticists including Nobel Prize winner Mario Capecchi from the University of Utah have come forward to declare that parent-child couplings have an exponentially greater risk of genetic defects in children than do first-cousin matches.[50]

Society does require a prohibition on incest, and the most compelling reason is to protect its children. The key issue isn't the biological link between the sexual partners—incest laws apply to stepparent and stepchild relationships, too. Nor is it that there has been an abuse of authority in these cases; there are abuses of authority in the business world too, but no one's arguing that a boss screwing his secretary is in any way equivalent. The best reason for prohibiting sexual relationships with nieces, daughters, sisters or first cousins is to prevent the normalization of sexual attraction in these relationships. To legalize the uncle-niece union would sexualize a relationship that begins long before the age of consent. Uncles could legitimately view their eleven-year-old nieces as potential partners as soon as they come of age; they could legitimately begin the process of seduction, just as the Order boys did with Christy's daughters. And this can only impoverish and endanger children.

In fact, the Order is an example of a society in which these sexual taboos have not only been normalized but protected by a culture of secrecy, one that employs decoy surnames to conceal biological relationships. For these reasons and others, attorney general Shurtleff, himself a high-ranking Mormon, has threatened to take a stand on more than one occasion. Sadly, nothing has come of it, so far. The last time he attempted to procure the DNA evidence he needed to prosecute, he decided to ask the Kingstons for their cooperation first—so obviously, they left town. That was in 2006, and it was no small embarrassment for the AG's office.

"It became known that we had obtained several dozen warrants," Shurtleff told me one day in his office. "We ordered them to be closed, secret, but someone—an attorney from that group or whoever—told the press and so it came out that we had these warrants set to go. The trouble was, we knew it would be difficult to serve those warrants and actually obtain DNA—how do you do that in a peaceful manner, how do you avoid looking like storm troopers coming into their churches and homes and grabbing children and swabbing their mouths? So we thought we'd take the peaceful approach and go ask their prophet to cooperate. Of course that backfired."

Shurtleff's tenure as attorney general has been at least partly defined by his approach to polygamy. It's a delicate game. On the one hand, he's trying to take down Warren Jeffs, and on the other, he's reaching out to polygamists through his Safety Net program, an effort to build bridges between polygamist groups and state agencies. But at one Safety Net meeting, he was accosted by Carleen.

"She was saying, 'Stop this, leave us alone, you don't need to go after the incest thing,'" Shurtleff told me later. "And I kept saying to her, 'Stop the practice or I will come after you.' One of the gentlemen there said, 'But what if we did the first-cousin or half sibling thing ten years ago? Are you going to put us all in prison?' And I tried to explain that if they come forward in a cooperative manner, I'm sure the judge is not going to put both parents in jail. But Carleen was just, 'No, it's none of your business.' It's very difficult. How do you do mass warrants and evidence gathering with a group that has indicated that it is not going to cooperate?"

In Texas, attorney general Greg Abbott wasn't so preoccupied with cooperation, and as a result he achieved a string of convictions, based on DNA evidence, and an understanding on the part of the FLDS that underage marriage will not be tolerated.

In Utah, with regard to the crime of incest within a cult, Mark Shurtleff appears to have made a different calculation. Over the last few years, he has preserved his good relationship with the fundamentalist community by continuing to wait for the perpetrators to "come forward." In the meantime, however, he has taken the decisive step of removing alcopops and wine coolers from Utah's supermarkets.

◆ The Sorry Ballad of Heidi and Daniel

Taking the issue of polygamy to any court in Utah is like taking the devil to court in hell.
— Letter to *The Salt Lake Tribune*, July 12, 1999

I cannot feel safe until I know [Daniel] admits he has done wrong. And I am afraid for the other members of my family who will know . . . that he can do it again, because he doesn't believe that what he did was wrong.
— Mary Ann Kingston's *Victim Impact Statement for the sentencing of Daniel Kingston—June 29, 1999*

What kind of house keeper do you think our Mother in Heaven is? Do you suppose that she rushes off leaving beds unmade and dirty dishes in the sink?
— *Order Family Handbook*

The attorney general's reticence in pursuing the Order is understandable. He would risk blowback from both church and state for again focusing attention on Utah polygamy, not to mention the prospect of a shrill fundamentalist lobby shrieking persecution. But he would also be given pause by his office's most recent skirmish with the Order. No, "skirmish" is the wrong word. The child custody case of Heidi and Daniel Kingston was a war.

The story begins with an incident eerily reminiscent of the Mary Ann Kingston episode: A hysterical fifteen-year-old girl runs down a wintry street to a nearby gas station, where she calls for help. She is fleeing a beating at the hands of her father, Daniel. And when the story ends, she will end up living happily outside the Order, with new adoptive parents, under an assumed name. Her name is Stephanie, and her crime is that she had her ears pierced without his permission.

What Stephanie unleashed with her flight to the gas station was altogether more complex and revealing about the Order than Mary Ann's case ever was. It not only exposed the cult's lifestyle, but also its methods and mindset. And, though the case generated enormous attention, the full story has never been told.

There were two girls—Stephanie and her sister Andrea—both guilty of pierced earlobes, and both placed swiftly into foster care with relatives. Stephanie appeared to rebel against her removal while Andrea embraced it, telling investigators of the harrowing life of beatings her family had suffered at Daniel's hands. And their mother, Heidi Mattingly Foster, fast became a polarizing figure. Her long record of neglect, compounded by her repeated noncompliance with court orders, eventually persuaded the court to remove ten of her children—all but her newborn baby. And yet, in the battle to win them back, Heidi also became a sympathetic rallying point. Somehow she was alone in this battle, this overburdened, pregnant and put-upon woman. Daniel was only required to provide child support payments, leaving him free to spend the rest of his time with his remaining family, an estimated fourteen other wives and 150 or so other children.[51] The case is still known as the Heidi Foster case, not the Daniel Kingston case.

News reports described a convoluted and peculiar trial. Certainly it was lengthy, with hearing after hearing and trial date after trial date as the children were moved between foster home, shelter and detention center. But certain events carried the particular ring of the Order. For instance, Daniel stumbled in court when asked to name the children he'd had by two of his alleged plural wives. "I'm going to have to count them," he said, flustered. "Stephanie, Kevin, Andrea, Jennifer, Melanie, Ronald . . . and I know I've got four other children there . . . Matthew. You'll have to excuse me, I'm very nervous up here. It's not that I don't know my children." Only after the judge warned that he might be incriminating himself did he take the Fifth.

Then a witness—Christy Tucker's son Jeremy—pointed out that one of the defense's paralegals, Laura Fuller, was also one of Daniel's wives, a fact the defense team should have revealed prior to the trial. This so irritated judge Andrew Valdez that he ejected her from the courtroom at once. But the Judge's irritation with the Order's idiosyncrasies only mounted as the proceedings went on—their preference for fictional surnames, for instance. At one hearing he demanded that the children's surnames be changed to Kingston since "it's their birthright." At another, he said, "I think we're running a child mill here," adding that if it were a puppy mill, it would have been shut down long ago.

Eventually, in an extraordinary decision, he ordered Heidi to break ties to the Order entirely—to give up her job, her interaction with her family and friends, her church. It was a straightforward attempt to break the cult's control over its followers. The guardian AD *litem*, Kristin Brewer, who represented the children in the case, claimed the measure was necessary because of the "groupthink" within the Order. But it was this move more than any other that turned the case into something that the Order had hitherto not experienced: a controversy. While Mary Ann's beating had elicited only loathing, the removal of Heidi's children aroused sympathy. It was debated in the media and camps arose on both sides. Some saw the state as the children's saviors and Heidi as one of Daniel's victims. Others saw the state as persecutor, a destroyer of families.

So the Order approached this case very differently from Mary Ann's. Harnessing the persecution complex that runs so deep through Mormonism, the Order took a stand, filling the courthouse with its members, organizing rallies and protests outside. Daniel didn't hide from the cameras this time—instead he strode boldly through the scrum of reporters to the courthouse steps and held a press conference. A website was even set up portraying Heidi as a civil rights martyr, the Rosa Parks of polygamy, a defender of the Constitution.

To counter these appeals for public sympathy, witnesses spoke of neglect, abuse, indoctrination, exploitation—even a sinister conspiracy to bomb the courthouse, invade the foster homes and kidnap the kids. Order members got into an altercation with the judge's son outside the courthouse, leading to the judge's removal from the case. Kingston detractors insist that old-school intimidation tactics went a long way to explaining why the new judge eventually granted the Order a victory of sorts.

Today, only Stephanie and Andrea live in new homes with new families under assumed identities. The rest of the children were returned to Heidi and Daniel, a result so demoralizing that it broke the spirits of many. Kristin Brewer resigned from her job as guardian AD *litem* and left Utah altogether, choosing to live in Washington State. Andrea Moore-Emmett, an antipolygamy journalist, left for California, as did Vicky Prunty of Tapestry Against Polygamy. I've spoken to members of the guardian AD *litem*'s office who have broken down in tears when discussing the case—this over a year after the verdict.

Heidi agrees to meet me one day at a Sizzler on Redwood Road in Salt Lake City. She promises to tell me "how it really went down, not what you read in the papers." But about half an hour beforehand, my phone rings. It's Carleen. "It's really emotional for Heidi to talk about it, so she asked if I can come along too," she says. And so they both pull up outside the restaurant in their large white vans—typical Kingston transportation, perfect for hordes of children. The Sizzler is typical too; polygamists love "buffet style."

We begin with the usual headshaking about Colorado City and Warren Jeffs. But the chitchat ceases when I bring out my recorder. I become a kind of interrogating officer, with Heidi as suspect and Carleen as her protective attorney. Her client can't confirm when she married Daniel ("Um . . . in the '80s") or what number wife she is out of Daniel's estimated fourteen ("Um . . . about halfway"). She does however let on that she was sixteen, half Daniel's age, when he asked her parents for her hand in marriage. They were married within weeks.

"Did you fall in love?" I ask her.

"Of course! Duh!"

"So what's he like, Daniel?"

She looks in her bag. "Is that my phone?"

"It sounds like the dishwasher to me!" laughs Carleen.

"I have a new phone," Heidi explains, "and I'm not used to the ring yet."

"I'm like that when I get a new phone," says Carleen, still laughing. And once the hilarity dies down, we pause a moment and resettle in our chairs.

"Can you describe Daniel?" I ask again.

"What like, five ten, gray hair?"

"No, what kind of a person is he?"

"Busy. Very busy." She looks to Carleen. "Help me out . . ."

And Carleen puts on her serious face and tilts her head to one side. "I'd say he's humorous, he's always cracking jokes. And he's actually one of the nicest men I've ever met. He was my supervisor at work for ten years, and he treated me like his own daughter." Presumably not his daughter Mary Ann, whom he beat unconscious in a barn one night. "That's why when the stuff came out in the media, I thought, 'That's not the man I know.' I've encouraged him to tell his story, but he won't, out of love and respect for his daughter. We told him, 'Tell your side, tell your side,' but he said, 'I don't want to hurt people . . .'"

From the outset, it seems, Carleen wants me to believe that Daniel, who pleaded no contest to battering his daughter Mary Ann, is not only innocent, but also a lovely man with a big heart and a great sense of humor. The kind of man, it wouldn't surprise me to hear, upon whose shoulders little songbirds are known to land. Why such a saint would accept public desecration and wrongful incarceration, neither Carleen nor Heidi will explain. "We're not here to tell that story," clips Carleen.

No, the story they're here to tell concerns a poor young mother and her brood, whose lives the state set out to ruin because they belonged to a polygamous church. It all started in 1994 when one of her kids called 911 for a lark and when the cops showed up, they found a young girl of nine or ten tending to six younger children. A caseworker was assigned to the family and little else came of it until 1996 when a school secretary alerted the DCFS that Stephanie repeatedly came to school tired because, she said, she was tending a baby at night. At the time, Heidi was living in a small three-bedroom home in Bountiful with six children. When investigators visited, they found a squalid hovel of filth and stench—rotting food in the fridge, dirty dishes heaped in the sink, diapers abandoned on the floors. They immediately placed Foster's three older children in shelter care, while the younger ones were placed with kin. That was the first time the state took her children away, and they kept them for fifty-four days. The oldest was eight and the youngest, one. The DCFS monitored Foster for three years before closing that case.

"It was just one of those days when everything was wrong. I was getting ready to move up to the Washakie ranch, where the barn is, but I'd just been in a car accident where I hurt my arm—I couldn't lift stuff up. Anyway, I was halfway packed and half unpacked, I had five little kids and I wasn't cleaning the house. So, yeah, it was kind of messed up."

"So the rotting food, the dirty diapers, the flies—is that all true?"

Heidi shrugs. "I can't remember. Keep in mind that fresh diapers on the floor are still 'diapers on the floor.'"

"You're saying they were clean, but the DCFS reported them as dirty?"

"I'm saying I don't remember."

The earrings incident with Stephanie and Andrea, however, Heidi recalls with crystal clarity. She insists that it was simply a dispute between two rebellious teenagers and their parents. Daniel didn't fly into a rage as Stephanie claims. "He was perfectly calm. Stephanie just ran. I was there!" Furthermore, the blame lies with Heidi's sister, Shari, and her brother Justin's girlfriend, Shawna, because they were the ones who signed off as legal guardians at the piercing parlor when they were nothing of the sort. That was the real crime, that the state intervened against parents in a matter that ought to be the natural preserve of parental authority, and that it sided with non-Order members who had a clear agenda to corrupt their children.

Before going any further into Heidi's account, it's worth noting just how far she has already strayed from what others claim to be the truth. Shawna, for example, finds her account laughable. "Oh please! This isn't about earrings! That's what they told the papers, but that's just bullshit."

A skinny thirty-something with a thing for motorcycles and a career in victim counseling, Shawna was never part of the Order, but her then boyfriend and current husband, Justin, was. Justin is Heidi's brother. Life in the Order so traumatized him that he won't have talk of it in the house, just to keep the memories buried. But two years prior to the earrings episode, he had promised Stephanie that if she ever wanted out, he would help her. That time came when Stephanie turned fifteen and was lined up to marry her uncle, Gary Kingston,* one of Daniel's half brothers. Gary was in his early forties at the time.

"It was Gary who gave Stephanie and Andrea a ride to the mall that day, since Heidi and Daniel were out. When they got there, I believe they ran into Shari, Heidi's sister," says Shawna. "And Shari was like, sure, go get your ears pierced, I don't care."

Later that evening, on a Sunday in February, Shawna was watching *The Simpsons* when the phone rang. It was Shari, screaming hysterically: "He's going to kill her! You gotta do something!" Stephanie had bolted from Daniel's office, run to a gas station and called Shari, shaking with fear at what Daniel might do. According to Shari, his rage was less about earrings than about their seeing Shari, an ex-Order member and apostate.

In the end, the police arrived before Shawna even left the house— they'd been summoned by the gas station owner. They found nothing particularly egregious at hand and sent Stephanie home with Daniel. But Shawna and Shari were determined not to let Stephanie's cry for help go unanswered, particularly since Stephanie kept calling. It was Presidents' Day weekend and Stephanie spent much of it talking to Shari. She wanted to leave but she didn't know how or whether it was right or what would happen next. So on Tuesday morning, Shawna went to the courthouse and filed a protective order for Stephanie and Andrea. And by Wednesday evening, she was outside the Order school with a police escort to collect them both—they were to live with her for the interim. She only found Andrea; Stephanie wasn't around. "They were hiding her," says Shawna. The Order had learned about the protective order. "So for two days we looked all over the valley. We found her in Daniel's office on Friday."

Needless to say, Heidi's account is wildly different. She accuses Shawna of meddling and lying and being an irresponsible guardian. She says that Shawna's home was too small to accommodate the girls, so Shawna would leave them at Shari's house instead, where they could fall prey to Arthur,

---

*Not his real name

Shari's husband—the same Arthur who had victimized Luann and Mary Ann Kingston growing up.

"The law says that any party can file a protective order on behalf of a child," says Heidi. "So you can file a protective order on Carleen's children. You can say, 'She's a bad mom, I'm scared she's going to beat those kids.' And the judge will say, 'Oh you nice kind man, here, you take custody of them for three weeks while we have a hearing to see if you were lying or not.' But you could be a child molester, a bank robber . . . there's no background check done on you."

There's actually some truth to Heidi's claims. Shawna admits that she wasn't subjected to any checks when she filed that protective order. She even admits that Arthur was a molester, though she couches it carefully. "Arthur is more a victim than a perpetrator," she says. "He was seriously abused as a child in the Order. He was whipped, forced to drink cleaning products . . . he was really on the horrific end of abuse. And between the ages of four to fifteen, it's true, he was forced to commit these sexual acts on other kids. But it was Gary who was forcing him. You know Gary, who Stephanie was supposed to marry?"

At this point, Stephanie seems to be surrounded by abusers, either sexual or physical: she's living with Arthur, she's supposed to marry Gary and her father is Daniel. But of them all, the one who most concerned Shawna was Gary, a notorious abuser about three times Stephanie's age. He was particularly dangerous because, at the time, Stephanie didn't object to marrying him. In fact, she rather liked him.

"It sounds incredible, but the Order is all the girls know," says Shawna. "And they're supposed to marry who they're supposed to marry. And Gary seemed nice compared to other Order men. After Daniel threw one of his rages, Gary would come over and help Heidi out, whether that meant money or fixing something or whatever. He comforted Stephanie and she would confide in him. He's a predator, basically."

Shawna maintains that Gary was in regular touch with Stephanie during her first two weeks at Shari's house. He encouraged her to rebel against her custody. "One time, Stephanie asked Shari if she could go for a walk. And Shari said, 'Of course'—she lives in a safe neighborhood. But it was just a plan Gary had concocted. He drove by and picked her up and took her off to have sex. She gave him fellatio and he performed oral sex on her. And he was very rough the way he did it. Biting labias and things. I think this all came out in court, years later."[52]

Arthur, on the other hand, was a different proposition. A damaged man, no doubt, but changed, in Shawna's view, despite the typically high recidivism rate for pedophiles. "It was absolutely safe for the girls to stay there. First, Arthur was only abusive in the Order because they forced him. And second, he worked two jobs, so he was out all the time. Shari was always there anyway. My worry was if I left the kids at *my* house, while Justin and I were at work, then Daniel would come and take them."

Heidi's take on Arthur Kingston, however, is quite different. At the Sizzler, she drops this passing bombshell: "Arthur is the real uncle who molested Mary Ann. And they know he did it, but Mary Ann wouldn't testify against him so they didn't charge him."

It's an incredible aside. On the one hand, it adds to the mystery of Arthur Kingston. While Order members tend to portray him as a heinous pederast who deserves to be punished, former members—with the exception of Luann—defend him as a victim and a reformed man. All that's certain is that he has never been convicted of these crimes, and that he's not talking.

But there are other reasons why Heidi's allegation is startling. The uncle they convicted of raping Mary Ann was David Kingston, Carleen's husband, whom Mary Ann had married. But now Heidi and Carleen are telling me that David is innocent too; Arthur was the real culprit. So the Mary Ann trial was built upon two colossal miscarriages of justice: both Daniel and David were convicted of crimes they didn't commit. Surely a case for the Innocence Project?

Within the Order, allegations have no end. They merely lead to other interconnecting rumors and lies, a labyrinth of dark tunnels like a sewer system. The only glimmers of light come from breaches in the network, when the lies are exposed and the liars shamed. When Jeremy Tucker told Judge Valdez that one of the paralegals on the case was married to Daniel, for instance. Or the time when two of Daniel's other daughters came knocking on Shawna's door, supposedly looking for Andrea, in an attempted sting operation. Shawna told them that they had to leave, owing to a protective order against the Order as a whole. "And it wasn't but minutes later that the cops show up and they want to know if I've got drugs," she says. "Turns out the girls just wanted us to open the door so they could say they'd smelled drugs. So I invited the cops in. They found nothing. And the following week we were back in court, with their star witness [Cheryl Nelson, Stephanie's half sister] on the stand. The attorney asked which drugs she smelled and she didn't know. This is what she said: 'It was just drugs.'"

According to Shawna, it was one of the Order's milder attempts to paint her and Justin as unfit custodians. Other ploys were more reckless and convoluted. Like the time Stephanie fled her custody and, with Andrea, hitched a ride downtown with a drunken stranger. By Heidi's telling, it was quite straightforward: the girls showed up at her office all but asking to come home, so she told them to go back, in accordance with the law.

But Shawna recalls an altogether more dramatic saga. Justin called her at work, at her victims' crisis center, to say the girls were missing. So she immediately reported them to the cops as runaways, praying that they would call. Eventually Stephanie did, late in the evening, panicked and scared. "She said that they'd taken the bus to go see their mom but then it got late and they didn't want to come back on their own. They were scared, so they hitched a ride with some drunk guy and he was dropping them off at the Delta Center downtown. And I don't know if this is a hoax or a kidnapping. At one point, I actually end up on my mobile to the drunk guy while I'm on the office phone to police dispatch. He wants me to go party with them, that's the only way I can get his address. But when the cops show up at his place, he's confused, he's saying, 'Wait, these girls approached *me* at a gas station, they said they needed a ride . . .' It turns out that he dropped them off and they flagged down the nearest cop with this bullshit story that they were abducted.

"Well, the next day I'm down at youth services, checking them in, because I figure they need to be at a shelter they can't run away from. And when I'm dropping them off, we have to go through their personal effects, and I find a couple of handwritten notes, which said to find a random bystander and hitch a ride. They even said what they were supposed to say when they called me. It was all written down. Someone came up with a plan to show that Justin and I were unfit to care for them. And later on, Andrea confessed, 'We saw Daniel and my mom, and they told us what to do.' But somehow we couldn't get that submitted into evidence in court."[53]

I'm not quite getting this story yet. Something's not adding up. Why do the girls want to run away from Shawna's house? Surely they'd gone to all that trouble of running away from home in the first place? And why did they tell Shawna that they'd hitched a ride with the drunk guy, but then tell the cops that they'd been abducted?

In any case, an almighty fight began to build between the Kingstons and the official agencies—DCFS, the Office of the Guardian AD *Litem* and the courts. The latter claimed that Heidi was ignoring their demands and resisting caseworkers, while Heidi insisted that she was trying to comply, but that the caseworkers were lying and trying to trip her up. On her website, Heidifoster.org (no longer active), she launched tirades against everyone she hated, not least Judge Valdez and Kristin Brewer. "Kristin Brewer has denied the children the right to be placed with individuals of the same religion, based solely on the fact that they are members of the same religion," her website read. "When will this stop? Who will be next? Catholics, Protestants, Methodists, Christianity in general, Muslims, Judism [*sic*] the LDS? When will we tell our government that WE GET TO DECIDE WHAT WE BELIEVE NOT THE GOVERNMENT!"

Her worst ire, however, she saved for DCFS caseworker Curtis Giles, describing him as a liar and a child abuser. Even during our meeting at the Sizzler, her venom is fresh. "He lied on the stand, he lied to our faces and he called us liars," she says. "He changed appointment times without telling us to make it look like we weren't complying. And that time he visited the school . . ." Evidently Giles had asked to see the children at the Order-run school, but when he showed up, Daniel, the alleged abuser, was there to greet him, rendering the whole exercise useless. But Heidi is indignant. "One of the school policies is that the child's parent is *supposed* to be present when they bring visitors. But Curtis refused to see the kids with Daniel there, and then he told this whole story about how we were holding the kids from him." (Giles refused repeated requests to respond.)

A group of construction workers arrive at a nearby table and start making a racket. Heidi uses the diversion as an opportunity to leave, so we head for the parking lot, where Heidi clambers into her transit and drives off. So it's just me and Carleen left, and her brow's furrowed, she's full of questions. What do I think of them? Which way is this book going to go? And I can't lie to her. So I tell her I have reservations about how insular and secretive the group is, with its own school and businesses, its sense of apartness.

"No, no, we have free agency," she says. And I have to cut her short.

"Carleen, if I had a dollar for every time I hear about free agency, I'd be a rich man."

"What do you mean?"

"You're only as free as your choices. And there can be an illusion of choice. If the only restaurants on Redwood Road were Burger King, McDonald's and Wendy's, then it looks like I have a choice of what to eat. But I don't—it's all burger."

"But what about Subway?"

"Okay, but even then there's no Chinese or Mexican."

"Yes there is, we have TacoTime. And what's that one with the chicken?"

"El Pollo Loco."

"Yes!"

"The point is, you need all these options to have a choice. Just burger won't do."

"What's that got to do with us?"

"Well, Heidi can choose who she marries, right? It could be anyone. She has free agency. But she needs to stay within the Order because otherwise it might mean leaving her church."

"But what's wrong with that?"

"Nothing necessarily. But then she hears that Daniel's asking for her, and he's the leader's brother, one of the most important members of the Order. Not only that, but he's also her boss; she works for him. It's possible that Daniel also employs several other members of her family. So you can see how that already limited choice might seem even more limited . . ."

Carleen shakes her head. Now she's upset. "No it doesn't! Heidi wasn't forced, we don't do that. Heidi has a choice. We believe in free agency . . ." There's panic in her eyes and I feel sorry for her. She's become a repository for talking points, incapable of deviating even in chitchat in a Sizzler parking lot.

It's a relief to hear that Carleen can't make it for my next meeting with Heidi. I arrive early at her workplace, an Order stewardship called Advanced Copy & Printing, tucked into the corner of a little strip mall— the shops on either side *no hablo inglés*, they sell tacos, Tecate beers and phone cards. It's an odd location for a polygamist cult to set up shop, but I'm not mistaken: there's Heidi's white van in the parking lot. And the staff have that Order look, that passing resemblance to Ortell—glasses, pallid complexions, ruddy cheeks.

"Hiya!" Heidi emerges from behind the reception, sucking on an ice cream cone. "Come into my studio." Heidi's a wedding photographer, one of the more ironic jobs she could have chosen. Christy once told me about Heidi shooting a wedding with a black eye—of course she denied it was Daniel. We sit on swivel chairs in a room stuffed with boxes of frills and backgrounds and props. We've reached the part of the story at which Judge Valdez told Heidi that she could only reunify her family if she cut all contact with the Order. So she had to leave her photography job and move out of her house because she was renting it from one of the Order businesses. She was being forced into the outside world.

"A couple of hundred people showed up at the hearing," she says. "They were all in the lobby and I couldn't talk to any of them. Some knew and some didn't. And when I came out, I felt like I was coming down the line of my own funeral."

Tears spring to her eyes. It's the first time she has cried in front of me, and it's telling that this should be the trigger. Her alienation from the Order is her most traumatic memory—not the estrangement of her daughters or their allegations of abuse. She was sent to live at the YWCA until she found a place of her own, and paranoia began to set in. She believed the attorney general had hired a burly, graying guy to follow her around and take pictures. Once, in a café around the corner from the Y, she was giving an exclusive interview to Brooke Adams of *The Salt Lake Tribune*, and the man was at the opposite table, glancing over occasionally. It so bothered her that they left and resumed the interview at Adams's house a few blocks away—a surprisingly cozy relationship between the Order and the *Tribune*'s polygamy reporter.

But her time at the Y was brief. The fundamentalist community was quick to rally, providing Heidi with a substantial loan for a down payment on a house, complete with movers, transport, everything she needed. A relative of Daniel's called Becky loaned her $3,000, no questions asked; Mary and Gary Batchelor helped box up her stuff; the Kelsch family, also associated with Principle Voices, helped with the packing and moving, and they let her stay at their place for that first night. None of these people knew Heidi before the trial. It was an outpouring.

But new home or not, little changed. Heidi continued to fall foul of the DCFS, and her children were moved out of the shelter and into a series of foster homes, setting off a convolution of visiting rights and times—for Heidi to see her kids with the proper supervision, for the kids to see their siblings, for the state caseworkers to see the kids and so on. And straight-away, the reports were disturbing. Eight of the children in foster care were found to have twenty-eight cavities between them. "Oh please," scoffs Heidi. "Did you know that one tooth can have several cavities?" Curtis Giles reported that Daniel used his time to give the children copies of the story of the biblical Daniel and tell them that their plight was a similar case of being persecuted for their beliefs. Giles also reported that the children were terrified of Daniel's visits.

Then Penny Hayes, a foster mother to four of Heidi's younger children, testified that the two girls, Jennifer and Kimberly, aged seven and five, were masturbating so often they were making themselves sore. She said they would pray while lying flat on their backs, legs spread apart. And when a female pediatrician attempted to conduct a vaginal exam, the older girl said, "Only the hand of God touches down there." Hayes said the girl had told her she usually felt the hand of God when she prayed with her father. The children were reported to be so scared of Daniel that they would literally soil themselves in fear before visits. Hayes testified that all the children between two and seven had bed-wetting problems that got worse before and after visits by both Kingston and Foster. On one day of Daniel's visits, the four-year-old, Michael, soiled his pants three times. When Hayes was cleaning him up one day in the bathroom, Michael asked her if she was going to hurt him. "I said, 'No, I'm not going to hurt you.' 'You're not going to stick your finger up there?' And I said, 'No, I would never do that . . .'"

Hayes's testimony of December 14, 2004 was disturbing stuff. She reported that not only Michael was afraid of being hurt at home, but Kimberly too, and Jennifer was worried that Daniel wouldn't be happy with her. "I didn't tell them they were going to see their parent one day and it was just fine," Hayes told the court. "Then we go in the car and 'Where are we going?' 'We're going to see your dad.' And by the time we got there Kimberly was uncontrollable, she was angry and upset. Jennifer was rude and she was bossy and jumpy. And Michael had wet his pants. And Ronald had messed his pants." Michael, who was four, once told Hayes that she was "Satan's whore" because she wore jewelry and could no longer have children. Apparently, the children considered many things in her home "evil" and "bad."

Heidi dismisses this all with a roll of the eyes. "Oh, Penny Hayes! It's all hearsay. First of all, our kids wouldn't say 'the hand of God'—they think 'God' is a swearword. They say 'heavenly Father.' They would have said 'hand of heavenly Father.' So we know they never said that. And the evidence that they had all came from an eye exam! Daniel even subpoenaed it." I ask Heidi for a copy of this eye exam—which seems to have nothing whatsoever to do with eyes—but nothing comes of it.

According to DCFS reports, Foster used her visits to turn her children against the state, the foster families and the court—whispered messages, private conferences in the bathroom. A court-appointed attorney for the children said that some of them were scared that the food in their foster homes was poisoned. And all the while, Daniel was reneging on payments. When Judge Valdez ordered him to pay $3,100 per month to Heidi in support, his lawyer Daniel Irvin pleaded that his gross income was only $2,200, a laughable amount, considering the size of his family. Judge Valdez shot back: "Maybe he should get another job or change career so he can pay for these kids."

One of the ugliest aspects of the trial was the ease with which Heidi and the Order's lawyers painted Andrea as a liar. "I think Andrea's testimony speaks for itself," Daniel Irvin told the Judge. "She lies for people that she likes, she lies to hurt people that she doesn't like." Irvin went on to attack the twelve-year-old's testimony for its lack of sufficient detail: "Some people say that you should remember a traumatic event but she doesn't remember if she was three or if she was four, if it was 1994 or 1995, it may have been warm, it may not have been warm. Her testimony is all over the place."

Andrea was an easy target because she was a lone voice. While she'd testified at length about Daniel's brutality—how he beat his children with a two-by-four, forced them to drink their own throw-up and dragged her pregnant mother down the stairs—her older sister Stephanie had told investigators that Daniel never beat his children, he just spanked them gently, never leaving any marks. Stephanie's sanitized picture flatly contradicted Andrea's bloody version. Having sparked the whole saga by fleeing Daniel's office, she appeared to perform an about-face, pleading to be allowed to return home to her family, whom she claimed to love.

As it turned out, Stephanie was just protecting herself in case she actually was sent back to the Order. Unlike Andrea, she had run away before, in 2001, only to be returned to her family, so this time, she was making a show of rebelling against the state and defending her family. But she did great damage to Andrea's credibility in the process. Still today, Heidi insists that Andrea is mentally unstable. "They diagnosed her as PTSD and I think she had a mental breakdown when they took her away," she says. "So she could have believed it was true when she said it. They really did a job on her, they had her on all kinds of antidepression drugs[54] . . . Basically you have nine kids saying, 'We're happy at home, no one hurt me, I miss my dad.' And one kid who's saying different. And she's the one who everyone believes."

"Andrea said Daniel threw you down the stairs. Did he?"

"No."

"Has Daniel ever beaten you or any of your children?"

"No. But you see, this is how the system sees it: If I can't admit that I'm a victim of domestic violence, then it's going to happen again. So I'm stuck: Do I get on the stand and lie? Or do I tell the truth and not get my kids back?"

"Is it possible that you were in denial? And these agencies were actually trying to protect you and your kids?"

"Well, you'd think that, but I knew they wanted to charge us criminally. They wanted me to testify against Daniel. Absolutely. That's why they wanted me to admit there was abuse. Me and my attorney were seriously trying to figure out how to admit to something without perjuring ourselves, but he said, 'You can't go on that stand and lie. If they ask you a question, take the Fifth Amendment.'"

Monday, February 8, 2005, was a particularly strange day in the trial.

Heidi was over at Becky's house in Riverton when Judge Valdez called, telling her to come to an emergency hearing. "I said, 'What hearing?' And he said, 'We decided to have one. You've got thirty minutes to get here.' I found out later he did the same thing with Daniel. So when I got there, Daniel was sitting there. That was the first time I'd seen him in four months. And there was media everywhere. They'd all been prenotified about this hearing but we hadn't."

Security was tight at the courthouse that day. Officers checked cars as they came in. A dozen bailiffs milled about in the lobby; others stood guard in the court itself. And the day's testimony would reveal why. Stephanie told the court how two of her half sisters, Cheryl and Krista Nelson, and her uncle Gary had concocted plans to abduct the children from their foster homes, and how they'd made death threats against the judge, the children's foster families, the caseworker Curtis Giles and state attorneys.

Carolyn Nichols (attorney general's office): What were the threats against Kristin Brewer?

Stephanie: That they was going to run her car off the road, blow her building up, shoot her.

The court: Shoot her? Did you say 'shoot her'?

Stephanie: Yeah.

Carolyn Nichols: Now, who was speaking about the threats against Kristin Brewer?

Stephanie: Gary.

Carolyn Nichols: Now you mentioned Judge Valdez. How is he going to be harmed?

Stephanie: Blow up the courthouse.

The court: Any other specific threats against me, besides blowing up the building?

Stephanie: Yeah, they would follow you around and take pictures of you so you would want to give the kids back to my mom so that would stop.[55]

The context of these admissions was that an Order member, Ethan Tucker, had been questioned by security officers after he was spotted photographing the area around the Matheson Courthouse in the middle of the night. And the two foster mothers who'd been caring for the girls' siblings testifying that they'd been followed by individuals later identified as Kingston relatives. It set the entire proceedings on edge. It transpired that cops had kept Judge Valdez's home under surveillance all weekend, and the judge had no idea why until he heard the testimony.

But perhaps the most disturbing revelation was the plan involving Stephanie's suicide. Quite why the Order might want Stephanie to kill herself is unclear—perhaps to deter other Order children against running away? Or to demonstrate to the state agencies just how distressing it was for children to be separated from their family and faith? Whatever the reason, it was a shock to Shawna when it came up. "It was the day when Stephanie went to her therapist," says Shawna. "And she said, 'I don't want to kill myself.' And the therapist was like, 'No shit!' That was when Stephanie finally stopped protecting her parents." The therapist contacted investigators at the attorney general's office who in turn notified Shawna about the potential threat and transferred the kids to a safe house.

Needless to say, Judge Valdez looked upon this all very gravely. But to Heidi, it was all high theater, wild exaggerations orchestrated to paint the Order in as scary a light as possible. "It's a conspiracy, it's just ridiculous, totally blown out of proportion," she says. "Ethan was taking photos at night for his homework. He was taking art classes at the community college and he'd just gotten off work at the late shift. Anyway, he was shooting the Internet shop across the street from the courthouse. I think it was a scam so that the foster homes could get free security equipment installed by the state. Penny Hayes probably got $10,000 of equipment in her house."

Certainly Heidi's mistrust of the state could scarcely have been higher when her therapists advised her to write a letter to the girls to patch over old wounds. Heidi sensed a trap. "Those letters weren't just going to the kids, they were going to the AG, the guardian AD *litem*—it was evidence for court. So I had three attorneys read my letter and make revisions. The same letter went to every kid, but I handwrote it. It was supposed to be an apology, so we worded it very carefully." The therapists said the letters weren't personal enough, so Heidi tried again, careful not to admit any wrongdoing on the part of herself or Daniel. It was at this time that her son Kevin fled a mental health facility after he'd been threatened by another boy. He ended up in a shelter and wrote three long letters describing what had happened to him. And Heidi milked the incident for all it was worth. "We sent copies to every TV station in the city. That was right before our April hearing."

The hearing only compounded the intrigue. While Heidi was on the stand, a scuffle broke out outside the courthouse between a dozen or so protestors—predominantly Order members—and the Judge's nineteen-year-old son, Tito. It seems Tito objected to the material the picketers were distributing; he found it defamatory. Ultimately, he was cited with disorderly conduct, and two days later, Judge Valdez ordered the state to begin the process of reuniting Heidi with her children. By the end of the week, he'd ruled that the visits should begin immediately and Heidi should have her children back before June. At no point had she acknowledged Daniel's abuse or her failure to protect her children. And by July, he'd left the case, saying that he could no longer be impartial, given the situation with his son. Still today, many see his exit as evidence of intimidation.

The case was transferred to judge Elizabeth Lindsley, and the momentum of recent months resulted in a decision. All the Kingston kids were sent home except for Stephanie and Andrea, for whom Heidi and Daniel had to give up their parental rights. There were court orders for Daniel to complete additional therapy and domestic violence counseling, but he paid them little heed. He reverted to his habit of failing to notify caseworkers at the DCFS when he would be visiting the children. The case continues to leave a bitter taste.

It can be argued that both sides, the Order and the state, emerged from this trial worse off. And yet in the final chapter, the victory was undoubtedly the Order's. In a state indoctrinated with the Mormon notion that "families are forever," the pressure to reunite ultimately trumped mountains of evidence of neglect, abuse and noncompliance. And at once, the conspiracy theories began to stir on the fringes—was the judge paid off, that sort of thing. But even sober observers remain starkly partisan on the case. And one issue that divides them is the media coverage of the trial, particularly in *The Salt Lake Tribune*. Those who felt betrayed by the verdict complain that Brooke Adams, the *Tribune*'s polygamy reporter, was overly sympathetic to Heidi and Daniel, and that she is overly sympathetic to polygamists in general. I've heard this from members of the relevant agencies—Kristin Brewer, Carolyn Nichols and Olivia Phelps—as well as former polygamists such as Rowenna Erickson, the Tucker family, virtually every nonfundamentalist that I came across in Utah. And on the other side of the fence, I'm yet to meet a fundamentalist who doesn't think the world of her. As Gary Batchelor says, "Brooke's a friend of fundamentalism. We like Brooke."

On May 26, for example, the day after reporters were provided with transcripts of the first interviews with both Stephanie and Andrea, Adams's story opened with this:

> They sound like two mixed-up teenagers who balk at their parents' rules—and are occasionally punished for it—but also are savvy when it comes to protecting their family's polygamous lifestyle. As far as evidence of wide ranging abuse, it doesn't come out in the pages of written transcripts of videotaped interviews with two daughters of John Daniel Kingston.

By contrast, Leigh Dethman of the *Deseret News* opened with this:

> Details of an abusive, dirty and neglected Kingston home surfaced Tuesday as transcripts of the testimony of two of polygamist John Daniel Kingston's teenage daughters were released. According to testimony from his 13-year-old daughter, Kingston beat her, her mother and her siblings and forced his children to eat rotten food he dug out of the garbage, drink rotten milk and worse.
>
> "He's . . . let them throw up and [made] them drink it," the girl said. "Arrest my dad and have him be in jail forever, or else do to him what he's done to us."

Admittedly, the *Deseret News* is a paper of bias, owned by the LDS Church. But nevertheless, the difference is stark. Adams denies that the interviews provide evidence of abuse, whereas the *News* highlights the abuse alleged in the interviews. It's true that the girls gave very different testimony—Andrea spoke of horrible violence at home, while Stephanie denied it. But Adams focused on Stephanie's testimony, quoting her six times in the story: how spankings were "not even hard" as a young girl, how babysitters were often worse than her parents and Daniel wasn't to blame for her crying on the day she ran away, she was just "moody." Andrea, on the other hand, is only quoted twice, and her interview is described as "disjointed."

By contrast, the *News* focuses on Andrea's testimony: how Daniel gave her sister a bloody nose, slapping the kids and then saying, "Quit crying or I'm going to do it again," how he hit her in the face for not saying "hi" to his mother. None of which Adams saw fit to print. While the *News* reports Andrea's allegation that Kingston "dragged Foster, who was pregnant, down a set of stairs by her hair," and that "Kingston hit his children one at a time with a two-by-four," the *Tribune* carries this neutered version: "The younger girl reports seeing her father hit her mother and another sibling and said sometimes they were spanked with a board"—which is immediately followed by a proviso: "But the older girl says she has never seen her mother hit, and even slaps were rare for the children."

Adams's defense is that she'd covered the details of the dirty home in previous stories, and she also noted that Andrea said that she hates her father. But it's easy to see why fundamentalists love Adams. She didn't focus on the alleged abuse so much as the question marks surrounding the testimony. She also helped sustain the Kingston argument that the whole thing was an overblown dispute over earrings.

Heidi is a fan of Adams's coverage. "That's why I gave her an exclusive," she says. "She showed both sides. And she cared about getting it right. She agreed to call and read it to me before it printed. Which reporters don't really do."

"She read you the piece before it went to press?"

"Yes. She wanted it bad enough."

It appears that the *Tribune* was offering "courtesy reads," in the midst of one of Utah's most high-profile polygamy cases, to one of the parties in the case, a woman accused of failing to protect her children from abuse. And Heidi isn't the only polygamist who claims Adams offered her a read-through. The Darger family from Herriman, who have appeared often in the Tribune, told me that they were given the same treatment, prior to a story about their lifestyle appearing in the Sunday paper. Adams insists that she was only checking accuracy, not for "content or stylistic suggestions," but it's all too reminiscent of Hollywood celebrities demanding copy approval, a privilege of only the hottest stars. In Utah, polygamists are celebrities. They're the state's biggest story. And they're beginning to realize their clout.

It was partly Adams's coverage that made Foster a *cause célèbre* within the fundamentalist community. The threat of the government seizing your children is a primal fear among polygamists, and not without reason, as events in Texas show. But it was the civil rights aspect that stoked the greatest outrage. By Heidi's incendiary framing, the issue is, "Does the court have the right to tell you that you cannot go to church?"

But in other ways, Heidi's victimhood is plain. She began life in Huntington Canyon, in a trailer that was flattened when a boulder came crashing down a mountain when Heidi was just a young girl, killing one of her sisters.[56] And by all accounts, she was a bright girl. This is what everyone says about Heidi, how she was at the top of her class and how her IQ is off the charts. In typical Order style, this A-student was married off to "one of the brothers"—Daniel, who had married her older sister Kelly a couple of years earlier. And immediately, her education stopped and a life of pregnancy and child rearing began, one for which she seemed particularly ill equipped.

Perhaps there is something sympathetic about Heidi's constant denials that anything was wrong at home. If indeed Daniel was beating her, it's tragic that she would reject the opportunity she was given to live outside the Order. Furthermore, her willingness to paint her children as liars speaks to a certain desperation.

But in her denials, Heidi has all the support and indignation of the fundamentalist community, and this has only calcified her position over time: Daniel is a loving father, her children were brainwashed by the state, she is the victim of a gross miscarriage of justice. And yet the fact remains that Stephanie and Andrea have done all they can to distance themselves. Both girls were adopted on the same day and are now living happily under assumed identities. Stephanie joined a Mormon family in South Jordan. She was baptized in the church; she graduated from high school. Andrea too has found a smaller nuclear family, and they live in Washington. "I don't know how to contact them," says Heidi, shaking her head. "I still live in the same house with the same phone number. I don't know why they're not contacting me. We were told that they didn't want to come home, but what were they told? Because I know *we* were lied to."

And this story leaves me asking similar questions. Who's lying to me? Heidi's and Carleen's insistence on Daniel's lily-white innocence is hard to stomach, given the charges against him. And yet they have the support of some of the most discriminating voices in the fundamentalist community, who angrily charge the state with fabrication and dirty tricks—the very charges that the state's supporters direct at the Order. Again and again this case boils down to instances of he said/she said.

But the core allegation here concerns Daniel. And the only people qualified to comment are those close enough to have witnessed any potential abuse firsthand. I've heard from Heidi. Now I need to hear from the girls—Stephanie and Andrea. The only trouble is, they've consistently refused to speak with the media ever since their cases were closed, and their new names are a closely guarded secret.

Still, this isn't over yet.

◈ Spies and Lies

> Secrecy is the freedom tyrants dream of.
> —Bill Moyers

On the morning of Utah's favorite public holiday, I'm aware of only three things—I have a hangover, my motel room stinks of last night's chow mein and I don't have a picnic to go to. The first two I can handle, but the picnic? That hurts.

I've been trying for months now to get invited to the Order's annual Pioneer Day picnic. It's a big day out for Order members. They head up to a patch of land called the "Home Place," near Carl Kingston's house in Bountiful, where they tuck into a feast of sugarless treats and green drink. The "Home Place" is where the "Holy Spot" is, where the founder, Elden, supposedly saw the Savior.[57] Order members turn to face this "Holy Spot" three times a day, when they say their prayers—it's the Order's Mecca, and this picnic is their Hajj. So if I could go, I'd get my chance at long last to meet the Prophet Paul Kingston. I had the whole thing worked out.

But then last night, Carleen called. "Sorry, Sanjiv, but I've talked to Paul and we really think that your presence will make our people uncomfortable."

"I'll only be five minutes, Carleen. I'll be very low-key . . ."

"The answer's still no. We just can't have a journalist at the event."

For six months, Carleen and I have been going back and forth about whether I can go to this thing or not. At first she doesn't know, then she needs to talk to Paul, but Paul's always busy. *Six months*. And now it's past 10 AM on July 24, and I'm left with only two real options. Either I sit here in America's Best Inn while the rest of Salt Lake City is out watching the Pioneer Day parade. Or I walk two blocks and join the fun.

So half an hour later, I'm out on the streets with the revelers, waiting for the Advil to kick in. There's a huge queue for the portaloos, kids sitting on the asphalt, men snoozing on deck chairs with 7-Eleven balloons tied to their wrists. And there's nothing to do but watch the floats go by, all just variations of each other—giant confections of tinsel and tiaras and fake trees and mechanical animals. They trundle by like big putrid cakes, with pageant winners jammed into the icing, waving like robots. Never has so much effort been expended for so little. And yet every year, people camp out on the sidewalk like upscale hobos, happy to wave and whoop at Dante's conveyor of small-town beauty queens and high school marching bands and police motorbike squads doing their dainty little maneuvers. Here comes the float with all the black people in Utah. Way to go, black people! And here's the prophet of the Mormon Church in a dropped-top Sebring. Whoo! That guy is pals with God!

By the time the pioneer fetishists come by with their prairie dresses and covered wagons, I'm looking through my cell phone for rescue. I must know someone who's having a beer on this public holiday. Maybe Ron and Christy Tucker could be persuaded? Ron did say he was making up for lost time.

"Tell you what, just come over!" says Christy. "Do you play poker?"

A quick nap and a shower and I'm heading over to the Tuckers' game room in the basement where a full crowd has assembled. Christy and Ron and all their kids and Christy's sister Elaine and her husband Sean and all theirs. Throw in a few cousins, a half brother here, a half sister there and we're about twenty-five strong, all ex-Order but me. And spirits are high. We're all betting away, sinking beers and eating nachos.

It turns out that poker night at the Tuckers is something of an institution—a chance to reminisce about the old days, a form of group therapy. Oh, the lies they told us, the underage marriages, the exploitation, but here we are with our families, we made it. Sean and Ron swap stories about the mine, the awful conditions, their heartless boss, the gruesome injuries. Each story seems to outdo the next. "I was earning six-dollars-something an hour when I left," says Ron. "I was on less than five," says Sean.

Then at around midnight, the doorbell rings and Christy runs off to see who it is. When she comes back a few minutes later, she's looking anxiously at me and talking in a whisper. "There's a boy here, he's from the Order," she says. "Sometimes he comes by and visits. We never get any warning, he just shows up. And he's scared to come in. He said, 'Is anyone from the Order in there?' And I said, 'No, but Sanjiv's here, he's a reporter, he's doing a book.' And he's really nervous about it. So can I just ask . . ."

"That's okay, Christy, I don't mind. It's past my bedtime anyway."

"No, no, I'm not kicking you out! I just want you to promise that you won't tell anyone who he is or that he came here. Because if the Order finds out, he'll catch such a beating."

"I promise, Christy."

"His name's Hyrum.* Just act normal."

It's impossible to act normal. Hyrum doesn't make a normal entrance. He loiters in the kitchen doorway, peeking occasionally to make sure he's safe. Then he sidles quietly over to the table, sits in the corner and looks at his feet, avoiding eye contact with everybody. Christy introduces us, and he nods. "I saw you before. I know who you are," he says, still looking at the floor. His hands fidget nervously with his phone, his cheeks are red as beets. I'm guessing he's maybe sixteen, a skinny little teenager whose shyness fills the room.

"So where you been Hyrum, up at the Home Place?" asks Ron.

"Yeah."

"How is it?"

---

*Not his real name

"You know." Shrug. "Same old thing."

He's obviously uncomfortable talking, so Ron leaves him alone and continues his conversation with Sean about how corrupt the Order is. We're all pretending that nothing's happened, but it has. An Order member is here, and the awkwardness is suffocating.

Suddenly Hyrum's phone goes off—a loud ring that gives us all a start. He springs up and leaves the room, mumbling, "Sorry, excuse me . . ." and doesn't answer until he leaves the room. And only then do I ask—who is he, why's he here?

"He's one of Daniel's boys," whispers Ron. "I think he comes over to see what life outside the Order is like. And I try to show him that it's okay, you know. It's better."

"Did you see how he was holding his phone though?" says Jeremy. "I think he was recording our conversation."

"Why would he do that?" I ask.

"Maybe so he could listen to it himself later, maybe it'll answer some questions for him, or help him do his own research into the Order like we did," Ron says.

"But maybe he's going to take the recording to Daniel," says Jeremy. "You can never tell with Order people. Until they actually leave you can never tell."

"You mean he's a *spy*?" I ask.

And Christy shrugs. Ron shrugs. "I don't know," he says. "Sometimes people call us up saying they want to leave and they want to get in touch with certain people. But we've found out later that Daniel put them up to it. We have to be careful."

Hyrum returns, apologizes and sits down at the table, mouse-like and contained, fidgeting with his phone. The conversation resumes, this time about the lack of proof for the Book of Mormon. But again, Hyrum's phone goes off. He looks pained and stands up. "I gotta go." And just before he leaves the room, he turns to look at me. "Please don't say anything. You promised." He looks terrified.

Before I leave, I ask Christy to give Hyrum my number in case he ever wants to talk to me. But I hear nothing. Weeks go by and I return to L.A., telling myself it was just another mysterious encounter at the fringe of a mysterious cult. But something about that night bothers me. Christy hasn't heard from Hyrum either, he's stopped dropping by. And I wonder if maybe he was on the cusp of leaving the Order that night, maybe he came to ask the Tuckers' help but then my presence put him off? It's impossible to say now that Hyrum has retreated back into the secrecy of the Order.

Then late one night in August, my cell phone rings. It reads PRIVATE, so I ignore it. No one calls me at 12:47 AM. But the message is intriguing—a young girl saying, "Well, I guess you're not there, so I'll try again later." No number, no name, no way of getting back to her. I assume it's a wrong number. Then a half hour later, it rings again: PRIVATE. I pick up.

"Hi, um . . . are you the guy that's writing the book?"

"Who's this?"

"Are you doing the book about polygamy?"

"Yes, who are you?"

"I'm from the Kingston family . . . I found your number on Carleen's desk."

"What's your name?"

"I don't want to say. I don't want to get found out. I'm Daniel's daughter and so . . . I'll get in trouble, you know? Are you talking to Carleen?"

"Yes."

"Well, she's a liar. She just lies all the time. She's a bitch."

"Why do you say that?"

"If you're talking to Carleen, then you should know that. That's all. She doesn't speak for herself. She goes to Rachel Young or Paul, they tell her what to say. And she gets scared because in the Order we grew up like, you know, not telling anyone anything. But now she can say stuff, so she's scared she doesn't say the wrong things."

"How do you know Carleen?"

"Um . . . I'm working at one of the stewardships she's at. I just saw your phone number on a Post-it on her computer. So I memorized it."

"You didn't write it down?"

"No, in case, you know, someone found it in my pocket."

It's a peculiar conversation. I don't know whether to trust her, whether she's a spy just trying to tease out my prejudices and get me to say something incriminating. I already know that the Order likes to record phone calls—Jeremy said he even found a transmitter in one of their phones once. But at the same time, she sounds so credible. She tells me herself that the Order monitors the calls out of its steward-ships, so there's no way she could call me from work. She can't use the home phone, because her parents would see the bill, so she's on a cell, sitting in a car outside her house, while her family sleeps. She's too scared to give me the number or even her email—"They check all that." And she sounds like a real teenager. When I tell her that I live in L.A., she says, "Oh neat. So um, do you like meet Britney Spears and Paris Hilton and stuff?"

We agree to set up another call. And a few days later, again after mid-night, my phone lights up: PRIVATE. She's back in her car outside the house on her cell phone. And then the week later, another call. And another.

Here's what I learn. She's twenty and still unmarried, which is rare in the Order. She says she's been under pressure to get hitched ever since she was fourteen, but she has always resisted, much to the dismay of her father. But Daniel, she says, is two-faced and has a vicious temper. He's not as violent to the older kids anymore because he's afraid that they might report him—a legacy of her half sisters Mary Ann and Stephanie, who ran straight to the cops. But he still beats the younger ones. He beat her growing up—proper belt-buckle whippings with bruises and welts. She's been thinking about leaving for six years, but she's afraid she'll never see her brothers and sisters again. She misses Stephanie and Andrea and Mary Ann—it has been years since she's spoken to them.

She tells me so many things, this mystery girl, much of which I can't repeat because it might blow her cover, like where she works, who her mother is, where she was at the time when this incident happened or that. And she provides no proof for the allegations she's making. It's possible that she's enacting some elaborate prank. But as the weeks pass, I find her increasingly credible. She's a naïve and lonely girl sitting outside her house in her car, making secret calls to a journalist whom she's never met. It's exciting, it's different, it's someone she can talk to. And whatever the truth of her message, it is unwavering: Carleen and Laura Fuller will lie to you, Daniel *is* a violent man, he brutalized Mary Ann and he beat Stephanie and Andrea, too.

"I'm just waiting for the state to hurry up and do what they said they would do," she says. "I can't leave until Daniel and Paul are in prison. That would be so *awesome*."

And something about that just pushed my buttons. "You know you're not the only one that wants to leave," I tell her. "There's a guy about your age. He's been to see ex-Order people like the Tuckers."

"Oh, Hyrum? It's Hyrum, isn't it?"

"Well . . ." And I buckle. "Yes, it's Hyrum. But you can't tell anyone."

"No, of course. I know Hyrum. He's my brother."

The Tuckers reckon my caller's name is Julie. So does Rowenna. And I'm waiting to spring this on her when she calls next. But this time my cell shows a text message:

```
is this Sanjiv?

                              —yes

its hyrum I now marlynes* calling you, she
is using my phone but she forgets to delete
the number. I've just been waiting for her
to say some thing to me.

                     —lets talk on the phone

Sorry I can't talk right now cause there
are people around but I can call you later
tonoght

                              —ok

I can't believe she didn't talk to me aboute
this its been like a week and I've known
aboute this does she no anything? Please
don't say anything to her. Thank you I will
try and call you later.

                              —ok
```

*Not her real name

Now I'm torn up. I feel rotten. Ashamed. I gave Hyrum up after he specifically asked me not to. I flick back through my conversations with this girl—this "Marlyne"—and I just get more and more confused. Was she just playing me to get Hyrum's name? Was she put up to this by Daniel? Then what about everything she told me about him, all those stories about the beatings and how she wanted him in prison—were they all lies? But why?

A couple of restless hours later, my phone lights up again. The text messages are streaming:

Hi its hyrum I just talked to marlyne/i gues
you didn't no her name
I m not mad aboute what you said but if she
calls you please don't say anything else
even if she asks you, sorry to bring you
into our crazy messed up world
I do want to talk to you I just need to wait
for things to settle down/ things are kinda
crazy right now and I'm kinda in trouble for
a couple of things

> —Did she say we talked? Pls tell her not to
> worry I will never reveal her identity or
> yours. Anytime you want to talk let me know

ya she told me every thing how you ran into
me at the tuckers I know every thing

> —I guess I misunderstood how bad things are.
> She told me she wanted to see Daniel in
> prison. I figured she was trustworthy . . .
> Sorry.

I trust her I just didn't want any one to
no/if daniel was to ask her she could say
she doesn't know anything

> —I understand. I shouldn't have said
> anything. Won't happen again.

```
It's ok its not your fault its mine I should
have called you before she did no hard
feelings, good luck on the book.
```

Nothing happens for a couple of days. Then Hyrum calls to explain what has been going on. He paints a troubling picture. It seems Hyrum and Marlyne really are brother and sister. They have the same mom, they live in the same house. I can't reveal Hyrum's age, but he says that Marlyne is only sixteen, not twenty as she claimed. On the face of it, Hyrum and Marlyne would appear to have everything in common: the same family, the same fear of Daniel, the same disillusionment with the Order. And like Marlyne, Hyrum would leave if he could, but he feels he must stay to look out for the younger ones in his family.

But until I blew Hyrum's cover, they had never even talked between themselves about how they felt about the Order. Rather than forge an alliance, they maintained their Order facades, even in their most private brother and sister moments—such is their fear of appearing disloyal. It's a haunting image, two siblings trapped by their fears and secrets, unable to escape the lies that define their lives. And more peculiar still is the fact that even when their secrets are out, nothing changes. I had hoped for some kind of exhalation or release, but instead, Hyrum and Marlyne preserve their distance, the status quo. There has been no great bonding experience.

The key to this intriguing dynamic between the two is Hyrum. I suggest to him that perhaps Marlyne cannot be trusted, since she used his cell phone knowing that Daniel would check his bill at the end of the month. But he shrugs it off—he doctors his phone bills before presenting them to Daniel, anyway. He's been doing it for years. Marlyne, however, is just a young girl who looks up to her brother and goes to him with her problems. He helps when he can, but he doesn't share his own life with her. "He's always been like that," says Marlyne. "Real secretive. Sneaky and stuff." But that's how Hyrum protects his sister: the less she knows, the less she can reveal. Because Hyrum isn't keeping ordinary secrets. Behind that painfully shy front is an incredibly determined and courageous young spy, on a mission to break the Order's stranglehold over its people, something he can only do from the inside.

In 2007, he started to supply information and documentation to the attorney general's investigators. He lets them know, for instance, of every incestuous marriage that has recently taken place or is about to take place, often with evidence in the form of wedding invitations. (Nothing has been done.) Hyrum also started up a Myspace page in January 2008 under the name "what is a cult?" which he later changed to "searching for freedom." It provides a forum for both "exorder and order people to come to the truth." Within three days, he had forty-six friends and hundreds of comments, almost all of them from young Order members and ex-members spouting off about the lies they'd been taught, the corruption of their leaders, the secrets they live with. It's a brilliantly subversive community, a rebuke to the control of the Order's leaders. With typical mischief, Hyrum identified himself in his profile as Rachel Young, Paul Kingston's sister and chief Order propagandist. "If satan is the god of all lies," he writes, "who is the order's god?"

Once the site had been up for a couple of days, Hyrum personal-messaged me through Myspace: *"this is hyrum, on this site i go by young please dont say anything to any one . . . every one is going crazy and paul is trying to find out who made it."* It's little wonder that Paul Kingston is on the hunt for the culprit. The comments, like this one from DeAnne, are often unrestrained: "I was born and raised as a 'Order Member', however I do not have the Kingston blood so I will not make it into the Celestial Kingdom unless I marry a 'Kingston' and practice polygamy. I will become nothing and no one will ever participate in my friendship or have anything to do with me because . . . I do not have the royal blood!!!!" But these comments are often countered by Order members who argue that those who leave are spreading lies. And at times the exchanges become vicious and personal—arguments about who is and who isn't a current Order member, who's secretly posting on behalf of the leaders. When some of Paul Kingston's wives were named on the site as women who live in poverty, the Order's hierarchy protested to Myspace and had the site shut down. But it was up and running again soon enough, as was another group exclusively for people who'd left polygamy. Only this time, Hyrum isn't the administrator. He's passed the baton.

Hyrum's Myspace page, however, was not his greatest revelation. It was the time he called and asked me straight: "What do you want?"

"Proof! What can you give me?"

"All the lessons they teach at Sunday school."

"Everything?"

"Everything."

And a week later, an unmarked CD arrives in the mail. No note, no return address. Just 350 megabytes of PDF files—booklets, primers, journals, teaching manuals, handbooks, textbooks. Over fifty documents in all.

◆ What I Learned at Order School

Those of you who are more robust and individual than others, will be encouraged to leave and find ways of educating yourself—educating your own judgement. Those that stay must remember, always and all the time, that they are being moulded and patterned to fit into the narrow and particular needs of this particular society.

—Doris Lessing, *The Golden Notebook*

The Order operates two schools at present, both in the southwest of Salt Lake City—The Ensign Learning Center, which is the elementary school, and Ensign Junior High, which operates out of their church building. Roughly 90 percent of Order children attend these schools, though there is a small portion who attend other schools. The Sunday School lessons take place at the high school.

Taken together, the documents Hyrum sent me reveal a group obsessed not so much with the welfare and growth of its children, but with itself—its history, doctrine, separatism and, above all, its mission to rear the next generation of Order members, loyal to Paul Kingston. It's a chilling read.

The boys graduate through a series of militaristic titles, from Young Lions (twelve and thirteen years old) to Stripling Warriors (fourteen and fifteen years old) to Honor Guard (sixteen and seventeen years old) until finally they become Men of Zion (ages eighteen through twenty-three). The girls' titles are more chaste and servile, from Rosebuds to Maids of Promise to Noble Maids. Both genders are subjected to an intensive program of indoctrination and behavior modification that begins at the cradle: there are instructions for teaching babies to pray, lessons on eternal marriage for four-year-olds, and warnings for eight-year-olds not to dance more than two dances with anyone they're not engaged to.

These tips, for instance, come from Family Steps of Progression, a series of booklets intended to help parents monitor the progress of their children within the Order:

0–3 year olds
PRAYER

6–11 months—Your child should be able to start folding their hands and bowing their head during prayer. They should know what it means to stay quiet during prayer. If you are having family prayer every morning and night they should be getting plenty of practice.

1–2 yrs—You should start having them face the Holy Spot, helping them fold their hands and recite their prayers after you.

3 yrs—Your child is now old enough to help you say the blessing, and should be able to understandably recite their personal prayers. Make sure they are in the habit of thanking heavenly Father for their blessings, especially their parents, family, the leader and their membership in the Order. They should also start asking heavenly Father to help them be baptized when they are eight, and to help them marry the right one.

APPRECIATION

1 yr—Start having the children thank heavenly Father for their things when you help them pray. Especially for their parents, the leader and their membership in the order.

4–7 year olds
MEMORY GEMS

It is my firm resolve and fixed purpose to give my all to the Lord; my time, my talents, all that I am or ever expect to be, to the establishment of Zion, and the building up of the Kingdom of God upon the earth.

If the order doesn't have it, we don't need it.

J is for Janitor. I would rather be a janitor in the house of the Lord than anything in any other kingdom.

K is for Kiss. My first kiss on the lips will be on my wedding day during the ceremony with my husband or wife. I will not hold hands with anyone as a boyfriend or girlfriend until I am engaged to be married to them.

L is for Loyalty. I will not betray the trust of any of my brothers or sisters of the Order.

PRAYER

When we pray we face the Holy Spot. Ask your parents where the holy spot is if you don't know. Make sure you kneel up and fold your hands reverently. Keep your eyes closed and bow your head.

8–11 year olds

Remember these guidelines/standards while at the dance:

You do not dance more than two dances in a row with someone you are not engaged or married to.

You dance in regular dance position.

You don't pair off. Sit by your parents, or someone appointed by your parents.

A child's cult identity is one of the first things he or she learns at Order school. The following section is taken from *Teacher's Manuals*, specifically from Course B-2, for six-to-seven-year-olds:

Point to each child and ask, "Who are you?" Have each child answer by stating his or her name. Explain that each of us is a unique person. State very clearly: "I am a member of the Order." "We are members of the Order."

The teachings go on to expound about the moral and physical superiority of Order members, all the while encouraging children to lie to protect the Order. Loyalty is placed above truth, just as Order members are placed above outsiders. This from the same Teacher's Manuals for six to seven-year-olds, page 276:

What is loyalty? It is when we do not do or say anything that will hurt the people we love, like our family and other Order members.

How can we be loyal to the Order and our families? We can give our time and talents to the Order, we can shop at Order stores, we can turn in our money, we can be a help to our parents. But one very important thing we can do when we go to school; we can see to it we do not talk to the people there about the very special things about the Order and our families.

What does it mean to cast pearls before swine? Pearls represent things that are precious and valuable like our Sunday School meetings, our home evenings and the things we are taught there; and the very special families that we have. The swine represent the people that do not understand the precious things of the heavenly Father and only ask questions because they are curious or want to make fun of us . . .

What are the rules we should follow?

Don't start talking about Order things ourselves. Sometimes some of us seem to think it makes us look smarter if we tell everything we know. It really makes us look not so smart.

If someone asks us a question, it doesn't hurt us to say, "I don't know." There again, people will think we are not smart to say we don't know. It is a lot smarter not to tell everything we know.

Let's give a little example. Suppose you lived in Nauvoo in the days of Joseph Smith. Suppose that a mob was after him and was going to tar and feather him. Suppose he came to your house to hide from the mob. If the mob came and knocked on your door and asked "Is Joseph Smith in your house?" What would you say? Would you tell the truth and say yes so they could take him and tar and feather him? Of course you wouldn't. You would say no to protect the Prophet Joseph. Sometimes we have to say no to protect the Order.

From a young age, Order members are taught the virtues of sacrifice and deprivation; children are encouraged to deny themselves income, books, pleasure, even food for the sake of building up the Order's wealth. In a series of workbooks for twelve to seventeen-year-old boys called the *Coop*

Training Personal Progress Journal ("Coop" seems so much more fitting than "co-op"), members are instructed to work without getting punched in, maintain strict monthly budgets and eliminate all unnecessary purchases from their lives. Typically the recommendations go to an extreme:

Go one week without wearing any clothing that has a mark or emblem on it. Imagine you are living in a tent and have just given up all worldly possessions; including burning your pictures. You have made the choice to dedicate your life and all you are to the Lord, no matter what the sacrifice.

Go two days without using any soap. Imagine you are living in a tent and have just given up all worldly possessions; including burning your pictures.

Sleep on the floor for three, five or seven nights in a row without using any pillows. Imagine you are living in a tent and have just given up all worldly possessions; including burning your pictures.

Go two days without using any mirrors. Imagine you are living in a tent and have just given up all worldly possessions; including burning your pictures.

And at all times, the leader Paul Kingston demands absolute devotion and obeisance. In the Thanksgiving lesson, children are encouraged to thank heavenly Father first for their health and second for "our leader Brother Paul." Their church comes fourth; their parents come eleventh. Teachers are told to show Paul's picture in class and have the children repeat his name in unison. They're to explain how "we need him today just as the people of Noah's time needed Noah." They're to discuss how Paul's commandments have brought blessings.

I came upon a school test completed by Christy's daughter Julie when she was eighteen. The title of the course was "Conduct on a Stewardship."

Q 4. Who stands in for the Lord as the man on the watch tower?
A: Brother Paul
Q 5. Name at least three ways we can show loyalty to our leader.
A: Be on time and never miss his meetings, listen to his instruction as if it were the savior, show support
Q 12. If we are called on to say a prayer or to speak at a function where there are nonmembers present, what things should be left out of the prayer or speech?

A: *Don't say anything sacred. Don't say any names. Don't say Brother Paul's name.*

(Julie scored an A.)

There's no question that the Order is a cult in the classic sense, thoroughly engaged in brainwashing its young. I think I now understand a little better the peculiar interactions I've had with Order people so far—the evasions of Heidi Foster, the Stepford repetition, the glassy glaze in Carleen's eyes. I expect they will be horrified if they read this chapter—not just that a grubby Gentile has gotten his hands on their sacred teachings, but that he's exposing their "most precious pearls" to the world. But they can be comforted on at least two counts.

Among their precious pearls are stories of those who have hurt the Order and come to a sticky end. The implication is plain: injuring the Order makes God mad. So by rights, I ought to get mine.

And they can be reassured that I've only revealed a miniscule portion of what I have. There's simply not room to communicate the sheer volume and numbing repetition of these documents. They left me dulled and tranquilized by the drone of doctrine ringing in my ears. By the time I reached the end of these files, I could finish the Order's sentences and complete the puny anecdotes about Brother Charles and Brother Elden and how so very worthy they all were. I can recite the mantras. The Order is in my head.

❖ Laura Fuller and the Exoneration of Daniel Kingston

> There are no choices without personal freedom, Buckeroo. It's not us who are dead inside. These things you find so weak and contemptible in us—these are just the hazards of being free.
> —David Foster Wallace, *Infinite Jest*

The mystery calls from the Kingston camp continue as summer turns to fall. I'll be at home in L.A., watching a *Deadwood* rerun on the sofa with the wife, and the phone will ring: PRIVATE. Grab the phone and my glass of wine—"Just one of those top-secret Kingston spies, dear, I'll take it in my room." It's either Marlyne asking me how to get into the fashion business, or it's Hyrum passing on some classified snippet, like how he sent a private letter to the AG.

But then one afternoon, I get a call that throws me way off.

"Hello, this is Laura Fuller. Hello? Can you hear me? Yes, hi, I'm Laura Fuller. From the Davis County Cooperative." Laura Fuller is one of Daniel Kingston's wives—number eleven by all accounts.[58] She's also the paralegal whom Judge Valdez ejected from the courthouse in the thick of the Heidi Foster case. Now, it seems she's a full-blown appellate lawyer, at least in California[59] (the Utah bar has denied her application), and she's determined to defend the Order against all comers.

"I can show you exactly why we will prove that Daniel is innocent of the crimes he's been charged with," she says. "I'll take you through the evidence. Are you interested?"

So within a week, I'm sitting in the lobby of the Placentia Library in Orange County, waiting for someone I've never met to tell me things I've never heard for reasons I can't quite fathom. The Kingstons are notoriously secretive, and yet this time one of Daniel's wives called *me*. One of the group's lawyers wants to *volunteer* information that she hasn't shared with anyone before. I'm suspicious. I'm excited. I'm not convinced this isn't some kind of setup.

Here's Laura now walking at a fierce pace—jeans, green blouse, lank mouse-brown hair and a bloodless complexion, no makeup. She waves hi and marches straight past—"Follow me." We thread our way through to the back of the library, to the children's section, where she motions for me to sit across from her, on a kiddie chair at a tiny table. There are toys on the floor all around us.

"Okay, I've brought a tape recorder," she says rummaging around in her bag. "Because I'm going to record this conversation." She looks determined, flinty, a little enraged. "I just want to be clear that if I'm going to talk to you, then there are some ethical things we have to talk about first. Does that make sense? I want to be clear that I'm not giving you any legal advice. Does that make sense?"

She sounds impatient. I'm evidently not getting it quickly enough. While she scratches away at the plastic wrapping on a packet of cassettes, she hurriedly gives me the necessary background as though one process were in a race against the other. Apparently she's close to qualifying—this is her eighth and last year at law school—and she's just about to embark on her life's mission, to defend the Order in court. She went back to school when Daniel was in jail for crimes against Mary Ann because, "I was horrified that a man could go to jail for something he didn't do." And she's been involved, to some extent, in most of the Kingston lawsuits ever since. She was one of the many defendants in the Mary Ann civil suit (until she was later dropped), and she worked for four months on Heidi's case as a paralegal (until she was kicked out). It was Heidi who encouraged her to talk to me. And clearly the Order's senior-most lawyers—Daniel Irvin and Carl Kingston—have given her permission.

"I know I instigated this meeting," she says, urgently rewinding and playing the tape. "But there are some things I need to know from you. Because if I'm going to sue you, I really don't want to talk to you!"

"What do you mean, 'if you sue me'?"

"If what you print is not true, it's very possible. That's why we're recording the interview." She's still fumbling with her recorder. "I think my batteries have run out. If you don't mind, we can just go around the corner to buy some. It's not far."

"That's fine, I've got my iPod, I can record it if you like."

"But that's your recording. I need my own recording. So I'd still like to get some batteries. You can come or you can wait here. It's up to you."

And so we march out of the library, clutching our bags and recorders, and we get into her tatty little car, sunbaked in the parking lot. She says it's okay to record our conversation as we drive to the ninety-nine-cent store.

"Over the last eight years, the way in which we have dealt with people has changed," she says. "Because we are being punished far worse for the lies than we ever would have been for the truth. Does that make sense?"

"No."

"If you're hiding behind a rock, and there's a hundred guns pointed at you, do you stand up? For generations we said no. But when the rock is gone, and the guns are still pointed, what do you do? Before, we would be quiet because if we stood up we knew we would be shot. But not anymore. That's why we will sue you if you lie about us."

"Hasn't that always been the way?"

"Not in the past, nobody's had the time or money. That's why I'm concerned that if you're prejudiced, you're going to misconstrue what you're hearing. Someone indicated that you thought Heidi was forced into her marriage because she was working for Daniel at the time."

"Oh, that was Carleen."

"I remember when Heidi came into the family, and me and my older sister—who both ended up in Daniel's family—thought it was sickening the way she pursued him. We couldn't believe she was following him around that way. So for you to say she was forced . . ."

"I didn't actually say 'forced'—I just said she's only as free as her choices."

"But what makes you think that our choices are limited?"

"You need to marry within the church, which is a small group. And if your boss asks for your hand in marriage, and he also employs other family members . . ."

"No, no, you don't understand it at all. You really don't. You're saying that if she said no, then their relationship would be somehow damaged and they wouldn't be able to work in the way they used to."

"It's a possibility, you have to admit."

"No, I don't have to admit! That is where we are unique. There was a gentleman who asked for my hand in marriage who was married to my best friend. And that seemed like a wonderful option for me until Daniel talked to me and I turned him down. At first I was afraid that this would hurt my relationship with my best friend and him. But it didn't."

"That's not the same thing. I'm talking about when a boss asks his secretary, 'Do you want to go out tonight?' The secretary can legitimately feel pressured."

"But we are different. We're not like people in the world."

It's an astonishing argument—arrogant and exceptional, but actually quite suited to the self-declared Chosen of God. The fleshly motivations of power, greed and sex, these are symptoms of the fallen world outside her fundamentalist bubble.

We buy the batteries and return to the children's section of the library, where she's getting increasingly frustrated with the recorder, popping the double A's in one way, then another.

"I'll give you an example of how we're different. When I first worked outside of the co-op in 1996, for Salt Lake County, there was a girl that worked for me that quit. And I never talked to her again. And that was odd to me. In our society, if you quit your job, you still see the people you worked with on Sunday. You might get in trouble at work, but you still pick up your boss's kids from school because you're part of her car pool. So you learn to leave the work emotions at work."

"I can see that. But the flip side is that there's arguably even more pressure precisely because you're going to see this person every other day, in all these circumstances . . ."

"There's not, though."

"It sounds like the kind of system that would only work if everyone was Christlike."

"Yes, and isn't that the goal? Here's another example. When Mary Ann made allegations against Daniel and David, I thought, 'What is this going to do to those brothers' relationship? Is David going to feel badly that Daniel's daughter is making these allegations?' But the love between Daniel and David did not alter even for a second."

She's right, it's a great example of how different Order members are. Following Mary Ann's beating, Laura's primary concern was for the relationship between David and Daniel.

I ask her the question I asked Heidi and Carleen that day at the Sizzler: "If he's innocent, why did Daniel plead no contest to the crimes?"

"I was very upset when he did that, but he said it was to protect the witnesses. When the witness list was submitted, DCFS pulled the kids out of school and questioned them, and they didn't know how to answer questions about their families. That was their big fear as they sat waiting to go onto the stand. To admit that you're living something illegal, you would risk being prosecuted yourself."

Like Heidi and Carleen, Laura maintains that Daniel sacrificed himself for the rest of the Order. "He figured that if he were in jail, everybody would be happy," she says. "Primarily Mary Ann but also Rowenna and all the others who were after him. That thirst for blood would be quenched."

"So he went to jail as a martyr."

"Yes."

"Like Christ."

"Absolutely."

We move to a picnic table outside where Laura lays out a heap of documents and files, flapping in the breeze. She has a case to make—not only that Daniel is a saint-like figure, but that his daughter, Mary Ann, is a filthy liar and borderline Jezebel. These files contain the meat of the case the Order never got to present in Daniel's defense back in 1998.

"Is it going around?" She holds up the tape recorder. "What's the problem? It can't be the batteries . . ."

"Maybe it's on pause. That red button on the side."

"Oh good! Okay, listen to this—this is March 20, 1998. A tape of Mary Ann calling her boyfriend Ryan Adams."

"Boyfriend? Wasn't she married to David at the time?"

"Yes, exactly. Listen." She presses play. The sound of a phone ringing and then two mumbling, monosyllabic teenagers making inane conversation. "What you doing?" "Nothing." "Huh." "Okay." And then:

> **Ryan:** So you pregnant?
> **Mary Ann:** I don't know.
> **Ryan:** You haven't gone and checked yet?
> **Mary Ann:** Uh-uh.

Laura clicks off the tape and gives me one of those looks—"you see?" Evidently Mary Ann had made the call from Valley Coal, an Order stewardship where, according to Laura, everyone knows that all business calls are recorded.

"When her dad heard that conversation, on March 23, he took her to the health clinic to find out if she was pregnant," she says. "She hadn't had a cycle for three months, from December 23 to March 23." She fishes through some papers and pulls out the test certificate. Mary Ann wasn't pregnant after all, but the implication is clear—she was screwing around.

On tape two, Mary Ann is talking to Chris, another boyfriend, on May 14—something about going to a motel. And on tape three, we have Mary Ann and Chris again a week later, May 21—a series of calls this time. At first Chris tells her that he's just got into a fight. Then he tells her that he's running from the cops. And then he comes up with this cock-and-bull story about how he's moving to Brazil because he just bought a condo there. And Mary Ann, bless her, believes him.

> **Chris:** I'm leaving Saturday, that's when my plane gets me—Saturday morning.
>
> **Mary Ann:** No sir! My heck. Uh-uh.
>
> **Chris:** Sucks, huh?
>
> **Mary Ann:** You are not moving.
>
> **Chris:** I am . . . have to send you a plane ticket. I'm moving to East L.A. too, I got a place there.
>
> **Mary Ann:** Really? Well dang, so you're like leaving, huh.
>
> **Chris:** Yeah, so I want to see you tonight if I can, say good-bye to you.

So Mary Ann arranges to go see Chris around midnight. One of his friends, Vincent, picks her up outside her house on Thirty-ninth Street. And it's what happens next that Laura wants to clear up for me. Three days later, on May 24, she was badly beaten and bruised and, according to Mary Ann, it was Daniel who did it. But Laura claims that she was beaten well before Daniel got to her—the culprit was either Chris or his pals.

She shows me a transcript of a report by the DCFS caseworker who did the first interview with Mary Ann after she ran to the gas station. It reads: "I was at Brigham Hospital on another call when Deputy Maughn brought OV [oldest victim] into emergency. He reported that he had picked her up out at a service station in Plymouth and that she had originally reported that she had been in a fight. She then reported that she was married and that she had left her husband and gone to her mom's home."

"You see?" says Laura. "She changed her story. She originally said she was in a fight."

Then a month later, on June 26, Mary Ann told the SLC County sheriff that Vincent had taken her to an apartment in Sugar House where "they had this white stuff" and they were trying to send her out to sell it, but she didn't because there were too many police around. Laura has that look again: "So there's obviously something about drugs going on."

According to this interview, she stayed the night in this apartment with the guys and had them drop her off the next morning in a field near Valley

Coal. She couldn't face going home; she even considered sleeping in the trailers round the back of the yard. Then she called her mom, Susan, and told her that she was going to the hospital for the day (Laura's improbable explanation being that Mary Ann didn't want to stay with her *mother*). But in the end, she did actually go home, getting back on the night of June 22, the very night that Daniel took her up to Washakie.

She's homing in on a theory here, Laura—Mary Ann was mixed up with nasty drug dealers who beat her up. According to Heidi, "That's how [Mary Ann] paid for the drugs—she let [her boyfriend] beat her up. You've heard of people doing that, right?"

Laura's theory is mildly saner. "She got in a fight like she originally said and she came home with bruises. She called her mom, Susan, and said, 'I'm going to stay at a hospital.' Theron [Mary Ann's uncle] will tell you that she was high on drugs. Daniel took her to Washakie and dropped her off and then left for California. She walked to the gas station, called the cops and said she got in a fight." What this "fight" was about, Laura can only guess—a drug deal gone wrong, perhaps, or her refusal to sell for Chris and his pals.

"So you're saying she got those bruises a few days before the twenty-fourth."

"Yes," she says. "And we can prove it because those bruises were green by the time they took the pictures. Bruises don't go green if they're fresh."

The green bruise theory is iffy, but it's true that there are inconsistencies in Mary Ann's story. At first she said she was in a fight, then she said she'd tried to escape from her husband David Kingston, and her father Daniel had beaten her for it. During David's trial a year later, she admitted to having said things in her earlier interviews that weren't strictly true.

But it's only to be expected that a sixteen-year-old girl who's been raised in a cult, raped by her uncle and beaten mercilessly by her father might give confused answers to state agencies. Inconsistency is a natural outcome of fear and mistrust, factors that Laura refuses to consider since in her view, Mary Ann is a liar and a harlot. When she points out that Mary Ann had boyfriends, it's simply to tarnish her halo as a victim. And yet she also shows me testimony that makes her sympathetic. In an interview with Detective Hadlow on June 25, Mary Ann recalled the times when her uncle Arthur raped her at the age of eight or nine—the same Arthur who's currently married to Shari, with whom Stephanie and Andrea stayed after leaving home.

> **Detective Hadlow:** Did he get undressed?
> **Mary Ann:** Yes.
> **Detective Hadlow:** Was it lit in there so you could see?
> **Mary Ann:** There was a hanging light bulb but I don't remember.
> **Detective Hadlow:** Do you recall what you were thinking?
> **Mary Ann:** I was kinda thinking that it wasn't bad because you know, he's a good guy.

It gets worse. Arthur wasn't the only uncle involved—Gary was there too, the same Gary to whom Stephanie was promised in marriage. According to Mary Ann's testimony, Uncle Arthur was maybe seventeen or eighteen at the time, and he'd bribe her with candy to go down into the basement with him. And in a clear sign of confusion, she tells the detective that she doesn't want to press charges against Arthur—"He's changed a whole lot, and he's probably my favorite uncle." On David, however, she is unequivocal: "I couldn't stand him. I hated him my whole life."

Laura shows me these transcripts in triumph as if her case has been made: The rapist uncle was not David but Arthur, and the beating was not Daniel's doing, but that of her boyfriend Chris and his druggie pals.

"But why would Mary Ann knowingly protect the guilty and convict the innocent?" I ask. "Especially her own father and uncle?"

"Good question. Because she's a heartless brat."

"But she must have hated them for some reason."

"It makes about as much sense as her protecting Arthur. I don't understand anything she does."

"So in your mind there's absolutely no possibility that Daniel might be guilty."

"Absolutely not. I've been with him for eighteen years, and I've seen him with my kids. And I've talked to Daniel. He said he didn't do it and I believe him."

"But here's my problem: Daniel either beats his kids or he doesn't. And everyone in his family knows the truth, so there are a lot of liars on one side or the other. You're asking me to believe that it's not Daniel or you or Carleen or Heidi. The cold-blooded liars here are three teenage girls—Mary Ann, Stephanie and Andrea—who all claim to have been beaten, who all went through a hellish trial and lost most of their friends . . ."

"Wait—you're saying that Stephanie said Daniel beat her?"

"That's the point of the case, surely?"

"No, Andrea said that. Stephanie didn't. She has never said she's been physically abused as far as I know."

It's true that Stephanie didn't file an affidavit concurring with Andrea's account; all that's on file is her initial denial. And this is why Stephanie is Laura's favorite witness. "Stephanie fought to come home," she says, "but Judge Valdez said, 'As long as you are loyal to your parents, you never will.' So she said, 'Okay, well, I guess what Andrea is saying is true.' And then they cut off the parental ties and she never came home. Valdez lied and she fell for it."

"If she wanted to go home, why does she now have no contact with her parents?"

"Because she was surrounded by people that hate us for so long that she took on their personas, the little clichés they say, their perspective. Children are very impressionable. You can tell a child just about anything and get them to believe it when they're young enough."

The irony is unbearable. If only I could show her the Sunday School lessons that Hyrum sent me, the bit about teaching three-year-olds to worship the leader of the Order. Is she mocking me with these arguments? Or is she just being openly dishonest? At one point, she insists that "nobody says 'Order.' We say 'co-op' or 'church.'" But throughout the Sunday School lessons, "Order" is by far the more popular term. Children are taught to recite, "I am a member of the Order." They are also taught to lie to protect the Order. Is this what's happening here?

We spend several hours together, Laura and I. It's as though I present a challenge to her obstinacy, her lawyerly need to persuade. When I tell her that Order people are weird about inviting outsiders into their homes, she takes me to her apartment in Fullerton, a pool house in the yard of someone else's home. It's obviously just her college digs—there are no kids here; there's a pool table in the living room and a wall hanging saying;

BEER IS THE PROOF THAT GOD LOVES US. And yet Laura still insists, "Now you've seen an Order home! You can't say we didn't let you in!"

She's an intriguing character. At once deeply cynical and wildly ambitious, she seems to carry a silent, simmering rage. She writes me long, angry emails that end with her urgent wish to help. She complains that I'm going to get the Order's history all wrong while at the same time refusing to give me the history herself ("It's too sacred"). At one point, she just sighs and says, apropos of nothing, "I don't know why I'm helping you, you're just going to stab us in the back." But then she tells me how she has managed to finish law school while raising several children, and she gets all excited. "I'm going to change the world," she says. "You're going to hear about me, you watch!"

The last time I see her, however, is twenty minutes after she calls with this tantalizing message: "Are you in Salt Lake City? I need to see you in person. I can't talk about this on the phone." She gives me an address of one of the Order's buildings downtown where I find her standing in the pouring rain, impatiently waving a card over the wall. It's a grim brick office building, where Daniel sometimes works. And she's trying to swipe past a secret dot masked in the brickwork, which will snap the locks.

It's a gloomy scene inside, a damp gray foyer with toys strewn on the scratchy, peeling carpet. Laura ushers me up some stairs to a dismal cell of a room with a single bed, tatty wallpaper and three children's bikes stacked against the wall. I can't tell if this is an actual bedroom or storage or both.

"Okay, there were some arrests on Wednesday. The state came to the school and they had warrants and they took three ladies and several children from the school—Paul's wives and Paul's children. They're trying to prove incest." Laura says all of this very calmly. "I couldn't tell you this on the phone because it's not safe."

"Your phones are bugged?"

"Oh, we've known that for years," she says, and rattles off an example. Evidently one time, Daniel called someone to say that he was going to deposit a check of a certain amount—this when lawyers were trying to squeeze him for child support payments. Laura says that Carolyn Nichols, from the attorney general's office, informed Heidi's lawyers that this check was arriving, a fact they couldn't have known without surveillance. (Nichols denies any such thing. "Plain false," she says. "I never got an order for a phone tapping, never requested one and never heard of one being used.")

According to Laura, it was probably phone tapping that led to these alleged "arrests." She tells me that the Order's senior members use a system of secure pay-as-you-go phones that are only ever supposed to call each other, never an outside line because the state can detect outside lines, and thereby track the number from which that call was made. She believes that one of these women, one of Paul's wives, accidentally made just that mistake, enabling the authorities to listen in and pinpoint the location of Paul's wives.

"They got their DNA samples," she says. "So Paul has left town. So has Daniel. Paul's also dealing with the fact that one of his babies died a couple of weeks ago. I'm going to go to Daniel Irvin's office to challenge the warrants on the basis that they don't have probable cause. All they have is the hearsay of an anonymous source."

And with that she gets up and shows me the door. "If you want to keep in touch, I suggest we do it in person, not on the phone."

"But Laura, I live in L.A."

"Oh well."

"Can't we communicate on email?"

"They may be monitoring emails too. From my understanding they detect an email when it is sent. So we can do this—we can set up a hotmail account and leave messages for each other as saved drafts. Does that make sense?"

"Okay, sure." So we're out in the rain, scribbling down secret passwords and email addresses. It's all so clandestine, so exciting, the phone tapping, the surveillance—I want it all to be true. Here I am with a member of a hardcore cult intent on world domination, whose leader is being pursued by the state, and it's all happening now. That car across the street could be staking us out this very minute.

But then, coming from Laura, it's hard to believe. Her arguments are frequently disingenuous and she appears to be paranoid. This picture of the state as a sinister Big Brother suits her agenda perfectly. What's compelling about Laura is her conviction. This is her life's cause, and it's hard to ignore the support she has found among other fundamentalists, outside of the Order—the turnouts at the courthouse, the otherwise reasonable men who assure me that "I've seen Daniel's wives, they look very happy."

By all accounts Laura is winning. In February 2009, she writes to tell me that Mary Ann's civil suit has been dropped; the "heartless brat" has been vanquished. Evidently many of those whom Mary Ann was suing were removed from the suit by the judge—notably the businesses or "steward-ships" where all the money was tied up. And several individuals went on to countersue her for defamation, since she'd labeled them polygamists when they were, legally speaking, monogamists. So in the end, she chose to drop her remaining suits in return for the suits against her being dropped. Another victory for the Order.

I can't bring myself to buy Laura's version of events—all these lying, malicious daughters led astray by the Order's hysterical opponents. But how can I prove it? As it happens, even as I drive back to my motel through the pelting rainstorm, my answer is gathering herself at her desktop. She's about to write me an email, breaking a silence of two years:

> Sanjiv Bhattacharya,
> I was informed that you are interested in speaking
> with me about your recent book. I believe you
> already spoken to my biological mother Heidi and i
> am willing to speak with you also. You're welcome
> to contact me at (801) ***-****

It's Stephanie, now living under an assumed name. She wants to tell me the truth about her father, Daniel, but only if I swear never to reveal her new identity or where she lives. She's never spoken to anyone about what really happened during the Heidi Foster case because she's afraid the Order will come after her. "I've got a new life now, I just want to move on," she says. "So you have to promise."

I promise.

◈ Stephanie

Not all those who wander are lost.

—J. R. R. Tolkien

Serendipitous, the way it happened. Apparently Christy Tucker was taking her twelve-year-old to the orthodontist one day when she bumped into one of Stephanie's half brothers (ex-Order) at the hardware store. He mentioned that he'd seen Stephanie working at a nearby mobile phone store, but he couldn't remember which one. So Christy tried the ones she knew in the area, and sure enough, there Stephanie was, behind the counter, living and working under a new identity. So Christy thrust my contact details into her hands. And to her surprise and mine, she sent me an email that very day. This is her first interview since the case closed. Christy was breathless when she told me.

She looks like Heidi, walking out of her front door to meet me—the spacing of her eyes, the pronounced forehead, strongly built. She lives in one of those picturebook *Big Love* suburbs of Salt Lake that looks especially spotless on this crisp sunny day. We drive to a nearby Chili's for lunch, and the small talk begins. There's a bashfulness there, but also a confidence for a girl of twenty, the way she just chats away to this strange reporter guy with the accent. It's the kind of confidence that comes from having left the Order, endured two withering years of hearings, foster homes and media coverage, and then found a whole new life with a new family—and emerged from it all somewhat intact.

She tells me her new name. "But I don't want you to use that. I guess you can call me Stephanie in your book."

"Okay, Stephanie, no problem."

"No, don't call me that now! If I heard 'Stephanie' when I was at home with Heidi, then my mind would start racing to 'what did I do wrong?' I just knew I was going to get beat. Daniel beat me basically my whole life, as long as I can remember."

This is her story; it could not be clearer: Daniel is a vicious and unrepentant abuser who has hurt scores of children over the years. He has been protected by polygamy, by the smokescreen of secrecy and distractions about religious freedom and state persecution—the stuff that so exercises Laura Fuller. But Stephanie is unequivocal: The state acted honorably throughout. Shari and Arthur and Justin and Shawna were her saviors, though she might not have always seen it that way at first. Her account almost entirely matches Shawna's, but it is a world away from the story I've been told with force and passion by Laura Fuller, Carleen and Heidi. And these women, she insists, know better.

You can tick all the boxes on her Kingston upbringing, it was typical enough. She didn't know who her father was for much of her youth, she worked at Order stewardships from the age of eight and before the earrings incident, at the age of fifteen, she had quite a resumé. "Let's see, I worked at A1 Disposal, I was at Triple A Security working in dispatch. At Advanced Copy, I was customer service, and at Advance Emblem, I did emblems, sewing. Up at the ranch in Washakie I worked in the butchering part. You know, I did the slaughtering and butchering, skinning, deboning. I packaged up the meat." It's quite a picture—a fifteen-year-old girl spattered with cow's blood, sending whole flanks of carcass through the saw.

There was blood at home, too. "When I was growing up the only times my dad came over to my house, that I recall, was to hit me because I did something wrong. I don't know how to explain it. He talked so soft you know, but it's so deep and so intense—he could just hit me without any emotions at all. It's like it's not him. I don't know. I was scared to death of him. He hit us with two-by-fours. And he'd get mad at Heidi because she didn't discipline us enough. She'd yell at us and he'd say, 'The neighbors are going to hear.' So he'd tell her to hit us instead. It's quieter. You're not supposed to cry when they hit you."

"But Heidi says he never beat you, or any of your sisters or brothers."

"What?"

"That's what she told me."

She looks shocked, upset. She shakes her head. "I can't believe . . . I don't even know how she can say that and sleep at night. She saw it *herself*. She *knows*. I mean, that just proves she cares more about her loyalty to Daniel than she does about her own kids."

During one of Andrea's beatings, for instance, Stephanie says she begged her mother to make Daniel stop, but Heidi said, "If he wasn't doing it, I'd be doing the same thing." And when Andrea was sent upstairs, Daniel set about beating Stephanie. "It makes me feel so powerless talking about it," she says. "It's embarrassing."

The beatings were regular, at least once a month. And though Stephanie wasn't the only victim, she took the brunt because she was the oldest. She would shoulder the blame when her siblings misbehaved, to protect them. She now has back problems she attributes to Daniel. She remembers looking in the mirror at the hand marks across her face.

"I remember as young as six years old, I was sitting on my mom's bed just crying my eyes out and my sister walked in. I had blood all over my face, my nose was bleeding, cuts and stuff. It was just, like, dripping on my clothes."

And that wasn't the worst of it. She wrote about her worst beating on a website, under her new identity. The stomach churns. She was dragged across the floor by her hair, thrown into a wall, punched repeatedly across the face and whacked with a two-by-four across the legs and back for an extended period. Daniel only stopped when she managed to roll under the bed, where she cried herself to sleep. And when she awoke the next day, Heidi explained what had set him off: She hadn't come quickly enough when Daniel had called her to the van after church.

Such was Stephanie's alternative universe that it only dawned on her that hitting children might be wrong after an episode of *Dr. Phil.* "I remember thinking, 'If you're not supposed to hit your kids, what do you do instead?' I saw other parents in stores say, 'When you get home you're going to have a time out.' And I was like, what's a 'time out'?"

Laura Fuller argues that if the beatings were so common, then DCFS would surely have picked up on it during ten years of inspections of Heidi's home. But Stephanie has an explanation: Daniel stopped hitting his kids across the face and started on their backsides or backs so that DCFS wouldn't see. Naturally, the children didn't dare tell DCFS workers when they came over. "We're not stupid," says Stephanie. "Our parents could very well put a recorder in the room. We know our parents would do stuff like that. And we're not going to set ourselves up after DCFS has already failed us so many times."

The weekend of the earrings was merely the tipping point for Stephanie. It offered her an out and she took it. Her parents had been at a convention in Las Vegas for a couple of days, leaving her and Andrea to babysit the six other children—plus another four during the day from her aunt. So Stephanie wanted to make the most of her "freedom." She took Andrea and set off in Heidi's car to get their ears pierced. She'd never driven before, so they lurched their way to the mall where they saw Shari and persuaded her to authorize the piercing as a guardian. And so it was that they wound up in Daniel's office, being reprimanded.

"Daniel hopped over his desk and said, 'You have ten seconds to take them out, otherwise I'll rip them out.' And he started the countdown. When he got to, like, five, I said, 'I need a mirror.' So he said, 'Go get a mirror, you know where one is.' So I walked to the bathroom, and I saw the door to outside. And I thought, 'I'm outta here.'"

It didn't work. They made it to the gas station down the road, where they called Shari, hysterical. Meanwhile, the gas station owner called the cops, who showed up quickly and separated the sisters from the parents, one officer talking to the latter, while the other sat with the girls. Stephanie told the cop that she didn't want to go home, she knew she was in danger, but it fell upon deaf ears. "The other cop came up with my parents and made us apologize. He said, 'If my daughter got her ears pierced without permission, she'd be a lot worse off. Your parents are loving parents.' And my mom gave us both a big hug, which was really weird because she'd never hugged us before."

As soon as they got home, Daniel and Heidi let them have it. "They said, 'You just opened up the door. Now DCFS is going to come over. So Andrea you need to clean the house up, and Stephanie you need to take work off tomorrow and . . .'"

"You were working?"

"Full-time. I was fifteen. But Daniel told Heidi, 'You've got to get her in school because DCFS is going to come and ask.' So it looked like I was actually going to finish out the year in high school—I loved that."

Meanwhile, Shawna was busy working on getting the girls into care. Stephanie recalls the day that Shawna arrived at the Order school, the Ensign Learning Center, with the police. "I came and saw the cops outside," she says. "So I sneaked around to Andrea's class to find her, but they'd already got her in the car by then. And the other girls there were all crying,

'The cops took Andrea, they're going to kill her.' I'm like, 'Who's going to kill her?' And they're like, 'Shawna and Justin.'"

Heidi and Daniel accused Stephanie of planning the whole thing. They dragged her to a meeting with the leader Paul at the Order's law offices on State Street. According to Stephanie, Laura Fuller was also present.

"Paul told me what to say to the officials," she says. "He said, 'Don't say anything about the Order.' He said that we were the Kingdom of God and it was better for one person to perish than a whole nation. He said it was better that I perish, like a savior or something."

"Is that where the talk of suicide came from?"

"Daniel said that a custody case is normally over within a year. So a year from now, if you still can't come home, it would be better to just die so you can still go to heaven, instead of living a life of sin outside of the Order. I basically took that as: 'In a year, I'm supposed to die.' I thought about it pretty seriously. And I thought that if I didn't do it, they would."

Once Paul had said his piece, he left, and Daniel took charge. His temper flared. "He yelled at me but I yelled back," says Stephanie. "I knew he couldn't touch me. He told me to go home and pack a bag, so I did. But he didn't even come to our house that night, knowing it could be our last night at home."

The next day, Daniel and Heidi checked through her things to ensure she wasn't packing anything incriminating—"evidence of their marriage, pictures or anything like that." Then they drove her to the police station to hand her over. It was a heart-wrenching time for the young girl, saying good-bye to all her brothers and sisters and cousins, all her friends, whom Daniel said she might never see again.

But she would see Gary again, her uncle and intended husband. She'd long known that she was meant to become Gary's third wife—the second being Stephanie's aunt (Heidi's younger sister). "Daniel flat out told me I was supposed to marry him, and so did Gary. At one point I even thought I was married to him because he sexually abused me, and I thought it was because I was his wife. He said I was sealed to him, and when I said, 'No, we didn't get married yet,' he said, 'But Stephanie, we were married in heaven before we came to Earth.'"

The abuse began young, toward the end of kindergarten, at the start of first grade. By the time she was eleven, "it was more or less a way of life. He would call me in the middle of the night and tell me to meet him outside. He works in a security company, so he has keys to a lot of companies in downtown Salt Lake. So he would drive me to different companies and turn off the cameras, and . . . the abuse would take place in there. Sometimes in the middle of the day. It was always odd hours so his other wives wouldn't know."

As Shawna told me, Stephanie actually missed Gary at first. "At the age of fifteen, I saw that as love," Stephanie says. "I thought if I married Gary, I would belong to him and Daniel couldn't hit me anymore—that would be Gary's job. And I knew that wives sometimes withheld things from their husband so he would treat them better. I thought I might have some control that way. To Daniel I was nothing. But to Gary I would be a wife and the mother of his kids. I always hoped that that would mean something."

So when Gary told her to contact him, she did, despite all of Shawna's warnings. He told her to write him secret love letters and ask her guardians to let her go on a walk, so that she could secretly meet him somewhere. She did whatever he said. And Gary would pick her up, take her to the parking lot of an LDS Church and abuse her there in his truck. He'd tell her they would be married soon, and she believed him. Even today, Stephanie has nightmares about Gary. "If I meet a guy now and it's my first date, I dream about Gary and how he's so disappointed in me. Sometimes he kills the person or something happens to them. He's still there in my mind."

Stephanie's feelings for Gary in the early stages of this case spoke to a deeper turmoil. At the time, she was also loudly protesting her life in custody and her treatment by the state. She gave every appearance of wanting to return to the Order, writing pleading letters, which Heidi would give top billing on her website. It confounded investigators, frustrated attorneys and hurt the credibility of her sister Andrea. Why did she do it?

"I was scared to death," she says. "I ran away when I was eight and I was sent back. I ran away when I was thirteen and I was sent back. So the way I saw it, the state just failed me. And I wanted them out of the picture as soon as possible so I could run away on my own. I didn't trust the cops, I didn't trust anybody. Plus I had dragged my sister into it."

Her conflicted state of mind comes through in the events of that bizarre night Shawna had described—the one in which the girls found themselves in a stranger's car. It all started with time to kill after school. Stephanie and Andrea had three hours before they were supposed to meet Shawna, so they took the bus to the Order school to see their old friends and relatives, and then onto Advanced Copy & Printing, where they met Cheryl Nelson, Mary Ann's sister.

"She said, 'Hey, if you run away from them, then they'll know you don't want to be there.' And me and Andrea looked at each other and thought, 'You're right.' We were very happy staying at Shawna's, but in case we actually got sent home, it would be good to be on the Order's side."

This was the balancing act during that first year: while she wanted to leave the Order, she gave the opposite appearance just in case she was sent back. The previous time she ran away, in 2001, she told the authorities everything. "I said that my parents are planning on marrying me off, I eat out of the garbage, my dad beats us, he's never there, my mom's pregnant, the house is unfit. I was probably thirteen," she says. "And the judge basically said, 'All I see here is a defiant child.'" He sent her to live with her grandfather (now expired) and she became an immediate pariah. "People would spit at me when I walked out of church to the car. They'd throw rocks."

So she tried to appear as if she were a victim of the state—that was why she wrote the letter saying that she loved her family so, and why she put Shawna's home last on the list of where she'd like to be moved to. "I knew that anything I put on paper was going to go to their lawyers and my parents would see it. So I told Andrea, 'Play it safe—don't say anything that could hurt you.' I stayed on the fence until I knew we were going to be safe, about a year and a half later."

She had every reason to be nervous of the Order during this time. While she was staying at her foster home, Order members would stalk her and give her instructions. "They came to my work and said, 'What day do you have off this week? Tell your foster mom you have work, so we can pick you up and then drop you back at the end of the day.' Or they would call with instructions about what I needed to say in the next court hearing, and if I didn't say it, I knew they could get to me the very next day if they wanted to. Even when they put me in a lockdown facility, Order members were servicing the kitchen."

"Laura says that the state was brainwashing you and putting words in your mouth at the hearings. She describes you as a prisoner of war."

"That's not true. The only thing the chief investigator always told me was 'The truth will set you free.' And I didn't believe her at first, but now when I look back, if I had just told the truth from the beginning, it might have gone down better."

"Another implication that Order people have made—that it was Arthur who is the abuser here. Is it true?"

"He never touched me, nor Andrea as far as I know. Gary did things to me, and other people did things to Andrea, that's just how they were. So they're hypocrites to point fingers at Arthur. Arthur is a good man. I'm still close to him and Shari. I babysit their kids."

Nevertheless, there was that one night when Stephanie and Andrea decided to run away to leave the impression that they didn't like it at Shari and Arthur's. They took the school bus to Heidi's office, where they told her they were running away. Heidi told them that they could stay at the home of a relative called Colin—the keys were in the mailbox. But by this time it was dark and Shawna was worried. She had reported the girls missing, fearing that they'd been abducted when in fact they were at Colin's house, afraid to turn on the lights in case it alerted the neighbors that the house had intruders. They were two girls huddled together in a big, dark house letting their minds wander and scaring themselves.

They started listing their options on a piece of paper. Either they could walk the several miles home, or they could catch a bus, or hitch a ride. Perhaps they could stay at Colin's all night and claim they'd been kidnapped? In the end they opted for the bus home, but the buses had stopped—it was past 10 pm. So they walked. There was no real plan. "Honestly at that point I really didn't care what happened to me," says Stephanie. "I was like, I would rather someone just kill us right now, because I'm sick of dealing with everything. I feel like walking in front of that car. Andrea was like, 'Me too.'" A mile or so down the road, a guy pulled up and rolled down his window. He offered them a ride downtown, and they thought, "What the heck." They got in.

The man was drinking and smoking and ranting as he went—some sob story about how his girlfriend had left him and he'd never see his daughter again. He seemed distraught. The girls quickly realized their mistake. "He started rubbing his hand on my knees and stuff," says Stephanie. "He was like, 'You guys are so beautiful.' So me and Andrea were pretty scared. Then he stopped at this gas station and as he was going in, he handed me his phone. He said, 'Here's my phone so you can trust me.' And he gave us his driver's license and it was like ten years outdated. So I was panicking, trying to remember Shawna's number. Finally I got through and I said, 'Shawna, we don't know where we're at, we're at this gas station, with this guy, he gave us a ride . . .' And she's like, 'Get out of the car and run!' I was like, 'Okay, okay,' but right then he was coming out. So I just slammed the phone shut and he got back in the car. He had bought himself some more beers. And he tried to give us these like little chocolate milks or something."

At a red light downtown, the girls bolted from the car, hysterical. They kept running until they found a police officer who had just pulled someone over. He told them to wait by his car while he wrote up the ticket, so they had a few minutes to concoct a story. "I was like, 'Andrea, we're going to get in so much trouble. You can't just run away and get away with it. Let's say that drunk guy kidnapped us. But wait—we shouldn't have been out so late anyway. We can say we got lost on the buses . . .'"

And that was how they played it when the cop came over, blurting out this half-fact, half-fiction story that barely hung together. Seeing the policeman's skepticism, they then changed tack and told him the whole truth, about how they they'd left the Order but now they'd left their foster home too, but not because they didn't want to go back . . . but that sounded even less plausible. "The police didn't believe us anymore," says Stephanie. "So they just kind of made up the rest of the report on their own and took us home."

The girls were returned to Shawna, who was hysterical by this point. She took them off to a secure facility the very next day and it was there that she discovered the notes that they'd made at Colin's house, listing all the options for their night. I tell Stephanie what Shawna thought those notes were: a deliberate plan written by Daniel or someone in the Order to make Shawna and Justin look like unfit guardians. She laughs.

"No wonder she responded the way she did! Me and Andrea were like, what the . . . ? She just dumped us off the next day like trash!"

There were other notes in Stephanie's backpack that make her cringe today—sexual notes to Gary that he'd asked her to write, incorporating tips and techniques she picked up from *Cosmopolitan* magazine. "I really didn't know those things at that age—you know, sexual moves that guys like . . . So I just used stuff I saw in *Cosmo* or in films. At Shawna's house, I was watching some show called *Basic Instinct* or something where this lady's writing a book? I took a lot of lines from there."

By the time we finish up, I'm humbled. I've heard no story on this journey quite so filled with anguish and cruelty, and yet here she is talking me through it, with all the grace and courage of a true survivor. Though Stephanie's only twenty, there's a remarkable wisdom and steel about her. And it's hard to understand why she would fabricate her story. What a monument of lies it would have to be, and at what a price: Stephanie cannot see her siblings again, or her cousins, or anyone in the Order. She scarcely even has contact with Andrea any more. Stephanie has not only changed her name, but also the names of her parents on her birth certificate. The names Heidi and Daniel have been officially scrubbed from her life.

Still, she often thinks of Heidi. At first she saw her as a victim, the young mother who never had a chance to grow up, the pregnant teenager who kept having children just to feel their love. "That's what happens, the women feel like no one loves them, so they rush to have kids so that their kids will love them. And then they're stuck in the relationship with kids and no money." At one time, Heidi used to give Stephanie advice about how to cope with Daniel. "When I was saying that I wanted to run away, she said, 'There's times I feel like that too. You just have to wait it out until you don't feel those feelings anymore.'"

But now Stephanie sees Heidi as a coward. She had a shot at freedom but she didn't take it. "The time Heidi spent outside of the Order was awesome for her. When I met her during that time, she was telling me about her accomplishments, she was proud of herself. 'Look what I did, look at the friends I made, look at how I reached out to society.' They were things she could never do on her own before. And I thought, 'Oh my gosh, I see a future here, I can come home now.' But she chose the Order."

"But Heidi says her time outside the Order was awful and frightening. She missed church."

Stephanie shakes her head. "There's no way she can admit enjoying life outside. She has to make it look like she was in captivity, as long as she's alive, as long as she has someone she cares about that she doesn't want to have harmed."

It has been an unsettling discovery, the Order—a culture of secrecy and cruelty in which abusers are sheltered and victims are muffled for generations, and with effective impunity. It appears to strengthen the case for the decriminalization of polygamy. If the Order could join the open society, the truth about the leaders might be more easily exposed, as would their doctrines of fear, otherness and incest, the grand fraud of their fictional surnames and the depressing exploitation of their economic system. At the time of writing, Hyrum and Marlyne remain trapped within the cult, while criminals like Daniel and Gary carry on in comfort. Who are the Kingstons to harp on about religious freedom when their own children feel so shackled? These are the things I'd say to Paul Kingston, if only he'd meet me.

"Good luck with that," scoffs Stephanie.

"What do you mean?"

"Well, considering they believe that white people are God's people and other color people are Satan's people . . ."

"I keep forgetting it's a racial thing with these guys."

"You know, um, the N word? They use that all the time. Like Daniel would say to me, 'Aren't you glad that Mom and I aren't a bunch of niggers?'" She's gone bright red.

"You're kidding."

"No. I mean, I know it's really messed up. But I didn't know back then. That's what we'd call each other when we were angry. Other people might say, you're an asshole, but in the Order, people say, you're a . . . you know. Daniel said it constantly. If we got up on the furniture or whatever, he'd say, 'Don't act like a bunch of . . .' That kind of stuff."

"I was planning on getting up on the furniture if I met him, too."

"Ha ha! You should do that if you meet Paul.

The way Stephanie's story plays out over the next few years could not be more heartening. She finishes high school and graduates from college in sociology (she wants to become a marriage counselor). She meets a young medical student named Todd and they marry in the LDS temple (she's a vanilla Mormon now). They have two little girls. And she grows stronger

every day in this new life of hers. Strong enough to testify against Laura
Fuller in court, thereby preventing her from gaining admittance to the
Utah bar. Strong enough even to reach out to Heidi.

They first reconnected at Heidi's mother's funeral, a big Order affair
where Stephanie saw her siblings and uncles for the first time in years.
It was tense, but constructive. And the following Christmas, gifts were
exchanged. So when Stephanie's first child, Kennedy, was born, she invited
Heidi over to visit, and it went well. The only blip was when Heidi asked to
bring Daniel to see the baby—Stephanie forbade it, for now and forever.
But otherwise, the door was opened. And bit by bit, she reconnected with
her old Order family, her brothers Kevin and Jason, and her sister Melanie,
in particular.

"The kids are more rebellious now. They have their own cell phones;
they drink, they smoke," she says. "I think they realize that they can have
a say in their futures. When Daniel was hitting the kids, Kevin stood
up to him. He said, 'Knock it off and get out, or I'll call the cops.' And
Daniel left. Even Heidi is standing up to Daniel now, just a little bit.
When Daniel threatened to kick Kevin out of the family, Heidi said, 'No
you're not!'"

But it's difficult with Heidi. She won't give up on trying to bring Daniel
into Stephanie's life. She even threatened recently to refuse Stephanie contact with her siblings unless she agreed. But Stephanie didn't mince her
words. "I told her that Daniel was not my dad and he was not my children's
grandfather, so he needs to leave me alone. Period."

It's also the sightings that bother Stephanie. Living in Utah County,
she sees Order members out and about all the time. The other day, she
saw Paul at the movies with his latest young and pregnant wife. She even
bumped into Gary the other day. "He still doesn't think he did anything
wrong," she says. And then there are the random encounters, at the shops,
at bowling. "I'll go to a grocery store, and someone's there just looking at
me. But I can't quite place them; I don't know who they are."

So she and Todd have decided to put an end to it. They're leaving Utah.
Her babies have lung problems, so the doctor has advised that they live
near the coast, where the air is more humid. Todd has applied to medical
school in the southeast, near Florida, Alabama, or Tennessee. "I'll probably
never come back," she says. "And I can't wait!"

The thing about moving out of state is that wherever they end up, no one there will know her as Stephanie.

"You don't have to call me Stephanie in the book anymore," she says. "You can say my real name: Jessica Christensen. The Order knows who I am. I'm not scared of them. If anything, it's the other way around."

Why Jessica? It's the first name of Jessica Eldredge, the investigator for the attorney general's office who stood by her when she first ran. "She was the one who told me, way back at the beginning, that 'the truth will set you free.' She was so right."

Postscript

The news from the Order has been mixed in recent years. There have been no fresh scandals, which is encouraging, but by the same token, no action has been taken against the group. In fact, the attorney general has stopped even pretending to investigate. Mark Shurtleff told *Rolling Stone* magazine in June 2011 that he believed the Order was an organized-crime family, and yet his office continues to do nothing about it. Such is the way of things in Utah.

But there have been improvements on other fronts—internal shifts within the Order, for instance. According to anecdotal reports, the Order is less militant than it was, the attitudes have softened, and Daniel isn't beating his children nearly as much anymore. After Andrea and Stephanie, the group is more afraid than ever of causing a scandal, and it's also struggling to hold on to its younger members, who are now less afraid to leave than they once were. So conditions are improving. Teenagers are more likely to enjoy an education, even though the leaders still decide what it is the kids will study. And of those who leave (there have been several), some are even permitted limited contact with their siblings.

Before we get too excited, however, it's worth remembering that incestuous marriages still take place. The most extreme form—brother-sister marriage—is on the wane, because genetic deformities have become so common, but the other combinations are rife. And the family of Paul Kingston continues to grow at a rampant pace. I spoke recently with Hyrum, the spy, who reckons the prophet has roughly four hundred children by now, an entirely reasonable figure, given the number of wives he has.

It's hard for Hyrum to share this news. Having given the attorney general so much information over the years—taking such personal risks in the process—he finds the continued impunity of Paul, Daniel, Gary, and others deeply disillusioning. Like so many within the Order, Hyrum wants to leave, but he's conflicted. "I can't because my brothers and sisters are quite deeply in the Order, and I might never see them again," he says. "But I can't stay. I can't stand it anymore."

The extent of his anguish became clear when in March 2013, I received a series of texts:

```
Here's your update: I'm killing myself may
13th . . . I can't leave the order and I
can't live the rest of my life without
family I thought I could but I guess I've
known for the last 8 years I've been wanting
to leave. I really just wanna die instead.
```

May 13 is Daniel's birthday. Hyrum planned to leave a suicide note that revealed his every act against the Order.

Hyrum's misery is understandable. There's just nothing easy about leaving the Order. But roughly a week before his cry for help, I heard from a girl whose story might just offer some reassurance—not that leaving isn't painful, but that no matter how traumatic it is, a happy ending still awaits, eventually.

She had read the first edition of this book and decided to Skype me one day, knowing full well that hers would be the chapter that completes this saga. It's a story so dark and upsetting that it's a miracle that she has emerged from it whole. But she has. She appeared on my laptop one evening with a bright smile, cross-legged on a couch in her student digs. A pretty girl, she's studying sociology at the University of Washington. She wants to be a lawyer at the end of it. And I wouldn't doubt her for an instant.

"Hi Sanjiv! It's Andrea. Can you see me OK?"

Andrea Kingston first met her adoptive parents when she and her sister

Stephanie were living with Shawna and Justin. Andrea and Stephanie had run away from home at that point, and as Shawna was discovering, the girls needed monitoring when she wasn't around. So from time to time, Shawna would ask her friends Ryan and Lynette Newton* to babysit. It was a stressful time of court battles and intrigue. The girls wanted nothing more than to leave the Order, as the guardian ad litem, Kristen Brewer, well knew. So once the drama had settled, it was decided that they would transition into foster care. And straight away, the Newtons called. Lynette had followed the girls' case closely and wanted to offer to adopt Andrea. The Newtons made a compelling case.

Lynette (twenty-nine) and Ryan (thirty-two) were successful software engineers who'd been raised in the Mormon church, but weren't religious anymore—they smoked, had a glass of wine occasionally. In a way, they were an odd match: Ryan was tall and slim and quite particular about his appearance, while Lynette was obese and unkempt. Andrea describes her as "very masculine. She hardly ever wore makeup." But they had a lovely home in Washington, near Snohomish, and two young children of their own, a boy named Calvin (three) and a girl named Hayden (five). They planned to send Andrea to school and to take her on vacations. They would offer her the family life she never had. It sounded perfect.

But from the start, there was hostility in the air.

"Even before I moved up, Lynette said she didn't like that I called Ryan 'Dad,' but I called her 'Lynette,'" says Andrea. "I explained that I have a mom already, and I didn't want to betray her, but I never had a dad. Then when I moved up to Washington, she just treated me like shit. She kept reminding me that she didn't want to adopt me—it was all Ryan's idea. And all this bullshit about how I was trying to take over her family but he was not my husband, and his kids were not my kids. This was even before the adoption went through."

Andrea was going to therapy at the time, to get some help with this transition. But the therapist's advice was peculiar. She recommended that Andrea sleep in her parents' bed at night. It was a form of "attachment therapy," to help her bond with her new family. So she did. At fourteen, she started spending every night wedged between her new father and mother.

---

*The names of the Newton family have been changed.

Lynette's response to this was instant. While at first she was hateful and cruel toward Andrea, now she acted as though she was delighted by the new arrangement. She began hugging Andrea in public. "She liked to kiss me, too. Not a mom kind of kiss, on the cheek, but on the lips," says Andrea. "And she would keep doing it over and over. It was totally inappropriate, but here I am at fourteen, confused. I just want her to love me and treat me like her daughter, and I don't really know how to have a mom, or how that relationship is meant to be. So I just went along with it."

Then one day, on the way to school, Ryan asked Andrea a bizarre question. "He said, 'Did I touch you in any way last night?' I was like, 'Er, no, not that I know of.' And he said, 'Your mom says she saw me fondling you and touching you, and I just don't remember doing that—so I thought if you remembered, then I could make my apologies to you.'"

She said nothing had happened. But his question was disturbing. Surely he would know if he had touched her? And what was this about Lynette watching him? It instantly changed things. From that moment, all physical contact with Lynette was cut off. No hugs, no comfort. "If I did well at something or was sad about something, and I just wanted my mom to hug me, she would just roll her eyes and say, 'You're disgusting, get away from me.'"

To this day, Andrea isn't sure quite what was happening while she was asleep. "Of course, the Order completely prepared me for this situation," she says. "There was a lot of sexual abuse in the Order. When I was young, maybe five, some of the boys used to touch me when I was asleep, and I knew then to just sleep through it. So I'd been trained for this."

The day soon came when there was no doubt—she knew, lying there at night, that her father was touching her. And the next morning, they were both in the car driving to the airport to pick up her sister, Jessica (Stephanie), who was coming to stay with them. It had been agreed from the outset that part of the girls' transition into their new families would involve visiting each other and seeing for themselves that the other was being properly looked after.

Ryan asked her, "Do you remember last night, or were you sleeping?"

She sat in silence for a moment, playing dumb. But then she gave an answer that haunts her now. "I always think back to how I responded and how that could have changed the outcome of my teenage years," she says. "I decided to make a joke about it, just to see what would happen. I said,

'Yeah, you left me hanging.'"

He laughed. "Oh, so you want me to do it again, huh?"

Right away, she regretted it. "I thought, fuck, wrong answer. I just sat there quietly until we reached the airport. I was like, how am I going to bring my sister into this house after that?"

Jessica's visit was a disaster. Lynette argued with her; there was screaming and yelling. Of course, Andrea didn't dare mention a word to her sister about what had happened. And once Jessica was gone, the abuse just escalated. It became routine. Ryan would say that if only he were a decade younger and she were a decade older, they could run away together. It wasn't long before he was raping her. It was 2007, and she was fifteen years old.

A pattern set in at home, between her hateful mother and her pedophile father. "On the one hand, there's Lynette telling me how she wishes she never adopted me," Andrea says. "She literally had this fucking countdown where she's like, 'Only this many days until this bitch is out of the house! One day less where I don't have to see your face again!' But when I'd go to Ryan all upset, instead of consoling me like a father, he would have sex with me and then just send me on my way. It was hell."

Certain moments stay with her for their horror. Like their picture-perfect family cruise to the Bahamas later that summer. Andrea liked to tell her school friends that she had this wonderful family, that her foster parents were lovely, and that they had this terrific life—holidays in the Bahamas helped maintain that fantasy. But the reality was quite the opposite. Lynette chose the cruise to accuse Andrea for the first time of having sex with Ryan. She screamed at her in their cabin, in front of Ryan and the two children, who were four and six at the time. "She's yelling at me like, 'You're stealing my family from me,' and so Ryan suggests—he's such a hero—'Oh let me take the kids out of the situation so that you can continue to yell at our daughter that we just adopted and that I'm raping.' Then the next day, he gives me the third degree. We're out on the balcony looking out onto the ocean, and from a distance, it looks like a father and daughter having a lovely moment. But the conversation is, 'Did you say anything? What did you tell her?' It was like the fucking Order all over again."

Andrea takes a deep breath. She wants to tell me all this, but it's not easy.

It's never easy. "I think of it as someone else's life, not mine," she says. "As unhealthy as that is, it makes it easier."

For two years, she was trapped in the Newton family. Lynette's cruelty worsened. She would lock Andrea outside the house and force her to shovel the snow from the driveway before letting her back in. It did no good to plead to Ryan. "This is hard for me too," he would say, leaving her out there. And Andrea's therapist suspected nothing, even as Andrea's weight ballooned from 110 to 170 pounds. And it didn't help that she (Andrea's therapist) was also Lynette's therapist and Ryan's, too, with a distorted sense of professional boundaries. "At one point," says Andrea, "she actually asked me point blank, 'Your mom thinks that there's some sexual activity taking place between you and your dad. Is there?' I said no. I've been trained enough to lie."

There was, however, Kristen Brewer. Andrea would call her from time to time, hinting only that things were less than perfect at home; she didn't let on quite how hellish life had become. "Kristen always said, 'Look, if you want to get away, for the summer or whatever, you're always welcome here.' She was like an aunt or something. She lived in Washington, too, about three hours south of us."

One day, for example, Andrea was scheduled to visit a college in Portland, Oregon, for "Mom Day," to see if she wanted to apply. Lynette was meant to take her, but had changed her mind. "She said, 'You need to go with someone who's interested in being part of your life. I couldn't care less.' And Ryan typically said he couldn't go, either, because it might upset Lynette. So Kristen took me." She noticed Andrea's weight gain, but didn't suspect that Andrea might be in serious trouble. After all, Heidi is heavy too.

In the end, Andrea selected a private university in Tacoma. And it was her savior. As a foster child, she had a full scholarship, so she wouldn't need to ask her parents for any support—not that any would be forthcoming. And in the fall of 2009, a new chapter began.

It's not that the abuse stopped, exactly. She visited Ryan twice in that first term, and both times, he tried to have sex with her. And when she went home for the Christmas break, the routine abuse started up again. "He used to say, 'I wonder what our life is going to be like when you get married. Because you'll come over to visit with your husband, but we'll go and sneak off into this other room and it's going to be this crazy exciting thing that no one else is going to know about.'"

But college was changing her. She saw a way out. She rearranged her 2010 spring schedule to rule out any visits. She spent that summer with her sister Jessica, who was getting married. And that fall, she started dating a guy, a proper boyfriend with a loving family who soon wanted her to join them on vacations. There was a whole life beyond the Newtons. And that Christmas, her mind was made up.

"The way Lynette talked to Hayden was the same way she talked to me. Yelling at her about how horrible she was, what an ungrateful brat. That was how she told her daughter good night on Christmas eve. And me and Hayden look just like each other. She was, like, eleven at this time. She used to talk to me about how excited she was that she's going to get her period soon, and start getting breasts. I was like, 'Are you kidding me? Do you realize what's coming for you when that happens?' So that was it for me. I thought, 'This is not happening to her.'"

She confronted Ryan on the phone. Screamed at him about everything he had done. It was over. He would never touch her again. She had the power now; he could hear it in her voice. Then she told her therapist and, a couple of weeks later, after a few too many glasses of wine, her boyfriend.

"When I told Kristen, it was at her house. I was visiting her more regularly then. And we were going to go out and do some errands together, but I sat her down and told her everything. She was devastated. I could see in her face that I'd crushed her."

Andrea didn't know what to do next, whether to press charges or not. She wasn't sure how this would work. It was her sister, Jessica, who convinced her with a piece of simple logic: Andrea would report the crime if it had happened to anyone else she loved, so why not herself?

At first the Snohomish Police Department dismissed it as a weak case, one for the files. But Kristen Brewer persisted—perhaps they could organize a phone tap in which Andrea could get him to incriminate himself? The detectives refused. It was against the law, they said. So Andrea did the next best thing. She called Ryan while Kristen Brewer and Andrea's boyfriend were in the room taking notes, to witness the conversation and support her story.

But it soon turned out that the police were wrong; it was perfectly legal for them to tap Ryan Newton's phone. So a plan was hatched. On December 10, 2011, in the first semester of her junior year, Andrea drove up to the police department and gave Ryan a call. But he was busy, and the whole plan nearly fell apart.

"I said, 'OK, let's set up another time.' And I figured out when the detective was free, and I said, 'How about Tuesday morning?' But then I didn't hang up properly. I butt-dialed him back. And he heard me making plans with the police department about how the detective was going to drive down to see me this time and be there for the conversation. So come Tuesday, the detective picked me up at my college house. Everyone's studying for finals, and here's me, doing this. We drove to a parking lot down the street; it was just me and the cop. And we waited there two hours for Ryan to call back. He was paranoid. He said, 'Is someone else listening to the conversation? I heard you making plans with someone. Was that your therapist?' I denied it. I said, 'Remember, I have roommates.' And that I'd never betray him. And he admitted everything on the phone. The guy's an idiot. I always think, whenever I feel a little bit guilty about turning him in, I remember that moment. He knew. He wanted to be caught."

Ryan Newton was arrested in January 2012. At first he pleaded not guilty, but then changed his mind in June, so Andrea was spared having to testify about her abuse in an open court. Not that she would have shied away. At the sentencing hearing on September 4, 2012, she told Judge Ellen Fair just how Ryan's abuse had affected her. And the judge gave him six years, acknowledging the role of Lynette, who was present in court that day. "The way this family have treated you is unacceptable," the judge said. Charges may yet be filed against the therapist.

That day, Andrea left the Snohomish courthouse with Kristen Brewer, and they walked down to the beach together and sat on a bench, looking out at the sea. And Andrea asked her a question that had been on her mind for a while.

"I said, 'Would you consider adopting me?' I was really serious about it. It wasn't a hyperemotional conversation or anything. She's always been there since I was like, twelve, coming in and out whenever I needed her."

Kristen has no children of her own—just two dogs. But she'd always been there for Andrea throughout her ordeal. She protected her when she ran away from the Order. She believed Andrea when she spoke of Daniel's abuse. And during the trauma of the Newtons, she had been a confidante and source of support.

"She's been like some angel in my life," says Andrea. "So I told her, 'I've always wanted a healthy adult in my life. I think of you as my mom. Why not be my mom legally as well as emotionally?'"

Like her sister, she changed her name. She's Andrea Brewer now.

The True and Living Church

CHAPTER 10

◈ Who's Angie?

Just for the record, the weather today is partly suspicious with chances
of betrayal.
— Chuck Palahniuk, *Diary*

*I*T'S A LOW overcast day as I leave Salt Lake City. Splatterings of
showers from a dirty sky. The clouds have lowered their beards over the
mountain peaks, covering the snowy nipples, and it seems a fittingly chaste
gesture for my journey into the super-Mormon provinces of rural Utah.

I'm heading for Manti, the home of a polygamous group called the True
and Living Church of Jesus Christ of Saints of the Last Days (TLC), led by
the prophet James D. Harmston. Now in his sixties, Harmston has built
himself quite a reputation over the years. Former followers describe him
as a shrewd narcissist who considers himself the reincarnation of Joseph
Smith, a living messiah. In 1998, he was sued by a couple of ladies who
claim he swindled them out of $287,000, a case summarized by the head-
line "Two Women Sue Church When Christ Fails to Appear."[1] (The lawsuit fizzled out in the end, with no clear guilt established on Harmston's
part.) And by several accounts, he has a prophet's penchant for young
girls. In 2006, former polygamist John Llewellyn published a book called

Polygamy's Rape of Rachael Strong, arguing that twenty-year-old Rachael
had been spiritually coerced into marrying Harmston, who at the time was
married to Rachael's mother.[2]

Usually, bad publicity sends polygamist prophets scuttling for the
shadows. But Harmston has displayed a rare taste for the limelight. In the
late '90s, he even allowed A&E to make a documentary about his church
and consented to an interview. And he came across well on TV—gentle,
ursine and approachable. But when I mentioned him to Anne Wilde of
Principle Voices, she bristled. "Oh no, no, forget about him. He's *way* out
there on his own. You *definitely* don't want him in your book at *all.*" And
that settled it—I had to track him down.

So I'm driving south out of Salt Lake City down the I-15, listening
to some debate on NPR about Al Qaeda's plan for an Islamic Caliphate,
when about twenty miles out, the reception goes fuzzy—NPR's frequency
is swallowed up by Jesus FM. On either side lies a disheartening landscape
of industrial parks and trucks upon trucks, massed militarily by the road.
And the news crackles from "holy war" to "find Jesus," from "radical Islam"
to "heavenly Father." I'm crossing a barrier here, piercing the veil like Patrick Swayze in *Ghost*. I'm entering what locals call "real Utah," the farm-
raised, fetus-friendly Utah that dismisses Salt Lake as a Gentile-infested
Gomorrah.

The mountains are stunning out here—on the right day, under vast
skies and cloudswirls, they look like rugged chocolate cake with frosting,
the valleys gouged out by giant dessert spoons. But the human contri-
bution to the vista is underwhelming. The clusters of box-fresh homes
that developers love to build beside freeways peter out and give way to the
occasional Home Depot or Comfort Inn until eventually you're down to a
bereft-looking barn every seven miles or so. Those magnificent desert skies
are interrupted by signs fixed to shafts that jut into view like pop-up spam,
the signs that blight all American freeways—Denny's, Chevron, McDonald's, La Quinta, Motel 6, Subway. They herald the approach of a small
town that has been colonized by corporations. Freeways have become as
sterile, anonymous and spatially dislocated as airports. The small towns
have become the food courts.

The effect is compounded by the scriptural place names that Mormons
are so fond of—names like Manti, Nephi, Orem and Enoch. I'm traversing

through a Holy Land of Walmarts and parking lots. Canaan turns out to be a land of cheap burgers and the Denny's Heartland Scramble. And flags. In Real Utah, every home and business trumpets its patriotism. It's all flags and Mormon place names, national pride and religious zeal. The Promised Land indeed.

Coming off the I-15 at Nephi, the roads thin and wend through one drab hamlet after another. Some are the cute kind, with puppies and craft fairs, others are cluttered and unkempt, with fading signage and busted tractors on the lawn. On the way to Manti it's mostly the latter—houses surrounded by rickety sprawl, cobbled fences, rusted pick-ups and seesaw trailers left chin-up on threadbare lawns. The streets are deserted. Motels advertize COLOR TV, with each letter painted in a different color. Curves, the popular weight-loss franchise, is almost as big out here as McDonald's, the popular weight-gain franchise.

Manti, however, is a postcard. There's no clutter here, just a large white temple perched high up on a mound, keeping a matronly watch over the town. Mormons flock here every year for the Miracle Pageant, which celebrates the pioneer trek—but that's not for a couple of months yet, so the town is eerily quiet. When I check into the Manti House Inn across the street from the temple, the receptionist tells me I'm her only guest.

"Now what are you doing here?" she asks. Her name's Trish, she's a bubbly woman in her forties. "Ooh, polygamy!" She grabs a phone book. "I'll give you some people to talk to you. We had Jim Harmston come here the other night with some of his wives—I think it was one of their birthdays. They think he's a God, but he's just a sweet old man if you ask me. He always leaves a tip, you know. Have you talked to Rachael Strong? She'd be good. You know who she is, right? *The Rape of Rachael Strong*. That book."

"Well, I'd like to, but I don't know her number."

"You won't get it off anyone in the TLC! But people who've left might talk to you. There's the Harpers. They're divorced now, and I think she's living out in Virginia. But here's her number. Hey, I'll talk to you if you want—I was one of two wives. Yeah, that didn't work out, ha ha! I'll say. It's not for everyone."

We chat for a while, Trish and I, and I'm happy to have found a pal so quickly. Small towns can be lonely places for a stranger, given that everyone knows everyone else already and, this being Utah, there's no bar to break the ice. So I tell Trish my plans, sparing none of the details. I tell her that I'm here to try to meet Jim Harmston, but the only contact name I have is Merrill Jensen*—he's the guy that answers the emails on the website (the website has since been taken down). So I wrote Merrill a letter and we chatted on the phone and he said he would introduce me to Jim if he felt comfortable. So tonight, I've got an appointment at the Jensen house. Quite excited about it, actually.

"I haven't heard of Merrill Jensen," says Trish, thoughtfully.

"He makes harps, apparently. Apparently there's a big demand in the next life, what with all those angels."

"Ha! Do you like toffee? We've got loads. Grab some toffee and I'll show you around."

She introduces me to the girl doing the washing up and the girl doing the laundry. A couple of guests have popped in for tea and she says, "Meet Sanchez, he's doing a book about polygamy!" It's all very chummy. And by the time I'm in my bedroom, I'm beaming. I like Manti. I like small towns in Utah. I've got a pocket full of toffee and a new friend called Trish. Time for a nap I think, before dinner.

When I first spoke to Merrill on the phone, he gave me the usual spiel— "we don't like talking to outsiders, we're very private," and so on. But then we chatted for an hour. And by the end, he told me, "We haven't done any interviews in eight years, so you would actually be the first in the new millennium." And he sounded as excited about the prospect as I was.

Certainly his eagerness is apparent from the moment we meet on his front porch. A large man in jeans and a flannel shirt, he ushers me in and tells his kids to run along. Would I like water? Would I like to talk at the table or on the sofa? Perhaps we should go over some background first before getting into details? I pick the sofa, and one of his daughters brings me a glass of water. And immediately Merrill sets about a rudimentary history lesson—the origins of Mormonism, the Manifesto, the birth of fundamentalism. He has a schoolmasterly way about him, punctilious about semantics. He chuckles at his own observations as though he just came up with them.

---

*Not his real name.

"We don't refer to ourselves as fundamentalists," he explains. "See, we don't claim an authority back to the dispensation that was supposed to be given to John Taylor back in 1886. Our authority stems from angelic ministrations in fairly recent times to our prophet and leader, Jim Harmston."

I want to ask him what a ministration is—it sounds medical, or clerical, or something to do with soup. But a woman has appeared to our left, a squirming, uncomfortable presence. She's trapped between not wanting to interrupt and an obligation to say hello—a pincer of politeness.

"This is my wife Natalie,*" says Merrill, dismissively. I stand to shake her hand, but she just stands there, smiling awkwardly.

"We're just doing a bit of background here," Merrill says, filling the silence. "So . . . how are the kids?" But Natalie's frozen, speechless—her smile as pained and awkward as Carleen's from the Kingstons. "Well, you can stay or you can go," he says, releasing her with a shrug. She leaves at once.

"So anyway," he continues. "Joseph Smith received divine visitation by John the Baptist—and Peter, James and John, who were resurrected as angels and came in person to give him the Priesthood. Our authority stems from similar angelic ministrations to our prophet and leader, Jim Harmston."

"So Mr. Harmston isn't a follower of Joseph Smith, but a prophet of equal standing."

"That's correct. Four angels came and instructed him that they were to be referred to as Moses, Enoch, Abraham and Noah—four of the grand patriarchs of the Old Testament. This was in November 1990. He was at home, here in Manti. He was taken into a room, which was totally light everywhere, but there was no light source like there is here. He had a cognizance of which way was in front of him but he could see all the way around—which, by the way, is what happens in near-death experiences. And then these four men, who all looked the same but had distinct identities, they came from the four corners and laid their hands on his head."

It's a bold claim, and one that Merrill makes with pride. But there's something endearing about his enthusiasm. It's his convert's zeal. He wasn't raised in polygamy; he chose this life himself, sacrificing his old life

---

*Not her real name.

for a new one. And now he wants to show off how far he's come. "Only five or six men in the group actually practice polygamy," he chuckles. Yes, and he's one of them.

This is all too new for Merrill to feel jaded. He's only been living polygamy since 2004, and he's fifty-four at the time of our interview. He married Natalie in 1998 and Noralyn* six years later. They're forty-four and forty-eight, respectively. "It's not easy, this principle," he says, cheerfully. "We're all stressed to the limit, but that's how we grow—it's like weight training." At first they all tried living together, but that didn't work. "Noralyn is very meticulous and detailed, but Natalie is a bit whatever about some things." So now the wives have separate living quarters, with Noralyn's kitchen and bedroom up front and Natalie's at the back—two homes under the same roof—and John's workshop, where he builds his harps, farther back still.

They seem a little old for such a radical change of lifestyle, but this is often the way with converts. They emerge wounded from Mormon marriages and turn to their religion for consolation, only to find that the church has hidden whole chapters of doctrine. And the discovery inflames them—these missing chapters must be the answer, their hope for rescue.

Merrill's journey down that road began at forty-four, during what he calls "the most difficult year of my life." It was spring of 1997, and he was married to his first wife, a French woman. They were devout LDS Mormons and he was living and working in California as an air force engineer. But his life was falling apart. His marriage had long been disintegrating as had his trust in the church, and he had begun to discover these suppressed teachings about polygamy. It was around the same time that he found the website for the TLC. It possessed him. "I just became on fire, reading this stuff," he says. "I felt I had the spirit."

Within less than a year, he dismantled his whole life—he left the church, quit his job, left California and divorced his wife. Then he moved to Manti, to the court of the new messiah, Jim Harmston, and even persuaded his mother to join him—"my brothers have never forgiven me." It was a harrowing time. His sister died that year, and his ex-wife threatened him with never seeing his children again. He still has strained relationships with the

---

*Not her real name

children from his first marriage. But the upheaval and trauma only fortified his faith.

It's the typical convert story, for men at least. But accelerated. First the
disillusion with the church, then the intense zeal for the new doctrine,
the sense of scripture as a vortex of dogma sucking him in, closing off all
exits, slamming all the doors behind him. The old life disassembled by
excommunication, divorce, the sale of a home and the estrangement of
family. Then the rebuilding, brick by fundamentalist brick, the sense of
resolve only stiffened by the economic hardship and the social alienation
that comes with the cult life, until finally the convert looks back over his
previous life and revises his past to suit the narratives of the present—
committing the same sin as the Mormon Church, the discovery of which
began the whole cycle in the first place.

For Merrill, as hard as it's been, it's all been worth it, because he knows
for certain that Jim Harmston is the messiah—it says so in Isaiah.

"It's prophesied that the messiah will come in great power and save
God's people and destroy their enemies," he says. "We believe that James
Harmston is that leader. And you must understand, other people in the
Gathering came to that realization before Jim did. He was not real excited
when he found out."

I can see how Merrill would "realize" that the man for whom he'd given
up his life was in fact the savior of all humanity. But I'm impressed at
Harmston's cleverness in making his followers believe that this was their
idea and not his. There's something messianic about that alone. When 150
people insist that you have special powers, then by some definition, clearly
you do.

The presence on Earth of a living messiah becomes a lot more plausible
once you buy into the belief in an imminent apocalypse, because Isaiah
talks about the destructions too. And the TLC seems particularly doom-
centric. For Merrill, the end is so nigh it's scarcely worth setting the video.
He sees the end wherever he looks—on TV, on billboards, on the news.
God's laws aren't being obeyed, so in a giant celestial tantrum, He's going
to trash the place and start over.

"First, God will bring in the Assyrian," he says, "which is a metaphor
for an invading force that God will use to chastize people. And when that's
over, God will destroy the Assyrian, and Zion will be established. It says

'the slain of the Lord will be many.'" Evidently, only the TLC in Manti will be spared. They are the Lord's people, and their leader Jim will protect them. In Jim they trust.

"He's not a dynamic speaker with all the oratory tricks," Merrill says. "But you've never heard anyone so eloquently get to the meat of something. And he does make actual prophecies, unlike some other so-called prophets! When my mother came here for the first time, she committed to baptism, so I said to him, 'My mother will be here next Saturday to get baptized.' And he said, 'No, she'll chicken out.' And she did!"

"Does that count as an actual prophecy?"

"Of course! He predicted something and it was true."

"It sounds like a hunch or a guess to me. We all do that from time to time."

"That's correct also. But you have to know how this calling came about to fully understand. Before he was visited by angels, Jim had several very important spiritual experiences." Merrill stops and adjusts himself in his seat. He's not sure whether to tell me this stuff, whether it's a pearls-and-swine scenario. But he can't resist.

There was the time, for example, in a restaurant in Salt Lake, when "all of a sudden his mother, who had been killed in a car crash a year or two before, is standing before him and giving him instructions." It's always instructions with these angels. "And one other time—these are very sacred special things right here, but I'm just telling you in order to give you some perspective. Another time, Jim was given the gift to know the inner thoughts of the people around him. And it was given in such a way that he couldn't pick and choose or tune it out. So he'd go near somebody and he'd know immediately what they were thinking and feeling."

"Did he use his power on you?"

"I don't think so. This was before I knew him. He was working as a businessman at the time. He was a very successful developer, we're talking millions of dollars. But when he went to work he knew what his business partner was thinking. He'd pull up next to people at traffic lights—same thing. And largely the things he saw were vile. The private thoughts of men are a terrible thing. So he basically spent three days in the park alone so he wouldn't have to be plagued by this. He prayed to God that this thing be taken from him. And after three days it was. However from time to time he still has this gift given to him in times of appropriate need. I can see it reflected in his eyes in certain situations. I've never seen a man more able to discern character than he is."

"Merrill, I've got to meet this man. He sounds incredible. You hear about people who have these gifts, but to actually meet someone in the flesh . . ."

Merrill umms and ers. "Well, it's possible, sure. I think you're genuinely interested in what we're doing here and you have an open mind. Tell you what, why don't you come over tomorrow morning? I'm teaching a trig class around ten in the morning. You can see how we educate our children in the TLC. Then we can give you a tour of the assembly room and you can meet Dan Simmons, our church president."

"Great."

"And after that, depending on how that all goes, I can introduce you to Mr. Harmston. Then it's up to him if he wants to talk to you or not."

I'm so close, I can smell it. My first prophet! My first miracle worker and magic man! All those months driving up and down the I-15, all those Subway sandwiches and shit motels, the forced smiles and mixed socks, the move to America, the years of college, the superpower books I read at the library as a kid—it was all going to pay off. Me and the messiah, one on one.

Hallelujah. I love Manti.

I'm there at ten sharp. It's me and two sixteen-year-old boys, Jacob and Matthias, sitting at a cleared table in the middle of Merrill's living room, our notebooks out and pens at the ready. Merrill wipes the white board clean and introduces me.

"This is Sanjiv, he's from London. He's writing a book about polygamy and he wants to see how polygamists do trigonometry!" We all laugh. "I told him that our lives are pretty boring, but he doesn't believe me. So let's see if I can't prove him wrong!" He's loving it. It's the Merrill show. "I was explaining to Sanjiv last night that we don't usually let media report on us because they're so prejudiced. We've been quite badly burned by the media. That's why you've never read anything about the TLC for the last eight years. But I met with Sanjiv last night and we've spoken on the phone, and he's genuinely interested to see what our lives are like. So let's just have a normal class. Just pretend he's not there. Does that work for you?"

The boys nod. I nod. Everyone nods. Then the phone rings and Merrill stops. "Hold on a second." And he retreats to the rear of the house to take the call. When he returns, minutes later, he's glaring at me. "Okay, we're going to have to stop this whole thing right here. You have to leave."

"What?"

"No more interviews. We can't continue this. You have to leave."

"What happened? Who was that on the phone?"

"Did you talk to a girl called Angie?"

"Angie?"

"You're staying at the Manti House Inn, correct?"

"Yes."

"Well, you talked to someone called Angie there."

"No I didn't, I talked to Trish."

"Yes, and you also spoke to Angie. She says that you are here to do a sensationalist, antipolygamy book and you were asking for numbers of people who have left our group. So our interview is over. That's all I have to say. Now you must leave."

"B-but wait a minute. This isn't true! I talked to Trish and then I talked to you. That's it! I don't know anyone else from the group."

"Have you spoken to Rachael?"

"No."

"Well, that's not what I've been told. You have to understand, there are people who have left who will give you a very different and frankly a very false perspective. Have you spoken to a boy called Jacob?"

"No."

My mind's racing. What's happening here? Who's Angie? Is "Angie" Trish's real name? Is Trish a member of the TLC? Who's Jacob? Who just called him now? Why doesn't Merrill trust me anymore?

"Look, Merrill, I don't know what's going on here, but you know where I'm coming from. I'm not an antipolygamist. I don't believe polygamy should be a crime. I believe it should be demystified. We discussed all of this." I'm scrabbling for a hold, the rocks are loosening.

"I've been told that you've misled me," he says, grimly.

"Was that Angie that called just now?"

"No, it was Jim Harmston. He has spoken with Angie." His boot heel is poised over my fingers.

"But I never spoke to Angie!" Fingernails scraping down the cliff face. "I spoke to Trish and she recommended that I speak to lots of different people and she gave me some numbers. But I haven't rung any of them. I just accepted her help in the spirit in which it was given."

"So you're saying that Angie is lying?"

"I don't know who Angie *is*!" My branch is breaking, the rope's unraveling. Either Angie's lying, Jim Harmston's lying or I am. And by defending myself, I'm attacking one of them. I'm screwed.

"You need to leave. I've already said too much. You just need to leave."

It's the Vermillion Cafe all over again—the fat girl's sniggering, the patrol car's circling. The trig students watch me stand up and grab my bag. But I can't just walk out. I need some sort of an exit. "You tell me that your prophet can read hearts and minds," I say, a little louder than expected. "Well, if that's the case, why doesn't he read mine? I'll tell you why—because if he sat there and told me I had a conversation with Angie, then I would know for sure that he was a false prophet. He'd understand that I'm telling the truth, goddammit."

I make for the door and struggle with the latch. It's all going wrong. Merrill has to come and help. He seems to pity me somewhat. "What I'm hearing from you and what I'm hearing from Jim just doesn't add up," he says. "Who knows what he's basing his knowledge on right now?"

As I turn back to say good-bye, I see Natalie at the end of the room, looking alarmed. Jacob and Matthias staring. Merrill's standing at the door, his hands on his hips and his head tilted to one side, a rather fey pose considering the tension of the moment.

"Good-bye Merrill."

"Good-bye Sanjiv."

And the door smacks shut behind me. Walking to my car, listening to the pebbles crunch underfoot and my short quick breaths, all I can think is, "Shit, I shouldn't have said 'goddammit.'"

On the drive back to the Manti House Inn, I'm fuming. I pushed the boulder up the hill and some fucker pushed it back down again. And I need to know who. Trish can sort this out. She'll know who Angie is. I can't leave Manti like this.

So I march back into the Manti House Inn and find Trish on reception, sunny as ever. "Hiya, Sanjiv! You're back for more toffee, I know you are."

"Trish, someone's been telling lies about me and I don't know who it is. I feel like I'm in a fucking Kafka novel, excuse my French." I tell her the whole story, how I got kicked out of the house, falsely accused, the whole thing. And she smiles. "Now you know what it's like in polygamy. These people have secrets you know, if you start poking around . . ."

"But who's Angie?"

"You met her last night. She was the one doing the dishes. She's one of Jim's wives, basically. I'm not supposed to say, but she has a secret, and Angie's secret could ruin the TLC. The whole thing could fall apart."

"What secret?"

"I can't say. It's too big."

"Did you talk to Angie after talking to me last night?"

"Oh, we talked for a good hour. She said, 'He's here to talk to Rachael, I know it. He's going to write one of those antipolygamy books full of lies.' I think that's what she told Jim."

"And Jim believed her."

"Angie's a queen in that group. Whatever she wants, she gets."

"Is she here?"

"No, she gets here at 4 PM."

I look at the clock. "Four! That's five hours away. Can I call her at home?"

"I can't give you her number, I'm sorry. Here, try some of this fudge. Take as much as you like . . ."

Five hours to kill in Manti. I try watching TV in my room, but I keep pacing around, replaying the scene in my head. I try driving around town and traipsing around the shops, but it's no good. I'm a duck moving across a still pond—apparently calm on the surface, but paddling away furiously below the water. Why would Angie lie about me? Why didn't Trish tell me about Angie before? How can I salvage this?

So I head for the library and for a couple of hours I write a letter stating my case—one part indignant and one part conciliatory. Figuring this might be my last shot at the prophet, I decide to hand-deliver it to his home, a little green house opposite the TLC's assembly building. So I'm standing there, ringing his bell as it begins to snow around me. The wind chimes are chinking and I'm preparing my lines—"Hello, Mr. Harmston, I think there's been a misunderstanding . . ."

Eventually a small, crinkled woman comes to the door, smiling. "Hello, I'm Karen." She says she'll take the letter for Jim. "He's out now." Of course he is.

At 4 PM sharp, I head back to the Manti House Inn to confront Angie. There's no sign of Trish, just a couple of girls in the kitchen, one of them sitting up on a worktop eating ice, the other wiping down a surface.

"Are you Angie?"

"I might be," says the girl with the rag in her hand. She's pretty and petite, with dark brown eyes and big lashes.

"I'm Sanjiv. I think we have something to talk about?"

"Do we?"

"Do you want to go somewhere private to talk?"

"No, we can talk right here."

"Okay, then. Did you tell Jim Harmston that you had a conversation with me yesterday? About my book."

"Uh-uh. I didn't call Jim. Why would I say I had a conversation with you when I didn't?"

"That's not what Merrill Jensen said."

"Oh, Merrill Jensen, I wouldn't believe him. Why are you talking to him? He's just trying to flaunt his family because he's got two wives. But he's a bad example of polygamy. He's very arrogant."

"He says Jim called him and said that you spoke to him about me. You said I was writing a negative book about polygamy."

"Well, are you?"

"No."

"Are you here to talk to Rachael?"

"No, I don't know how to get in touch with her."

"What's your book about anyway?"

So I give her the pitch. And at every step, she questions my motives, my honesty, my credentials. "What makes you different than other journalists?" "How can you write about this if you haven't got any faith yourself?" "Why do you care, what's your agenda?" And she rejects my every answer. It's exhausting. I'm doing a backfoot jig here, doing all the talking while she bats back everything I say with a skeptical spin. The portcullis is up. The crocodiles in the moat are snapping. There's no way she's letting me in.

"Can I call you sometime?" I ask. "I want to continue this conversation."

"No."

"Is email better?"

"No."

"Well . . . do you want to talk to me again, or are you done?"

"I don't mind talking to you. If I'm here when you come back and if I'm not busy working, we can talk then."

"But Angie, I've come here from L.A. That's six hundred miles away. I can't just come up on the off-chance that you're here."

"That's not my problem."

"Can I at least leave you my details?"

"You can do whatever you want."

So I write them down on a piece of paper and hand them to her. But instead of taking the note, she turns around and walks away. "Leave it on the side."

My hope shattered, I leave Manti, still none the wiser as to how things took such a bizarre turn.

Then a few days later, the emails come flooding in. Four in a day, long urgent letters, all from Angie—full name, Angelinna Mower. This time her tone is warm and confessional. She apologizes for her attitude, for causing me inconvenience, and she wants me to forgive her.

"I had the opportunity to read the letter you wrote to Jim," she writes. "I thought that it was very well written and seemed sincere. I do not intend on staying in the situation I am in and so I am feeling extremely insecure about my circumstances at the moment. You see, I am only 25—I turn 26 in September. According to law I was a 'Child bride.' I have spent 50% of my life living this way. I risk a tremendous amount just by speaking with you over the email."

It seems beneath all that bristle is a nervous and sensitive young mother on the verge of a momentous decision. Angie doesn't only want to talk. She wants to leave Jim and the TLC and escape to California.

◈ The Prophetess Speaks

The best way out is always through.
—Robert Frost

This is her secret: On her sixteenth birthday, according to Angie, Jim Harmston "spiritually" married and had sex with her. He's forty-one years her senior, so that qualifies as statutory rape in Utah, and the evidence is in plain sight: she's had two of his children, James and Cora, the elder of whom, she says, was conceived before her seventeenth birthday. So they devised a cover story. Angie legally married one of Jim's younger followers called Jake, in order to give the impression that the children were his. But as Trish and everyone else in Manti knows, their marriage is a sham.

When I asked Angie for proof of these allegations, particularly the paternity of her children, she said that she would provide it all in court if necessary. She's aware that she could bury Harmston if she wished. But she doesn't. In her emails she reiterates that she doesn't want to hurt anyone and wouldn't dream of pressing charges. She just wants out. She went into this with her eyes open she says, and now, nine years later, she's had enough. And she wants to know if I can help her.

My wife and I had discussed this eventuality before I embarked on this project. "What would you do," she said, "if some girl passes you a note: 'Help me'?" Naturally, I assured her that I would not flinch—this would be my Popeye moment and there was only one choice. I would breach the walls, snatch up the damsel and bravely smuggle her out of the clutches of the cult, even bring her back to our little apartment if necessary. "She could go in the living room," I said. "We could borrow the neighbor's air mattress."

"What about the kids?"

"On the couch."

"All ten of them? We'll need another air mattress."

"I'll pick one up at Target."

But thankfully, Angie has no designs on our couch. All she wants is help in writing a letter to the members of her church articulating why she's leaving. She wants to explain herself. "I want to write it for a very specific reason," one of her emails reads, "that reason being an understanding offered to those within my 'church' that they currently do not have." Her emails are taut with stress. She wants to leave Jim but she can't find a way out. "It would bruise Jim's ego for me to leave him as a wife but still stay in the TLC. He won't accept that. So my only out is to leave Manti altogether. But Jim won't let me."

We schedule a phone call, and she's sounding stronger. She says she's coming to California soon to visit Disneyland with her kids and stay with her brother who lives near Temecula. "If I had my way, I'd never go back," she says.

It turns out she's been dreaming of escape for months. Ever since February, when life in Manti turned especially ugly. February was when Angie stopped having sex with Jim. He retaliated by making thinly veiled threats in church. "He talked about what would happen to wives who don't perform their covenantal duties, and I knew it was about me," she says. "He told me afterward that he was infuriated because I had withdrawn from him as a wife."

I want to ask her the details, but the time's not right. She's moving from fear to defiance and back again. One minute she says "I know what I want, I'm not going to be a doormat for anyone." And yet in the next breath she's afraid that Jim will come after her children using Jake, or that her kids won't adjust to life in California. "They've been taught that people outside are bad. They've been so sheltered. And my boy's only eight, he's quite attached to Jim." What's more, she's terrified by the risk of spiritual repercussions. "Part of the purpose in me marrying Jim was a very particular revelation. So for me to walk away would cause a lot of bad spiritual stuff."

"Like what?"

"Oh, I can't . . . It's complicated. There's so much."

I suggest that we meet, but Angie's not keen. She only agrees if I take certain precautions. "You need to drive a different car," she says, "because Jim has people watch my house. "When you were here before, he knew you were driving that Jetta. And come on a Sunday during church so everyone's there and I can skip out. I'll just say I've got work at the inn. And we can talk then for a few hours."

So a plan is hatched. I'm to fly up from L.A. on a Sunday, rent a car at St. George Airport, something innocuous like a pickup. If possible I should grab a Utah Jazz baseball cap, something to pull over my eyes as I approach the town, and when I check into the Manti House Inn, I can't leave the hotel room. No wandering around town. Strictly ninja stealth. Deep cover.

But things don't quite go as planned. The only car available at the airport is a silver Mustang with thick black streaks down the side. And I can't find a Jazz baseball cap because all the stores are shut on Sundays, leaving me to make do with a hooded top and sunglasses. So I roll into Manti looking like a dodgy Latino in the midst of a midlife crisis, parking his sports car outside a little country inn and skulking to the front door, looking over his shoulder. I may as well have been loading a television into my trunk.

The inn's empty when I arrive, so I hide in the dining room, away from the windows, and call Angie. Minutes later, she swings by to check me in, looking harassed and anxious. Her eyes are thick with liner, her cheeks caked with foundation—makeup as armor. She doesn't mention my ludi-crous car or look me in the eye as she fumbles with the keys.

"It's supposed to say ACE on the key, but . . . I don't know. How come you're so early? Did you even get any sleep?"

"I'm fine, Angie. How are you?"

"I'm . . . a nervous wreck."

She leaves me in room 204 and hurries off to church, promising to return. So for a couple of hours I lie on the bed, half expecting a cursing Jim Harmston to burst in with a couple of snarling wives in tow. I'm rehearsing my response to such an invasion, alone in my room like a crazy person, when Angie returns.

"Okay," she shrugs. "Ask me questions if you want."

She sits opposite the bed, breathing nervously and gripping the seat of her chair, white-knuckled. Her discomfort is palpable. She can hardly make eye contact. But over the course of the afternoon, punctuated by dif-ficult, squirming silences, she manages to tell me just how it was that she wound up in this mess.

She arrived in Manti at the age of thirteen, by which time she was already emotionally scarred, the weakened calf of the herd. Her life pre-Harmston had been chaotic and joyless thanks to the immense emotional deficits of her mother, Angel. Not that she blames her mother for anything—Angie's not a blamer. But the facts are plain: Angel became pregnant with Angie at fifteen and went lurching from one tragic choice of husband to another.

By the time Angie was sixteen, Angel had married four times, each time a disaster. Angie's craving for a father figure was such that when she found one in Jim, she married him.

Her biological father—according to both Angel and Angie—was a violent felon who ended up in prison soon after she was born. The step-father that followed wasn't much better: he was a heavy drinker who kept a stash of porn under his bed and never took to Angie or her sister. In part this was because their birth father, upon his release from prison, tried to murder the stepfather with scissors, an event that Angie witnessed at the age of four. When Angie turned ten, Angel turned to the Mormon Church to restore order to her life, but her eye for men remained unerringly poor. Husband number three had a hankering for polygamy and developed connections with the Apostolic United Brethren (otherwise known as the Allred Group), as well as with Harmston's outfit in Manti. And inevitably he experienced a revelation that Angie, his stepdaughter, was meant to be his wife.

"I cried my eyes out the day my mom married him," says Angie. "He was creepy. He wanted to get involved in polygamy simply because he wanted to marry young women. Seeing as my mom had two girls, he thought that would be a good match."

Both Angie and her younger sister, Daisy, told the Creep to go to hell. But at the time, they had other problems. The family was moving around a lot in those days, from city to city in Utah County, and Angie was fast going off the rails. By eleven, she was smoking weed and drinking, hanging around with gangs. So Angel looked to Manti as a way to save her, to escape the city and turn their lives around. It also helped that, by this stage, she'd been swayed by her husband to the promise of polygamy. And like everyone else in the area who was flirting with fundamentalism at the time, she'd heard of James Harmston, on account of a scriptural course he was teaching called "The Models," an intensive two-day lecture that covered all the usual polygamist topics such as the apostasy of the LDS Church and the necessity of plural marriage. What distinguished the Models were Harmston's embellishments about how angels came "across the veil" and gave him the authority to gather the saints for the last days. Here was a guy who was claiming it all—angelic visitations, the urgency of a gathering, the imminent destructions—and it got everyone excited. Angel and the Creep weren't the only ones who moved to Manti to get baptized.

As soon as she arrived, the young Angie felt that a bright new chapter was opening up for her. Her angry, ruinous life of petty crime and drugs was over. She was a churchgoer now, with a loving community around her. The warm reception was seductive, the sense of purification and purpose, the calm of the country, the comfort of prayer. The TLC became her rock, a respite from the turmoil at home.

But her arrival got the polygamist shark pool of Manti circling—here was a pretty thirteen-year-old girl, mature for her age, turning herself over to the ways of the Lord with the naïve zeal of a teenager. Soon enough, men in the TLC were quietly informing Angel that God was directing them to marry her daughter. And Angel found them increasingly difficult to dissuade. After all, these were Priesthood brethren, men who communicated with the heavens.

Angel had never been very good at standing up to the men in her life. But when the Creep demanded to marry Angie, she scored a victory of sorts. She pleaded with Harmston to release her from the marriage and he did. He sent her to become the second wife of another follower, we'll call him Nick. But Nick's first wife reacted violently to Angel's arrival and took to assaulting Nick with whatever came to hand. In the meantime, the Creep was provided with another wife whose daughter he molested. Only then was he expelled from the Gathering. Ultimately criminal charges were filed and he was convicted.[3]

Through all of this transferring of wives and expulsion of predators, Jim Harmston himself remained an aloof figure in Angie's life. He scarcely interacted with her and she thought little of him. But behind the scenes, he was busy maneuvering to work her into his harem. His strategy was elaborate and shocking in its calculation. As she tells me the story out loud, Angie can see just how clearly she was set up, but still she insists: "I don't want to criticize Jim. I don't want a negative story."

First, Harmston spiritually strong-armed Angel. He summoned her to his office one day ostensibly to discuss the issue of Nick's abusive first wife, but instead he asked whether she'd had any inspiration about whom Angie might "belong to." Angel replied that Angie was too young. So Harmston dismissed her, but over the next two weeks, he arranged for a number of his other wives to take Angel aside and persuade her that Angie was ready. When Angel was called back into Harmston's office, the denouement was inevitable: he said that he himself had received a revelation that Angie was meant to be his wife. And Angel's response reflects just how her faith had enfeebled her. She told him, "If God has told you that this is what is supposed to be, then God's will will be done, not mine." It was her way of acceding without officially giving him permission. Not that Harmston was asking. He was simply presenting her with a clear choice: either fall in line and be saved, or oppose him and be turned into a black woman. At least that's how Angel explains it when I talk to her later: "If I told Jim, 'No, you can't marry my daughter,' he would have turned my skin black. And he would have married her anyway. That was what I believed."

Even if Angel had protested, it's not clear that Angie would have listened. Angie and Angel were more or less estranged at the time—another facet of Harmston's plan. He'd noticed that Angie was frustrated with her mother's weakness and the succession of husbands, and like any fifteen-year-old, she yearned for independence. So Harmston had her move in with Laura and Gail, two of his wives who shared a home in the center of town. And once she'd moved, they told her that they were her new family and that Angel didn't want to see her anymore. A rumor began to spread among the congregation that Angel was insane and incapable of proper judgment—a humiliation that Angel, in her fragile state, not only endured but actually believed. When Harmston forbade her any contact with Angie, there was little she could do but meekly accept.

What neither Angie nor Angel realized, however, was that her new guardians, Laura and Gail, had a sordid history. They were former members of a polygamist cult called the Zion Society in northern Utah, which was led by Arvin Shreeve, a landscape gardener with a God complex. His group lived and worked in ten neighboring homes in the picturesque suburbs of Ogden, each with manicured front lawns and dainty flower beds. At its peak, it numbered close to one hundred followers, almost all women and girls, from infants to grandmothers. And he had free reign over them all—they worked for him and gave him their money and their bodies. His cult was more sexual than most. He had his flock produce lingerie for local strippers. There were lesbian orgies. They played a game called "Rape in the Dark" in which a designated rapist woman could perform any act she wanted upon another.[4] Fifteen-year-old girls were instructed to teach nine-year-olds how to sexually satisfy men and women.[5]

When investigators exposed the group, twelve adults were charged, convicted and sentenced for the sexual abuse of children, with Shreeve himself pleading guilty to two counts of sodomy on a child and two further second-degree felony counts of child sexual abuse. He died in prison in August 2009 at the age of seventy-nine, though many of his followers are free.[6]

Gail wasn't named in the convictions although former TLC members insist that she left just before the arrests were made.[7] But Laura was placed on the Sex Offender Registry, as was another lady named Rebecca, who also joined the TLC. They were part of the "Sisters" in Shreeve's group, they participated in the sexual exploitation of young girls. They were party to sodomy and were accessories to crimes of pedophilia.[8] Upon arriving in Manti, it seems Laura simply picked up where she left off. Though she'd completed her probation by 1995, she was still a registered sex offender in 1997 when she played a key role in Angie's marriage to Jim.[9]

With Angie in the grip of his wives and Angel effectively neutralized, Jim expedited Angie's endowment, or confirmation, an elaborate and secret ritual not unlike the ceremony that LDS Mormons go through, the details of which are not meant for Gentile ears. Even now, all Angie will say is that it took place on June 28, 1997, and it involved white outfits, a play about the creation of the Earth and several solemn covenants. In other words, it was an explicit and public avowal of religious commitment, a significant milestone for an impressionable young girl.

And the very next day, Jim called her into his office to announce that he'd received a revelation that she belonged to him for all eternity. She'd been cornered.

"It was gut-wrenching," she says. "I had just made these covenants, so how could I contradict what I just agreed before God?" She didn't want to marry him, but she didn't dare defy a revelation. And the pressure was intense. "Jim, Laura and myself went into prayer and asked if I should marry Jim. Laura and Jim said that they received a witness of the spirit that I should. I told them that I did not have that witness but that I would do it anyway. I felt coerced but I kinda put it to the side. I believed that I had made the right decision in joining the church. Up until that point my life had been pretty good, comparable to previous years."

Thus, Angie defends her choices—the very choices that put her here, gripping the sides of her chair, desperately trying to leave the group. She's still clinging onto the idea that the church was good for her, that it saved her somehow. "I'm not a victim," she says. "I hate those girls who leave polygamy and pretend they're victims so people feel sorry for them." And as much as I admire her toughness, I can't agree. Angie is a victim. When this all went down, she was fifteen, without a father, estranged from her mother and surrounded at all times by members of a fanatical, borderline-criminal cult. What choices did she realistically have?

As soon as she submitted to the marriage, she had to meet with Jim daily. And Laura, the registered sex offender, began instructing Angie in the sexual aspects of marriage. "How to be arousing for Jim, basically," Angie says. "How to look older. Anything that showed the female figure was good. But Laura is Jim's age, so it was all about just wearing tight, formfitting clothes. Flared skirts and snug blouses. It's what Jim wanted." It was enormously painful. It dawned on her that long before her endowment, the people who purported to care for her had merely been preparing her for the prophet. "I was the last one to know that this was coming."

The coercion continued—Harmston told Angie that their union had been prophesied and only when they bore children could the new millennium be brought forth. The apocalypse, the return of Christ, the future of the planet—it all depended on the virgin Angie, fifteen, submitting to the lust of Jim Harmston, fifty-six. "I know it sounds crazy," she says, shaking her head. But that doesn't mean she doesn't believe it. She reaches for a Bible from the bookshelf, and turns to Isaiah 7.

"'Therefore the Lord himself shall give you a sign; Behold, a virgin shall conceive, and bear a son, and shall call his name Immanuel. Butter and honey shall he eat, that he may know to refuse the evil, and choose the good. For before the child shall know to refuse the evil, and choose the good, the land that thou abhorrest shall be forsaken of both her kings.'" She hands me the Bible. "You see? It's all about the end of times."

"But how does it relate to you? It also says, 'the Lord shall hiss for the fly and the bee . . .'"

"That's the plague of insects."

"And 'the Lord shall shave with a razor.'"

"Mm-hmm."

"I still don't see how it applies to you."

"That part doesn't. My bit is here, look: 'And I went unto the prophetess; and she conceived, and bore a son. Then said the Lord to me, call his name Mahershalasha . . . something. I can't pronounce it.'"

"But your son's name is James."

"I know, but it's about him. The bit where it says 'before the child shall know to refuse the evil and choose the good'? That's my son. Before he knows right from wrong, basically, we would experience the last days. But now we're ten years down the road and I'm thinking, you know . . ."

"Can we hurry up with the apocalypse already?"

"Totally! My little boy's eight!" Sigh. "I never would have entered the marriage if I knew it was going to take this long."

For all the ballyhoo in Isaiah about how their union would bring forth a new dawn for mankind, the actual sealing ceremony was a solemn, shadowy affair. No flowers, no music, no celebration. It took place in deep secrecy at the stroke of midnight on Angie's sixteenth birthday, September 20, 1997. Not a moment was wasted once she crossed that threshold. The location was withheld from all until the last minute. Angel got the call three hours beforehand. She was told to wear white, and to sneak out of her husband's home, where a car would take her to the "Endowment House" in Fairview. And there she found her daughter Angie on her knees facing Jim on one side of the altar. Gail and Laura sat either side of her, and they were flanked by several members of the Priesthood Council, the quorum of twelve, all standing by in their whites, bearing grim and silent witness.

Angel burst into tears as expected. But they weren't the typical tears of a bride's mother, the mingling of joy, pride, reminiscence and love. As Angel tells me later, she was overwhelmed by other emotions—confusion, fear and anxiety. She was caught between trying to show the group that she was stable, not the screwup that Jim said she was, while at the same time struggling to understand how this could be happening if Jim was a true prophet. And there was no joy on Angie's part either. She recalls feeling numb, just robotically submitting to instructions. Once the sealing was complete, the new couple were driven back to Manti where Jim took her virginity, all of two hours into her sixteenth year.

And so it continued—sex and secrecy became the cornerstones of Jim and Angie's relationship. No one outside the group could ever know.

When Angie was pregnant with their first child, Jim engineered her legal marriage to Gail's son, Jake, who was twenty-one. By the time Jacob was born, roughly four months shy of her eighteenth birthday, Angie was already living with Jake and his first wife, Leah, in an extension to their Manti home. Jim would drop by twice a week. He'd have sex and dinner. Then he'd leave.

As the prettiest of Jim's wives, the "prophetess" commanded a privileged position. But it wasn't easy being the favorite. As the first of the younger wives, she faced the jealousy of the older women. And as more young women entered his harem—Margaret, Naomi, Amanda and Rachel—the bitterness just multiplied. They went at each other like barracudas and Angie was not one to shrink from battle. For a particularly fractious spell, she lived in a house with Margaret and Amanda, both of whom had left their previous husbands to marry Jim. They conspicuously gossiped about her and accused her of being a bad mother. They fixed dinner for their children but not Angie's. They didn't let their children play with hers, or invite them to birthday parties. It was petty and vicious but Angie gave as good as she got. She admits to a reputation of being snotty and overly proud of her appearance in Isaiah. "I'm difficult to live with," she says. "I don't deny it."

Through these endless wife wars, her relationship with Jim was slim recompense. He wasn't abusive but the age gap became increasingly difficult to stomach. She considered leaving, but each time she stayed as an act of will. She even consciously decided to love Jim at one point, and make nice with the other wives. "I was trying to make myself feel what I really didn't," she says. "And in going through the motions, I learned to not be so controlling. I changed the way I managed my jealousy."

This is the commonest refrain from unhappy plural wives, that polygamy builds character—a variation of "that which doesn't kill you." The challenge of overcoming jealousy, having to reconcile and compromise rather than dominate—it's supposed to help you grow. Never mind that Angie's marriage requires her to lie as a matter of course. The lie she usually tells outsiders is "I'm going through a divorce."

"When I was pregnant with my little girl, if I was seen anywhere with Jim, people would be like, 'I can't believe she's having a kid with him,'" she says. "You could see it on their faces. And it was just crushing." It got so bad that she couldn't bear the thought of having another child with Jim, so at the age of twenty-three she had her tubes tied. "I had to sit in that doctor's office and cry and plead. He didn't want to do it, he said I was too young. But Jim was all for it because he refuses to use condoms."

By this time, Angel had long left the group. After her marriage to Nick fell apart, she married a large, sanctimonious man named Randy, who declared himself the reincarnation of Brigham Young. But Randy got into a fight with Harmston and was expelled, after which his family fell apart. And Angel took the opportunity to strike out on her own, taking Angie's sister, Daisy, with her. This was in 2000. They kept in touch with Angie, trying to persuade her to leave as well, but Angie resisted. Daisy had started drinking, and Angie found little inspiration in Angel. Besides, she had two children in the group who, according to Isaiah, were supposed to save the world. So she would watch TV at nights, eagerly noting new calamities around the world, and hoping fervently for more—more pestilence, war and category fives. She wanted the world to end, if only to release her from marriage.

It wasn't until she moved out of her home with Margaret and Amanda into an apartment of her own, that she gathered the strength to take some steps toward independence.

"That was when I told him I didn't want to have sex with him," she says with a heavy sigh. "And that's when it all went crazy. He said I was a fornicator."

"But fornication means having sex, not withdrawing."

"No, 'fornication' means the alienation of affection." Angie is convinced of this. She picks lint off her jumper. She holds her head in her hands and lets out a deep, exhausted sigh. "And the other wives, they love it. Last week at church, he came up with this doctrine where wives have to stay with their husbands, otherwise they will be damned." Another sigh. She's on the cusp of saying something but she can't, so she just sits, breathing hard. She knows that at this minute in church she's being condemned, and her sister wives are loving it. She knows how they talked about Rachael Strong, the last of Jim's wives who left and talked to a reporter. They hate her. They wish her harm.

"Don't say I hate Jim," she says. "I don't want this to be a negative story like Rachael's."

"What *do* you think about Jim?"

"I think he's a good father. He dotes on the children," she says carefully. "He's very intelligent, he's very wise."

"What about the way he married you on your sixteenth birthday?"

"Maybe his motives weren't completely pure, but he's a man. That's how men are."

At every turn, she lets him off so that she can salvage the idea that she chose well. She's a prisoner of her own rationalization.

"If he's a good man, why are you afraid to leave him?"

"Because what if I'm wrong? What if I walk away and all that stuff does happen? The destructions and everything?"

Her phone rings—it's Whitesnake, "Here I Go Again." She looks at the number and switches it to silent. "I'm in trouble."

"Who is it?"

"Who do you think? The longer I stay here, the more suspicious he'll get."

It's six o'clock. We've been talking for four hours. Angie sits on her hands and rocks in her chair biting her lower lip, urgently flicking through the excuses she can use. "I can say I'm busy, but he knows there's no one staying here tonight—there's only one car outside. Your car."

"Well at least he doesn't know you're talking to me."

"Don't be so sure. There are TLC people at the phone company, so he can access cell phone records."

Again her phone blares Whitesnake. Again the lyrics hit the nail: "I've made up my mind, I ain't wasting no more time."

"I've really got to go. He's like this—he'll just call and call and call. But we can talk more later at my house."

"Okay, just give me the place and time, I'll be there."

"No, don't drive. He has his wives drive by the house to check the cars outside. I'll have my mom pick you up about eight."

And sure enough, Angel pulls up in her truck at 7:55 PM. Once again, I'm the guy in the hoodie, creeping out of the B&B. I get in and find Angel smoking, the cigarette quivering between her fingers. She looks older than her forty-two years, worn-down and disheveled. The truck is an ashtray. Everything about Angel seems nicotine stained.

"It's better this way, trust me," she says, sounding like Patty and Selma from *The Simpsons*. "He's got like sixteen wives, so it's easy for him to check. Plus Angie lives at a dead end so it's even more obvious if there's a new car parked there."

"Especially a silver Mustang."

"Ha! Yeah, Mormons don't drive Mustangs. Can't fit any kids in them."

She drives the five or so blocks down to Angie's place where she parks in the drive and has a quick check before we get out. "It looks okay. Just follow me up to the door. Put your hood up. And if anyone sees, we'll just say you're my new boyfriend."

Angie's apartment is cozy, tidy and fragrant—the antithesis of her mom's truck. The surfaces are all wiped down, there are no dishes in the sink and the kids are safely off in bed. Angie is evidently the disciplined one of the family, the designated driver, the equal and opposite reaction.

Mother and daughter sit curled up on opposite armchairs like cats. Angie quietly leafs through a book of Chinese astrology while Angel peppers me with questions. She wants to know everything about my book and me—why Angie, why polygamy, why I don't believe in God, what about my parents. The conversation only switches when I mention the failed father figures in her life. Angel looks at Angie, shocked.

"What, you told him about my marriages?"

"Yes, I told him everything," Angie says calmly.

"Well, I didn't know you were going to get into all that," Angel says and walks to the door to have a cigarette, smoking across the threshold, her hands trembling violently as she lights a match. After a few lugs, she says "You'll never understand the guilt that I feel for pushing Angie into this life. It's with me every day. I'm her *mother*. I should have protected her. But in my naïvety and my ignorance and my stupid obsession with righteousness, I caused her so much pain."

She's trying to make up for it now that Angie is ready to leave. Even though she and Daisy now live in Ephraim, they'll gladly move to California with Angie, if that's what she wants.

"I've got some money saved up," she says. "So we can afford to put a deposit on an apartment. And California's fine. It will be good to get some distance from Jim. Anywhere but L.A. You got so much crime and everything going on there."

"But, Mom," Angie protests, "Sanjiv says that waitresses in L.A., make good money."

"No, you read about that place in the papers. L.A. is no place to raise kids." It's the typical heartland prejudice, this idea that the population density in cities somehow squeezes out the morals, and family values can only survive in small towns. Towns like Manti where the cult of Harmston comprises nearly 10 percent of the population.

Angie wants to say something. She wants to read from her book on Chinese astrology—the part about roosters, because that's what she is. "It says here that roosters are 'irrepressible, staunch, multitalented, open-minded yet conservative,'" she says. "'They dress sexy, they're absolutists, they don't think in halves . . .' I never think in halves. It says, 'For the rooster, nothing is lukewarm, it is either hot or cold.' All of that's true! And listen: 'Life for a rooster is a roller-coaster ride, a crazy quilt of successes and setbacks.' This is so me it's amazing!"

"She's obsessed with that book," says Angel.

"But look at what it says about Jim," Angie continues. "He's a Scorpio dragon. 'You long to crawl into cave after cave with a series of passionate lovers who tickle and hurt and thrill all at once.' That's exactly what he's like! 'You dream of a lifelong moment of ecstasy . . . But when you choose a mate, choose a solid citizen, a rooster.' And it says here, 'The complex side of the rooster woman may prevent her from having a good time in bed until she is sure of her mate's intentions.' Which is exactly the problem with Jim . . ."

"You need to explain to Sanjiv what you mean."

"Jim says that I don't know how to love a man or even have a relationship and that's why I'm going through this phase. I just need to get over that part of me and sanctify it, then I'll be able to have sex with him again. He said the same thing about why I couldn't live with Margaret and Amanda—there was a part of my personality that I needed to sanctify. I've spent a lot of emotional turmoil trying to get rid of those characteristics. But according to this book, I'm just being a normal rooster. Those characteristics are me!"

It can be a lonely business wriggling free from a cult's indoctrination. But this book is her replacement magic at this sensitive cusp, giving her a simple explanation for why things are the way they are. Her relationship with Jim broke down because she's rooster and he's a dragon, it's that easy. And I'm a dog, that's why she trusts me. There's a light in her eyes—she's reclaiming her personality, even if it is coming out of a book.

"I've lived the life of a fifty-five-year-old, and I'm just finally realizing that all these years I haven't been myself, I haven't had the experiences that I desire," she says. "I don't want to be in bed with a sixty-six year old man."

It's encouraging to hear her talk like this. But there are still rivers to cross, fears to overcome before she can leave. The fear that she'll be destroyed, for instance, is common to many people who leave polygamist groups—Jessica from the Order, the Tuckers, Carolyn Jessop from the FLDS and many others have spoken of the same thing. It took Angel two years of anxiety attacks to conquer that fear after she left the TLC.

"I believed Jim had the power to destroy me," she says. "And when I did actually get in a car wreck three months later, I thought God caused it."

"Has Jim destroyed anyone before?"

"He's damned maybe a dozen people over the years. One actually died—Seth Jordan, who had a heart problem."

"You think Jim caused it?"

"Prophets have that ability. It's all over the Bible. Angie's afraid that she'll get in a car wreck and her children will grow up without a mother. Or, as Jim has proclaimed, God will take James and Cora from her. That fear is so deep it's uncontrollable. It keeps you up day after day."

Angie looks up from her astrology book. "I saw myself in a crash once," she says quietly. "Everything's fine and then I pass a semi not realizing that there's oncoming traffic and it's a head-on collision. I'm the only one in the car. I die. It scared the hell out of me."

In the TLC, dreams are to be believed. As Angel explains, "When you're doing everything God wants, He rewards you with special powers to see the future and the past." But if you were doing what God wanted, why would He want you dead?

Angie turns to her astrology book. "Roosters always believe that something bad is going to happen when they feel down," she says. The conviction in her voice has faded.

"Angie, you know that Jim can't hurt you, right?" I tell her. "His curses mean nothing. He's delusional."

She shakes her head. "You don't understand."

"Oh, he's delusional all right," says Angel. "He believes he's the Holy Ghost, he's part of the Godhead."

"Mom, we don't need to get into that right now," Angie says, protecting him, even now, after everything she's told me.

"Why can't we get into it?" I ask. "Because it makes him sound crazy?"

"No, because it's just not relevant."

"Of course it's relevant! Look, I know this isn't easy. But he's a fraud. You have to know this by now." And just to say "fraud" out loud feels so good.

"That's just how it seems to you."

"He's one of a long line of religious con men and phonies who are in it for sex and money."

"But that's not the story I'm trying to tell."

"It's what you have to believe before you can move on. You can't live in fear, Angie. He can't make you get in a car wreck any more than I can. True prophets don't check up on other people's phone records."

"That's just because he's been burned by the media."

"Oh come on! Jim's not the victim here. He's the one who came up with his bullshit prophecies about your children, just because he wanted to have sex with you. You told me the story yourself!"

"No!" Both Angie and Angel cut me off. "You're wrong!" Angie shuts her book and her mother looks sternly at me. "You don't know him. Jim Harmston is not a fraud. He truly believes that people came to him from across the veil and blessed him. That's his reality."

"And he truly believes that I'm broken and that's why I can't have sex with him," says Angie.

"As far as he's concerned," says Angel, "the world is coming to an end and he and his people will be the only ones left. His belief system is so deeply rooted that it produces behavior that just reinforces the beliefs. It's a vicious circle. The minute he does or thinks anything, he thinks it comes from God. He doesn't think, he *knows*."

It's past midnight and I'm exhausted. Frustrated. Defeated. They're right, I don't know Jim Harmston. I haven't met him, I haven't witnessed the devastating magnetism of his belief. And for a moment there, I forgot who I was talking to. Angie has spent a decade with this man. She's the prophetess, the mother of his children.

"Just tell me you're going to leave, Angie," I say, heading for the door.

Angie just smiles and returns to her astrology book.

❖ Jim

> The trouble with kingdoms of heaven on earth is that they're liable to
> come to pass, and then their fraudulence is apparent for all to see.
> —Malcolm Muggeridge

Does he believe this stuff, or is he a fraud? This is the perennial question
with the likes of Jim Harmston or Warren Jeffs or any leader possessed
of beliefs that appear to fly in the face of reason. According to Angie and
Angel, Harmston believes. His speeches have a messianic tilt, a sense of
divine sanction. His power stems not from the beliefs themselves, but
from the intensity with which he adheres to them. He has the charisma
of certainty.

I came across a video of Harmston once, hoping to witness this charisma for myself.[10] It featured the prophet at his pulpit, a stocky and
bearded man with a fat stack of scripture before him. But it wasn't the ora-
torical master class I'd been led to expect. Harmston didn't rock the house;
there was no fever to his pitch, just a mid-range monotone. He even says
"'mkay," like Mr. Garrison on *South Park*.

But when it comes to outlandish claims, he doesn't flinch. He declared,
for example, that he would show his people the way to the "throne room,"
and he left no doubt as to whom that throne was for. When discussing a revelation that was supposedly given to a man called John, he said: "Jesus then
approached the third man and said, 'Do you have the name of the living
God?' And the third man replied, 'The name of the living God is Harmston.'"

For Harmston, this kind of audacity goes hand in hand with certainty—
they're symbiotic, one fuels, even necessitates, the other. Once you claim
to have been visited by four separate angels who placed their hands on
your head and imbued you with supernatural powers—on November 25,
1990, in Harmston's case—then there's no longer any room for doubt. You
can't be iffy on the details. Like Warren Jeffs, Paul Kingston and others,
Harmston's trajectory shows a growth in both certainty and audacity: He
became increasingly sure of increasingly outrageous claims.

I wanted to speak to someone who knew Harmston during the nascent
stages of the TLC, so I paid a visit to Pauline Strong, one of his earliest

recruits. She'd been seduced in the early 1990s by the Models, Harmston's lecture series, particularly his argument about the apostasy of the LDS Church. At the time, she was in the throes of a traumatic divorce from a Mormon bishop. The divorce left her penniless and struggling to win custody, so she arrived in Manti distraught and found solace in the TLC. There was sweetness and positivity, the way people worked together and helped her get a job. Harmston noticed Pauline's plight and informed her that she belonged to him. Once her divorce came through, she became his third wife after Elaine and Karen.

She's a doddery old lady now, badly weakened by a battle with breast cancer. Though she has left the group, she still lives in Manti, alone, on a street where she's surrounded by TLC members, some of whom are her children, which is a source of continuing pain. She failed to protect them once before, a circumstance that led to the original divorce, and the guilt she feels is now compounded by having delivered them to Harmston. One of her daughters, Rachael, actually married Jim Harmston for a few months before leaving. Another daughter, Natalie, became Merrill Jensen's first wife. Then there are Becky and Michelle, both married to church members.

"In the early years, there was no talk of Jim being this great prophet. He didn't even practice polygamy until 1993," she says. "He was just this Mormon teacher who had been excommunicated by the LDS Church. Even when he did become the prophet, he had twelve apostles on the council. There were checks and balances."

But megalomania loomed. In September 1993, he issued a timeline to church members instructing them to anoint, curse and prepare for destruction all the "polluted temples of the LDS Church"—all except for the Manti temple, which he intended to take over himself. He declared that when Armageddon arrived, his followers would take possession of everything of value in Sanpete County. Then they would march to Salt Lake City to annihilate the LDS hierarchy, turning them all into "crispy critters and natural element." Former members[12] recall Harmston instructing his followers to pray that he become powerful enough to destroy both the LDS Church and the U.S. government in retaliation for the death of Joseph Smith.

By 2000, Harmston's eschatological fever was peaking. He predicted that the world would end on March 25, so he had his people gather for three days prior. There were baptisms for the dead and lengthy prayer meetings. Everyone showed up in their temple whites for what was meant to be a huge feast to herald the Savior's arrival. Some were so convinced by his prophecy that they maxed out their credit cards, even declared bankruptcy. And when Jesus didn't show, Harmston blamed them for their wickedness—the oldest trick in the book.

But bad prophecy never hurts prophets, it just makes them meaner. Angie remembers 2001 as the year that Jim took a more autocratic turn. Where once the church would feature several different speakers, now there was only Jim, and he was not to be questioned. According to Pauline, this change was prefigured by the arrival and growing influence of a certain group of women, some from the Shreeve group in Ogden such as Laura and Gail, and others including a former prison matron named Darcy and a former wife of Ervil LeBaron named Anna Mae. They called themselves "the Daughters of Light."

"They're the inner circle of women," says Pauline. "They come up with new ordinances and prayers. It's like Jim's the head, but these women are the neck. The head goes where the neck points it." She describes Harmston as a kind of randy king, with his wives as courtiers, scheming and plotting around him.

Of all the wives, Gail was the most powerful. She would receive revelations of her own, each of which worked to elevate Jim (and therefore herself) in the organization. "She said it was revealed to her that Jim was the reincarnation of Joseph Smith, and on it went, higher and higher, until he was the same as Jesus Christ," says Pauline. "Gail also revealed that she was Christ's wife in her former life. And Jim just backed her right up."

This is how power plays are conducted in polygamous cults. Through revelation, the courtiers raise up the leader to a pedestal of infallibility, thereby concentrating power in his hands while winning influence over him and diminishing potential dissenters. It happened in Short Creek with Leroy Johnson and the move toward one-man rule—no small reason for the mess the FLDS is in today. And the TLC is particularly prone to this kind of thing because of Harmston's doctrine of "multiple mortal probations"—reincarnation in a different wrapper. It creates an aristocracy of past lives for his followers, which unifies them on the one hand, by giving them a sense of instant superiority over outsiders. But on the other, this spiritual caste system sows division, which Harmston then exploits to cement his power.

In one instance, he vested a man named Phil with the gift to discern the lives that had been led by members in their prior "probations." Among the characters Phil recognized were Brigham Young and his right-hand man Heber C. Kimball, and the apostles Peter, James and John. Somehow the souls of several historical figures had been returned to a crummy church hall in central Utah where they were reembodied as former sex offenders, haggard fishwives and sweaty old men forever rummaging in their pockets. A fight broke out over Brigham Young—Angel's ex-husband Randy and a man named John both felt they had a claim to his soul. In the end Harmston settled it by saying that John was actually Brigham Young *Jr*.

Of course Harmston himself boasted the most splendid lineage. According to former members he has claimed to have been Isaiah, John the Baptist, Shem, Joseph with the Technicolor dreamcoat, King Arthur, Napoleon and—after seeing the movie *Braveheart*—William Wallace. But not everyone was judged so highly. And only the select could be raised up. Pauline, for instance, was torn down by Gail's revelations. "First she said I'd been a prostitute in this life," she says. "Then they had revelations that I had been a prostitute in my last life and Christ couldn't communicate with me because I was so wicked." Gail announced that Pauline's daughter Rachael—who was rebelling against her marriage to Jim—was incapable of receiving revelation, so Gail had to receive them for her, as a sort of spiritual proxy. And however oafish this scam sounds, in a world where the dreams of a few dictate the devotions of many, it works.

"The Daughters of Light would gather in a circle and pray, and say words that sounded like witchcraft, part Latin and this and that," Pauline says. "I know I've been cursed in these ordinances. They were vicious. Once, because I wasn't attending meetings regularly enough, Jim had them gather around me in a circle and yell and call me names. It was like a pack of wolves surrounding its prey."

The humiliation, the lack of solidarity among the wives, the power of the inner circle, the millennial fantasies—all the familiar tropes of polygamous cults are here in Manti. And to complete the picture, Jim's paranoia was escalating. Like Jeffs, he encouraged snitching and had his followers spy on each other, tracking movements and noting alliances. He'd know whether members were praying three times a day and wearing the appropriate robes. At one point he even had his senior apostles secure licenses to carry guns.

When I ask Angie about this later, she says she remembers Jim wearing a concealed gun. "But it was only a little one," she says. "I think he kept it in his shoe." It's typical of Angie to diminish Jim's excesses. But she has witnessed Harmston's paranoia firsthand. He kept an eye on her home for months. When she recently had some friends over to watch movies, Jim was lying in wait. "He saw a car in my drive that he didn't recognize, so he parked behind my house until they left and then he pulled up next to them and stared," Angie says. "Scared the living crap out of them."

Once he suspects one of his wives, he lets himself into her home and goes through her things. When Angie lived with Rachael, Harmston would come by and read Rachael's emails, even enlisting Angie as a co-conspirator. And she told no one, never imagining that she might be next. "I didn't like Rachael, so I think she got what she deserved—which is pretty awful to admit, actually!" she says. "But now it's happening to me, and all the other wives are sitting back and enjoying it . . ."

The truth is, Angie felt sorry for him. For all his dragon-like dominance, Jim elicits loyalty from his women in another way—he appeals to their sympathy, their instinct to protect and comfort. They know he has been hurt. Angie isn't the first of his wives to deny him sex. Rachael did the same thing in 2005 before leaving him, and before Rachael came Naomi who cheated on him with a guy she met in St. George, which reopened a wound left by his first wife, Elaine, who had had an affair some thirty years ago (though they're still together).

"He does have a soft spot that's easily manipulated," says Angie. "And he takes rejection hard. He flies into rages and bangs the table. But he's never violent. He just swears a lot. Stuff like 'shit,' 'damn,' 'hell'—you know. Not 'fuck.' He only uses 'fuck' in bed." (Pauline Strong also attested to Jim's language during sex. "He's a dirty old man in private. Very filthy-mouthed.")

Harmston takes sexual rejection so badly that Angie seems anxious to stress that she has no complaints in that department. "Sex with Jim wasn't bad," she says. "He was caring and loving and that's why I don't think he'd do anything to hurt me. But it was just sex. Women don't have much of a relationship with men in polygamy apart from the sex."

But sex wasn't enough for Angie. Jim thought his relationship with her was "normal" because they snuggled on the sofa and watched TV, but it was only because Jim wanted to. Angie never picked the channel. When I ask what her fondest memories of her marriage are, she struggles. "That's you know . . . it's tough. Our relationship was so lead-and-follow type of thing. I didn't even get a honeymoon. We went out, gosh, three years after we got married, through Bryce Canyon and Zion National Park—three nights and four days. I was pregnant with my little girl at that point. It was awful."

She didn't want to go to Zion National Park but when Jim asked she knew to obey. That's why she wants to leave—after ten years of marriage, Jim doesn't know her or care to. He just wants an obedient wife who provides for his needs for the sake of her own salvation. But Angie's not the lost young girl of a decade ago. She's a mother with a mind of her own.

"I've got a sense of humor," she protests. "But I have to keep that side of me quiet with Jim. There's no laughter with him." She sighs. "Typical Scorpio dragon."

My chances of meeting Harmston have looked slim ever since Merrill Jensen ejected me from his home. I never heard back after I sent him that letter, not even a cursory "no thanks." But Angie reckons that I should never have gone through Merrill Jensen in the first place. "Try Dan Simmons," she says. "He's the president in the church. He's much better." And she scribbles his number down for me. So I make the call. And he sounds friendly enough.

"Sanjeev you say? Now where's that from? Iran?"

"No, India."

"All right then, terrific. But you sound like an Englishman. My forefathers are from England you know . . ."

He says he's in Zion National Park with Jim; they're taking their families out for the weekend. "But I'll be back Monday. After 4 PM should be fine. I can certainly meet you and I can ask Jim at that time if you'd like."

I don't understand why Dan's being so nice, but he's obviously close to Jim, so maybe this is a fresh start. On the road to Manti, I call Merrill Jensen—I'll just tell him that the whole kerfuffle about Angie is all sorted out now, Dan's looking into it, so maybe we can pick up where we left off?

But Merrill doesn't pick up—his second wife, Noralyn, does. And she's furious.

"You shouldn't have called Dan Simmons just now. That was wrong, wrong, wrong."

"What?"

"Dan Simmons just called me. What did you think—we wouldn't know? If you think you can go behind our backs like that, then you've got the wrong idea, my friend."

"I'm not going behind your back! Dan said he could meet me on Monday. So I thought we should meet up too . . ."

"Oh dear, you really don't get it. Look, Dan Simmons was not happy to hear from you. We already told you that Jim wouldn't speak to you, so Dan wants to know why you're asking again. And that's not good, because we've already caught flak for talking to you in the first place."

"So Dan's not going to meet me?"

"No, he's not! And if you think about knocking on Jim's door again like you did before, he'll call the sheriff. It's harassment."

"But I'm half an hour away from Manti. Is there anyone else I can talk to?"

"I'm prepared to speak to you. But that's it. We've never let anybody in for eight years. You're the first and we've given you more than anyone."

"But you're just one family. How can I get a full picture of the TLC with just one family?"

"You can't, okay? Nobody outside the group can ever understand where we're coming from. To get it, you have to join the church."

In the end, Noralyn commits to giving me twenty minutes. But when I arrive she goes on for three hours. She's like her husband—a lecturer, a didact. They're like bicycle dynamos, the pair of them, offering dim light to the drone of their wheels turning. Had Merrill been around, I suspect Noralyn would have taken a back seat. But he's off picking up his first wife, Natalie, who's been away for a week. So this is her chance.

She tells a grim story. She had been married to a Mormon who sexually abused their children, an experience that prompted her to ask her bishop a touchingly naïve question: "How come God didn't tell the bishop that this man was not worthy?" Not, "How come God didn't tell me, his wife?" or "How come God put my children in harm's way?" Having accepted the premise that God speaks first to bishops before other mortals, Noralyn's faith wasn't diminished, just redirected. So with husband number two, she abandoned the LDS Church and headed for Manti, for the promise of polygamy. But husband number two didn't buy into Harmston the way Noralyn did, so they split up and she married again, this time to someone within the TLC who was such a bad match that Noralyn just rolls her eyes and moves swiftly on. Cue Merrill Jensen, her fourth.

"Plus I'd lost some children in joining the TLC—they were teenagers and they didn't want to be a part of it so some went into foster care and others just moved away. *And* my parents won't have anything to do with me." She chuckles. I think it's supposed to impress me, the sheer emotional wreckage that she has caused by joining Jim's cult—it's a badge of her commitment. And as she regales me with her beliefs, that pride prevails: this is who she is and this is what she stands for.

She doesn't believe in an arbitrary minimum age for marriage because "some young girls are mature beyond their years." She believes suicide is a sin and fully expects the apocalypse in her lifetime, you've only got to see all the earthquakes on the cable news. She believes that Jim Harmston is Joseph Smith reborn and that she herself is one of the "elect of Israel" and that it's not racist to deny black people the priesthood. "Those black people won't be black in the next life unless they choose to be," she says. "It's the view that this is the only life there is that's racist."

"But you just said the apocalypse is coming in our lifetime, so there's no time for a second life. Does that mean if you're black today, then you're damned?"

"Listen, God can do what he wants. Who's to say that He can't turn black skin white?"

Later that evening, Pauline Strong, Natalie's mother, tells me why Natalie and Merrill weren't around when I dropped by. A week earlier, Natalie had taken a fistful of pills. It was her second suicide attempt. Natalie had been molested as a child, and her marriage to Merrill Jensen had become increasingly unsteady when Noralyn arrived.

"They wanted to keep it a secret," says Pauline. "I only found out because my son Don called asking for Natalie, and a little child answered the phone. He said 'Natalie's in the hospital, she swallowed too many pills.'"

"But I was just talking to Noralyn about suicide," I tell her. "She said it was a sin."

"Oh, it's terrible to say, but I'm sure she'd like to be the only wife. And I think this gives her more status. But that's just my belief."

The TLC seems more and more like a refuge of damaged people, the battered backwash of the Mormon Church. Perhaps I've chanced upon a particularly broken circle here with the Jensen family and Pauline Strong, Angie and Angel. But the effect is dispiriting. The women arrive with a string of divorces in their wake, often including at least one child abuser; the children arrive confused, molested, desperate for stability; and the men are either pederasts or fools.

But they all come to Manti with a purpose, like the original pioneers, to start afresh, having been ravaged by their previous lives. They know from Mormonism that Armageddon looms and a prophet will lead them to salvation. So they come to remake themselves by another man's light, drawn like moths to his conviction. Harmston appears to be nothing so much as a sophisticated scavenger of these hobbled spirits.

As I drive to the local Chinese restaurant in Ephraim, a ray of light: Angie calls. She's in California with her mom and sister, staying with her brother somewhere near San Diego. And she sounds strong.

"I like it here," she says. "California's awesome."

"What, you've left already?"

"No, we're just on vacation. We went to Disneyland, we did Sea World in San Diego and I think we're going to stop by Vegas on the way home. But then we're basically coming straight back, all three of us."

"You're definitely leaving?"

"Yeah, it's now or never. Angel's maxed out her student loans and now's the only time we'll have enough money for it. We'll drive back to Manti tomorrow, pack up all our stuff and get a U-Haul, basically."

"That's great news, Angie. Let me know if you need anything. I can do that letter if you want."

"No, there's no point. The people in the TLC have already made their minds up about me."

"Well, I could help with the packing . . ."

"No, there's too many eyes on me already. Listen, we'll be fine. I'll email you when I get there. There's more I want to tell you about my marriage to Jim."

◆ Freedom

I think I can. I think I can. I think I can. I know I can.
—Watty Piper, *The Little Engine that Could*

The first email is a shock. It's a forward of the long and heartrending email she sent to Jim, the one explaining why she's leaving after ten years of marriage. She prefaces the letter with a note to me: "I guess I have tried to be overly optimistic about my situation . . . But strangely our conversations have helped me come to terms with the reality. In a way, your anti–organized religion type of attitude and cynicism was exactly what I needed to pull out of the fearful perspective I was carrying. Even your harsh opinion of Jim stung at first but certainly helped me view things in a new light."

What follows is an abridged version of her letter to Jim. She wrote it from her home in Manti in the week she spent preparing to move. It was a fraught time. The rumor was out that the prophetess was going to leave. So she decided to cool things down by communicating with everyone by email alone. It was a wise decision, and bold, but not surprising. As her letter shows, Angie has grown in strength, maturity and resolve since we first met. She's no longer gripping onto the sides of her chair, struggling to find the words.

Dear Jim,

You have led me through many years and I have followed. I feared my damnation and condemnation if I did not perform exactly as you saw fit and so I based so many of my decisions on what you believed . . . But I have come to a point where I need to base my decisions on my own insight, understanding and knowledge and you will not let me do that. When I tried you told me that what I felt and believed was wrong and your "revelation" superseded what I felt.

I have endured a lot of hurt and pain. But, this last year has hit me to the absolute core. It broke me in a sense, but also saved me by revealing who and what I really am. I cracked—you are right. I am not cut out for this. I am not strong enough. I realize now that the person I was trying to be for you is not the person I really am. My own hard headedness is what pushed me through.

It feels like many of your wives only tolerate me for your sake. They are concerned superficially, only because they see you hurt. Is anyone truly concerned about the pain I feel? My heart is aching. I have given my entire life to you, Jim. I grew up under your guiding hand. This is where I believe the problem originates. If I had entered your family as a woman rather than a child maybe I would feel differently. Maybe I would not see you as a father figure and instead see you as a husband.

I will take responsibility for my decision to enter your family at only 16 years of age. I walked into the situation in ignorance, fear and naïvety. If I had based my decision on what I truly felt rather than fear of damnation I would not be where I am today. But I can't live like this anymore. I want to be happy. I want my kids to be happy and we aren't. The days of pretending have to be over now. One of the things that hurts most is having so much to say, and not being able to say it. My whole heart, my life and all of my efforts have been invested in you and I thank God for all of that, but I can't do it anymore. I can't face another meeting. I can't face anymore hurt. I can't watch you hurt, it's all too much.

I am so sorry that I failed to be what you wanted me to be. I am walking away and I will not do anything to cause you further hurt. I will never be your enemy, it's not in me. You are who you are and you will always have a place in my heart.

Love

Angie

Jim's response was immediate and disarming. "I agree with all that you said in your email," he begins. "I will always love you and I am determined to support you in every way possible." There's no rancor, no anger, no self-pity. And he makes all the right assurances about keeping things civil in the aftermath. He goes on to suggest that during their remaining week in Manti he could take the kids fishing and shopping and on playdates with their friends. He says that he will pay $600 per month to pay for their flights to and from Manti, and he's going to convert his prayer room into a bedroom and stock it with clothes so they won't have to pack when they visit. "We'll have lots of fun things for them to do and I'll email you pictures," he writes.

The sudden metamorphosis into Superdad makes Angie suspicious. "He has never been so involved," she writes to me. "Now that he's lost us he wants to jump in all the way." She forwards me an email she received from

Jim's first wife, Elaine, full of sympathy and support, but again, Angie's skeptical. "Here she is trying to save me," she writes. "But she never bothered to pay attention to the kids while she had the chance."

In the week leading up to her departure Angie's resolve only stiffens. She picks a Sunday to leave—May 27—because the group is in church from 11 AM until 3 PM. So she, her mother and her sister pack up their U-Haul and she tells the children they are off to spend the summer in California. And as they set off, they pass Jim's daughter Wendy's house, where Jim has gathered a group on the front lawn. There's no confrontation, no drama—they just watch the truck pass in silence. And all Angie can think of are the times Jim said that she and her children would die if she ever left him. She grips the steering wheel all the way to California.

When I see her a few weeks later, the fear of curses has given way to more practical concerns. She's living with her brother in his little two-bedroom place in Ramona, a sweet, dusty little town some way past Temecula. But there's just no room for them all—Angie, her two kids, her mom, Daisy and her baby. And moving out's going to be tough because rents in California are higher than in Utah. And jobs are scarce.

She's visibly stressed, getting into my car. "Can we go get a margarita?" she says.

"Sure."

"It's just been a nightmare. Jim's playing mind games already. All that stuff he said in his email—well forget that. I let the kids stay with him and he pulled a lot of crap. He took them to Sunday meetings, he even tried to get James baptized. And when I got them back, my daughter was saying stuff like 'I belong in Manti, I want to go and live with my dad'—stuff she just got from him. And he's being difficult about the dates. It just goes on and on."

"Remember, Angie, if you want to prosecute, you could put him in prison. He's in no position to push you around."

"I know what my leverage is. But I'm not capable of hurting anybody."

We find a little Mexican place down the street and order two margaritas, and she lightens up a bit. She says she's open to dating even though her mother says it's too soon. The prospect of a guy her own age! She wonders too about her former faith. She saw a DVD about polygamy that debunks Joseph Smith, and now she's not sure if he was a true prophet at all.

I tell her that she's come a long way and fast—she's already shaking off her religion. "Oh yeah, the indoctrination has worn off, but now what? I need a job, I need an apartment. I've got two kids involved in this."

Sadly, her California experiment doesn't come off. It's just too expensive. Even though all three of them work—Angie waitressing, Angel at a kids' center and Daisy at the local Wendy's—they still only scrape by. Jim doesn't pay the child support he promised—Angie has to beg him for $100 here and there. And even though Angie loves Cali, her mom and sister hate it.

So they return to Utah County in November, where they lived before the whole Manti saga began. First Orem, then Provo. Angie gets a job at a residential treatment facility helping teenage addicts and goes to school to study community health. She also finds an apartment of her own, just her and her kids. And visitation with Jim becomes more manageable. He gets forty-eight hours every other weekend and the kids are back with Angie by Sunday.

The last time I see her is for a drink at Club 90. Angel picked the venue—a budget megaclub for fogies, a place where the knackered Gentiles of Salt Lake County can get their drink on, have a dance and maybe meet a divorcee. It's a huge place, heaving with forty-a-day grandmothers and grizzled old men drinking jugs of beer. There's a covers band onstage and a couple of women twirling on the dance floor. Cheap carpet, stackable chairs, glitter ball. And the family Mower are up for a night out—Angel, Angie and Daisy. Angel's all lipsticky, done up on a Friday night. "Look at you with three women!" she says. "You're a polygamist!"

Angie seems disappointed at first—she was hoping for a proper nightclub with people her own age rather than Jim Harmston's. But she soon settles in. It's not Manti anymore and the relief is visible in her face. "The weight that has been lifted," she says, beaming. "I don't think I've ever been happier."

We order drinks and play pool and chat. It's not that there was nothing of value in her former life, she explains. One vestige of the TLC, for instance, is that she still leans toward the subservience of women in a relationship. And there are things she learned from Jim, like to not be so hasty and let things play out. "I should probably have learned that from a father figure," she says. "But I realized I've been treating Jim like a father-daughter relationship, except with sex. Oh, he mentioned you."

"What did he say?"

"He said he researched you on the Internet and you were a sensation-alist with a smooth tongue."

"So I guess an interview's out of the question."

"I guess. But why would you go back there anyway? Ugh, Manti was suffocating. People can't breathe in those situations, always trying to be perfect for God. They go crazy. I was going crazy."

"But now you're free at last, free at last."

"I know! I still talk to Jim about when to get the kids or whatever, and he still drops these little things, about how the end of the world's coming and I better be ready. It's sad really. I think he's brainwashed himself. He doesn't have any other purpose than to be this prophet and he can't imagine any other kind of life. He doesn't get why I did what I did. He thinks I'm insane for giving up what I had. He doesn't have a clue what I went through and why. He thinks I'm still scared, but I'm not! If the world's going to end, I want to be at ground zero. I'm single, I'm free and I'm going to enjoy my life."

She cues up for a shot, and stops. "Listen!" It's the band, they're playing that Whitesnake song. "It's the story of my life!" And she sings along, cueing up for a pot. "I made up my mind. I ain't wasting no more time . . ."

Death by Rumor

CHAPTER 11

One dog barks at something, and a hundred bark at the bark.
—*Chinese proverb*

*T*HE KNOCKBACK FROM Harmston wasn't easy to take. I tried consoling myself that he hadn't done media in years, he'd been burned, all the usual excuses. But in truth, I thought I had a shot—a real chance at a one-on-one with a bona fide, God-complex polygamist prophet. The odds of getting Paul Kingston were always slim. And forget about Warren Jeffs. But I got close to Jim. I knocked on his door. I'm friends with the prophetess.

I know I'm meant to bounce back at this point, all chipper, with a positive mental attitude and all that. But I'm no longer the sunny optimist who set out on this journey. Six months in and my spirit's waning. I'm getting pudgy and sallow from all the junk food and long drives. I've got polygamy fatigue, is what it is. I couldn't tell you exactly when it set in, but it was in one of those $40 motel rooms in the asscrack of rural Utah. I'm in one now, sitting in bed, eating Cheetos and flipping channels, trying to avoid that "your mattress is freeeee" commercial. All summer long I've gone from Triple 8 to Motel 6 to Travelodge, and all the Inns—Comfort, Days, Sleep and Best. I've had the breakfast buffet in the lobby. The bruised bananas and the Styrofoam bowls.

None of this is polygamy's fault, admittedly, but polygamy has other ways of wearing you down. This isn't a book about ice cream or daisies. Listening to stories of abuse, oppression and despair doesn't do anything for one's general perkiness. Nor does encountering suspicion at every turn, especially here in Salt Lake City, where polygamists hide among the Gentiles and are that much more paranoid as a result. One of the labors of the job is the relentless self-pitching to people who just don't trust me, and quite like it that way. Every time the same questions—"Is it going to be positive or negative?", "What are you, Islamic?" And always the sneer, the variation of, "Yeah, *sure.*"

Of course I understand how very sensitive it all is, what with the mean state and the nasty media. But—here's the fatigue talking—give me a break, guys, I didn't arrest your grandfather. These victims of prejudice sure know how to dish it out. It's got so I can't even fake the smile anymore—that affable smile, forced but friendly, which saw me through so many fundamentalist interrogations and housewifey non-jokes. It makes my jaw ache. In fact, this morning, at a diner, this baby was gurgling at me from a neighboring table, fixated the way babies get. And I couldn't smile back. I had to turn away. From a *baby.*

All this came to a head after the poisonous events of the previous week. It started when I moved into a hostel on account of my dwindling budget. I figured I could rough it because I wouldn't even be in most of the day— I'd be out in the field chasing interviews, shaking off this fatigue thing. So I checked into a place called the Camelot, a blue and yellow eyesore in downtown Salt Lake City, run by a man called Arthur. Presumably he got a kick out of the whole Camelot/Arthur thing at one time. Not any more. On the day I moved in he threatened me with the cops. "We have rules here, my friend, and if you break them, I'll just call my friends at the police department and you'll go straight to jail," he said. "Are we clear?"

Crystal clear, Arthur. I'm not here to break rules, I'm here to relight my fire. I embraced my cramped little cell with its barf green walls and little welded seat-table thing in the corner. This cubicle was going to epitomize order and industry—the shoes in rows, my papers stacked and a laundered shirt hanging from the door. I'd eat salads, not Cheetos. I would be a model prisoner, working my way to freedom, with the soundtrack to *Rocky* playing in the background. I even tried to bond with the "Camelot

Community," a bunch of oddballs who clattered around in the kitchen. I said hi to the guy with a twitch playing video poker and the grunting Shrek creature, who called himself "the concierge." I had a beer with Ralph, a printer salesman from Montana, who liked to copy my English accent. I think he thought it was going to get him laid.

But all that momentum ground to a halt when one day I discovered that the fundamentalist community was cutting me loose. Suddenly, all I heard was *no*.

The penny dropped when the Apostolic United Brethren, one of the largest groups in Utah, stopped taking my calls. Of all the groups, it's probably the most open and has a history of working with researchers and social scientists. Anne Wilde had taken me to a church service up in Bluffdale where I'd met Lamoine Jensen, their presiding prophet. Jensen had referred me to one of his apostles, David Watson, a towering man with a white beard and five wives, whom I'd visited at home. We'd talked for hours—myself, David and his wife Marianne. It had gone so well, we'd resolved to get together again soon. But then David stopped returning my calls and emails. And so did Marianne. I tried passing messages through Anne, but it was no good. Then one day by chance, I managed to get Marianne on the phone and she said, "I shouldn't tell you this, but we're not comfortable talking to you anymore. A lot of people feel that you've deceived us about your book. I have to get off the phone but I recommend you look up Brooke Adams's blog."

It turned out that the previous week, as I was checking into the Camelot, *The Salt Lake Tribune*'s polygamy reporter, Brooke Adams, posted a piece about me on her blog, *The Plural Life*, which turned the whole fundamentalist community against me.

■ AUTHOR MAKING FUNDAMENTALISTS NERVOUS ■

Writer Sanjiv Bhattacharya has been crisscrossing the state to meet with fundamentalist Mormons, many of whom have welcomed him into their folds with open arms as he gathers material for an upcoming book.

Last week, one plural wife stumbled over a blurb about Sanjiv's book on the Miss Snark blog (misssnark.blogspot.com), which focuses on the publishing world. It said:

NON-FICTION: GENERAL/OTHER

Journalist and filmmaker Sanjiv Bhattacharya's TO BE A GOD: A *Journey into American Polygamy*,* a humorous and compelling study of America's definitions of faith through the stories and facts regarding abuse, incest, forced marriage, and religious fervor within Mormon Fundamentalism . . .

That description alarmed some of those who have met with Sanjiv and shared their stories. Didn't they read his newspaper piece on Warren Jeffs titled "The Man With 80 Wives?" later made into a small documentary? He is, after all, a writer who specializes in writing about celebrities. He has a certain tone and voice, which no doubt helped him land the book deal.

It wasn't an assassination, just some sniping from a territorial journalist who resents an intruder. The sniffiness of "small documentary" and "specializes in . . . celebrities" and "certain tone and voice." But it takes only a droplet of doubt to poison the well. The fundamentalist community is extraordinarily sensitive to gossip, and it holds Brooke Adams in high regard. So the damage was done. I posted a reply on her blog but it was no use, the doors were closing all around me. Having been turned down by Paul Kingston and then Jim Harmston, I was now being spurned by David Watson and Lamoine Jensen of the AUB, and even the chatty Winston Blackmore, the notorious polygamist from British Columbia who makes the occasional appearance on Larry King. My hopes of meeting a prophet were fading to black.

It's a tall order maintaining a sunny perspective at the Camelot at the best of times. The grubbiness, the tyranny of the pube in the shower. My standards start to slip—the Cheeto packets return, the clothes are in a heap. I reminisce about the halcyon days in Centennial Park. I miss the trust and warmth down there. Salt Lake City's so full of whispers and intrigue. Anne Wilde has washed her hands of me—"You've had a lot of access already, Sanjiv, you should be happy with that." Mary Batchelor was kinder. She said, "Why not try the Dargers? They're a great family." The trouble is, the Dargers are so overexposed and well rehearsed that when I visit them one evening, they trot out a tired

---

*1. *To Be a God* was the working title of this book at the outset.

performance, a series of bland fundamentalist talking points. There's a fatigue about the Dargers too—only last week, they gave Brooke Adams an exclusive.

Within a few halting days, I find myself alone in a messy cell of a room, thinking: Is this it? Am I done here? For all my efforts at trying to understand polygamists, I've ended up a pariah of the community, ruined by the snippety pen of another reporter. I thought getting stitched up by the media was something *polygamists* complained about.

"Hey, Sanjie, want to go and get a pint, mate?" It's Ralph doing his rubbish English accent. He might be the only person in Salt Lake City who wants to talk to me right now. So we go to the Spot, a chintzy little dive a few blocks away. All the way there, Ralph twitters on about printers and football and this other English guy he knew once. At the Spot, there's a bartender he's trying to impress, so he regales her with his favorite stories—the time he won a grand in Vegas, the time he was in a pile-up but survived . . . and here it comes: the English accent. "I said corblimey officer! Can I have a cup of tea?" Is this how my journey ends? Watching Dick van Dyke try to get some action?

The next morning, my cell phone starts bleating at an unkind hour. It's Arthur. He's shouting. "Your time is up my friend! Did you hear me? You are no longer welcome at the Camelot. You're on private property, so you better get out or I'll call my friends at the police department and they'll be there in two minutes. Are we clear?"

A few days ago, I'd asked Arthur for a bigger room, and this seems to have set him off. Apparently I should have done it online and not bothered him on the phone. Whatever. Arthur's only finishing what the fundamentalist community started. First they chucked me out of the Vermillion Cafe, then it was Merrill Jensen's house, and now I'm being kicked out of a rancid, smelly hostel by a pilchard named Arthur.

It's 10 AM in the brutal sunlight, and I'm dragging my suitcase back to the car across the crunching gravel. Shrek is at the door giving Arthur a running commentary over the phone. "Yes, he's out of the room. He's taking his suitcase to the car. Yes, he's alone . . ."

This is going to be a long, long drive back to L.A.

• • •

A Chevron in Sandy. Filling the car with gas. Giant bag of Cheetos for the road. And the phone rings.

"Guess where I am!" It's my wife.

"Where."

"Pulling into LAX. I'm coming to see you!"

"What, now?"

"Don't sound too happy about it."

"But I'm done. I'm finished. I'm driving back. It's a long story . . ."

"No you're not! I've bought my ticket, I'm flying in like an hour. I managed to get a week off work, so I thought we could have a holiday. We can hang out with your polygamist friends."

"But I haven't got any."

"What, you've been up there all that time and you haven't got any friends?"

"I guess."

"Don't be ridiculous. There must be *someone*. What about that guy who looks like Fabio?"

She means Christopher Nemelka, the guy Vicky Prunty married after Gary, who claims to have translated a whole new book of scripture using the gold plates and all the rest of it. I first met him back in April, but then I got sucked into the Order and Harmston and dropped the ball.

"What are his wives like? Are they cute? Do they drink wine like the ones in Centennial Park?"

"Well, he's not strictly a polygamist. I mean he used to be, but he's not anymore . . ."

"Okay, whoever then. And afterward we can go to Park City and have dinner. And I want to see the Salt Lake. Can you go boating on that thing? How far is it from the Grand Canyon?"

I turn the car around and trek back to Temple Square to look for a hotel. Maybe she's right about Nemelka. He might not be a polygamist, but from what I recall, he's even better—he's a prophet. Or a madman. And he may be the only one out here who hasn't been poisoned against me. He's not really part of the fundamentalist gossip circle.

It's time to get back in the saddle.

Christopher Nemelka

CHAPTER 12

◈ The Walmart John the Baptist

Matilda said, "Never do anything by halves if you want to get away with it. Be outrageous. Go the whole hog. Make sure everything you do is so completely crazy it's unbelievable . . ."

—Roald Dahl, *Matilda*

$\mathcal{A}$PRIL 1. THE girl behind the information desk at the Salt Lake City library tells me there's a "science fiction club" going on downstairs in one of the meeting rooms. And I guess you could call it that. But the fifty or so people who have come to hear Christopher Nemelka speak might take exception. They're not here for the fiction. They're here for the facts. "You know that I only bring you the truth," says Nemelka. "My mission is to prepare you for death, or in other words, for life—so you can understand things the way they really are."

He's a brawny, stubbled man with long hair, boots and jeans, bit of a tan. Vicky was right—he does look a bit like Fabio. He stands at the front of the hall with nothing but a radio mike clipped to his jumper—no script, no overhead projector; he's a prophet unplugged. But Nemelka doesn't need props. His sermons are incendiary enough on their own. Within the first ten minutes he has declared that all other religions are false and promised that in the year 2145, beings from another planet will come to transform this world forever. He knows this because he chats with them. He also has superpowers. "Could I perform miracles? You bet I could, but I don't want that kind of persecution. Did they listen to Christ?" In any case, he explains, what we consider to be superpowers are just manifestations of superior technology, the kind he receives from his pals on other planets. "In the future, let me tell you," he says, "they've got technology the size of a quarter which produces enough electricity for L.A., Las Vegas and San Diego put together!"

The crowd accepts all this without so much as a murmur. They've read Nemelka's books—*The Sealed Portion* and *666 The Mark of America, Seat of the Beast*—so this is old ground for them. But it's not for me. And I can't make head or tail of what he's on about. I'm sitting up the front, in a row of senior citizens, scribbling down quotes like "these beings are one thousand years advanced" or "if you create a galaxy, then you can't live in it, it's that simple." Clearly Nemelka is no run-of-the-mill preacher. At one point he reveals he has a job at Walmart unloading trucks for $9.20 an hour. And this segues somehow into his philosophy on human happiness, which is what he's here to spread. "My best friend at Walmart is a mongoloid or Down syndrome or whatever," he says. "You know, retarded? Is it okay to say 'retarded'? Well those guys have got it going on! They live in their own little world. That guy's happy!"

His audience is a curious bunch. There's none of that clean-cut Mormon formality here—they put their feet up on chairs, they don't shave, they wear shorts, their children sit on the floor playing with toys. One guy's just lying on the floor by the wall. He might be asleep. Most are middle-aged or elderly, but there are some college types among them, with tattoos and piercings. It has the feel of a fringe lefty movement of conspiracy theorists and objectors. When Nemelka opens up the floor for questions, people ask about energy independence and world hunger and the thirteen families who control the world. They also ask him, "What does the spirit look like?" and "Is Lazarus walking the earth today?" Nemelka answers them all without hesitation. He's the oracle. "I'll debate the smartest men in the world, just me and them, and the audience will be there, and I will not lose—I will not. Why? Because I know reality."

But Fabio's not fooling everyone. One elderly man at the back announces to the room that Nemelka's book *The Sealed Portion* is a fake. "I have video where you actually said that you faked it," he declares. "If anyone is interested, give me your email at the end of the meeting."[1] It's a confrontational move and creates a stir. Nemelka calmly retaliates by pointing out that the man's grudge is personal. "I almost sued your brother when he said 'Uncle Chris is crazy,'" he says. "Don't defame my character, sir, or I will sue you." But the man continues. He accuses Nemelka of stealing $10,000 from a woman called Patte, and the meeting quickly degenerates into a squabble. Some other detractors weigh in, Nemelka's followers protest, and before long, the prophet is no longer expounding on extraterrestrial humanoids and advanced civilizations. He's bickering about a credit card bill. "No sir, Patte was a cosigner on the card. And the fact is, I paid the $8,900 remodeling costs while I was married to Jackie and then I took out a home equity loan to pay off the credit card in December 2000 . . ."

We've gone from *Star Trek* to *Judge Judy*. It's the most bizarre religious meeting I've ever attended. And in the middle of it all, Nemelka looks up at the clock, grabs his bag and leaves. His Walmart shift starts at 4 PM and he can't afford to be late. As a convicted felon, there aren't many jobs he's even eligible for, so he can't afford to lose this one. I run out after him to ask for an interview.

"Sure, young man," he says. "Set it up with Julie."

I've met Julie, Nemelka's assistant. She's a fifty-something divorcee and exile from the Mormon Church—that common prelude to membership of a fringe cult, faith and family all lying in a heap. She'd been a self-confessed Molly Mormon before that, who taught seminary and practiced food storage. But divorce had left her with eight children and a mortgage that the church refused to help her with. It was at this time that she discovered *The Sealed Portion*. And now she's Christopher's personal secretary, the keeper of his schedule, his greatest champion and defender and even the cowriter of his autobiography.

It was Julie who invited me to the event in the first place. I contacted her through thesealedportion.com and she was nothing but helpful. None of that fundamentalist paranoia about the evil media, the tiresome Mormon persecution complex—Julie just wants to help, she wants to chat. After the lecture she offers me a ride downtown, so I clamber into her smoky little car, squeeze in between the clutter of Nemelka's books, a computer monitor and a bag of clothes.

"Sorry about the mess here," she chuckles.

"What's that sticker on the bumper, Julie? It says, 'Finally . . . the truth 666America.com.'"

"Oh, that's Christopher's latest book. It was dictated to him by a homeless man who's one of those people who never age," she says. "You should read it. People see the 666 and they just think it's all about the devil. But it's not. It'll answer every question you've ever had."

There's an air of faded glamour about Julie—she's all put together, fragrant and charming. And she's a nippy little driver, whizzing about town in a stick shift, chattering away as she goes. She says she's his biographer too and I suspect she may also be his lover; it's hard to tell. She's certainly besotted with him. What time she has left after her day job selling time share at Trends West she devotes to Nemelka's cause. He's the man in her life right now, even though she insists it's not a physical thing. Julie fell for Chris long before she ever set eyes on him.

She first heard of Chris back in 2001 when her divorce went through, after thirty-three years of marriage. Her world had collapsed and she was in dire straits financially. Her ex-husband was no help and neither was the church, so she had to sell her house to survive. It was a miserable time. Then she met a man called Jay at an LDS singles dance who told her about this Christopher character down in San Diego who claimed to have translated the Sealed Portion of the Book of Mormon.

The Sealed Portion is a huge deal for Mormons. The story goes that only a fraction of the gold plates were translated by Joseph Smith, so witnesses say[2]—the rest were sealed for a later date, and Mormons have been waiting for that day ever since.[3] So when Jay said he'd met Christopher and was convinced that he was the real deal, Julie was enraptured. All she needed was a man to confirm it. "Women are more easily swayed by things, men are not," she explains. So she rushed home and read *The Sealed Portion* in a fever. It blew her away. And only then, once she knew that Christopher truly was a prophet of God, did she meet him.

"I wasn't wowed like some women are with him," she says, screeching around a corner. "I just want to protect the work that he's doing. It's so vitally important. Now, you know he's not a polygamist, right?"

"Yes. But he was for a few months, wasn't he?"

"You could say that, but he's not any more. That's very important. He doesn't agree with all those other fundamentalists in your book."

"Got it."

We pull up next to my car. She turns the engine off and turns to face me.

"Okay, what did you think of what he was saying? You can be honest."

"Well . . . he's pretty out there," I say, weakly.

"You know what? He is! And a lot of people aren't ready for it. Like that guy today who started arguing. But Christopher always says 'There are enemies of truth out there.' They went after Christ in the same way."

"You think they might go after Chris?"

"I'm sure he'll be killed one day. It happens to all the great saints. They get persecuted. Look at Joseph Smith."

"Do you believe that Chris is the reincarnation of Joseph Smith?"

"No, I don't. How could he be if he meets with Joseph? No, he's not Joseph. He's someone else."

"Who do you think?"

"Oh I don't *think*. I know. Oh yes. He's John the Baptist. Can't you just see him eating locusts and honey and wearing animal skins? Think about it.

◆ Ask the Stones

Dan, don't you agree that truth, if only a pinch, must season every false-hood, or else the palate fucking rebels?
—Al Swearengen, *Deadwood*

We're at the Village Inn in Sandy—Julie, Chris and I—at a booth by the window, looking at laminated menus on formica tables. It all looks good this morning, all the glistening eggs and crispy hash browns, bathed in sunlight and Muzak, the sound of Anita Baker singing "Sweet Love." And Chris is beaming, his eyes as clear as the morning.

"So, Sanjie! You're interested in writing a book about polygamy, huh? Well, I can certainly help you with that. I can explain polygamy to you, how it got started in the Mormon realm. This has never been explained before in public, except to a few people. Most people don't know. They haven't a clue. Fundamentalists don't understand it, the Mormon Church doesn't understand it—how did Joseph Smith come up with the idea? Well, I'm going to tell you. And you're going to be the first one to understand and say 'Gosh, Chris! This is real! It makes sense!'"

He adores the sound of his own voice, Nemelka. It's a bumpkin's brogue, the kind that goes well with dungarees. But he's precise—everything is enunciated, all his 'k's and 't's are hard. He likes to say "the fact is" a lot. And he refers to "reality" as though it's something only he has a grasp on. It's clear that he's here to teach me, not answer my questions. I'm the audience, a potential conscript and ally in the media. So every fresh lesson comes with a "But wait, there's more!" like a pitchman on a late night infomercial—you're the first one to hear this truth, it's a brand-new kind, you can't get it in the stores, so dial now with your credit card number . . .

"So, Sanjie, we're sitting here having breakfast at the Village Inn. None of us would question that. But there are people out there, I guarantee you, who would. If we told the world, 'We had breakfast at the Village Inn,' there's people who'd say, 'No you didn't, you're lying, you're deceiving, you're making it up.'" He chuckles. "I'm just giving you an example. But the fact is, we're here. It happened. We can show 'em the receipt."

"So evidence is important."

"Oh, very important."

"No point having truth without evidence because you'll never be able to share it."

"That's right! And the claim that I've been with beings from other planets sounds to some people absurd. But once you think about it, it makes sense. Once you think about the human race evolving. Can we go to the moon? Yes. Will we be able to go to Mars in a few years? Of course we will. Does it make sense that there are colonies of humanoids out there in the solar system that have advanced far beyond our technical means? And if there are, why would they pick one bearded ding-a-ling guy like me to talk to and say 'We have a message'? That's what people ask: 'Why you?'"

"Okay. Why you?"

"Ask yourself, 'How does he live? Does he make money from this? Does he have a following?' I don't have any of that."

"You have a foundation that raises money." His Worldwide United Foundation claims to have the solution to world poverty: simply demand that governments give everyone foodstamps. After all, the pamphlet says "Money is just an abstract human illusion."

"I don't make a penny from that foundation, Sanjie, and I don't make a penny from my books. All of the sales are donated to the WUF. You can look at all our accounts. Just ask Julie. I'm all about the truth. Some people say 'He's crazy, he just has dreams.' No. If you were to get to know me, you'd know that I'm a pragmatic, sensible thinker. I don't believe that there's any God or spirits that speak to you. It's all in your mind."

"But I thought that's what happened to you—some spirits spoke to you."

"No, I had *actual beings* from other solar systems present themselves to me. Now, at the moment that they did, I thought it was a religious experience. I thought it was an angel, quote unquote. But that's what people don't understand. They're humanoids—they look like me, like us . . ."

He stops for a moment as the waitress comes to refill my coffee. It's as though he knows he sounds crazy—that people who chat about meeting humanoids from distant galaxies are probably rowing with one oar out of the water. But it's just an intermission. Once the waitress leaves, he's straight back into it. After all, crazy has always been the nutmeat of religion. No self-respecting prophet can afford to be squeamish about sounding nuts. And Nemelka knows this. Nemelka brings the crazy.

Over a monkish breakfast of fruit and water, he explains that there are people on Earth who don't age. They live for hundreds, even thousands of years. These people have told him that they're from another planet just like ours, where the technology is so advanced they've conquered the aging gene. They've also mastered a form of interstellar transportation that involves manipulating their DNA in a way that enables them to take off and zip from planet to planet, no spaceship required. (Apparently our DNA is what keeps us grounded to the Earth like magnets, a force we mistakenly call "gravity.")

"See, according to our Neanderthal science, electrons are what make up the atoms. The power and mystery of all life lies in what we call electrons, but they're really just forms of energy that undulate at different frequencies. These beings have advanced to such a degree that they control their electrons. And their electrons have the ability to control other electrons. And once you can do that, you can do anything you want."

"So why don't they give us that technology?" asks Julie. "Why don't we have it today?" It's a fair question, but odd that she should ask. She's just helping Chris to steer the conversation. She's a plant in an audience of two.

"That's right, Julie. Do we give it to Hitler? Do we give it to George Bush?"

"Not George Bush, you gotta be kidding!" says Julie. They're quite the team, these two.

"That's right. People will misuse it. And these beings won't allow that because they exist for one purpose only: to use their knowledge and the power they have over their electrons to serve us, so that there's peace and we can experience happiness. I just described God to you, basically. That's what God is."

I'm not sure how to respond to all this. He may as well have told me that he flew to the moon last week on an albatross made of marzipan. It's becoming noise. He's simply ignoring the fact that I haven't yet bought into his fairy tale and I might need persuading. Back when he was talking about evidence, I saw a glimmer of a chance of a normal conversation. But he barely opened that window before slamming it shut again. And now he's off, unstoppable, using up all the oxygen. The only available role for me is as a sidekick, like Julie. Maybe if I keep him talking, he'll open the window again.

"So, Chris, how many times have you met these humanoids from the future?"

"Well, you say the future, but these humanoids have already lived through a world like this. There's worlds out there that are in the 1950s right now. And worlds that are way advanced. Look at it this way—and this is a quote from Joseph Smith—'As man is, God once was, and as God is, man may become.' He understood these things because he was taught by the same being I was taught by—a guy named Moroni."

Moroni is the angel who told Joseph Smith where to find the gold plates, the angel whose golden statue sits atop the Salt Lake City temple. According to Nemelka, he's also an advanced being from another planet.

"He's a handsome, good-looking kinda guy. I'm trying to think of an actor . . ."

"You said Brad Pitt," says Julie.

"He's just one of those guys, if women were to see him they'd go 'Oooh!'"

"A sharp dresser?" I ask.

"He just wears white. Kind of biblical robes, but not exactly. They're more fitted than that. They're made of a material that doesn't get dirty. You never have to wash it. If you think about bacteria, well, this is nonbacterial clothing that they have. And the fact is, we're going to have it too. But not until they come to save us from ourselves."

I take the bill when it arrives. No one stops me. It seems fair—he provides the meaning of life, I provide breakfast. And he agrees to continue our conversation back at his place, or at least, the place he's staying right now. It's a trailer belonging to his girlfriend, Sherry, who's not around today. He's not due at Walmart till 4 PM, so we've got a few hours.

"I only stay there sometimes," he says as we leave the diner. "Sometimes I need to keep moving so I can continue with this work. That's why I got my van." He points to an *A-Team*-style van in the parking lot, one that Julie bought him last year. He slides the door to reveal a swivel chair in the back and a desk with a computer, a small bed and a rack of clothes. It's surprisingly tidy—the shirts are all laundered, there are no clothes or papers lying around. And judging from the rumpled bedding and the whiff of cologne, Nemelka may have woken up here this morning.

I'm quietly disturbed. Why so undercover? There's something creepy about a van parked on some suburban street, with passersby oblivious to the fact that some Fabio-resembling prophet type is typing away inside.

"Sometimes I need to get away and do my work where people can't find me," he says. And Julie nods, seriously. "That's why I bought him the van," she says. "There's a lot of people out there who would stop his work if they could."

"All those people at the library, they used to be staunch LDS members until they read *The Sealed Portion*," says Chris. "Fact is, I'm taking people away from the church. Tithe payers."

"Are people after you?"

"Probably more now than ever. I'm not paranoid, but do I think that people are out to kill me? Yes."

"We have to take precautions," says Julie. "His work is too important. We'll get into it back at Sherry's." She taps the side of her nose. "He's translating Isaiah."

This is Nemelka's grandest boast—that he translates scripture, just as Joseph Smith did 180 years earlier. And he does it in more or less the same way, by using magic stones, the very stones that Joseph Smith used, in fact. So when we arrive at Sherry's trailer, in the Mountain Shadows RV trailer park in Sandy, I ask him how he came by these stones, how it all began, this work of his. And he needs no encouragement. He tips back on his La-Z-Boy and kicks off his shoes.

It was 1984 and he was a staunch Mormon of twenty-two, fresh from his mission in Argentina and working as a security guard at the Salt Lake Temple. But the experience was disillusioning. He began to see the church leaders as corrupt, in part because he says he dated a couple of their daughters and they told him all about them. He's never wanted for female attention, Nemelka, and he doesn't mind saying so.

Questioning his leaders, he explored the temple buildings, rifling through the bishops' files and digging around in the archives. And one day, he came upon an opulent room, decorated with high-backed chairs and hung with oil paintings of each of the twelve apostles. And he was sickened—the ego of these men! How could the church be true if it was led by these people? In time-honored fashion, he fell to his knees weeping, and right on cue, Joseph Smith appeared before him, barefoot and bearded and wearing one of those antibacterial white robes. In a David Copperfield flash, the gold plates appeared on the table, Sealed Portion and all. And Joseph informed him that he had been chosen to translate it.

"Now I'm a very humorous guy," says Nemelka. "I said, 'Man, you know how much this is worth?' And there was a little smile out of Joseph—he said, 'I was tempted the same way. Just let it go.' He said, 'One of the reasons we picked you is because you won't have anything to do with money.'" And with that, Joseph touched him and charged him up with knowledge and light.

"There were these bands around the plates, and they broke at that moment. I was like 'woah,'" he says. "Then the bands disappeared—just like that. I said, 'Jeez! This is magic stuff!' And I'm just thumbing through the plates like this going, 'Wow, this is awesome . . .'"

At this point the story gets complicated. The plates were magicked away and entrusted to a man called Timothy, who never ages. And Timothy only gave them back to Nemelka in December 1987, by which point he had gotten divorced from his first wife, Paula, over religious differences. Timothy's instructions were plain: go and find a suitable place to translate the plates but keep it on the hush, even from his then wife, Jackie. So he gathered his family—Jackie and four children—and they set off in a bus and a travel trailer, moving from state to state like hippies. They went from Missouri to North Dakota to Seattle. He claims that an apostle at the Mormon Church leveraged his contacts in Washington to get him fake IDs and social security numbers, even set him up with construction work out in Portland. "We had to protect the plates," he says. "The claim at the time was that I was Amish. It's a long story." It's true that he did go under the alias of Christopher Abraham Stohl for a while. But typically with Nemelka, it's hard to separate fact from fantasy.

The confusion continues. His first wife, Paula, won custody of her children, which so upset Nemelka that he kidnapped them back and was eventually thrown in prison (there would be a second prison spell later for violating his parole). The mysterious "Timothy" returned to take the "plates" back off him in 1991, not returning them until 2003. And in 1992, he dabbled in polygamy, bringing in a couple of extra wives to join Jackie—Vicky Prunty, who went on to found Tapestry Against Polygamy, and Marcee,[4] the cousin of Mary Batchelor, one of the founders of Principle Voices. This was back when he was the toast of the fundamentalist community for his bold claims about *The Sealed Portion*.

It didn't last. For a couple of months in early 1993, they lived together in Vicky's house. But then he dumped both Marcee and Vicky, claiming that he never believed in polygamy in the first place—this after fathering children with both women.[5] According to some, he also declared that *The Sealed Portion*, which he'd been raving about, was all made up—there were no plates, he was just trying to show the fundamentalists how gullible they were (something that Nemelka now denies).

But within a few years, the story appeared to change once more. In March 2001 he was sentenced to a year in jail for violating a restrictive order, and the *Salt Lake City Weekly* ran an interview at that time in which he confessed to having concocted *The Sealed Portion* to defraud the LDS Church.[6] The allegation was supported six years later in an affidavit by his then cellmate, an alleged drug offender named Jeffrey Michael Richins.[7] It describes

Nemelka as an arrogant and ebullient con man who was writing a lost book of Mormon that he planned to sell to the Mormon Church. It was deceitful, sure, but "he was deceiving people for their own good," Richins claims, and he tried to recruit him into his scam—Nemelka suggested that, when they were both out of jail, they should take a trip out to the desert to build some boxes and return pretending that the gold plates were inside. "He wanted me to say I saw a shaft of light come over him," the affidavit reads. "He wanted me to tell a girl who he had believing that he was a prophet, that I saw a shaft of light. And to confirm to her that he was a prophet . . . He told me he had so much control over her that he could have her give sex to other men for money, and have her believing that it was what God wanted her to do . . . He said he could even arrange for her to give me sex if I wanted." According to Richins, Nemelka promised him wealth and a harem of women if he wanted. "He thought he was irresistible to women and he could 'nail' any woman he wanted. He said he would go to the LDS singles dances [because] the women who went to those dances were really vulnerable."

Today, Nemelka characterizes the entirety of Richins's statement as "bullshit." Furthermore, he denies ever wishing to defraud the Mormon Church, though he admits to telling the *Salt Lake City Weekly* that he'd made up *The Sealed Portion*. He lied, he says, in order to persuade the judge in his child custody battle that he wasn't crazy. This from the man who told me "I'm all about the truth, Sanjie."

The part of his story I like best is the magic stones. They sound like a double act, these rocks, like Abbott and Costello. They're called the Urim and Thummim—a double act that lost its dentures. My wife calls them the Uma Thurmans. Apparently you place them over the area you want to read, like a magnifying glass, and the translation appears in the stones. It works for anything. To translate Isaiah, all he need do is plop the stones on the relevant page of the Bible.

Nemelka supposedly found these stones while he was rooting around the secret church artifacts. "I put 'em together and the stones lit up. It's like when you open your cell phone, you know, the backlight. See, they're kinda like a small computer that pretty much translates things. But they only work if a person's DNA energy allows them to. So they work for me and they worked for Joseph. Those rocks were the same ones Joseph used. I have them with me now."

"Can I see?"

"Sure, I'll show you. It just looks like a couple of rocks but if I were to take them in my hands and touch them together, my body creates a circuit. All it is, is this computer that was embedded in the molecules of these rocks a long time ago. That's all it is. Before there were plastics or any of these things. They're mentioned in the Bible—all the ancient religions talk about seer stones."

"Go on, Chris, get the stones."

"Okay, but you and Julie have to go outside because I can't have you know where I keep 'em."

Julie and I are like infants now, all excited. We step outside and pace around. "You know I haven't even seen the Urim and Thummim yet," she says. "You're really lucky to see this!"

Then a few minutes later, Nemelka opens the door looking sheepish. "I'm sorry, but I can't show you them. The rocks didn't tell me that it was okay, I don't know why. These advanced beings can hear everything that's going on in this room. There's a few of 'em watching right now."

"But why would the beings object to me?" I protest. And Nemelka looks genuinely apologetic. "Maybe another time, Sanjie. I know your heart. I know you're interested in truth. Come by another day, we'll ask the rocks again."

It's three months before I see him again. When I call Julie to set up meetings, she says he's busy translating scripture with his magic stones— "sometimes he goes off and I don't hear from him for weeks!" But it gives me time to read some of his material. There's plenty of it—*666 America* and *The Sealed Portion* clock in at over 1,500 pages between them. And he never stops. His latest is *Sacred, not Secret*, a book about the secret LDS endowment ritual.

The volume that catches my attention is the unpublished autobiography, *As I Have Loved You: An Autobiography of a Modern Day Revelator*. This is no translating job, but Christopher in his own words. And as the title suggests, it's largely a trumpet solo, a work of unrestrained egotism and circular logic. On several occasions he quotes *The Sealed Portion* to prove his point, relying on the premise that it was revealed to him, rather than something he made up. He even claims surprise at the verse that reads: "The name of this last divinely appointed Prophet, Seer, Revelator, Brother, Friend and Servant of all . . . is Christopher Marc Nemelka who is indeed the 'Bearer of Christ.'" He insists that he had no idea his name was going to pop up like that—he's just taking dictation from a couple of stones. He didn't even want this calling, he says; it chose him.

In among the mythmaking, however, there are other windows into his character. He comes from well-known Utah stock—mention "Nemelka" in Salt Lake, and they don't talk about Chris, the prophet, but about his grandfather who once ran for mayor of Salt Lake City; or his uncle Dick, the BYU basketball star who became an eminent attorney; or his attorney brother Joe. Nemelka describes his father, a devout Mormon, as a womanizer and a man he yearned to please. And when his parents divorced, he protests that his stepmother didn't love him enough. It's all a piece of his recurring dissatisfaction with women who, in his narrative, have either disappointed and abandoned him in his youth, or fallen for him so hopelessly as an adult that they feel disappointed or abandoned when he doesn't reciprocate.

Nemelka's track record with women isn't pretty. The court battles are many. To be fair, his defamation antennae are so sensitive that he has also challenged Tapestry Against Polygamy, the author John Llewellyn and even the LDS Church[8] in court (never with any success, however). But it is his conflicts with his ex-wives—or women who consider themselves ex-wives[9]—that are the most telling. In among the tussles over child custody, child support or protective orders, there are uglier allegations. Vicky's account of how he threw her to the ground,[10] for instance, or Marcee's allegation that Nemelka once smashed down a door to snatch back his children.[11]

The most extraordinary charge of all, however, comes from Christine, a businesswoman from Las Vegas, the "girl" that Richins mentioned in his affidavit. Of all the women that entered Nemelka's orbit over the years, no one fell quite so far and so fast. When she met him, she was a dynamic businesswoman with the world ahead of her. Within a year, she was shattered and destitute, grasping at what remained of her sanity. And it was her faith that propelled her into this mess. Christine may have been the most Mormon woman in Nemelka's life.

A graduate of BYU, she read the Book of Mormon thirty-two times. She broke all her mission records and wrote a book about her methods, which was widely distributed. Her second book, about how to raise your children as better Mormons, is still in print. Upon graduation, she married a nice Mormon boy, bore several children, played a key role in her local church, practiced baking and food preservation and even found time to win several beauty pageants.

But then, a series of traumas. First, a divorce in 1997 followed by excommunication from the church, a wrenching experience. It took her three years to get rebaptized. And then, one night in New York, she was raped by a biker, a wanted criminal, and the legal process that followed felt like an extension of the assault. The investigators wanted her to testify even though she was terrified of retribution, and the biker's defense lawyer argued forcefully that she asked for it. Ultimately, no case was filed. And by the time she met Nemelka, she was acutely vulnerable, both wounded by the rape, disillusioned with the legal system and yearning for righteousness. She was perfectly primed to fall for him. And she did.

It was October, at an LDS singles dance at Wheeler Farm, a dismal Mormonized affair stripped of cigarettes and alcohol—a high school dance for adults. Nemelka told her about the Sealed Portion and the gold plates, and she was completely taken in. Something about the conviction in his voice, the earnest look in his eyes. She'd had a dream in which her future husband looked a little like Nemelka. And so she jumped with both feet. By December, they were spiritually married in the Luxor hotel in Las Vegas, or so she believed. And by January, under Nemelka's guidance, she had given up her home and moved into a homeless shelter in Salt Lake City. She sent her children off to live with their father, telling them that she was "on a mission," and in a way, she was. And in order to support Nemelka's all-important calling, she had agreed to make the ultimate sacrifice for the Lord's work. She had agreed to become Nemelka's prostitute.

She tells me this from her home in Las Vegas where she lives with her children and her partner, a part-time photographer. She's in her forties now, blonde and motherly, with a soft childlike voice that drops to a brushy whisper when she comes to the bits of her story she'd rather not remember—which are many.

"Who was the first, Christine?"

"It was someone I knew. I was dating him. That was the thing—I thought I was married to Chris, but he told me that I had to be with other men."

"How did you persuade your date to pay Chris?"

"I told him, you know, let's just play a fantasy. And the account number I gave him, I said it was to help the poor. He had no clue. It was sickening."

"Did Chris pick the men?"

"Oh absolutely. They put the money in, and Chris would say 'Go!' And he wanted proof."

"What kind of proof?"

"He wanted me to write about every little detail. I gave him some pictures, just me by myself, never with the people. But all the time I'm thinking 'If this is false, I'm going to hell, so it doesn't matter, I'm worthless.' And remember, I was really conservative at that time. I wore my dresses below my knees. This was no small thing for me."

She stops and gets up. And sits down again. There are tears in her eyes. "Mormons believe there's sex in heaven," she says. "Like in the Lord's Prayer—'on Earth as it is in heaven'? And he told me that for celestial people, sex was not a sin. And furthermore, the world would never know—ever— the sacrifices that I was asked to do, to bring forth the Sealed Portion."

She won't say how much money was paid—she didn't always know— and she cannot bear to tell me the specifics of these trysts, or how many suitors there were. But she fervently believed Nemelka's promise that by enduring this degradation, she would not only fund Nemelka's momentous work, but also win rewards for her sacrifice in heaven. It was painful and disorienting. Holiness and humiliation became one and the same. Her thoughts turned to suicide. It was only when she met Richins—who was released from prison prior to Nemelka—that she realized just how thoroughly she was being exploited.

Inevitably, Nemelka's version is wildly different. He denies marrying her or convincing her to live in a homeless shelter or even ever claiming to be a prophet. By his account, Christine slept with those men of her own free will in order to persuade them to invest in her business and he neither requested it nor profited from it. He describes her as a nymphomaniac, a repressed Mormon woman who discovered orgasm—"she was a squirter, Sanjie", he told me, ever the gentleman—and all he did was reassure her that her promiscuity wasn't a sin, so spiritually speaking, she was in the clear.

"I just felt sick for her, Sanjie, I wanted to help her," he says. "So I sent her some religious-oriented emails and letters saying 'If it makes you and the other person happy, then go ahead.' And I'll say it again—if that's how you get things done, and no one's getting hurt, then have at it! What do you think marriage is? Marriage is modern-day prostitution for most women. Think about it."

But Nemelka's account is a Swiss cheese—hole-ier than thou. A wealth of emails and letters passed between Christine and Nemelka during this time, which trip him up, time and again. His insistence that he never claimed to be a prophet, for example, runs counter to an email in which he enlists Christine as a secretary, likening himself to Joseph Smith.[12] In another letter, he describes a revelation that demands Christine's obedience and support until the translation is complete,[13] and assures her that her sins of the flesh would reap great rewards.[14]

According to Nemelka, the idea to give up her children and move into a homeless shelter was Christine's, though it seems a bizarre strategy for someone who was trying to raise capital for a business that concerned children. "All I said was 'You don't need that big expensive home, you need a littler place!'" he protests. "And I think one time I said 'Why fight your ex-husband over custody, just let him take care of the kids!' That's what I *said*, but what she *heard* is a different matter." It's clear from his letters, however, that he approved of her squalid living conditions. "Where else would a true disciple of Christ be found?" he writes.[15] He also encouraged her to tough out this period of testing, "the trials and experience,"[16] to give up her possessions[17] and to be stoic about the absence of her children, in the style of "our mother in heaven."[18]

Most telling of all, however, is Nemelka's email of January 10, 2001, in which he wrote: "When you sleep with these men you will make them earn the priviledge, [sic] and those earnings shall help the Lord's work in more ways than you can imagine. Your orgasams [sic] will be a sign that the Lord is pleased and you will praise His name. At times you will see me and feel me as you become physical with these men, and you will know that I love you and will one day be your only God."

The same email required Christine to make out a promissory note for $75,000 to Patte Nattrass, an elderly lady on whose credit card Nemelka was a cosigner. (Nattrass would later accuse Nemelka of ripping her off to the tune of several thousand dollars.)[19] Nemelka claims it was simply a money-laundering scheme, a way to protect Christine's earnings. And yet Christine clearly saw it differently. In an impassioned letter dated January 11, 2001, she wrote: "By gosh Chris—I have already paid a price before God, including the horrors of last night where I was in agony preparing to be a sex slave for someone I loathed for 4 years ($1500 worth or 15 sessions a month for 50 months until I paid the debt) and who I think may be Mafia connected. If this was what it took for this work to be truly supported, then I was preparing myself to do it. For your work, Chris! For God!"

That Christine was injured by her faith here is plain. But then she took it further than most. She yearned for special recognition in the eyes of the Lord, a kind of superiority. She tells me how she believed that, once she'd suffered her debasement, "Jesus would hold me up as an example to all of heaven." No doubt, it takes extraordinary naïvety to succumb so fully to these fantasies, not to mention narcissism and a degree of emotional desperation too. These are the women who surround Nemelka—wounded dreamers, suckled by the church and torn asunder by divorce. They come to him, their hearts open, wanting to believe again.

For his part, Nemelka finds nothing extraordinary about Christine's story. He sees her as typical of the women in his life, a continuation of a pattern: the women desire him sexually, sometimes to the point of obsession, and when he rejects them they become bitter and scorned. He describes Christine as sex-crazed. He says the same about Vicky Prunty. He sleeps with these women because he either wants to help them, or he feels sorry for them. He portrays his foray into polygamy, for example, as a rescue mission. The reason he married Marcee and Vicky and then quickly dumped them was to save them from fundamentalism. "I was getting them out of polygamy! Otherwise they'd probably still be in it!" And with both women, he maintained a sexual relationship after their split because, by Nemelka's account, they begged him to take them back.

"Look, Sanjie, I *am* a romantic, I *am* a charismatic man," he says. "But I guarantee you, if I was out to get women, I can get a lot prettier women. I don't say that out of arrogance. It's the truth. You've met Vicky, you've met me. Think about human nature. The fact is, I could have stayed with any of those women—Marcee, Jackie, Vicky, Christine. If I stayed faithful to them, as their one and only, they'd be right there by my side now. No doubt in my mind."

In his autobiography, he claims he went to a therapist to find out why he can't find a long-term companion, but the therapist fell for him. He's also the author of a book (though he claims it was just a student project) called *Diary of a Player*, about a man who knows how to "play" women. It's purportedly a work of fiction, but he names three of the characters in the book after his wives, "Victoria, Jacqueline and Marcee." And Vicky Prunty has accused him of giving a copy of the book to one of his daughters, who was fifteen at the time.

If I want to know the truth about that whole period with Christine, he says, I should call Sheri Johansen, his ex-wife. It seems there were at least two other women in Nemelka's life during Christine's humiliations, each of whom knew little to nothing about the others—Jackie (his legal wife) and Sheri, who met Nemelka shortly before Christine did. Jackie refused all requests for an interview. And according to Christine, Sheri was very much a co-conspirator. But nevertheless, I give Sheri a call.

I say, "Chris urged me to call you, he said you'd tell me the truth." And she bursts out laughing.

"Oh, Chris probably thinks I am still under his magical spell, but I'm not," she says. "But neither am I angry. Chris thinks that every woman that he's been with either worships him or they're scorned. It's his answer for everything."

Now a mortgage advisor in Salt Lake City, Sheri was twenty-eight when she met Nemelka, and thoroughly disillusioned with the Mormon Church. She'd had enough of the "brainwashing," and wasn't about to fall for any talk about the Sealed Portion or gold plates. So Nemelka didn't bring it up. Though he appeared to Christine as a prophet around this time, he presented himself to Sheri as an atheist. He was an unbeliever for as long as she knew him.

"I never believed he was a prophet and I don't think he believed it either," says Sheri. "I do think he believes that he is so superior to other people that the world needs him, so he has to present his philosophy in a way they can understand. If they believe in Joseph Smith, then that's how he'll dress it up."[20]

Sheri doesn't see Nemelka as evil or a swindler, necessarily. But she was instrumental in getting him a psychiatric evaluation while he was in jail, as per the judge's orders, and a Dr. Nancy Cohn diagnosed him as having narcissistic personality disorder—that is, grandiose ideas about himself, a need for admiration, fantasies of his own brilliance and a tendency to be exploitative. When the judge denied him probation, she noted "Mr. Nemelka continues to victimize others, manipulate and misrepresent facts." And most of his victims are women.[21]

"I do think he's got that disorder," says Sheri. "He has this need to create drama in his life and he really believes that he's going to change the world. But I don't know if he's malicious. Maybe that's me being naïve. You look at the string of women he's left behind and how unhappy they are, and you wonder—is it malice, or is it mental illness?"

At the time of writing, Nemelka is married to another woman called Sheryl, whose trailer we use for interviews. But besides her, Julie is the most prominent woman in Nemelka's life. And I like Julie. She's a decent soul who's had a hard go of it. After a hellish marriage and a traumatic divorce, she came to *The Sealed Portion* very much out of the frying pan. Oddly enough, she suspects her ex-husband of having a "narcissistic personality disorder," though she would never say such a thing about Nemelka. She's infatuated with him. It seems inevitable that she'll end up feeling used like so many of the other women in Christopher's life.

So I take Julie to lunch one day at a nice little Italian place downtown, to broach the whole "what if he's nuts?" conversation. I thought I'd just wade in with double-barreled skepticism, the argumentative equivalent of shaking her by the shoulders. It worked on Angie.

"Oh, I get it. You think I'm a sap, right?" she says, before we've even ordered. "I told you I wasn't wowed like some women are with him. But when he looked at me, I thought, 'Oh my gosh, he's stared into my heart and seen all my sins.'"

"Julie, come on. That sounds like you were totally wowed."

"But I'm not attached to him in the same way. I'm not his wife or his girlfriend. I just have a sense in my heart of who he is. Those women didn't have a clue. They didn't know who he truly is."

There is no saving Julie. We get talking about the Worldwide United Foundation, whose mission statement is to cure global poverty by simply persuading world leaders to give everyone food, shelter, clothing and health care for free. I tell Julie just how cretinous it all sounds but she's already handed over roughly $100,000 of her savings—the money from the sale of her house following her divorce.

"I believe no one deserves to go without food, without shelter," she says with a big smile. "It kills me what's going on in Africa. How many cars has Jay Leno got? And there are children that don't even get one meal a day." For a woman in her fifties, she sounds like a child. Can she hear herself? "We just need a spokesman. I've tried Oprah, Anderson Cooper . . ."

"Oprah's never going to endorse Nemelka." I feel like a parent.

"Look, will we get the WUF off the ground? I don't know. But will I die trying? Will I sacrifice just about everything I have? You bet. Will my kids get their inheritance? They might not, but it won't matter because they're surviving fine." In her childlike innocence she's robbing her own children. Little wonder some of them won't speak to her anymore.

She tells me that the foundation will pay her back. It hasn't yet, but there's nothing to worry about. "Christopher cannot be tempted by money. He's received offers of millions of dollars." And even if he did turn out to be a fraud and run off with the money, she wouldn't mind. "Already what Christopher has given me with the Sealed Portion, oh my God, there's no value you can name."

And with that, our meal comes to a close.

A month later, I'm back in the trailer with Julie and Nemelka, and he's explaining why the rocks said "no" last time around: they magically disappeared. "I put them in the same place every time, but when I looked they weren't there!" he says. "And when you left, they came back! You don't have to believe that, you can believe whatever you want."

This time it's different: he knows I don't believe him, so we're having an altogether testier exchange. But that's okay; I'm done letting him get away with nonsense like "I had special enhanced memory from the beings, that's why I did so well in my exams." No more kid gloves for John the Baptist. And possibly to repair his credibility, he does show me the Urim and Thummim this time.

It's the same routine: Julie and I step outside while he retrieves the rocks from their supersecret hiding place. Neither Julie nor I are nearly so excitable this time. We hear him call from inside, like a game of hide-and-seek: "Okay! You can come in now!"

On the table is a leather wrap with a box on top, which he opens ever so slowly, milking the drama of the moment. And—ta-da!—he reveals two grubby lumps of quartz, each one the size of my palm. Carefully taking a piece of cloth in each hand, he picks up the pieces and gingerly hands them to me, as though he were handling explosives. No one says a word.

"I need to use the cloth, otherwise I might make the circuit and they'll light up."

"But that's what I want to see, Chris."

"No, I can't show you. Because even if I did, you'd just say, 'He's a great magician.'"

"No I wouldn't. If you show me how you communicate with beings from another planet using these rocks, then I'm signing up, Chris, I swear. I'm donating my wages."

"Can't do it, Sanjie, because, see, it would take away your free agency. You'd believe anything I say. I could say 'Drink this Kool-Aid, because that's what these beings told me.' The advanced beings know you're not supposed to interfere with free will. People have to progress logically . . ."

"It's not logical to believe that rocks light up. Not unless you show me. And even if they did, I can still refuse the Kool-Aid."

"Okay, so let me give you another example. If a being came down right now and said, 'Sanjie, we're taking your sex drive away.' No doubt you'd say 'No thanks!'"

What's he talking about? Sex drive? "Look, people take vows of celibacy all the time. That's not the point. The question is whether these beings even exist!"

"Oh they exist all right. You can say what you want but those rocks work exactly like a cell phone." He's squirming. He's not enjoying this, and neither is Julie. She takes the rocks from me and starts putting them together, trying to create a diversion. "Does it matter which way you put 'em together?" she asks. "Like this? Or end to end?"

"I put 'em end to end," says Chris.

"What about if they're flipped over?"

"It doesn't matter."

I turn to Julie. "Don't *you* want to see them work?"

She laughs. "No, no. I don't need to see them work, because I already know."

"You don't know, you believe," says Chris.

"That's right, I believe."

"The reason you're convinced is because of the fruits."

"Yes, the fruits."

"You see, Sanjie, I'm the only one who has ever been able to answer her questions."

"Look, Chris, I'm not saying you're a liar." But I want to. The word "liar" hangs in the air for a moment. "But you can't just expect me to believe you. You have to *show* me."

"Joseph Smith didn't show the stones to many people. Joseph Smith didn't show those plates to many people." Nemelka's smile has faded. "And those were the same stones he had, and they worked for me on the same plates." He stands up. It's my cue to leave. "Look, you might as well forget about the Urim and Thummim working. I can't show you. I'm under strict orders. Matter of fact, they might not even work if I used them now. Because *they* can force them to not work."

I drive out of the trailer park feeling both indignant and regretful. I doubt I'll be invited back to John the Baptist's place in a hurry. I wanted to understand Nemelka, to penetrate his shell, but he got to me—his arrogance, the way he bangs on. What was he thinking when he brought out those ridiculous stones? Did he think I was that naïve?

It's embarrassing to admit, now that I'm scowling at eighty miles per hour down the I-15, but there was a time when I quite liked him. He seemed delusionary, potentially nuts, but also harmless and clownish. So I focused on the positives. He doesn't proselytize. His followers like a drink and a smoke and they don't have a problem with black people or gays. And however dodgy it looks, it's not obvious that Nemelka's bilking them through his WUF. He doesn't appear to be overtly cash-conscious—his followers don't tithe, his books are all free downloads. And he's churning them out, each one a giant tome of scripture-speak. Verily I say unto you, he speaketh not in the tongue of man, but in the tongue of the sages. Perhaps it isn't so hard after all. A couple of whereuntos and a smiting, and you're there. There ought to be software—Microsoft Prophet 2.0.

I think the main reason I warmed to Nemelka was his openness. He was the first prophet to invite me in. And that may be his fatal flaw. Exposure ruins a prophet's magic. It becomes harder to ascribe a mythic life to him, a lesson that more successful—and more aloof—prophets like Paul Kingston and Warren Jeffs seem to understand.

But Nemelka can't resist the limelight. It isn't long before I see him again. This time I bring my wife. He's holding a meeting under a tree in Liberty Park—Nemelka with his Jesus ponytail, jeans and T-shirt sitting in a picnic chair surrounded by a circle of maybe forty of his devoted. It's the usual ragtag entourage, from undergraduate to geriatric, this time with coolers and sunhats. There are a few young mothers with infants, a pierced guy and an elderly couple knitting. Julie's taking notes. And the prophet is typically unleashed, taking on judges, corporations, the president.

"I showed Sanjie here the Urim and Thummim," he says, and a "wooh" goes up from the crowd. "And Sanjie tempts me like the devil! He says, 'I want to see these work. If you make them work, it'll change my whole life, blah blah blah . . .'"

"'And I'll pay you too!'" says Julie. "Ha ha!"

"Well, it ain't going to happen. Because even if I did, he'd think I was a magician."

I'm not going to argue. There seems little point. He's a huckster again, a bumpkin oracle. These people are not here for a debate, but for the reassurance that their prophet still thrives, his fire undimmed. They were weaned on the Joseph Smith story and therefore susceptible to Nemelka's protest—"If Joseph was a prophet, then why not me?" And he has a point. Both men spun similarly tall tales and produced giant, turgid works of scripture; they both had a gadabout, unsophisticated appeal to them and an appetite for women. Both were accused of fraud and neither made the slightest attempt to prove their claims.

In fact, the only proof that Nemelka does offer is that if you take the Mormon Church as your premise, then your conclusions may lead you, on a Sunday afternoon, to join one of many clusters under the trees in Liberty Park and listen to a convicted felon reveal the great news that out there in the celestial cosmos there's a planet similar to Mercury where only couples exist. And another planet like Venus which is populated only by women and children. And another realm entirely that is populated only by eunuchs.

As I say my good-byes to Julie and walk toward my car, Nemelka's ramblings grow fainter on the breeze. "And yes it's true, they did have in vitro fertilization during Christ's time, I can prove it…"

The Rock

CHAPTER 13

◆ Apocalypse Bob

> If trouble comes when you least expect it then maybe the thing to do is
> to always expect it.
> —Cormac McCarthy, *The Road*

*M*ORMONS ARE DEFINED by the apocalypse. It's right there in the
name: Latter-day Saints. They're waiting for Mormogeddon, which could
come any day now. In fact, it's long overdue. Both Brigham Young and
John Taylor predicted that the destructions would follow the Civil War,
which duly prompted a flood of last-minute plural marriages, frantic
believers grabbing what they could before it was too late, like the end-of-
season sales at Macy's. When the end didn't come, many asked to be let
out of their hasty unions. It's not clear what God's return policy on wives
was back then, but they're not like toasters. You can't just bring the receipt.

Of course, Mormons are far from unique in this obsession. Christians
have long looked nervously at the skies. As have Jews, Muslims, Hindus,
Parsis, Mayans—it's a long list—not to mention those communities outside
of faith like physicists, economists and environmentalists. And somehow
this sense of doom seems particularly strong in America. It might be the

history of genocide and slavery festering in the basement of the national conscience—that quote by Jefferson, "I tremble for my country when I reflect that God is just." Or perhaps it's the flip side of a get-rich-quick society: just as we believe we can become gazillionaires off a lottery ticket, we fear destruction in the gazillions by earthquakes or terror or meteor showers.

Whatever it is, I get it. What I don't get is how anyone can *not* be obsessed by the apocalypse, what with the banks collapsing, the Middle East going mental, the oil crisis, bird flu, shoe bombs and plain old megaton bombs that could turn Manhattan into a quarry quicker than it takes to blend a Frappuccino. Not to mention all the CNN Planet in Peril stuff about quakes and tsunamis and cyclones and floods and melting icecaps and drowning polar bears. And the bees—have you heard about the bees? They're all dying, which means nothing grows except the cockroach and the scorpion. Lab coats call it Colony Collapse Disorder, which is science for We're Toast. Roll credits, people. It's *Armageddon*, starring Bruce Willis. Except this time, Bruce is toast too.

Okay, deep breath. Count to three.

Maybe science will save the bees. Maybe we're fixated with the apocalypse because it's a metaphor for our own death. Perhaps all religion is an effort to comprehend the void that bookends our existence, before birth and after death. The apocalypse is part of our id, that's all. And "id" is a cute little word that couldn't hurt a soul.

But I can't buy into all that, much as I want to. I read the papers, I watch TV. I've seen towers fall, and polar bears drown. I've flipped from earthquakes in China to the collapse of Lehman Brothers to the Real Housewives of Orange County. And I'm scared. When Vicky Prunty first told me about the Rock at the beginning of this journey, it made sense to me. She described it as "a big rock in the desert with all these polygamists living inside getting ready for the end of the world." I had this picture of scowling women in a giant cave, gathered around a fire, banging rocks. It sounded like the outer limits of fundamentalism, the clock wound back millennia rather than just a century or so; a life of scripture and survival; the cave as a giant helmet for when the sky falls on our heads.

But Gary Batchelor put me straight. "It's not *The Flintstones* out there," he said. "The houses are amazing, much nicer than ours. Go and ask for

Bob Foster, he's the guy who started it all." He scribbled a number down on a piece of paper.

So now I'm looking at this number, pulled over on the side of the road outside McCarran Airport in Las Vegas. I just saw my wife onto a plane bound for L.A. She said, "Why don't we just drive back together? Who else have you got to talk to?" And she's right: I'm still toxic in the fundamentalist community. No one is taking my calls. But I can't go home like this. Not after Nemelka left such a bitter taste. Not without giving the Rock a try, a last surge before the final troop withdrawal. I muster my phone voice and dial the number, telling myself that he probably won't pick up, and he probably won't reply to my message, but never mind, I have to leave one, I have to play my role here . . . but then a man answers. It's Bob, and he's in such a good mood, he's singing and chuckling at the same time. "You're in Las Vegas? Well come and see us! We'd love to have you!"

It's a joyous drive up to Moab. Once more up the I-15, but this time, I branch east toward Fish Lake and Richfield, and the landscape transforms. Just breathtaking stuff—vast walls of cascading plates, the strata tilted like wonky shelves jutting into the air creating profiles, all kinds of noses and eyebrows. It's canyon country here, red rock for a million miles, and right in the middle, there's Moab, the hiking Mecca, a little strip of a town with a hippie vibe. Coffee shops with spacey art on the walls. White guy with dreads on a mountain bike. It hardly feels like Utah at all. The Rock is another twenty-two miles south and east, down into the sage brush desert. You turn off at Looking Glass Rock and follow the tracks until you see a giant terra-cotta lump off to the right. And there it is. From a distance, you'd never imagine it was inhabited. But close in, and you can see the houses up on a ledge, their facades set into the rock, the faint drone of engines, the laughter of children.

I ask a kid playing on his bike where Bob lives. He points up to a house with its door wide open and a cage of yappy little Yorkies to the side. So I climb the stairs and hover at the door. "Hello?"

"Aha! Hello! Come in! Come in!" Bob emerges from inside, a tall, lean old man, squinting into the sun. He ushers me into his living room to sit on one of his two battered couches, the only furniture in the room. There are flies everywhere, tapping at the windows, swarming around our heads, but Bob pays them no attention. "See how cool it is? That's the Rock—temperature stabilized. Warm in the winter, and cool in the summer. Free air-conditioning!"

He's an engaging old man, Bob, pushing eighty-four and effortlessly cheerful. The lines on his face describe a life spent chuckling. And he's filled with pride at this Rock, his Big Idea. He came here in 1979 with three wives and a burning conviction that it was time to prepare for the end of days. The Rock was just a rock back then. But today there are eight homes and several apartments, perhaps seventy residents at capacity. The homes vary in style and size, some as big as six thousand square feet, nattily designed with rugged ceilings and walls and fireplaces. There's water in the huge tanks out front and a thirty thousand gallon tank up on top of the Rock, all of which is pumped right out of the ground by the desert sun. There are solar panels up on top of the Rock, and banked down below where the vegetables grow, the mini-orchard, where Rock residents motor about on four-wheelers.

"We've got twelve panels for now," says Bob, "but we're getting twelve more. There'll come a day when you won't be able to get gas or water or electricity or any of those things . . ."

The community keeps growing. Bob's latest project is the "Charity House," a two-story arrangement of twelve apartments, stacked either side of a chapel, a baptismal font, conversation pit, lounge, balcony and giant dining area out back. It's well on its way: the apartments are almost ready and nine are occupied, mostly with construction workers. "I originally built it as a homeless shelter," he says. "But it's just for whoever the Lord sends when the end comes. And it's coming, mark my word. We've got twenty years left on the lease, but you'll be lucky if you get another twenty."

He started hearing the voices when he was eighteen, an army boy who married a Mormon girl and lived in a log house up near Mount St. Helens. They told him to live polygamy or be damned, but he didn't heed them at first and pressed on with his Mormonism, teaching seminary school for years. The religious experiences, however, kept coming.

"The first time I felt the Holy Ghost," he says, "the whole house looked like it was a raging fire. I thought it was going up in smoke! Remember when Moses saw the bush burning violently but not being consumed? That's the spiritual fire they're talking about. It purifies. You need that fire, otherwise nothing's active. You need to go through *the gate*."

Bob believes most polygamists today are deficient in both fire and gate categories. He admits that some have the priesthood, as does he—Bob was ordained three times, once by Anne Wilde's late husband, Ogden Kraut— but Bob can go one better: he also has the Holy Ghost. "I knew I could ask God for things and get them," he says.

There was a time in the '70s when Bob actually met God in the throne room of heaven. "We were out on a little planet near Kolob, which is the greatest of all the suns in our galaxy," he explains. There was a splendid room of "columns and pillars" in which a "beautiful angelic man" showed him parchments—a man so heavenly Bob didn't dare even look at him. "It wasn't Jesus, just one of the high ones. And to this day I can't remember one single thing I read off those parchments, it's all just blotted out. But then He said 'I'm going to leave now.' And finally I looked up at heavenly Father, and He's looking into this huge Urim—it's like a great magnifying glass. And suddenly I was filled with what He was seeing. It exploded in me."

The tears are flowing now. "There isn't anything save He knows it! You know people who talk about God going to college, taking advance classes so He can learn new stuff? That's just stupid. He knows it all."

"Who says God goes to college?"

"A lot of Mormons think God is off getting further education."

I've not heard this one before, but now's not the time to get into it. Evidently, having filled Bob with knowledge, God then filled him with love, "which just about blew me to pieces. " Then there were some other instructions, which he has since forgotten, and then: "Phewsh! Twenty billion light years away, I was back in my bed!" He claps his hands. "And that's how God works."

It's hard not to be charmed by someone who admits he forgot most of what happened on the day he met God. But his wife at the time wasn't having any of it. After twenty-five years of marriage, she ran off with a priest from their local church. "And this old priest managed to kill her in a car crash several years ago. Oh, I rejoiced! But I was rejoicing to have her in a safer place. She's still mine; she'll be mine forever, I believe."

Bob was in his forties, divorced and on fire for the Lord, when he became a polygamist. He caused a scandal by marrying two of his seminary students—first Susan, then Karen—both of whom were half his age. After the church excommunicated him in 1972, the family moved to Arizona, then Kansas. Bob took a job catering to college fraternities and sororities, and that was how he met wife number three, Carla. The way Bob remembers it, they started talking about the gospel, and soon afterward, Carla asked to join his family. He accepted, they married and off they went on a honeymoon to Vancouver.

But there were complications. Carla's roommate told her parents that she ran off with a middle-aged man, so when the honeymooners returned, Carla's parents were waiting at the school, none too pleased.

"We just packed her stuff. Didn't say anything about getting married. I was chatting with her dad by the car and I didn't know if there was going to be a fistfight or what. Then they hauled her back to Kansas. But she called me up. She said, 'You gotta save me—they're sending me to Denver to stay with my sister.' So I went to Denver and collected her. She left a note on her sister's dresser: 'Don't try to find me because you won't.'"

Carla's parents charged Bob with bigamy and had him extradited to Arizona. Bob pleaded guilty and served twenty days in jail; the charges against the wives were dropped. It was 1974. There hasn't been a stand-alone conviction for polygamy in America since.

Four years later, he became possessed with his next big idea, a huge sandstone refuge where he could practice polygamy in peace. The Bureau of Land Management owned most of the sandstone desert near Moab, but the state owned a few pockets, which they were open to selling. So Bob went to the state capital, where they offered him a lease of two hundred acres at $1,200 a year. And he took off into the desert with a topographic map, identifying all the acreage that was available to him. He had a feeling about the Rock the moment he saw it. It was the Lord's direction. This was the place.

"I didn't know if there was water or any of that stuff," says Bob. "I don't question the Lord." He tells a magical story about how the place was built from scratch, how everything he needed was provided, often by passing strangers. "I told the boys 'I won't ask for your help or your money. The Lord will provide both.' And He has. It's been very miraculous."

Miraculous, perhaps, but not easy. The cold nights and baking days, the tents and sleeping bags. It's hard work blasting chunks out of a sandstone monolith. Dynamite's tricky to handle. And to do all this with three wives and a rapidly expanding family? "Oh my wives, just fabulous women," he says with a wink. "They came from wealthy homes and I took them out into the desert and dressed them in rags." Inevitably, they took up careers. Carla went into medicine and Karen, accounting. They bought houses nearby, so they could live in relative comfort while the Rock was under construction. And work moved swiftly. Before long, the Rock became a viable bed-and-breakfast called Rockland Ranch, which was quite the hit with European tourists until September 11 killed it off.

Today, Carla lives up in Sandy, Susan stays with Bob at the Rock and Karen stays close by, visiting often. His thirty-eight children are largely scattered to the winds. Only a handful remain here at the Rock, still true to the doctrine of plural marriage. But the others keep returning. The Rock's B&B welcome remains.

"Okay, you hungry?" He's holding up two tins of Campbell's soup. "Split pea and ham or chicken noodle?" It's time to prepare lunch, so we set about the task as a team. We're having soup, banana bread, tinned peaches and raw cow's milk. (Bob loves milk, he drinks pints of the stuff every day.) But it's us against the flies. They're everywhere, all over the food, our hands and plates. Bob hands me a swatter and I go to work. They seem to have gathered by the window, so I go to open it up, keeping my mouth shut so nothing can fly in. And there on the counter are hundreds of dead flies, strewn along the edge, heaped on the sill. How long have they been there? And why so many? I gather them into a big crunchy pile and sweep them into the bin.

"Tell me about the apocalypse, Bob."

"Okay, right you are! Half the population of the United States will be obliterated overnight. We will be nuked—we know this for a fact. The bloodshed will be so bad in this civil war that the Russians and the Chinese will decide to stop it and nuke us—three hundred megaton bombs."

"Hold on, what civil war?"

"It could happen tomorrow! You stop the gasoline, the lights, the power, the water—stop any of it and people will go crazy. That's why we're trying to get totally independent out here. We don't want to need their fuel, their lights, water or anything."

"So there's an economic crisis in America, followed by a civil war. Then the Chinese and the Russians attack."

"Yes! They'll loot the land—that's what Daniel said.[22] But then disease will take them, and strip them down. Very few will get out alive. And out of all that the Lord of Heaven plans to bring the ten lost tribes back in, out of the north. Some Jews, some remnants of the Mormon Church—they'll come in. The Lamanite people—the Indian people, probably Mexican. And you'll have a gathering in central Missouri, which the Lord refers to as the city of Zion. Here, have some more banana bread. This is good stuff."

For Bob, the writing is on the wall. You've only to look at the energy crisis and the phony wars in the Middle East, to say nothing of Big Pharm controlling us with drugs and the government manipulating the weather (Katrina) and cooking up diseases (AIDS). These things are facts, this is where Bob begins. He's a sponge for apocalyptica; every conceivable portent is folded into his recipe for doom.

"It's just like John the Revelator said: 'All nations, kindreds and tongues on the Earth will worship the dragon.' That's Lucifer, our archenemy. They already are and they don't know it. Satan is in control: he owns the cities, he rules the government. I don't want to sound like some kind of doomsayer but there's going to be a collapse. We've just got too many rotten things going on. You sure you don't want more banana bread?"

"What rotten things?"

"Oh, you know, homosexuality, lesbians, oral sex."

And my heart sinks. Bob the lovable eccentric who lives in a Rock is about to go and ruin it. "What's wrong with oral sex?"

"The scriptures say 'Do not defile yourself with women.' But that stuff goes on in oral sex, all the time!"

"I still don't get what's wrong with it."

"Well . . . I don't like to talk about it really. But we know what's wrong with homosexuality, don't we? Homosexuality would eliminate having children. What has sunk every major country that was ever born? Homosexuality! You never heard of Sodom and Gomorrah?"

"But Bob, gays are just a minority, like left-handed people."

"Oh, I know what you mean, but the Lord doesn't. He abhors it. And He stops it when it gets so far. Look at Egypt, Greece, Rome, when homosexuality kept piling up and up." A sweep of the hand: "Finished! And then there's pornography. You know the difference between art and porn? You know when Michelangelo made all these beautiful sculptures of the human body?"

"Michelangelo was gay."

"You're right. You can't name anybody that was great or important that didn't go gay. Michelangelo, Leonardo, up and down the line. But just because it's nude art doesn't mean it has to be dirty. It's when you see the stuff that kids see on television now, women getting it at both ends from different men and in the mouth and the whole business."

"What channel's this?"

"I don't really watch TV, haven't watched it in years. But I know it goes on."

And for a while we sit at his breakfast counter, shooing flies away, eating in silence. Something has changed. It might have been the "women getting it at both ends"—it sounded like he was working off some kind of visual. Or maybe he realizes that going all Jerry Falwell about gays didn't sit so well.

Either way, it's a sad end to our little chat. I still like Bob, he's a lovely old man. Maybe I will have some more banana bread.

◆ Promises, Promises

One of the saddest lessons of history is this: If we've been bamboozled long enough, we tend to reject any evidence of the bamboozle. The bamboozle has captured us.
— Carl Sagan, *The Demon-Haunted World*

The next day, Bob and I are up at the Charity House making small talk about the weather and Armageddon and such like. Then suddenly, looking out of the window, he turns serious. There's a FedEx van trundling through the wilderness toward us.

"I'll bet that guy's looking for me," says Bob. "He's got a scam on his hands. Some people called me the other day saying, 'We got a $150,000 sweepstake, and we're sending the money out but you need to pay the man three hundred-something dollars. This guy's going to deliver a package and he'll want a check,' they said. Well, my check will bounce, but you know, their check's going to bounce too. I've been involved in these sweepstakes somewhat. I've got quite a bit of money coming. Nobody knows that."

The FedEx guy gets out of his van with a package and looks around, a little lost. "Ah . . . here he comes," says Bob. "This is going to get interesting. These people sounded like Mexicans or Argentineans or something. They said they were sending me a cashier's check for $150,000."

But the FedEx guy just drops the package off at another house, gets back in his van and drives off. No scam, no sweepstakes, no Argentineans. "Oh, he's leaving. Good move," says Bob. And he turns to me, as though he's about to make an announcement. "Okay, now have you heard of Novatech?"

"No."

"They're very wealthy and powerful people and they're spending millions of dollars to try and stop death with science and technology. I'm on a mission to help these guys. They're brilliant people, but they missed the gospel."

"Bob, I'm a bit lost."

"Come here, I want to show you something."

We head downstairs to his office, a chilly, musty little cellar that smells of dust and grandparents. It's his hideaway. There's a bed and a cramped little kitchen in the back. Pictures of his family on the walls and shelves, a packed bookshelf, vitamin supplements. And on his desk and tables—on every flat surface that I can see—there are stacks of mail, piled up neatly in rectangular columns. Hundreds of envelopes, all face up, all of them opened. He reaches for a pile and extracts a letter, reading from it with enthusiasm.

"This is from a man in New York," he says, putting his glasses on. "'We've discovered that you're a Beyonder. The only heavenly body that has any effect on you is the sun. You've done without way more than you should have, and we're going to fix that.'" Bob looks over his glasses. "What do you think of that?"

He pulls out another letter. "'This letter is about two unexpected events that concern you, more specifically a money-related event with a considerable sum that involves you personally. What we're talking about, Mr.

Foster, is sufficient to definitively keep the wolves at bay for years. That's why Liza and I immediately decided to send you a valuable gift.'"

"Who's Liza?"

"She's from Switzerland, she's psychic. This letter is from her and her friend, who's psychic too. I don't know how they got my address. I'm not going to tell you too much about this, because it's pretty private. I haven't even told my family."

"Psychic women from Switzerland are writing to you out of the blue?"

"Not just from Switzerland, they come from all over the world," says Bob. He reaches for another neat stack on his desk and flicks through the letters, each one ready to action, with words underlined and notes in the margin "This one's from the Netherlands. Now, let's see, there's California, New York, Europe. They're telling me that I'm heading for an astronomical moment in my life. Look: 'The first will happen in a few days—money. An unexpected amount. A heaven-sent windfall that will enrichen you far beyond anything you can hope for. The second is directly linked to someone whose destiny will meet yours.' A lot of them say I'm about to meet my soul mate."

All these promises of wealth, true love and happiness to an eighty-four-year-old polygamist whose life would appear to be full enough—he's been married four times and he's met God. But Bob is flattered by his mailbag; clearly these people have heard how special he is. One letter from a Roger Grimstone alludes to the fact that Bob has led a tragic life, which is about to change. And Bob agrees: "They're reading me like a book!"

"But how is your life tragic?"

"Not tragic, hard. Because I've always been scrambling for enough money to get by. Like my phone's going to be cut off tomorrow. Oh, don't worry, I've got millions coming very soon. But I can't pay my phone bill today." He grabs another pile of letters. "I don't know who Professor Bernard Von Drass is, but he's been writing me regularly. And here: Prosperity Forecast by Lady Charlemagne. Oh, she's funny!"

"Do you know her?"

"I know of her."

Yet again my heart sinks, but much lower this time. Bob's being had by an army of frauds—scam psychics and pretend gypsies, secret societies and junk mail clairvoyants. The sheer volume of their attack is disconcerting, and the way Bob keeps their mail so meticulously like important business correspondence. Letters that begin, "Mr. Foster, I am going to make you a millionaire," or "The Most Important Letter You've Ever Received." Letters from "One of the richest men in Europe," or "Kreskin, the world-famous mentalist." Bob treasures them all. "Roger Grimstone says the money's going to come like an avalanche, and Kreskin says tidal wave," he says, chuckling. So he sends them the little sums they ask for, the twenties, even hundreds.

Perhaps his credulity is a kind of elderly regression, a return to the naïvety of his youth. Perhaps it's a product of his separation from the world, his unfamiliarity with its ways. But I suspect Bob's being fleeced for the same reasons that he built the Rock in the first place—a boundless capacity to believe in fantasies. The fire of his faith is scalding him.

"One psychic said 'You have one woman in your life who's going to regret the way she's acting.' He's touching delicate places in my life that nobody else would know!"

"But Bob, everyone knows a woman who's a pain in the ass sometimes."

"Yes, but he's talking about one of my wives. She's been giving me flack for years."

And with that, he pulls out a series of three huge volumes, each one over one thousand pages long and marked "Nouveau Tech." This is the "Novatech" group he mentioned earlier. "Multimillionaires, worldwide, very powerful secret society," he explains. "They're trying to put their own men into power so they can break up the IRS. And they need exactly what I've got to tell them. One of their Nobel Prize winners was writing me letters. He said, 'That man is engulfed in double sine waves, we need him here.'"

Bob doesn't know what double sine waves mean or signify. And he has never met these Nouveau Tech people, but he says they're the Illuminati, the Enlightened Ones, and it's his mission to reintroduce them to the prophets. I flick through these enormous volumes, each one marked "Limited Heirloom Package, specially printed for Robert Foster." They're a peculiar format—giant novels, essentially, with fictional characters embarking on all kinds of quests. And the scam could not be more transparent. The book titles alone: *The Earth's First Immortals*, *The Greatest How-To Book Ever Written*, *The Greatest Kept Secret of All Time*. And the chapters: "Stop Ageing," "Become A Genius," "Ride a Prosperity Explosion

That Will Make You a Millionaire." And even "Diet Down to the Body You Always Envied."

Bob has gone through these pages with a highlighter, making notes in the margin. He believes the characters are real—people like Frank Wallace, the gambler who cannot lose, and his genius sidekick Mark Hamilton. Bob believes he'll meet them both soon enough. He's going to save them, and they're going to make him immeasurably rich. It's a tragedy. A broke old man is being ripped off and it can't be stopped. He's been hooked by a classic one-two: flattery and a false promise. The scammers first tell Bob how gifted he is; they send him diplomas and fellowships at pseudo-scientific academies, admission to elite societies and karmic medals. Then they promise him riches, love, immortality, eternal happiness, everything that anyone could ever want. It's not so far removed from the Mormon flattery elevating saints over Gentiles, promising them godhood, eternal families, planets of their own. Bob has lived his life believing these things; it is his greatest charm and his greatest flaw.

There was a mantra I used to recite, in the days when I believed, and it translated to something like: "Keep God in mind but do not hanker after the goal." Of course, I was all about the goal—I wanted superpowers, sexual magnetism, I wanted it all. But even then, I knew that something felt off: you shouldn't find God because of what you want but because of what you no longer need.

And yet in fundamentalism, the carrot is the key. Without the prize, the path loses its meaning. No doubt, arguments can be made about free day care and the benefits of large families, but even the most functional of plural families will admit that Mormon polygamy isn't exactly a recipe for happiness. "The Work" is meant to be strenuous and difficult, the hard path toward a payoff sometime in the candyland hereafter. And there is no limit to what people will do for these fantasy futures. Christine prostituted herself; Angie married a man who could have been her grandfather. Happiness is so hard to find in this life, so maybe the next.

"Bob, Nouveau Tech's a scam." I have to say *something*.

"No, that society is rock solid," he says. "There's a lady who is in communication with them, and she sent me a revelation that I was going to go there and straighten this out."

"What lady?"

"This psychic lady I know. She didn't name them, she just said 'an organization that helps people'—and that's exactly what they do."

I'm feeling helpless here. Faith can be a kamikaze business. Bob says he hasn't told his kids, but I'm sure they know; these letters are in plain sight, they go back over a year. Is it enough to politely suggest that perhaps he's being hoodwinked? Is decorum even ethical at this point?

"Bob, all these psychics—they just want your money."

"I know what you're saying."

"Don't trust these people. They're preying on you. You're on some mailing list or something, they think they've found a sucker and they're just—"

"Yes, yes, I know why you would say that, given your background," says Bob. "But I've been studying these people for a year and a half. You don't know the dreams I've had."

And he continues to sort through his stacks of empty promises. "Robert you are a potential grand winner of $25,000." "The Tomorrow Fund. This letter is highly confidential. Things are about to happen!" "I am about to offer you the potential solution to practically every problem you have!"

◆ The Overlook

> We must respect the other fellow's religion, but only in the sense and to the extent that we respect his theory that his wife is beautiful and his children are smart.
> —H. L. Mencken

Bob says he has to go away for a few days. Important business, probably related to Nouveau Tech, he won't say. It's top secret. "Why don't you go and meet the gang?" he suggests. "Try any one of those houses. They're nice people. We're trying to build a friendly place here."

So I wander down to the first house and stand on the porch, knuckles poised. The dread returns at once. The number of times I've been in this position on this trip—knocking on strangers' doors, like a pollster or a salesman. Or a Mormon. Except this time, given my current status in the fundamentalist community, I fully expect to be sent packing, in no uncertain terms. Perhaps Bob hadn't heard the rumors, but the younger ones, they'll be plugged in . . .

But instead, a miracle: I'm invited in. The first house I try is Anna's, Bob's daughter with Karen. "Come in! Come in!" she says, and staggers back to her sofa, panting. Anna's pregnant, but she doesn't let it get in the way of her basic hospitality. She offers me lemonade and biscuits and uncensored opinions. Like Bob, she's an open book, except she's not a polygamist and has no plans to be, either. "We're all products of plural marriage here, we've all seen the heartache and the pain. But God also wants you to have joy, you know? Me, I just say, 'I'm Mormon.'"

Anna has lived most of her life at the Rock. She spent nine years here before getting married in 1992, and she's lived here ever since. Growing up, she says, it was this big fun place to camp out with her brothers and sisters, a dirty basin of dust and mud where dad would blow stuff up with dynamite—a blast in every sense. But now it's more of a haven. She uses the words "idyll" and "oasis." It's not about the apocalypse—"that's just Dad's thing"—it's about escaping Gomorrah, the iniquity of cities, the pollution of the media. She doesn't own a TV and doesn't care to. No one watches TV at the Rock. They had the Internet installed a couple of years ago, but Anna's not bothered about that either. God doesn't mind if you're out of the loop. The first she heard of 9/11 was when Bob drove up with his radio on, and they all gathered around. She didn't see the television footage for two weeks. "This, for me, is a manageable world," she says.

As we talk, people keep coming to the door and joining in. Melinda from three doors down, then April and Angela—all women. And I'm just bracing myself for the chitchat to peter out and the grilling to begin. But instead, we have a conversation about polygamy in which I'm just another voice, another person who's met people and seen things. And along the way, Melinda asks if I'd like to stay at her house. Except the way she says it is, "I'd be honored to have you stay in our spare room."

Just when I'm thinking that this couldn't get any better, Catrina drops by. Skinny and blonde with sparkling blue eyes, she looks like the actress Mena Suvari, the one in *American Beauty*. She's with her sister wife Lillian, a slender brunette with big brown eyes, long chocolate hair and movie-star teeth, all of twenty years old. Both of them in blue jeans and T-shirts.

They're hands-down the two hottest plural wives I've seen on my travels.

"So, do you have plans for lunch?" asks Catrina. "We're having burritos."

Turns out the lucky guy is Enoch, one of Bob's sons by Carla, a rangy thirty-year-old with a forthright, earnest manner and a big handshake. He's lived at the Rock from the age of one, on and off, hopping around from Salt Lake to Colorado to Missouri in the interim. It was in Missouri that he met Catrina, two years his junior, and as soon as he turned eighteen, he married her. She'd been around polygamists before—she was raised by an independent fundamentalist father. At the time, Enoch was working as a framer for Jared Zitting's crew—Jared from Centennial Park—but he came back to the Rock soon afterward. That was six years ago.

Lillian joined the family two years back. She too, is no stranger to polygamy, being the daughter of Addam Swapp, the man who blew up the stake center in Kamas (she has never strayed too far from dynamite). Since she was only eleven months old when it happened, she knows her father mostly through prison visits. But she's proud of the Swapp name and regards him absolutely as a moral man. She met Catrina through Enoch's sister, with whom she was friends. There has long been a connection between the Rock and the Swapps. Catrina felt strongly that Lillian should be part of her family, so she prayed on it, and went to Lillian. Lillian prayed on it too, and then they both approached Enoch.

"It's called the law of Sarah[23] where the first wife instigates the plural marriage," explains Catrina. "I had a good feeling about it and so did Lillian. And when we went to Enoch, he said he had the same feeling."

I'll bet he did. However you cut it, Enoch's doing all right. He spends his days blowing stuff up with dynamite, and when he gets home, he's got two hot wives waiting for him, along with ten kids and a cozy little temperature-stabilized hearth, way out in the beautiful wilderness of canyon country, not to mention the approval of the creator of the universe, which means he gets the same deal in the afterlife. This isn't "the Work," this is "the Vacation."

But Enoch's not the only one enjoying life at the Rock. It's an easy place to like. Today, for instance, I woke up at Melinda's place and joined the family for breakfast, the canyon view flooding through the windows. Morning stroll down the ledge to say hi to Ann, wave at Angela and pop into the Charity House to get on the Wi-Fi and check my email. Quick chat with Enoch, who's jamming a huge drill into the rock face and jagging away—he's building a new house, with huge windows, plenty of daylight. Meanwhile, back at the house, Catrina and Lillian are busy canning cherries—food preservation, that classic Mormon pastime. You can hear the rattle of the jars boiling in their kitchen. All the kids are out helping, dragging great buckets of fruit up from the orchard, washing and draining and pelting them at each other. Now, now kids, you'll be grateful for those cherries when the apocalypse comes.

At mealtimes, Enoch likes to engage me in a spirited debate about God, the Universe and Everything. Needless to say, neither of us emerge much swayed from our positions. I'm a curiosity to Enoch, a puzzle—all the places I've visited and the books I've read and still all I have is questions, not answers. He's staggered that I believe in evolution. Haven't I read the work of Kent Hovind, the man behind the Dinosaur Adventure Land theme park in Florida? The park that was built on the premise that dinosaurs and humans lived alongside each other, like in *The Flintstones*?

But Enoch is a puzzle to me, too. Certainly, he's living proof that you can subscribe to a Fred-and-Barney version of history and live an immensely content life. Who am I to question his happiness? Catrina tells me: "We enjoy our life, we don't see polygamy like 'we'll suffer it to get to the afterlife.'" And Lillian tells me "I can't imagine myself being any happier than I am now." Some women in plural marriage claim to be happy but it seems as if they're brainwashed—they don't know what true happiness is. But I look at Lillian, who's twenty and still hasn't seen the sea, and she looks perfectly happy to me. She has Enoch and Catrina and all kinds of wonderful stories to explain her world. Her cosmos is complete. She doesn't need the sea.

When Enoch returns to work, I borrow a four-wheeler and chug leisurely around the Rock's ample perimeter. It takes a while on account of the Rock's scale—some ninety acres of scrubland around. But it also brings home the scale of Bob's belief, the spiritual fire he was talking about. I've always admired the boldness of Mormon fundamentalism. Bob didn't hedge; he went all out. He read the book, listened to the voices in his head and lived his life in their service—that's what religious life is supposed to be. I like to think that there's something intrepid about my own life, coming from London to L.A. and hanging out with polygamists, way out in the desert. It's how liberals like to think of themselves: broader, more

adventurous than those fearful Bible-blinkered conservatives. But polygamists are the real rebels. They've stepped outside society's conventions and
laws in their pursuit of happiness. A giant rock in the desert? That's what
I call opting *out*.

Faiths often create for themselves homes of overwhelming solidity—
giant monoliths, vast temples of stone—as though to compensate for their
reliance on airy notions of spirits and dreams, the general flimsiness of
their evidence. Their buildings overstate their permanence—they doth
protest—and perhaps the Rock is one such overstatement. Certainly, the
durability of fundamentalism cannot be denied. After a century of exile
from its mother church and society at large, the Rock stands as a rebuke to
those who would have Mormon polygamy just wither. Here in the desert,
like certain rugged shrubs, it's thriving.

I'm reminded of Centennial Park, a young group, full of the invigor-
ating energy of growth. Size difference aside, they have much in common:
two desert communities, committed to isolation, who share a friendliness
to strangers and the absence of a lording prophet. Bob might have been
the Rock's prophet; he certainly made all the right claims about chatting to
God and so forth. But he lacks the grim ambition for the job. And he's far
too chummy, which is entirely to his credit. Chumminess is key. Chumminess and doubt.

I visited Centennial Park again with my wife for the Fourth of July
weekend and caught up with Nephi there. He wasn't sure whether to stick
with the ten kids he had, or to take a few more wives and have twenty more
kids, the way his forefathers had before him. "I'm just not sure that's what
I want," he said, scratching his head. It was a crisis of faith. And it gave me
such hope. Faith always ought to be in some kind of crisis, a state of refine-
ment or evolution.

In Centennial Park, we went to a huge community breakfast in the
morning, and then Jared and Carol took us hiking with the family up a trail
called the Narrows, returning down the creek where the boys all took turns
dive-bombing into the water. Then it was back for cocktails and lunches
and more cocktails. Talk about oasis—they've got margaritas bubbling
out of the ground in Centennial Park. But if I had to choose, I'd take the
Rock. There's no shadow of old sectarianism here, no fractious history or
prairie dresses; the Rock's polygamists are easier to blend in with. And here

more than anywhere, the people seem comforted, not cowed by their faith. They're free to leave and return as they please, with no need to hide or lie, and no council of elders watching over them. That anxious look of Carleen's, the accretion of secrets and fears and which-lie-did-I-tell—you don't find that in Rockland. In fact, the Order and the Rock exist at opposite poles of the polygamy spectrum in many respects. What a thing it would be if Paul Kingston ruled his clan from remote sandstone caves instead of the suburbs of northern Utah. Imagine the scandal of a girl like Mary Ann running to her freedom through the sagebrush desert, the feeding frenzy for those film rights. But such a thing would never happen at the Rock. Hysteria stems from secrecy and separation, and Bob isn't about to run a fence around the place or command his children to keep quiet.

The need for apartness is core to fundamentalism. It feeds its exceptionalist self-image. It's why the Order couldn't invite me to their homes as the Rocklanders have, or allow me to attend their precious picnic. It's also why polygamists don't actually want legalization. To be included into the great wash of society would neuter their cachet. Even if polygamy were legalized, I suspect fundamentalists would still opt out. They'd just have to find another reason to satisfy their urge to march out into the desert and live in a giant cave. And I get it, in part, this need for separation. In a nation of strip malls, Twitter and Glenn Beck, fundamentalism is at least partly a plea for simplicity. Perhaps a hopeless plea, an ostrich move, but nonetheless, comprehensible.

But apartness can also be ugly in its implications of superiority and purity. And correspondingly, it's a similar sense that keeps a Christian country from legalizing polygamy: the fear that the institution of marriage would be corrupted. Christian institutions contaminated by Mormons, Mormons by Gentiles—and among the Gentiles it continues, between Brahmin and Dalit, Muslim and infidel. Isn't it wrong to base a religion on what divides rather than what unifies us? And yet this is the bedrock of many faiths, this distinction between chosen and damned, high-born and low, pure and contaminated. Certainly, the virus of hierarchy has infected every polygamist bubble I've seen, either through the corporate masthead of a church or the fabricated aristocracies of bloodline and past "probations." Perhaps this is only to be expected in a culture built upon an *a priori* denigration of black people and gays. Even the affable Bob Foster blames the decline of civilization on the likes of RuPaul. And as usual, I did little to disabuse him. What would be the point? I can no more persuade Apocalypse Bob of the merits of *Rent*, the musical, than I can budge this giant rock I'm driving around.

On my last day at Rockland, Catrina says "You have to see the canyons while you're here. Why don't I take you?" So we hop into my car and drive twelve miles down the road to Needles Overlook, climb over the safety rail and sit on the ledge. And she's right—I did have to see the canyons. We're sitting at the rim of a Martian apocalypse. It's infinite, brutal and magnificent, a whole hemisphere of buttes and arches and crazed jutting Gorgons of red rock throwing jagged shadows across each other. A few feet away is a drop to the center of creation, so huge it makes my legs spasm. And there's no one here but us and a silhouetted bird hanging in the far sky. The silence is colossal.

"Look at that," says Catrina. "Doesn't this make you think there's a higher power?"

Of course it does. It's awesome and humbling. Faced with these canyons, I feel like a speck, immeasurably puny. There was a time when I liked to imagine the magical hand of a creator, and feel comforted that a kernel of his power was within me. But I can no longer put myself in the company of the forces that created this, much less believe that I possess a similar capacity. I imagine being deposited on one of the distant peaks and left there to squirm like an offering to the pterodactyls. I can't conceive of witnessing this landscape and thinking not of my insignificance, but the opposite—that, by virtue of my virtue, I too would one day have the power to build canyons like these, in a matter of weeks at that.

Leaving the Rock, I feel a swell of emotion. The rituals of good-bye tend to tug at me—the handshakes and promises to stay in touch, the waving in the rearview mirror. But more than that, my journey feels over. I've found fundamentalism here at its most open, beautiful and generous, and still there remains a gulf between us, a chasm the match of any canyon. I can never share the contentment they feel here, the consolations of scripture, of literalism. But equally, I will never feel the tremor of a believer whose magical prospects start to totter when prophets go postal and pennies start to drop. Our lives are so deeply defined by the stories we tell ourselves.

As I drive back to Los Angeles, the desert freeways have the effect of sifting my memories, one skyline erasing another like the tide. Back to St. George and down through Nevada, I leave behind an archipelago of fundamentalism, each island bubbling with ferment: Bob's psychic fantasies and the FLDS furor in Texas; Emma and Carol in Centennial Park dueling over the décor; further north, Angie exploring her freedom while an ageing prophet reels from his loss; and further still, the madness of Nemelka and the darkness of the Order.

I'm going to miss polygamy. Not the bigotry or the dogma or the claustrophobic little communities, but the intensity. Wild beliefs make for a dramatic life; they raise the stakes and force your hand. You don't find adventure by way of skepticism and a sober assessment of the arguments. You jump—top board, eyes closed. Test the depth of the puddle with both feet. Happiness is a risk, and Mormon polygamy is full of gamblers, all committed to their grand ideals and magical eternities, leading lives of purpose and drama, all the things that I want in my own life. But I won't jump. I can't find the right ledge.

Even as Las Vegas looms on the horizon, I feel I'm heading toward a calmer, saner frequency. The cacophony of strip clubs and prime rib specials are reassuring; give me the blare of Gomorrah over a quietly seething Canaan any day. It's not the cities but the small towns that fill me with dread now. Always the quiet ones. I've made this drive so many times, but never with such urgency—past Baker, down to Barstow, then west through Pasadena to L.A. I can feel Zion receding and I like it. At home in the city of the unfound and rootless, I'm anonymous and free, one of a million cars in a grid. All the possibilities of America are before me.

I come home to find my wife holding a knife and telling her friend she'll have to call her back.

"Notice anything?" she says to me. "Yes, my hair. Duh. But look at the color. There's a new guy at the salon who's really good. Want a mojito? I'm cutting limes. Can you get me the mint in the fridge? Okay, so I've got like a bunch of stuff to tell you, but you first, come on! Did you find that Rock place? Were they cool? Oh, I made your favorite: turkey osso bucco!"

I think that wives, as with all things, work best in moderation. One's fine; why spoil things? Monogamy has been good to me. As the old routines reestablish themselves—the gossip and cocktails, cozy on the sofa with the dogs—I feel restored, realigned. We laugh and drink and make plans and change them. All our triumphs and setbacks are understood here; anxieties are shared, and hopes are nourished.

Fundamentalists would ask, "What, you don't believe in *anything*?" But I do. I believe in this home, filled today with the soft hum of love and the smell of my favorite dish. I believe in the goodness of people, the magnificence of nature, the possibility of happiness. This too is a simple life. There are no cosmic certainties, but hope persists, even so. There's magic in hope. Atheists are believers too. When *Big Love* starts up on HBO, I get the clicker and she brings the chips. Neither of us have a clue what happens when we die. This, for me, is a manageable world.

Sources and Endnotes

1. Dropping In for Coffee

1. "[Ron] looked back at Dan and said, 'Thank you, brother, for doing the baby, because I don't think I had it in me.' And Dan replied and said, 'It was no problem.'" From testimony of accomplice Chip Carnes in the 1996 trial, in *Under the Banner of Heaven*, by Jon Krakauer, Anchor Books, 2003, p 284

2. "Church Bomber Apologizes for Actions," by Jason Bergreen, *The Salt Lake Tribune*, March 13, 2007

3. *Mormon Polygamy: A History*, by Richard S. Van Wagoner, Signature Books, p 214

4. "16-year-old Girl Testifies of Beating," by Ray Rivera, *The Salt Lake Tribune*, July 23, 1998. John Daniel Kingston subsequently pleaded "no contest" to charges of child abuse, a third-degree felony, and was duly sentenced.

6. Interview with Brent Jeffs, nephew and student, August 2006

7. Interviews with Ross and Lori Chatwin, Richard Holm

8. "Life At Polygamist Ranch Was Austere, Controlled," *Associated Press*, April 3, 2009

9. "Fugitive polygamist sect leader caught near Las Vegas," *CNN*, August 30, 2006

10. The Vermillion was later sued for discriminating against non-FLDS customers when two former FLDS members brought a case. The owner, Bygnal Dutson, settled with Arizona authorities. "Diners Settle Suit with Ex-FLDS," *The Salt Lake Tribune*, December 12, 2007

2. The Campaigners

1. See endnote 4 in chapter 1: "Dropping In for Coffee"

2. Salt Lake City Police Department records, April 27, 1996

3. See endnote 5 in chapter 1: "Dropping In for Coffee"

4. *The Essential Lennie Bruce,* edited by John Cohen, Ballantine Books, 1970

5. In a later email, Gary and Mary Batchelor add the following: "The divorce was an anguished period in our lives because of the immense resentment and conflict. We did pray through that horrible, painful time and we believe that God ultimately heard our prayers and helped us to forgive. Forgiveness freed us from the anger and torment. It did not free us from the responsibility to do better in the future. In that spirit, in spite of what Vicky chooses to say or do, Mary and I shall not engage in the duel of defensiveness and finger-pointing. It's not conducive to the peaceful home life which is in the best interest of all our children."

3. Mormon Polygamy—The First Century

1. As reported to Wilhelm Wyl in *Mormon Portraits, Joseph Smith the Prophet, His Family and His Friends*, Salt Lake City, 1886, as cited in *No Man Knows My History*, by Fawn Brodie, Vintage books, 1995, p 297

2. "Admonitions for the Priesthood of God," by Harold B. Lee, *Ensign*, January 1973

3. "Hallowed Be Your Name," by Marilynne Robinson, *American Scholar*, Spring 2006

4. *No Man Knows My History*, by Fawn Brodie, Vintage books, 1995, p 32

5. *Ibid.*, p 37

6. *Ibid.*, p 54

7. *Introduction to the Study of the Book of Mormon* by J. M. Sjodhal, as cited in *No Man Knows My History*, by Fawn Brodie, Vintage books, 1995, p 78

8. *The American Religion*, by Harold Bloom, Simon and Schuster, 1992, p 85

9. *Is the Book of Mormon from God?*, by Dave Miller, Apologetics Press: Scripturally Speaking

10. *View of the Hebrews; or the Ten Tribes of Israel in America*, by Ethan Smith, Smith & Shute, 1823

11. *American Indian mtDNA and Y Chromosome Genetic Data: A Comprehensive Report of their Use in Migration and Other Anthropological Studies*, by Peter N. Jones, IIIRM.org, 2004

12. *The Teachings of Lorenzo Snow*, ed. Clyde J. Williams, 1984, p 1

13. *In Sacred Loneliness, The Wives of Joseph Smith*, by Todd Compton

14. *Ibid.*, p 12–15

15. *Ibid.*, p 14

16. *Ibid.*, p 38

17. *The American Religion*, by Harold Bloom, Simon and Schuster, 1992, p 93

18. "I go emphatically, virtuously, and humanely for a Theodemocracy, where God and the people hold the power to conduct the affairs of men in righteousness"—*Nauvoo Neighbor*, April 17, 1844, as cited in *No Man Knows My History*, by Fawn Brodie, Vintage books, 1995, p 364

19. *Mormon Polygamy: A History*, by Richard S. Van Wagoner, Signature Books, 1989, p 110

20. *Ibid.*, p 112

21. *Ibid.*, p 128

22. *Ibid.*, p 185

23. *Ibid.*, p 183

24. *The 1886 Visitations of Jesus Christ*, by Lynn L. Bishop and Steven L. Bishop, p 172, as cited in *Modern Polygamy and Mormon Fundamentalism*, by Brian Hales, Greg Kofford Books, p 158

25. Testimony of Moroni Jessop, by Moroni Jessop, p 22, as cited in *Modern Polygamy and Mormon Fundamentalism*, by Brian Hales, Greg Kofford Books, p 161

26. *Mormon Polygamy: A History*, by Richard S. Van Wagoner, Signature Books, 1989, p 156

27. *Ibid.*, p 185, a quote from *The Salt Lake Tribune*, July 26, 1937.

4. When the Saints Come Marching Out

1. "The Mormon Moment—The Church Of Latter Day Saints Grows By Leaps And Bounds," by Jeffrey L. Sheler, *U.S. News And World Report*, November 5, 2000. "In the 170 years since its founding in upstate New York, the LDS Church has sustained the most rapid growth rate of any new faith group in American history. Since World War II, its ranks have expanded more than 10-fold, with a worldwide membership today of 11 million—more than half outside the United States. In North America, Mormons already outnumber Presbyterians and Episcopalians combined. If current trends hold, experts say Latter-day Saints could number 265 million worldwide by 2080, second only to Roman Catholics among Christian bodies. Mormonism, says Rodney Stark, professor of sociology and religion at the University of Washington, 'stands on the threshold of becoming the first major faith to appear on Earth since the prophet Mohammed rode out of the desert.'"

2. *The Donner Party*, by Ric Burns, PBS, 1997. Narrator: "William Eddy crawled out of the white tomb where the dead and dying emigrants lay and managed to relight the fire. Someone cut the flesh from the arms and legs of Patrick Dolan. They roasted the meat and ate it, averting their faces from each other and weeping."

3. *Mormon Polygamy: A History*, by Richard S. Van Wagoner, Signature Books, 1989, p 93

4. "Teen Pledges Barely Cut STD Rates, Study Says," by Ceci Connolly, *The Washington Post*, March 19, 2005. "Although young people who sign a virginity pledge delay the initiation of sexual activity, marry at younger ages and have fewer sexual partners, they are also less likely to use condoms and more likely to experiment with oral and anal sex, said the researchers from Yale and Columbia universities."

5. "Utah Has New Tool to Stop the Silent Epidemic of Teen Suicide," release by Mark Shurtleff, attorney general of Utah, November 14, 2005: "The Utah suicide rate for young males is the highest in the nation. Youth suicide is the third leading cause of death for those between the age[s] of 15 and 24 and the second leading cause of death for college-aged students."

5. Centennial Park

1. *The Penis Book*, by Joseph Cohen, Broadway, 2004

2. "The Frog and Peach Sketch," Plymouth Theatre, New York, 1973

3. Warren Jeffs may still be the FLDS prophet, though he's abdicated the presidency of the church, a position now held by Wendell Nielsen

4. "For I have given him the keys of the mysteries, and the revelations which are sealed until I shall appoint unto them another in his stead." Doctrine and Covenants, chapter 28, verse 7.

5. Doctrine and Covenants, chapter 43, verses 1–7

6. Ibid., chapter 85, verse 7

7. "In Every Dream Home a Heartache," by Roxy Music, *For Your Pleasure*, Island Records, 1973

8. "Happiness Is Easy," by Talk Talk, *The Colour of Spring*, EMI Records, 1986

9. "Vatican Issues a Qualified Ban on Gays in Priesthood," by Tracy Wilkinson and Maria De Cristofaro, *Los Angeles Times*, November 23, 2005

10. *The Bell Curve*, by Charles Murray and Richard J. Herrnstein was indeed slammed eventually but was widely welcomed at first, as reported by Jim Naureckas in FAIR ("Racism Resurgent," January 1995). Richard Cohen of *The Washington Post* wrote: "Both Murray and Herrnstein have been called racists. Their findings, though, have been accepted by most others in their field, and it would be wrong—both intellectually and politically—to suppress them." Geoffrey Cowley of *Newsweek* wrote: "As the shouting begins, it's worth noting that the science behind *The Bell Curve* is overwhelmingly mainstream." In fact, most of the research Murray and Herrnstein used was funded by the Pioneer Fund, a far-right organization with overtly racist roots. The fund's first president, Harry Laughlin advocated sterilization for the genetically unfit. A later fund treasurer, John Trevor Jr., praised South Africa's apartheid policy as "well-reasoned." Other

scientists cited in the research and/or funded by the Pioneer Fund have argued for eugenics, school segregation and the "phasing out" of "incompetent cultures."

11. From *Lectures and Lay Sermons*, by T. H. Huxley, University of Michigan Library, 1926 p 115, "No rational man, cognizant of the facts, believes that the average negro is the equal, still less the superior, of the white man. And if this be true, it is simply incredible that, when all his disabilities are removed, and our prognathous relative has a fair field and no favour, as well as no oppressor, he will be able to compete successfully with his bigger-brained and smaller-jawed rival, in a contest which is to be carried out by thoughts and not by bites."

6. Texas 2008

1. The number of children removed seemed to keep changing, a symptom of the complexity of this case and the difficulty the Texas authorities had in handling it. The quoted figure in May, a month on, was 468 children, but that was soon judged a typo, the real figure being 464 children. By late June, the figure was readjusted to 440 children, until September 5, when the Texas Child Protection Services spokesman Patrick Crimmins told the *Deseret News*, "we think the number is 439 instead of 440."

2. The sites are www.CaptiveFLDSchildren.org, www.FLDSTruth.org and www.truthwillprevail.org.

3. Ben Stein on CBS

4. "Costs top $12.4 million for raid on FLDS," by Ben Winslow, in *Deseret News*, November 21, 2008

7. To Be a God

1. *The Crisis*, by Thomas Paine. 1776

8. Legalize It

1. The historical background came from *Mormon Polygamy: A History*, by Richard S. Van Wagoner, and from interviews with Mary and Gary Batchelor, Anne Wilde and attorney Brian Barnard. Details about specific cases like *Holm*, *Bronson/Swenson*, came from *The Salt Lake Tribune* and *The Deseret News*.

Reynolds v. United States, 98 U.S. 145 (1879). Chief Justice Waite declared in his opinion that "Polygamy has always been odious among the northern and western nations of Europe, and, until the establishment of the Mormon Church, was almost exclusively a feature of the life of Asiatic and of African people."

2. For example, *The Moral Animal: The New Science of Evolutionary Psychology*, by Robert Wright, Vintage books, 1995; "The Ethnographic Atlas," by George P Murdock, *World Cultures*, vol 2 (4), 1986 and "A Peculiar Institution?

Greco-Roman Monogamy in Global Context," by W. Scheidel, *History of the Family*, vol 14 (3) 2009

3. "Polygyny in American Politics" by Laura Betzig and Samantha Weber, *Politics and the Life Sciences*, vol 12(1)1993, Beech Tree Publishing

4. "Polygyny in Cross-Cultural Perspective: Theory and Implications," by Joseph Henrich, Canada Chair in Culture, Cognition and Coevolution, University of British Columbia, 2010

5. "Polygamy has troubling implications for any society," by Daphne Bramham, *Vancouver Sun*, July 16, 2010

6. Laura Betzig has a large body of work documenting the relationship between polygamy, despotism and stratification in early agrarian states. Notably "Despotism and Differential Reproduction: A Cross Cultural Correlation of Conflict Asymmetry, Hierarchy, and Degree of Polygyny," *Ethology and Sociobiology*, vol 3(4), 1982, and "Harem Polygyny Codes," in *World Cultures* vol 5 (2), 1990 and "Sex, Succession, and Stratification in the First Six Civilizations: How Powerful Men Reproduced, Passed Power on to Their Sons, and Used Power to Defend Their Wealth, Women, and Children" in *Social Stratification and Socioeconomic Inequality*, vol 1, edited by Lee Ellis, Praeger, 1993, p 37–74

7. There is no law against polygamy per se, only bigamy. But bigamy's where polygamy begins—with two.

8. Interview with Anne Wilde

9. *Lukumi Babalu Aye, Inc. v. City of Hialeah*, 508 U.S. 520, 535 (1993)

10. *John Geddes Lawrence and Tyron Garner v. Texas*, 539 U.S. 558 (2003)

11. "In 2003, the U.S. Supreme Court dropped a cluster bomb in *Lawrence v. Texas*. For the first time in its history, a majority of the Court rejected morality as a legitimate justification for a state criminal law." Taken from "When Will Bisexuals Drag Homosexuals out of Polygamy Closet?" by Janet M. LaRue, www.townhall.com, Dec 22, 2006.

12. *Ibid.*

13. "In every society, the definition of marriage has not ever to my knowledge included homosexuality. That's not to pick on homosexuality. It's not, you know, man on child, man on dog or whatever the case may be." Rick Santorum, in *USA Today*, April 23, 2003.

14. "Slippery Slop," by Dahlia Lithwick, *Slate*, May 19, 2004

15. "Academic Cross-dressing How Intelligent Design Gets Its Arguments From the Left," by Stanley Fish, *Harper's*, December 2005

9. The Order

1. *God's Brothel*, by Andrea Moore-Emmett, Pince-Nez Press, 2004, p 85. The $200 million estimate is disputed, however, largely because the co-op itself is silent upon the issue. Another figure that has been cited is $150 million, albeit several

years previously. Greg Burton wrote in "Kingston Journey: Insiders to Outcasts," *The Salt Lake Tribune*, August 16, 1998: "[John Ortell Kingston] built it up into a business empire worth an estimated $150 million, funding its growth on strict profit reinvestment."

2. From interviews with several former Order members

3. There are no accurate figures for membership of the Order, since we rely upon information from the Order itself, which tends to change. While Anne Wilde was told 1,500, Rachel Young tells me 1,000. But as we've seen, telling outsiders the truth isn't high on the list of priorities—the Order receptionist reflexively lied about whether Rachel Young was in the office or not.

4. From interview with Kingston lawyer, Laura Fuller

5. From interviews with Rowenna Erickson, Christy and Ron Tucker, Rebekah Wood

6. These numbers are anecdotal and come from former Order members. In her interview with state investigators, Andrea Foster estimated that she had between 110 and 120 siblings—this was in 2004.

7. "Sex Abuse Victim Sues Kingstons," by Ashley Broughton, *The Salt Lake Tribune*, August 29, 2003

8. Most of the defendants were dropped in installments over the years, most particularly the Order businesses, which the judge has ruled are not relevant to the case. And according to Laura Fuller, those individuals who were dismissed then countersued Mary Ann for labeling them "polygamists" when they were, in legal terms, monogamists. By February 2009, Mary Ann agreed to drop her case in return for the cases against her being dropped. In April, it was put to rest. See section on Laura Fuller, "Laura Fuller and the Exoneration of Daniel Kingston" in Chapter 9, "The Order."

9. "The Kingstons wanted economic communalism, Short Creek wanted separation and the urban polygamists wanted assimilation. That three-way split continues today." D. Michael Quinn quoted in "Kingston Journey: Insiders to Outcasts," by Greg Burton, *Salt Lake Tribune*, August 16, 1998

10. *Laman Manasseh Victorious: A Message of Salvation and Redemption to His People Israel First to Ephraim and Manasseh*, by William K. Ray (Charles W. Kingston and Jesse B. Stone), Printcraft Shop: Idaho Falls, Idaho, 1931

11. *The Autobiography of Charles William Kingston*, (photocopy in my possession)

12. "1940 New Year's Meeting, 8.40am to 12.30am," by Charles Elden Kingston

13. Interview with Laura Fuller

14. Interview with Ronald Tucker

15. *The Autobiography of Charles William Kingston*, (photocopy in my possession), plus interviews with Rowenna Erickson, Ronald Tucker

16. The niece mentioned confirmed the quote to me on record, but insisted on anonymity

17. Teachers Manual Course C-6, Age 8–9, p 192 (PDF in my possession)

18. "Kingston Journey: Insiders to Outcasts," by Greg Burton, *The Salt Lake Tribune,* August 16, 1998. Also confirmed by former members of the Order Ronald Tucker, Rowenna and several others.

19. Interview with Ronald Tucker

20. "Kingston Journey: Insiders to Outcasts," by Greg Burton, *The Salt Lake Tribune,* August 16, 1998

21. "Social Security Numbers Blur Maze of Kingston Businesses," *The Salt Lake Tribune,* April 25, 1999

22. "Paper Fortress Guards Kingston Clan Fortune," by Ray Rivera, *The Salt Lake Tribune,* August 16, 1998

23. Interview with Laura Fuller

24. In her interview with state investigator Jessica Eldredge, Andrea Foster said: "Coreen never had kids. She was pregnant and Ladonna pushed her down the stairs and she lost her kid.' Eldredge asked, "How did you know that Ladonna pushed her?" Andrea replied, "Everybody knows."

25. Interview with Luann Kingston

26. "Probe into Death in Clan Reopens," by Jenifer K. Nii, *Deseret News,* August 25, 1998

27. Interviews with John Ortell's son Ron Tucker and daughter Luann Kingston

28. *Adult Order History 1*—Chapter 39: "Fasting"

29. Interview with Elaine Peterson

30. "Suit Filed over Coal Truck Driver's Death" by Geoff Liesik, *Deseret News,* December 16, 2009

31. "Immigrant Miners Take On Kingstons," by Mike Gorrell and Rhina Guidos, *The Salt Lake Tribune,* October 12, 2003. On September 22, 2003, C W Mining in Huntington Canyon fired seventy-five miners for attempting to unionize but were forced to take them back months later. The mine's problems, however, only magnified after that. A prolonged labor strike and numerous roof collapses meant that it couldn't make good on its contract to provide coal to a Missouri public utility company, Aquila, from 2004 to 2006. Aquila sued and C W Mining was judged to owe Aquila $24 million. The mine filed for bankruptcy in January of 2008 and lost its appeal in November of that year.

32. "The Chosen," by Linda Sillitoe, *Salt Lake Observer,* January 14, 1999

33. Interviews with Ronald Tucker, corroborated by a written list of numbered rankings from Rowenna Erickson

34. The American Cancer Society writes: "Experts strongly warn consumers not to eat or drink anything that contains comfrey . . . Several studies have shown that comfrey contains toxic compounds called pyrrolizidine alkaloids or PAs, which can cause severe liver damage. Animal studies have also shown that these chemicals lead to the development of liver tumors."

35. Teacher's Manual Course B-2, Age 6–7 (PDF in my possession)

36. The estimates of former Order members and current family members.

37. Racism within the Order is corroborated by all former Order members that were interviewed

38. "The Sacred Things of the Order," by Clyde Gustafson, (photocopy in my possession)

39. This relationship with money within the Order is confirmed through interviews with all former Order members mentioned in the book and many others who requested anonymity

40. Ron showed me several of his account slips and transaction records, corroborating the Order's unusual system of finance

41. "Polygamist Heads to Jail for Incest," *The Salt Lake Tribune*, January 27, 2004. Article reads: "With one of his 3 purported wives and 4 of his 17 children looking on, Jeremy Ortell Kingston was sentenced Monday to a year in jail for 'marrying' and having sex with a 15 year old cousin."

42. Further corroborated by Rowenna Erickson and Sharon Kingston

43. Further corroborated by Jessica Christensen (Stephanie), who says that the reason she was given for the stillbirth was that the mother had eaten too many ramen noodles during her pregnancy

44. Exodus 21:20–21: "When a man strikes his slave, male or female, and the slave dies under his hand, he shall be punished. But if the slave survives a day or two, he is not to be punished; for the slave is his money."

45. Psalm 137:9: "How blessed will be the one who seizes and dashes your little ones against the rock." Or, 1 Samuel 15:3: "Now go and smite Amalek, and utterly destroy all that they have, and spare them not; but slay both man and woman, infant and suckling, ox and sheep, camel and ass."

46. "Genetic Counseling and Screening of Consanguineous Couples and Their Offspring: Recommendations of the National Society of Genetic Counselors," The *Journal of Genetic Counseling*, vol 11 (2), April 2002 (C° 2002).

47. "Forbidden Fruit," by John Dougherty, *Phoenix New Times*, December 29, 2005

48. "Hypocrisy on Adult Consent," by Jeff Jacoby, *The Boston Globe*, August 28, 2005

49. "Polygamist's Sons: Incest Will Bring Back the Line of Jesus Christ," by Susan Duclos, digitaljournal.com, May 1, 2008

50. "Incest Law Focus of Draft Bill," by Jennifer Dobner, *Associated Press*, November 2008

51. Estimates from former members Rowenna Erickson, corroborated by Christy and Ron Tucker and Rebekah Woods. Family sizes in the Order are strictly guarded, so these estimates are arrived at by means of projection and educated guesses.

52. There are no court records to this effect, though in a court hearing July 18, 2005, Kristin Brewer references an affidavit by Stephanie from April that details her sexual abuse by Gary. The reason it didn't come out in court was because it was the subject of a criminal investigation. A further corroboration of Gary's predatory tactics here is Andrea's interview with Jessica Eldredge in which she confirms that

Gary's number was the last number to call the house before Stephanie went out for her "walk."

53. This account from Shawna will later be found to have inconsistencies

54. In a recent interview Andrea corrects Heidi's allegations: "My diagnosis was chronic PTSD and the doctors believed that I'd had the condition from the age of five. It had nothing to do with leaving the Order and everything to do with my family life under Heidi and Daniel. They did put me on antidepressants, that's true too. But I didn't have anything like a mental breakdown. Everything I said to the investigators was true and I stand by it to this day. Leaving the Order was the first time in my life that I could see clearly what was going on." She's presently attending college in Washington.

55. Hearing of February 8, 2005, p 66

56. Interview with Elaine, former Order member

57. According to former members Christy and Ron Tucker, Rowenna Erickson, Rebekah Woods

58. The number eleven came from Stephanie, Daniel's daughter, and was supported by former Order members Rowenna Erickson, Christy Tucker and another closet Kingston wife who wishes to remain nameless. I asked Laura Fuller during a discussion about the number codes that are assigned to Order members for the co-op's own records—a way of masking their names from outsider's eyes. She refused to tell me her personal number code, but she wrote it down on a piece of paper for me, on condition that I never reveal it. So I won't. But part of her code was the number 15, which is Daniel's number.

59. Since this interview took place, Laura has passed the California Bar and is applying to practice in Utah

10. The True and Living Church

1. *Associated Press*, April 28, 2005

2. *Polygamy's Rape of Rachael Strong: Protected Environment for Predators* by John R. Llewellyn, Agreka Books, 2006

3. Interviews with both Angel Mower and Angie

4. "A Prophet and His 'Sisters,'" by Lynda Wright, *Newsweek*, Aug 19, 1991

5. According to Amber Dawn Lee, former member of the Zion Society, as cited in "Ex-Polygamy Cult Member Shares Tale of Sex, Control," by Charisse Yu, *10 News, San Diego*, June 19, 2008

6. "Ritual Crime in the State of Utah: Investigation, Analysis, and a Look Forward," by Lt. Michael R. King and Lt. Matt Jacobson (Salt Lake City: attorney general's Office, 1995)

7. Interview with Pauline Strong, Kaziah Hancock

8. A Prophet and His 'Sisters,'" by Lynda Wright, *Newsweek*, Aug 19, 1991

9. Interview with Jack Ford of Utah Department of Corrections

10. Video in my possession, undated

11. Interview with Kaziah Hancock

12. Christopher Nemelka

1. The man's name is David Bishop, a Mormon thorn in Nemelka's side for many years now

2. ". . . the leaves were divided equi-distant between the back and edge by cutting the plates in two parts, and united again with *solder,* so that the front might be opened, as it were on a hinge, while the back part remained stationary and immovable and in this manner remained to him and the other witnesses a *sealed book,* which would not as yet be revealed for ages to come, and that event the prophet himself was not as yet permitted to understand." *The Reflector,* Vol II, Palmyra, March 19, 1831.

3. Book of Mormon, 1 Nephi 14:26: "And also others who have been, to them hath he shown all things, and they have written them; and they are sealed up to come forth in their purity, according to the truth which is in the Lamb, in the own due time of the Lord, unto the house of Israel."

4. Marcee refuses to go on record

5. Confirmed in interview with both Vicky Prunty and Nemelka

6. "True Believer," by Ben Fulton, *Salt Lake City Weekly,* December 27, 2001

7. Affidavit was submitted to Third District Court, Salt Lake County, April 20, 2007. (Richins could not be contacted for interview).

8. Memorandum In Support of the Smith Defendant's Motion for Judgement on the Pleadings, civil # 070910537. Denis P. Smith and Hyrum W. Smith are named as defendants as well as The Corporation of the President of the Church of Jesus Christ of Latter-Day Saints.

9. Nemelka has argued about the definition of "wife," since several women who consider themselves his wives, and are mothers to his children, are not married to him in the legal sense (esp. Vicky, Marcee).

10. Salt Lake City Police Department Records, April 27, 1996: "R/O spoke with A/P and under Miranda, admitted that he shoved comp to the ground." Also, a Petition For A Protective Order, #960902897SA by Vicky Prunty, May 30, 1996: "Without warning, Respondent then pushed Petitioner with both hands and with great force causing Petitioner to fall down and strike the gravel and rocks upon which the parties were standing. Petitioner struck her elbow and buttocks hard on the hard gravel and rocks."

11. Salt Lake City Police Department Records, Jan 30, 1999

12. Email is dated February 6, 2001, and reads: "Christine it is wisdom in the Lord that you copy these revelations much the same way that the scribes of Joseph

Smith copied his revelations."

13. The revelation is dated March 16 and refers to Christine as "Selah": "And this I say unto thee for cause of my daughter Selah, who I have blessed because of her exceeding faith. She shall be commanded to honor thee [Nemelka] in thy calling and support thee in thy needs, but she shall not rise above thee and do that which I have not commanded her by thy voice."

14. The same revelation as above continues: "Give [Selah] my blessings and ease her mind regarding her dealing with the arm of the flesh. If it so be that her mind stays single to my glory and my work, the iniquity that she supposes her actions to be shall be turned to righteousness."

15. In a letter from prison, Nemelka wrote: "I received your letter which was sent from your indicated address at a downtown Hotel room exclusively for the homeless, downtrodden, sick, inflicted and needy of our society."

16. From letter in my possession: "These are the days of your probation, for you have not yet earned the status of eternal motherhood. But you are passing through the trials and experience that are preparing you for that role."

17. From letter in my possession: "What of these 'things' you have lost? Were these things with you when you were born? Would these be with you when you return from whence you came?"

18. From letter in my possession: "Our mother in heaven—what does she do? How many of her children has she suffered by? How many has she lost because of the 'things' of the world? Does she miss them? Does she long for them and want to hold them close? Do Her tears cause the heavens to unfold and reveal her loving arms, or does She wait in patience for them to return and become as she is?"

19. In a letter to the Utah attorney general's Office, of February 5, 2002, Nattrass wrote: "He exploited and coerced and persuaded me to get me to sign under false pretenses . . . If I have to pay $10,000 on a debt because I am old and didn't know what I was doing, Nemelka might as well be in jail as to victimize some other poor soul whom he charmed and schmoozed and coerced into investing in his folly."

20. In an email to Jackie on December 27, 2000, a matter of days after he'd "married" Christine in Las Vegas, he made much the same point, about using religion as a mere tool. "I hate religion. However, I see religion's need in the life of others and I am simply attempting to do my part in helping others open their minds. I am staying out of the picture and want nothing to do with it other than my ability to write scripture that is convincing."

21. Nemelka's views on women creep into his correspondence—in an email to Jackie, December 27, 2000, he writes: "The only way I could handle it [knowing that Jackie was with another man] is if you allow me to raise the kids... Nothing would make me happier, short of you respecting, loving and accepting everything about me. Because I know you will not do this, I realize that you are no different

than any other woman."

22. Daniel 11:24 "When the richest provinces feel secure, he will invade them and will achieve what neither his fathers nor his forefathers did. He will distribute plunder, loot and wealth among his followers."

23. The Law of Sarah stems from Genesis 16:1–4, in which Sarah allowed Abraham to have sex with Hagar, their female slave, in order to bear children. Hagar, being a slave, likely had no say in the arrangement. It's cited in the Doctrine and Covenants section 132, whereby the first wife is given the right to consent or prohibit her husband from taking additional wives. But it's hardly a choice—if she refuses, then God makes it very clear that He will destroy her. From D&C section 132:64–5: "And again, verily, verily, I say unto you, if any man have a wife, who holds the keys of this power, and he teaches unto her the law of my priesthood, as pertaining to these things (plural wives), then shall she believe and administer unto him, or she shall be destroyed, saith the Lord your God; for I will destroy her . . . she then becomes the transgressor; and he is exempt from the law of Sarah, who administered unto Abraham according to the law when I commanded Abraham to take Hagar to wife."

Photo by Louella Boquiren

Sanjiv Bhattacharya has written for *Esquire, Details,* and the *Guardian*. He has appeared as an expert on polygamy, discussing his Channel Four documentary, *The Man with 80 Wives,* on MSNBC Live, *Montel Williams,* and elsewhere. He lives in Los Angeles.

Printed in the United States
by Baker & Taylor Publisher Services